Strategic S Consul[ting]

Methods, Models & Mastery

Martin J. Grigg

Intentionally blank

Strategic Security Consulting:
Methods, Models & Mastery
Martin J. Grigg

First edition 2025
ISBN 978-0-9927250-1-3

Copyright Notice

Intellectual Property Statement

Authorship Statement

This book was developed using a human-led approach, with all core ideas, structural elements, and the overall narrative conceived and produced by the author. Artificial Intelligence tools were employed selectively to support the author's work, serving only to enhance accuracy, refine language, and verify factual consistency. Within this supporting role, AI collaboration was applied primarily in three areas: writing, where sentence structure and clarity were refined without altering the intended meaning; data analysis, where relevant datasets and research findings were organised and summarised for review; and literature review, where credible sources were identified and summarised to strengthen key arguments. All critical thinking, conclusions, and contextual insights remain entirely the work of the author, ensuring that the content reflects human expertise, professional judgement, and practical experience.

Disclaimer

The information contained in this book has been drawn from reputable sources and the professional experience of the author. While every effort has been made to ensure accuracy, the author cannot guarantee that the content is free from error, complete in every respect, or universally applicable. This book is intended as guidance and should not be relied upon as definitive engineering or security advice for any specific situation. The author is an independent consultant and does not endorse any product, company, or organisation referenced within this publication, whether directly or implied.

Model and Framework Disclaimer

The Grigg Evolved Equilibrium Resilience Model (GEERM) and all associated diagrams, terminology, and explanatory material presented in this volume are original works developed by the author through professional consulting and applied research practice. At the time of publication, the model remains in a pre-review stage and is undergoing preparation for academic and professional validation. It is included here as a conceptual and analytical framework intended to advance professional understanding and encourage further study.

tectec-press

Dedication

To Jerry,
whose love, patience, and quiet strength restored my confidence – and
reminded me what it means to think freely, work purposefully,
and give something back to the profession that I care about.
You are, in every sense, my compass and my calm.

And to Omar,
who, over coffee by the sea in Pescara,
planted the seed and gave me the push to begin again.
Your optimism and encouragement helped turn thought into action.

Intentionally blank

Foreword

Security consultancy is a profession that lives in the space between risk and resilience. It is not a branch of engineering, a form of policing, or an academic exercise – it is the disciplined practice of thinking clearly amid uncertainty and acting with integrity where stakes are high. This book was written to capture that practice: to define what it means to consult well, to explain how judgement is formed, and to give structure to the intuition that separates experience from expertise.

Over the past two decades, the field has changed beyond recognition. Systems have converged, threats have globalised, and expectations have intensified. Yet, at its heart, consultancy remains human work. It depends on listening, questioning, and the courage to say what others avoid. Clients still value clarity over complexity and trust over tools. For all the new acronyms and analytics, the consultant's craft is still about earning that trust through competence, transparency, and proportionate advice.

This guide is not a catalogue of technologies or standards – there are already many of those. It is a manual for thinking: how to frame problems, challenge assumptions, and translate risk into strategy. Each chapter reflects lessons learned from practice – some through success, others through error – but all through experience in environments where theory alone was never enough. The models and frameworks presented are tools for reflection as much as for design, intended to help practitioners make sense of complexity rather than to prescribe formulas.

Writing this book has been an act of consolidation. It gathers what has worked, questions what has not, and connects disciplines that too often remain separate. It recognises that consultancy is evolving, and that future practitioners will need to combine systems thinking, digital fluency, ethical independence, and personal resilience in equal measure.

If the pages that follow help even a few readers to think more critically, act more independently, or advise with greater confidence, then this work has achieved its purpose. The security profession deserves consultants who see the bigger picture – who can connect purpose to protection, and protection to progress.

— *Martin J. Grigg*

Intentionally blank

Contents

Figures

Tables

Intentionally blank

Introduction

Security consultancy is not a technical discipline dressed in management clothes. It is the art and science of protecting people, assets, and operations through structured thought and practical action. To consult in security is to stand between risk and resilience – not as a guard or a gatekeeper, but as an interpreter of complex realities. This book was written to demystify that position: to show how consultants think, how they add value, and how security can become a force for good rather than an obstacle to progress.

Over the years, the role of the security consultant has shifted from installer and specifier to strategist and integrator. The modern consultant must navigate a world of hybrid threats and converged systems – physical and digital, procedural and human – while understanding that clients rarely buy "security" in isolation. They buy confidence. They buy the ability to act, expand, and recover when the unexpected happens. Yet, too often, consultancy is reduced to compliance checklists, vague risk assessments, or product-driven advice. The result is a profession that talks about resilience but rarely measures it.

This book begins from a different premise: that good consultancy is a thinking profession. It requires intellectual discipline, ethical grounding, and the humility to recognise that expertise is only valuable when it connects meaningfully to the client's world. The chapters that follow are not a manual in procedures, but a framework for how to think, decide, and deliver like a professional consultant – one whose recommendations are trusted, defensible, and proportionate to the risks at hand.

A Profession of Thought Before Tools

Every consultant begins with knowledge – of standards, technologies, and threat environments. But the mature consultant learns that knowledge alone does not create value. What clients seek is insight: the ability to make sense of complexity and offer a path through it. The consultant's craft lies in bridging worlds – translating engineering into risk, policy into design, and intent into implementation. It is not enough to know what a camera does or what ISO 27001 says. The consultant must know *why it matters, when it applies,* and *how it interacts with everything else.*

1

That is why this book treats consultancy as a form of applied critical thinking. Tools, templates, and procedures matter, but only when anchored in purpose. The same methodology that designs a data centre's security system can also guide a cultural change programme or a resilience audit – if the thinking is clear. Each decision, each diagram, and each clause in a specification should have a reason behind it. The consultant's duty is to make those reasons visible and defensible.

From Layers to Systems

The traditional view of security, built on layers and perimeters, is no longer sufficient. Threats cross boundaries, and so must our thinking. The Grigg Evolved Equilibrium Resilience Model, which appears later in this book, was developed to help consultants visualise this interconnectedness: the way physical, cyber, procedural, and people factors converge around governance and resilience. But even before models, there must be mindset. True integration begins with curiosity – asking how systems interact, how people behave under stress, and how organisations learn from failure.

The best consultants are systems thinkers. They see how an access control policy shapes culture, how a software update can disable a gate, or how the wrong tone in an evacuation message can cause panic. They also understand that clients live in the tension between business goals and operational risk. The consultant's task is not to eliminate risk but to make it understandable and manageable – to design environments that bend, not break, under pressure.

The Consultant's Character

Technical skill can be taught. Professional character cannot. Integrity, discretion, and intellectual honesty are the quiet constants of consultancy. The consultant occupies a position of influence without authority, trusted by the client yet accountable for independent judgement. That trust is earned through consistency: showing that advice is based on evidence, not convenience; that conflicts of interest are declared, not disguised; and that the consultant's first loyalty is always to truth and client outcome, not to manufacturer or margin.

Ethical consultancy is not an abstract ideal. It is the foundation of sustainable practice. In every project, decisions about cost, scope, and risk have moral consequences. Choosing to specify an unproven system, overlooking procedural weaknesses, or ignoring the human factor can

2

undermine years of investment. This book invites readers to consider ethics not as a constraint but as a design principle, one that underpins professional credibility and long-term client relationships.

From Compliance to Value

A central theme throughout this book is the difference between compliance and value. Compliance is the floor, the minimum condition for acceptance. Value is the ceiling, the level at which security contributes to performance, reputation, and return on investment. Many consultants spend their careers working at the floor, navigating regulations and ticking boxes. The professionals who stand out operate closer to the ceiling. They translate standards into strategy and turn mandatory requirements into opportunities for improvement.

That transition demands a change in language as well as mindset. Instead of "meeting the standard", consultants should ask what the standard is trying to achieve. Instead of "installing a system", they should define what outcome the system must enable. Clients rarely remember the make of camera or model of controller; they remember whether the system worked when it mattered. The consultant's ultimate product is not drawings or reports but clarity – a coherent path from intent to implementation that allows the client to make informed choices.

The Learning Journey

This book is structured as a journey through that transformation – from technical competence to strategic consultancy. It assumes that the reader already understands the basics of security systems and risk assessment. What it offers is the professional layer above: the habits of thought, communication, and collaboration that turn a specialist into a consultant.

Readers will learn how to frame problems, conduct meaningful assessments, and communicate findings in ways that influence decision-makers. They will explore how to manage scope, navigate politics, and handle the commercial realities that shape every project. The aim is not only to build capability but to cultivate judgement – the consultant's most valuable asset.

Each chapter distils lessons drawn from professional practice across sectors such as critical national infrastructure, hospitality, and healthcare. The examples within are illustrative. They are designed to reinforce the principles and reflect situations that many consultants will recognise, rather than recount specific projects. They show what happens when theory meets the realities of construction sites, client committees, and cultural differences. While the book offers principles, it avoids prescriptions. There is no single "right way" to consult, only a disciplined way to think.

The Consultant's Landscape

The consultancy environment is evolving rapidly. Digital transformation, artificial intelligence, and the growing convergence of physical and cyber systems have blurred old boundaries. Clients expect faster, smarter, and more transparent services. At the same time, geopolitical uncertainty and regulatory complexity demand stronger governance and resilience.

Against this backdrop, the consultant becomes a navigator, guiding organisations through uncertainty while maintaining ethical independence. The ability to integrate disciplines, understand risk, and communicate value is now more important than any individual technical skill. This book therefore treats consultancy as a *meta-profession*: one that sits above individual domains and brings them into purposeful alignment.

Why This Book Exists

Security consultancy has never lacked technical guidance. Standards, codes, and handbooks exist in abundance. What has been missing is a text that speaks to the *practice* of consulting – the thinking, reasoning, and human factors that determine whether a project succeeds or fails. This book fills that gap. It aims to prepare readers not just to design systems, but to design trust.

The pages that follow are built on three convictions:

1. **Security must serve purpose.** Protection without purpose is obstruction. The consultant's first task is to understand what the client values and design protection around it.
2. **Integration is a mindset, not a diagram.** Physical, cyber, procedural, and human factors only converge when the people managing them do.
3. **Resilience is measurable.** It is not a slogan but a performance outcome, achieved through alignment of governance, technology, and culture.

By the end of the book, readers will be able to recognise these principles in their own work and apply them with confidence. They will understand how to structure engagements, develop defensible recommendations, and communicate with authority. More importantly, they will see themselves not as technicians but as trusted advisors – people who make a measurable difference to safety, continuity, and value.

How to Use This Book

The book is written for reflection as much as reference. Each section builds upon the previous one, moving from theory to method to application. Readers are encouraged to pause, question, and adapt the material to their own context. The examples, checklists, and models are there to guide, not to constrain. Consultancy thrives on adaptability.

Whether you are a new entrant learning the craft or an experienced professional seeking to refine it, this book is designed to be used actively – annotated, challenged, and revisited as your practice evolves. The ideas within are not static. The profession will continue to change, and so must our frameworks and language. The goal is not to offer final answers but to enable better questions.

A Note on Context

Although many of the examples draw from projects in the Gulf region and the wider Middle East, the principles are globally applicable. The cultural, regulatory, and environmental conditions may differ, but the consultant's mindset transcends geography. The book's perspective is that of an international practitioner: one who respects standards but is not confined by them, who values experience but remains open to innovation.

In a world of increasing automation and artificial intelligence, human consultancy remains vital because it deals with meaning, not data. Machines can process information faster than any analyst, but they cannot yet interpret intent, ethics, or organisational culture. The consultant's role is to bring these dimensions together – to make decisions that are not only efficient but right.

Looking Ahead

As you read, remember that consultancy is not a solitary profession. It exists in dialogue – between client and consultant, between disciplines, and between theory and practice. The stories and frameworks that follow are meant to invite participation. The industry will only mature if consultants share knowledge, challenge assumptions, and collaborate across boundaries.

If this book achieves one thing, let it be this: to help you see security consultancy not as a narrow service but as a strategic discipline that enables progress. To protect is to empower. The consultant's success lies not in preventing change, but in making it safe to happen.

Part 1 – Foundations

Security consultancy is built on more than technical expertise. At its core, it is a profession that requires clarity of role, resilience in practice, ethical judgement, and the ability to integrate across disciplines.

The chapters that follow explain what a security consultant really does, the skills and disciplines that underpin long-term success, and the professional ethics that govern practice. They also set out how consultants operate within project ecosystems and how they distinguish themselves from adjacent roles such as designers, integrators, and operators.

This part frames the consultant not only as a provider of technical solutions but as a guide who shapes decisions, balances risks, and builds trust. By the end of Part 1, you will understand the mindset and principles required to operate effectively in the field, and how these foundations prepare them to use the practical tools introduced in Part 2.

Chapter 1 – What a Security Consultant Really Does

Security consultancy is often misunderstood, yet its value lies in providing independent, accountable advice that identifies problems, tests assumptions, and delivers credible solutions across diverse contexts. This chapter introduces the core responsibilities of the consultant, clarifies how the role differs from related professions, and highlights the mindset and methods that distinguish consultancy from purely technical practice.

By the end of this chapter, you will be able to:

- Distinguish the role of the security consultant from designers, integrators, and operators, and justify why clear boundaries preserve independence and effectiveness.
- Identify and challenge common misconceptions about consultancy with constructive responses in practice.
- Explain why AI tools cannot replace professional judgement and state the limits of automated outputs in high-risk environments.
- Describe how responsibilities vary across sectors (critical national infrastructure, corporate, public, humanitarian).
- Analyse a short case to infer the underlying problem behind a client's stated request.
- Apply structured methods (Five Whys, SWOT, PESTLE, red teaming, tabletop exercises) to test assumptions and develop robust recommendations.
- Articulate the consultant's defining attributes – independence, accountability, ethical reasoning, adaptability – and defend their importance for credibility and trust.

Introduction

Security consultancy is a profession built on independence, clarity of thought, and the ability to bring order to complexity. It is not about selling equipment or managing day-to-day operations, but about guiding organisations through decisions where safety, resilience, and reputation are at stake. The consultant's value lies in defining problems, testing assumptions, and shaping solutions that are not only technically sound, but also workable in the environments where they must be applied.

The role is distinct from that of designers, integrators, or operators. While those professions focus on producing drawings, installing systems, or running facilities, the consultant occupies a different space: identifying and interpreting threats, framing options, and ensuring that security outcomes are aligned with wider organisational objectives. Independence allows the consultant to stand apart from commercial interests and provide advice that can be trusted as impartial.

The need for such expertise has grown as risks have become more complex and more global. Threats cross borders easily, and multinational organisations must reconcile different regulations, cultural expectations, and operational realities. At the same time, technology is advancing at speed, with new systems promising solutions to yesterday's problems, but often creating fresh challenges of integration and management. In this shifting landscape, the consultant provides a steadying influence – translating technical possibilities into practical strategies that safeguard people, property, and assets.

Professional consultancy also demands breadth. A consultant may spend the morning in a boardroom, framing security in terms of risk, continuity, and reputation, and the afternoon on a construction site, observing how procedures function in practice. The ability to move fluently between these different contexts, and to communicate effectively at each level, is what distinguishes a consultant from a purely technical specialist.

Above all, consultancy is about responsibility. Clients expect more than information – they expect judgement that can withstand scrutiny. While automated tools and artificial intelligence may offer useful support, they cannot replicate professional accountability, ethical reasoning, or situational awareness. The consultant is the person who carries the responsibility for recommendations, and who must defend them in front of clients, regulators, or the public if outcomes are challenged.

This first chapter introduces what security consultants really do. It clarifies how their role differs from related professions, addresses common misconceptions, and explores the skills and mindset that underpin effective practice. It sets out why independence, adaptability, and critical thinking matter as much as technical expertise, and why consultancy begins not with tools or checklists, but with the identity and integrity of the consultant themselves.

The Many Faces of Security Consulting

Security consulting is a discipline that adapts to context. Unlike professions with rigidly defined tasks, the consultant's role shifts according to project stage, sector, and client needs. To understand what consultants really do, it is essential to distinguish them from related professions.

- **The Consultant** is the independent adviser, engaged to identify needs, assess risks, and guide the client towards the most appropriate solution. They ensure outcomes are coherent, defensible, and aligned with wider objectives, standing apart from commercial interests.
- **The Designer** translates requirements into technical drawings, specifications, and schematics. In some projects this work is undertaken by the consultant, in others by architects or engineers, but the focus is on producing precise instructions for delivery.
- **The Integrator** installs and commissions systems, working with manufacturers and contractors to bring designs into operation. Their value lies in problem solving on site and coordinating with other trades under time and budget pressure.
- **The Operator** runs the systems once live – monitoring, responding to incidents, and managing day-to-day procedures. Their effectiveness often determines whether technical measures achieve the intended result.

To illustrate these differences, consider four brief scenarios:

- At an airport, the consultant identifies risks in baggage handling and recommends strategic improvements; the designer produces camera layouts; the integrator installs the cameras; the operator monitors the images and responds in the control room.
- On a corporate headquarters project, the consultant aligns security with business objectives; the designer integrates requirements into building plans; the integrator delivers the installation; the operator ensures smooth daily use.

- In critical infrastructure, the consultant advises on compliance and resilience; the designer specifies protective measures; the integrator implements them under strict regulatory oversight; the operator maintains continuity in operations.

- In a public facility, the consultant balances security with accessibility; the designer adapts layouts to match; the integrator addresses technical issues during construction; the operator provides frontline service to staff and visitors.

These examples illustrate how each role contributes differently to the project lifecycle. Designers translate requirements into technical drawings, integrators deliver installations, and operators manage daily use.

Role	Orientation	Accountability	Lifecycle Position	Typical Outputs
Consultant	Risk-informed, client-centred, independent of supply chain.	To the client and governance structures.	Initiation to handover.	TVRA, strategy, performance specifications, evaluation reports.
Designer	Technical, solution-focused, standards-based.	To design codes and client brief.	Concept to detailed design.	Schematics, layouts, specifications, schedules.
Integrator	Implementation-oriented, technology-driven.	To contract and system performance.	Construction and commissioning.	Installed systems, integration protocols, test certifications.
Operator	System use and incident response.	Operational continuity, performance against SOPs.	Commissioning to operations and maintenance.	Event logs, incident reports, maintenance records.
Owner	Governance and strategic outcomes.	Oversight of value, risk, and assurance.	All stages.	Business case, budget control, acceptance sign-off, performance metrics.

Table 1 Comparative Orientation of Security Roles

The consultant's distinct value lies in maintaining impartiality and providing continuity across stages, ensuring that these contributions remain coherent, neutral, and aligned with the client's objectives.

Misconceptions About the Profession

Despite the growth of the industry, the role of the security consultant is still often misunderstood. Misconceptions persist both within the sector and among clients, shaping expectations in ways that can diminish the consultant's value if they are left unchallenged. Confronting these myths is part of professional practice because it helps set realistic expectations, reinforces independence, and clarifies the distinct contribution of consultancy within the wider security field.

"Consultants are just report writers.": Many assume consultants deliver a document and then disappear. Reports are just one product of a process that spans many project stages – from scoping and design validation through procurement and commissioning. The consultant's value lies in continuity and coherence, not paperwork alone.

"Consultants slow projects down.": Threat, Vulnerability and Risk Assessments (TVRA) and specifications are sometimes viewed as bureaucratic hurdles. In practice, they reduce delays by clarifying requirements, preventing disputes, and ensuring contractors work to a consistent brief. Effective consultancy accelerates delivery by removing ambiguity early.

"Consultants only repackage existing information.": With standards and regulatory guidance readily available, it is sometimes assumed that hiring a consultant is unnecessary. This view overlooks the critical distinction between information and expertise. Compliance with prescriptive guides may demonstrate adherence to minimum requirements, but it does not necessarily produce security, because the authors of those guides cannot anticipate the specific circumstances of each organisation or site. The consultant's role is to interpret requirements in context, filter what is relevant, and assess the real-world consequences of each option – moving beyond checklists to provide recommendations that are proportionate, defensible, and genuinely effective.

"Consultancy is only for large projects.": Because high-profile assignments often involve major infrastructure, consultancy is mistakenly seen as exclusive to large budgets. In fact, smaller organisations – from schools to healthcare facilities – often benefit most from independent guidance that avoids costly errors.

"Internal managers make consultants unnecessary.": Internal security managers know their organisations intimately, but they are also constrained by politics, budget, and institutional history. Consultants complement this perspective by bringing independence, benchmarking against wider practice, and the freedom to challenge entrenched assumptions. They draw on experience gained across multiple sectors and organisations, offering insights that internal teams alone may not encounter. The two roles are therefore complementary rather than interchangeable.

"Consultants are only technical.": While technical knowledge is essential, consultancy extends to strategy, communication, and stakeholder management. Translating complex risks into language that boards, regulators, and communities can act upon is as important as understanding locks, cameras, or networks.

"Consultancy is one-size-fits-all.": Some expect standardised solutions that can be applied universally. Good consultants adapt recommendations to local law, culture, and operational realities. A measure appropriate in one jurisdiction may be unworkable in another. Independence requires tailoring, not template application.

"Consultancy is an unnecessary cost.": Organisations sometimes believe training staff to produce in-house assessments is cheaper. Yet internal teams may lack independence or exposure to broader benchmarks. The apparent saving is often offset by hidden costs in poorly scoped systems or inefficient procurement. External consultancy frequently pays for itself in avoided mistakes.

Misconceptions endure for many reasons – negative experiences, misuse of the title "consultant" by vendors, and the illusion that free access to information equals expertise. The consultant's task is not to argue defensively but to demonstrate value in practice. When clients see that consultancy prevents scope creep, improves procurement fairness, and strengthens operational resilience, the myths lose their force.

Why AI Cannot Replace Professional Judgement

The rise of artificial intelligence (AI) has prompted questions about whether professional consultants remain necessary. Large language models can generate apparently authoritative text, summarise regulations, and suggest system components in seconds. To some clients, this raises the possibility that automated tools could provide the same guidance as a consultant at far lower cost. This assumption is misleading.

AI produces information, not professional judgement. A system may generate lists of technologies or summarise general security measures, but it cannot interpret the physical layout of a site, assess cultural and organisational dynamics, or weigh the trade-offs between resilience, cost, and usability. For example, an algorithm may recommend "access control" or "CCTV" as standard measures, but it cannot recognise that a façade design creates hostile surveillance risks or that staff behaviours undermine existing controls. Computers can list options, but only a human can see how they fit the situation.

Accountability further separates consultants from machines. When professional advice is provided, the consultant assumes responsibility for its validity and carries the liability if recommendations fail. They are expected to justify their reasoning in boardrooms, regulatory hearings, or courts. AI systems carry no such burden of accountability; they produce text without a duty of care. Acting on those outputs without professional oversight introduces unquantified risk.

Ethics also highlight the limits of automation. Many security decisions involve considerations beyond the technical. Introducing facial recognition, for example, raises issues of legality, privacy, and public acceptance. Consultants must help clients navigate these questions, balancing operational objectives against ethical standards and reputational risk. AI tools do not engage with such complexities and therefore cannot provide defensible guidance in sensitive or high-risk environments.

Even within technical domains, AI lacks adaptability. Security projects evolve as budgets shift, regulations change, or unforeseen vulnerabilities emerge. Consultants are expected to respond to these dynamics, reshaping advice and mediating between competing stakeholders. AI provides static outputs divorced from political, financial, and cultural realities. If relied without question, AI can lock in errors or blind spots, leaving organisations less resilient rather than more secure.

AI can support consultants, but it cannot replace professional accountability. When employed carefully, it can support consultants by accelerating research, highlighting recent studies, or generating preliminary material that professionals can refine. Its role is that of an assistant, not a substitute. The consultant remains responsible for testing outputs against evidence, contextual realities, and ethical obligations.

Clients do not engage consultants simply for information. They engage them for interpretation, independence, and accountability – qualities that machines cannot provide. In a landscape where errors can carry severe financial, reputational, or safety consequences, the professional consultant's judgement remains indispensable.

A Day in the Life – Sector Snapshots

No two days in security consultancy are the same. The role demands quick adjustment to very different settings, from strategic discussions in boardrooms to practical reviews on construction sites. In every case, the consultant is expected to deliver independent, well-founded advice that combines technical accuracy with an understanding of organisational realities.

In critical national infrastructure, consultants are often required to assess sites against strict regulatory and resilience frameworks. This involves identifying vulnerabilities, reviewing how existing measures align with standards, and framing findings in a way that regulators and operators can act upon. The task is not only technical but also diplomatic: consultants must highlight weaknesses clearly while preserving the client's confidence in the overall security programme.

In corporate projects, consultants often work with architects and IT specialists to integrate security into building design. The challenge is to preserve functionality and aesthetics while addressing risks. This requires fluency in the language of multiple disciplines and the ability to justify measures in terms of resilience, brand protection, and cost.

In the public sector, consultants navigate complex stakeholder environments. Police, planners, community representatives, and politicians may all be involved in a single project. The consultant's role is to structure discussion so that consensus can form without diluting the integrity of protective measures. Recommendations must be clear, proportionate, and defensible under public scrutiny.

In humanitarian contexts, the consultant may advise non-governmental organisations operating in conflict-affected regions. The work often involves balancing dignity and protection: ensuring security at refugee camps or supply chains without imposing measures that resemble imprisonment or undermine community trust. Success depends not on technical sophistication but on solutions that can be sustained in fragile environments.

In technology-driven sectors such as data centres, consultants monitor contractor installations, verify compliance with specifications, and brief boards on emerging risks such as insider threats. Here, technical accuracy is vital, but so too is the ability to explain vulnerabilities in strategic terms that secure executive buy-in.

Across all these settings, the consultant acts simultaneously as strategist, translator, and inspector. The profession is defined not by routine tasks but by versatility, independence, and the ability to interpret and translate complexity for diverse audiences. This variety illustrates why consultancy is not a narrow technical specialism, but a discipline grounded in adaptability, credibility, and trust.

Underpinning that trust is a shared ethical foundation. Security consultants hold privileged access to sensitive information, strategic plans, and personal data. Maintaining independence, discretion, and integrity is therefore non-negotiable. Ethical consultancy means declining assignments where conflicts of interest exist, protecting client confidentiality, and ensuring that advice is not shaped by commercial or political pressure. The credibility of the profession rests on this discipline: without trust in the consultant's motives, no amount of technical expertise can sustain a client relationship.

Illustrative Example: The Parking Garage Problem

One of the clearest ways to understand the work of a consultant is through real-world examples. This case is based on common industry experience, and it illustrates how projects often present themselves with a stated problem that turns out not to be the real issue at all.

A client approached a consultant with what seemed like a straightforward request: design a new CCTV system for a multi-storey parking garage that was experiencing thefts from vehicles. The facilities team had already concluded that the problem was inadequate surveillance – they believed that adding more cameras would deter offenders and provide evidence for investigations. On the surface, this appeared reasonable, and many practitioners would have started drawing up camera layouts immediately.

The consultant, however, began by asking questions. What types of vehicles were being targeted? At what times of day did incidents occur? How were offenders gaining access? What measures were already in place, and how effective had they been? This line of inquiry quickly revealed that the garage already had a modest but functional camera system covering key entry and exit points. The thefts were not happening in unobserved corners, but in well-lit areas under direct camera coverage. Footage showed offenders moving freely through the garage without challenge, often breaking into vehicles within minutes.

Digging deeper, the consultant discovered the true issue: the garage had uncontrolled pedestrian access. Stairwells and side doors were regularly left propped open, and the access control system was poorly maintained. Offenders could enter without resistance, roam for long periods, and then leave without triggering any intervention. The security team were reactive and over-stretched, responding only after incidents were reported. Cameras, in this case, had provided plenty of evidence but had not deterred or disrupted the crimes.

The consultant reframed the project from a technology upgrade to an access management and operational problem. Recommendations included repairing and monitoring pedestrian entry points, tightening access control procedures, and retraining staff on active monitoring and response. Cameras were still part of the solution, but their role was now properly integrated into a wider security strategy. The cost was lower than the client's original plan for a blanket CCTV expansion, and the impact was far greater because the measures addressed the root cause of the thefts rather than the symptom.

This case illustrates several truths about security consulting. First, the stated problem is often not the real problem – clients may ask for a particular technology when what they truly need is a reassessment of processes or behaviours. Second, effective consulting is not about selling more equipment but about delivering outcomes that actually reduce risk.

The value of the consultant lies in structured curiosity, the discipline of questioning assumptions, and the confidence to challenge a client's initial request when experience shows a better path forward.

The parking garage problem shows how easy it is for projects to drift into wasted expenditure when no one is asking the right questions. It also demonstrates how a consultant's independence and critical thinking can save money, reduce risk, and build long-term trust with the client.

Never accept the first problem you are given. The consultant's craft begins where the client's assumption ends.

Critical Thinking Toolkit

The parking garage case illustrates one of the most important truths about consultancy: the problem a client presents is rarely the real problem, or at the very least, the whole story. The consultant's value lies in asking the right questions and refusing to accept assumptions at face value. This discipline of thought is what separates consultancy from technical service. Critical thinking is the consultant's core toolkit, the method through which information is tested, assumptions are challenged, and conclusions become robust enough to withstand scrutiny.

At its simplest, critical thinking begins with curiosity. The consultant does not stop at the first explanation but digs deeper, asking why events occur, why they matter, and why a proposed solution may or may not be appropriate. A technique as straightforward as the "Five Whys" demonstrates this principle. By repeatedly asking why thefts were happening in the garage, the consultant moved beyond the surface issue of surveillance and uncovered the real vulnerability in uncontrolled access. This way of thinking prevents projects from drifting into superficial fixes and ensures that recommendations address causes rather than symptoms.

Structured frameworks add rigour to this curiosity. Tools such as SWOT and PESTLE provide a way of organising information so that patterns and priorities emerge from complexity. A consultant examining a port facility, for example, might use PESTLE to highlight political influences such as shifting trade regulations, economic pressures from fluctuating import volumes, technological change through automation, and environmental risks like coastal flooding. A complementary SWOT analysis might then show that while experienced staff are a strength, outdated perimeter fencing is a weakness, new funding is an opportunity, and organised smuggling represents a persistent threat. Together these insights create a map of the landscape in which risks must be managed. The value of these frameworks is not in filling boxes but in creating clarity, giving both consultant and client a shared language for identifying what matters most.

These approaches also connect directly to formal risk management frameworks such as ISO 31000:2018[13]. The consultant who uses SWOT and PESTLE is not engaging in abstract exercises but is building the internal and external context required by ISO's risk identification stage. This link to internationally recognised standards makes the analysis defensible if challenged by auditors, regulators, or courts. It also reassures clients that the work is not subjective opinion but part of a structured and transparent methodology.

When dealing with intelligent adversaries, consultants often need to adopt an attacker's perspective. Red teaming provides this shift, encouraging the consultant to think not about how to defend a facility but about how it could be penetrated. Walking a perimeter while asking, "If I wanted to get in, where would I try?" can reveal blind spots that conventional inspections overlook. Simulating social engineering attempts or testing how easily procedures can be bypassed exposes vulnerabilities that technical reviews alone may miss. This change of perspective forces clients to confront uncomfortable realities and prevents consultants from being lulled into complacency by reassuring checklists.

Tabletop exercises extend the toolkit into collaborative territory. By bringing stakeholders together to walk through scenarios step by step, the consultant exposes gaps that only emerge under pressure. A fire alarm triggered during a protest outside a building, for instance, raises questions about decision-making authority, communication channels, and potential points of confusion. The exercise is less about the specific scenario and more about how people respond when events unfold unexpectedly. In these sessions, consultants act as facilitators, guiding discussion, recording insights, and ensuring that lessons are turned into practical improvements. The value lies in building shared understanding among stakeholders, something that technical documents cannot achieve on their own.

Critical thinking also requires awareness of bias. Clients arrive with assumptions shaped by recent experiences, and consultants bring their own preferences and enthusiasms. A client who has suffered theft may fixate on cameras as the answer to every problem. A consultant excited about a new technology may unconsciously steer solutions toward it, regardless of context. The discipline lies in challenging these biases, asking what evidence would disprove the current line of thought, or deliberately considering the opposite perspective. By testing their own reasoning as rigorously as they test the client's assumptions, consultants protect their independence and avoid losing objectivity by defending answers that they assumed from the start.

Listening is another part of the toolkit. Many of the most important insights arise not from formal analysis but from informal remarks, the guard who mentions that a door is always propped open, or the executive who hints at staff frustrations with access systems. Active listening allows the consultant to hear not only what is said but what is implied, reading hesitation, discomfort, or silence as signals that merit further inquiry. These subtleties cannot be captured in checklists, yet they often shape the difference between a design that works in theory and one that functions in practice.

Communication is inseparable from analysis. Discovering the real cause of a problem is of little value if it cannot be explained in a way that decision-makers accept. Methods such as the Pyramid Principle [17], long used by management consultants, demonstrate how to structure findings: begin with the conclusion, then present the supporting evidence in a clear hierarchy. Instead of delivering pages of technical argument before revealing the point, the consultant might start with, "The core issue is uncontrolled pedestrian access," followed by three concise reasons why. This approach respects limited attention spans and ensures that the message is not lost in detail.

The real strength of the toolkit emerges when methods are combined. A hospital facing equipment theft might prompt a PESTLE analysis that reveals economic pressures leading to increased reliance on temporary staff. A SWOT analysis might show weaknesses in loading bay management. Red teaming might identify contractor access as the easiest theft path. A tabletop exercise might reveal that staff are uncertain about escalation procedures. Each tool sheds light from a different angle, but together they form a coherent picture that supports clear, defensible recommendations. Without this structure, the hospital might simply have installed more cameras and seen thefts continue unabated.

Consultants also face the challenge of working with incomplete or ambiguous information. Threats change, data is patchy, and clients may be unwilling to disclose sensitive details. In such environments, critical thinking does not eliminate uncertainty but provides a way of making judgements that are transparent and reasoned. Clients may not agree with every conclusion, but they will respect the rigour of a process that is systematic and explainable.

Critical thinking is not about making problems more complicated, but about stripping away the noise to reveal what really matters. It provides a discipline of inquiry that moves from symptoms to causes, from raw data to insight, and from analysis to action. It is both a mindset and a method: curiosity and scepticism on one hand, and practical tools such as Five Whys, SWOT, PESTLE, red teaming, and tabletop exercises on the other. Together they ensure that consultancy is not guesswork or repetition of assumptions, but a professional practice grounded in evidence, independence, and clarity.

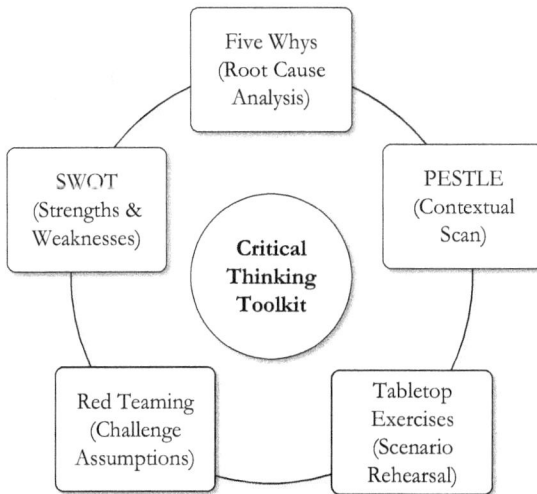

Figure 1 The 5 Critical Thinking Tools

Practice Guide

This first chapter of the consultancy guide has established what makes the security consultant distinct: independence of judgement and the ability to diagnose root causes rather than accept symptoms at face value. New consultants often stumble by accepting client requests without question, allowing boundaries between consultant and client to blur, or relying too heavily on readily available information and AI outputs without exercising professional judgement. Others risk focusing on technology while neglecting the organisational and human factors that determine effectiveness. Communication presents another common challenge, as overly technical reporting or insufficient adaptation to local context can undermine otherwise sound recommendations.

The key point is that consultancy requires disciplined inquiry, not compliance with initial assumptions. Protecting independence is essential: once the consultant becomes aligned with suppliers or day-to-day operators, credibility is compromised. AI and other information tools can assist consultancy, but only when their outputs are examined and shaped by professional judgement. Solutions must integrate people, processes, and technology in balanced ways; technology-led measures without sufficient organisational integration rarely succeed. Advice must be communicated with clarity, sensitivity to culture, and awareness of regulatory expectations so that it is both understood and acted upon.

You should now be able to distinguish consultancy from related roles, challenge misconceptions, explain why AI cannot replace professional accountability, describe how responsibilities vary across sectors, apply structured critical thinking methods, and appreciate the defining attributes of independence and credibility. These foundations enable you to deliver advice that protects people, assets, and organisational reputation. As threats evolve and governance expectations tighten, future consultancy will require sharper ethical judgement, clearer communication with non-specialists, and evidence-based recommendations that stand up to regulatory and public scrutiny.

Chapter 2 – The Mindset of a Successful Security Consultant

Success in security consultancy depends on far more than technical expertise. What separates effective consultants from those who struggle is mindset – the ability to think critically, communicate with clarity, and sustain performance under pressure. This chapter introduces the ways of thinking and working that shape a successful consultant's mindset, showing how established consulting frameworks can be applied directly to security.

By the end of this chapter, you will be able to:

- Differentiate between the roles of technical expert and trusted adviser and explain why this shift underpins credibility.

- Apply structured, hypothesis-driven analysis using the MECE principle to break complex security challenges into clear, defensible parts.

- Use the Pyramid Principle to communicate recommendations clearly to both technical and executive audiences.

- Employ critical-thinking techniques (socratic questioning, root cause analysis, red team perspectives) to test reasoning and challenge assumptions.

- Manage incomplete or politically sensitive briefs by clarifying objectives, mapping stakeholders, and maintaining progress under uncertainty.

- Develop mental, physical, and professional resilience strategies to sustain long-term effectiveness.

- Analyse a case of a politically sensitive security review to illustrate how mindset and structure produce constructive outcomes.

- Implement reflection tools (performance audits, learning loops) to embed continuous improvement and professional growth.

Introduction

The effectiveness of a security consultant is determined as much by mindset as by knowledge. Technical expertise provides the foundation, but it is only one part of the equation. Clients rarely hire consultants simply for what they know. They hire them for how they think, how they frame problems, how they communicate solutions, and how they guide organisations through uncertainty.

This chapter explores the mindset required to make that leap – from being seen as a capable technical contributor to being recognised as a trusted adviser. In this role, the consultant is not just solving narrow technical problems but is guiding decisions that affect wider organisational resilience, reputation, and strategy. The chapter explains the mindset behind this shift and shows how consulting frameworks can be applied directly to security.

The material is structured around several key themes. First, we consider the transition from technical expert to trusted adviser, examining why credibility and influence often matter more than raw technical detail. We then explore structured approaches to problem solving, drawing on McKinsey's hypothesis-driven method and the MECE principle to demonstrate how security challenges can be broken down into their core components. Building on this, we examine the Pyramid Principle as a way of communicating with clarity and authority, especially to time-pressured executives.

Next, we turn to the realities of practice: the consultant's ability to operate when the brief is incomplete, ambiguous, or politically charged. Here, mindset becomes not just a tool for analysis but a shield against confusion and conflict. To sustain performance over time, we also consider resilience – the combination of mental, physical, and professional habits that prevent burnout and ensure longevity in a demanding career.

The chapter provides a practical Illustrative Example in de-escalating a politically sensitive security review, showing how these mindset tools come together in practice. It concludes with reflective techniques that allow consultants to audit their own performance and embed continuous learning.

Mindset is not abstract but expressed in how consultants think, act, and sustain themselves. When mastered, it turns technical competence into trust, clarity, and resilience – the marks of a successful security consultant.

From Technical Expert to Trusted Adviser

Many security professionals begin their careers as technical specialists. They may be engineers, system designers, or analysts whose work is defined by detail, precision, and compliance to standards. This foundation is essential, but when those individuals step into consultancy, they often discover that success depends on far more than technical accuracy. Clients are not only looking for someone who can configure a system, design a perimeter, or write a risk assessment. They are looking for someone they can trust to guide them through uncertainty, make sense of complexity, and influence decisions at senior levels. Making the shift from technical expert to trusted adviser is therefore a central mindset change for any consultant.

The technical expert mindset is rooted in solving problems at the micro level. The expert identifies a fault, applies knowledge to resolve it, and delivers a solution that meets defined criteria. Success is measured by correctness. While valuable, this approach can limit the consultant's impact when the problem itself is ill-defined, the objectives are contested, or the decision-makers do not speak a technical language. In such situations, focusing only on the detail can leave the consultant sidelined, with their recommendations misunderstood or ignored.

The trusted adviser mindset, by contrast, is solution-oriented and contextual. It requires the consultant to look beyond the immediate technical issue and consider how the problem connects to organisational goals, regulatory obligations, commercial drivers, and reputational concerns. Influence comes not just from the accuracy of analysis but also from how advice is positioned, communicated, and received. This mindset is about being proactive, shaping the conversation, and becoming a partner in decision-making rather than a vendor of information.

Alan Weiss, in *Million Dollar Consulting*[23], captures this difference by describing how consultants move from providing deliverables to creating outcomes. A deliverable may be a risk register or a technical specification;

an outcome is a more resilient organisation, reduced exposure, or improved stakeholder confidence. Clients ultimately value outcomes over deliverables, and consultants who frame their work in those terms are more likely to earn trust. For security consultants, this might mean shifting emphasis from producing a technical audit report to showing how the audit supports business continuity or regulatory compliance.

Consider a review of a logistics hub. One consultant lists technical deficiencies: outdated CCTV, non-compliant fire doors, and poor perimeter lighting, etc. Another begins with the risk to the hub's ability to meet delivery targets in peak season, linking each deficiency to potential disruption, reputational damage, and regulatory exposure. Both are technically correct, but only the second connects directly to outcomes the client cares about and is therefore more likely to be viewed as a partner in the business. Similarly, an access control system failure can be described as a hardware issue, but it becomes more compelling when framed as a risk to revenue continuity if staff or customers cannot access facilities. The trusted adviser translates the technical into the strategic.

Developing this role also requires presence and communication. Clients respond not only to what is said but to how it is said. Clear, confident communication in the client's language builds credibility, while jargon or unnecessary technical detail risks alienation. Consultants who can explain complex issues simply, listen actively, and frame recommendations around the client's objectives quickly establish authority.

Trust is reinforced by integrity. The trusted adviser does not simply echo what the client wants to hear. They are prepared to challenge assumptions, highlight uncomfortable truths, and point out risks that others may overlook. What distinguishes them is the diplomacy with which this is done – offering difficult messages in ways that preserve relationships and create room for constructive action.

The pathway from technical expert to trusted adviser can be described as a series of practical shifts in mindset: from detail to context, from deliverables to outcomes, from passive to proactive, from jargon to clarity, and from isolation to integration. For new consultants, developing this mindset means engaging with senior stakeholders to understand their priorities, and practising the art of reframing technical findings into strategic impacts.

Many technically excellent reports fail to create change because they overlook client priorities. By contrast, some consultants with limited technical depth achieve lasting influence through clarity, framing, and outcome-focused advice. Technical knowledge is essential but not enough. What elevates a consultant is the mindset of the trusted adviser – a shift that creates opportunities for lasting credibility, influence, and career growth.

McKinsey-Style Problem Solving

Successful consultants distinguish themselves by their ability to bring structure to complex and ambiguous problems. In security consultancy, where clients often present incomplete briefs or politically sensitive concerns, unstructured analysis can lead to wasted effort and inconclusive reports. A disciplined, hypothesis-driven approach ensures clarity, efficiency, and defensible recommendations.

McKinsey & Company are widely recognised for this structured method. Their approach is straightforward: define the issue precisely, break it into logical parts, focus on the most important elements, test assumptions against evidence, and synthesise findings into clear advice. For security consultants, adopting this discipline provides a way to turn confusion into actionable outcomes.

The first step is to clarify the problem. Client requests are often framed as solutions: a ministry may insist that "more guards are needed" or a corporation may state that "a new access control system is required." Taking these at face value risks entrenching a predetermined outcome. By probing further – asking what risks lie behind the request and what objectives truly matter – the consultant changes the brief into a strategic issue. This act of reframing demonstrates value before a solution is even proposed.

Once defined, the problem must be structured in a way that is both comprehensive and avoids duplication. The principle of being "mutually exclusive, collectively exhaustive" (MECE) is useful here. For example, concerns about a data centre can be set out under three categories: threats (terrorism, insider action, natural hazard), vulnerabilities (access control, redundancy, staff competence), and consequences (loss of service, reputational damage, regulatory penalties). This structure shows that security is not a vague concern but a set of interrelated elements that can be addressed systematically.

Prioritisation is the next discipline. Not every factor deserves equal analysis. A consultant who treats all issues alike risks diluting focus and exhausting resources. The professional approach is to identify the most critical drivers and direct attention there. This demonstrates judgement and respects the client's priorities.

With priorities established, the consultant formulates initial hypotheses about likely solutions. Hypothesis-driven work does not begin with exhaustive data gathering but with an informed best guess that is then tested. For example, if a transport authority reports rising vandalism on metro lines, the consultant might hypothesise that poor monitoring of CCTV coverage is the main factor. Evidence – such as camera placement, monitoring practices, and incident patterns – is then gathered to confirm or refute the hypothesis. If disproved, the hypothesis is revised, perhaps pointing instead to inadequate lighting or poor community engagement. This iterative process avoids aimless analysis and ensures data collection has purpose.

The final step is synthesis – bringing evidence and analysis together into a clear story that leads directly to action. In the metro example, this might be expressed as: 'Vandalism is undermining passenger confidence and revenue. Three drivers were assessed: deterrence, access control, and environmental design. Poor lighting and weak monitoring proved decisive, so immediate improvements should focus on these areas, with other measures considered later.' This type of conclusion is unambiguous, defensible, and actionable.

Security consultancy is shaped by ambiguity: threats are uncertain, intelligence is partial, and stakeholders are rarely aligned. Consultants who rely on instinct or unstructured inquiry risk producing reports that lack focus or credibility. Those who apply structured, hypothesis-driven methods provide clarity, demonstrate professionalism, and deliver recommendations that withstand scrutiny from boards, regulators, and public authorities.

Critical Thinking Tools for Security Consulting

Structured methods such as hypothesis-driven analysis provide discipline, but they must be complemented by techniques that test reasoning more deeply. Critical thinking ensures that recommendations are not only logical but also robust against hidden flaws. Three approaches are especially valuable in security consulting: socratic questioning, root cause analysis, and red team perspectives.

Socratic questioning challenges surface assumptions by asking a sequence of probing "why" and "how" questions. A client may assert that "more guards will reduce risk." Instead of accepting this at face value, the consultant asks: Why is more manpower necessary? What risk is being reduced? How will effectiveness be measured? This method uncovers gaps in reasoning and reveals whether the proposed solution addresses the true issue.

Root cause analysis prevents consultants from treating symptoms rather than causes. If repeated breaches occur at a facility, the immediate response might be to strengthen locks or add cameras. A root cause approach digs deeper, perhaps showing that staff training, procedural lapses, or poor supervision are the real vulnerabilities. Addressing these underlying causes delivers more durable solutions than reactive fixes.

Red team perspectives introduce deliberate challenge by considering how an adversary would exploit weaknesses. By adopting the mindset of an attacker, or inviting a colleague to take that role, consultants test whether their assumptions hold up against determined opposition. This perspective often exposes blind spots overlooked by conventional analysis.

Together, these tools sharpen judgement. They do not replace structured problem solving but enhance it, ensuring that recommendations are challenged from multiple angles before being presented to the client. For security consultants, the discipline of applying these methods is what turns structured analysis into advice that is both credible and resilient under scrutiny.

The Pyramid Principle – Communicating with Clarity

Advice is only valuable if clients can understand it and act on it. Many reports fail not because the recommendations are wrong, but because they are buried in detail or delivered in ways that lose the audience. Senior executives in particular expect the conclusion first, with evidence to follow.

Barbara Minto's Pyramid Principle provides a disciplined structure: start with the answer, support it with a few grouped arguments, and place detailed evidence beneath them. The result is a pyramid – conclusion at the top, key points in the middle, data at the base.

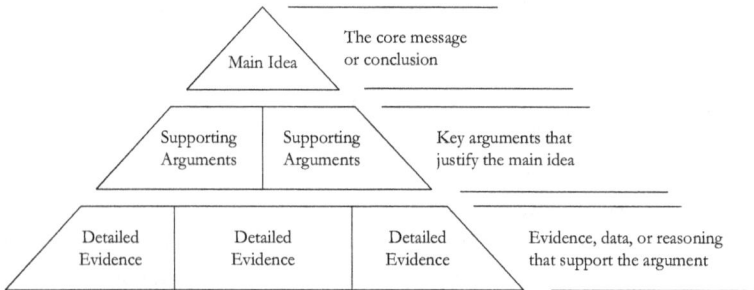

Figure 2 The Pyramid Principle

For example, a conventional headquarters security review might begin with survey notes and specifications before eventually recommending a lobby redesign. The pyramid approach reverses this: "The lobby design must be changed to prevent tailgating and ensure regulatory compliance." Supporting arguments then follow: tailgating incidents are frequent, CCTV placement is ineffective, and design alternatives exist within budget. Detailed evidence such as logs and diagrams sits beneath each argument. The executive immediately knows the action required and why it matters.

The same discipline strengthens presentations. Instead of leading with background slides, the consultant opens with the recommendation: "Upgrade perimeter detection within twelve months to address critical vulnerabilities." Three grouped reasons then follow, each supported by concise evidence. Technical detail remains available in appendices but does not obscure the key message. This prevents overloaded presentations and ensures that the recommendation is heard before attention fades.

The point of the Pyramid Principle is to make the logic obvious. Put the answer first, then show why it follows, either from rules or from evidence. A rule-based line might read: the standard requires two-factor authentication; the site currently uses one; therefore, a second factor must be added. An evidence-based line might read: recent breaches exploited single-factor logins; sites that added a second factor saw incidents fall; therefore, the stronger control should be adopted. When set out as a pyramid, i.e. conclusion, grouped reasons, key facts, the chain of thought is clear and easy to test.

The temptation to recount every investigative step is strong, but it risks burying the conclusion. The Pyramid Principle demands discipline: lead with the answer, group arguments logically, and keep detail in supporting layers. Clear structure signals clear thinking. Clients perceive concise, logical recommendations as authoritative, while disorganised reports undermine confidence.

Clients remember clarity long after they forget detail. Lead with structure, finish with sense.

The Pyramid Principle is more than a presentation technique; it is a mindset for communication. By ensuring that advice is correct, comprehensible, and actionable, it turns technical findings into decisions that drive change.

Managing Ambiguity in Security Consulting

Ambiguity is a constant in consultancy. Unlike engineering, where inputs and outputs can be specified, security assignments are shaped by incomplete information, shifting priorities, and political sensitivities. Threats evolve, intelligence may be withheld, and different stakeholders often push in conflicting directions. Because ambiguity is inevitable, the consultant's role is not to remove it but to manage it constructively.

Ambiguity in security projects has several sources. Information may be incomplete – for example, a client might choose not to disclose insider incidents. Stakeholders can clash, with ministries emphasising compliance while operators concentrate on cost. Political sensitivities may complicate recommendations, such as when the use of armed guards risks provoking public resistance. Rapid change also plays a part, as technologies or threats evolve during the life of a project. By recognising these drivers, consultants can anticipate challenges and plan ahead instead of being forced into reactive measures.

Progress depends on creating clarity step by step. The first task is to define the objectives, which rarely happens in a single discussion. Consultants need to ask questions such as "Why is this being done now?" or "What will success look like for the client?" to sharpen the brief. When data is lacking, the best way forward is to frame a working explanation, essentially an informed guess, and then test it against available evidence, refining the explanation as new facts emerge. Stakeholder mapping helps the consultant understand the political landscape: who holds influence, whose priorities matter most, and where resistance may appear. Throughout this process, openness is essential. Consultants who show the options available and explain their assumptions earn trust, while those who present uncertain conclusions as if they were definite, soon lose credibility.

Ambiguity can also be an opportunity. A loosely framed request for "better security" allows the consultant to broaden the agenda, linking security to business continuity, compliance, and reputation. For example, when a city authority wanted safer transport hubs, analysis showed that crime was concentrated in poorly lit areas. By framing the issue as one of environmental design rather than levels of policing, the consultant proposed practical improvements that delivered results without triggering political backlash. This type of reframing shows how ambiguity, if handled well, can open space for solutions that are both effective and acceptable.

Ambiguity should not be seen as an exception but as the norm in security consulting. Consultants who accept it as part of the job, and manage it with structure, adaptability, and transparency, turn uncertainty into confidence for their clients. In doing so, they position themselves as trusted navigators in complex environments.

Resilience Skills for Long-Term Success

Security consultancy is demanding. High-stakes projects, tight deadlines, and constant travel create pressure that can erode performance if resilience is neglected. Technical ability and mindset matter, but without resilience, careers shorten through burnout or disengagement. With resilience, consultants sustain performance, credibility, and influence across years of assignments.

Resilience can be understood in three dimensions: mental, physical, and professional. Each requires deliberate attention. Mental resilience is the ability to absorb pressure without losing balance. Reframing setbacks as feedback, maintaining a growth mindset, and setting clear boundaries prevent overwork and preserve confidence. Simple tools such as maintaining a lessons log after each project help identify patterns and strengthen adaptability.

Physical resilience is equally important. Irregular travel, long hours, and stressful environments diminish energy and decision-making. Sustainable routines of sleep, nutrition, and exercise are not optional extras but core to professional credibility. Planning high-concentration tasks for peak energy periods and building recovery time into travel schedules ensure performance is maintained when stakes are highest.

Professional resilience secures long-term career viability. Consultants who diversify skills, maintain networks, and protect their reputation adapt more readily to changes in technology, regulation, or client demand. Regular "career audits" help to check progress against goals, ensuring growth is intentional rather than accidental.

Consider a consultant securing a new airport under shifting regulations, political pressures, and budget cuts. Without resilience, the strain may cause withdrawal or decline in output. With resilience, the consultant maintains perspective, protects health, and adapts skills to emerging risks, finishing the project stronger and more credible.

Resilience is not innate. It is built through deliberate routines, reflection, and recovery. Consultants who treat it as a core skill, rather than a background consideration, sustain effectiveness over time. In security consultancy, consistent high-quality output is the ultimate measure of success – and resilience is what makes it possible.

Illustrative Example: De-escalating a Politically Charged Security Review

A multinational energy company commissioned a review of a critical facility in a politically sensitive region. The consultant's technical findings were a weak perimeter security, inconsistent response readiness, and limited insider threat controls. Although the findings were accurate, they provoked hostility from local management and government representatives. The consultant faced a dilemma: dilute the findings or risk losing the project altogether.

The breakthrough came by reframing the role from external critic to trusted partner. Instead of defending technical detail line by line, the consultant presented the issues in grouped categories of deterrence, response, and insider resilience, which reduced defensiveness and encouraged systemic discussion. Adopting a Pyramid Principle style, the revised summary began with a positive conclusion: compliance could be achieved within eighteen months by addressing three priorities. Evidence followed in support, showing a practical path to improvement.

Stakeholder mapping revealed competing interests: government actors wished to avoid reputational harm, while the multinational's board required regulatory assurance. By positioning recommendations as both compliance measures and opportunities to demonstrate international leadership, the consultant aligned both camps. Throughout, resilience was tested, absorbing criticism, maintaining calm, and keeping communication constructive under political pressure.

The revised report was accepted. Upgrades began with perimeter improvements and response drills, followed by insider threat measures. The government presented these changes as progress, and the board gained the assurance it required. The consultant's success lay not only in technical accuracy but in mindset: reframing, structuring, communicating clearly, and maintaining composure. The point is that in politically sensitive environments, influence depends as much on how findings are positioned as on their technical content.

Personal Performance Audits and Learning Loops

Resilience and clarity of thought are strengthened when consultants commit to deliberate reflection. Security consultancy often involves complex projects where multiple factors interact in unpredictable ways. Without a structured way of reviewing performance, consultants risk repeating mistakes, overlooking personal blind spots, or failing to recognise areas of growth. Reflection therefore becomes not an optional extra but a professional discipline, one that ensures each engagement contributes to long-term development rather than simply adding to a catalogue of experiences.

A useful tool for this is the personal performance audit. At the end of each project, consultants can assess their own contribution systematically, asking questions across several dimensions: technical quality, client influence, clarity of communication, and personal resilience. This process moves reflection beyond vague impressions into something concrete. For example, a consultant might conclude that while their technical recommendations were sound, they struggled to frame them in language accessible to executives. By recording this insight, they set a specific focus for improvement in the next engagement.

Another valuable approach is the use of learning loops. A single loop of learning involves evaluating an action, drawing a lesson, and applying it to the next project. A double loop goes further, questioning the assumptions or mindset that underpinned the original action. In consultancy, where much depends on how problems are framed, double-loop learning can be especially powerful. A consultant who repeatedly encounters client resistance might, through reflection, realise that the issue lies not in the recommendations themselves but in how they are introduced, prompting a deeper change in communication style.

Journalling can also support reflective practice. Brief notes captured during and after projects provide a record of challenges faced, decisions made, and outcomes achieved. Over time, patterns emerge, highlighting strengths and weaknesses that may not have been obvious in the moment. Sharing these reflections with a mentor or trusted peer adds further value, as external perspectives often reveal blind spots that self-assessment misses.

Importantly, reflection should also encompass resilience. Consultants can ask not only "Did I deliver the project effectively?" but also "At what cost to my health, balance, or motivation?" Noticing when a project has drained energy excessively allows consultants to adjust, whether through better time management, improved boundary setting, or more deliberate recovery practices.

Embedding performance audits and learning loops into professional life ensures that each assignment is a source of growth as well as delivery. The consultant who reflects consistently becomes not only more skilled but more self-aware, avoiding the complacency that can undermine long-term success. Reflection, when treated as a structured habit, turns experience into expertise and ensures that every project strengthens the mindset required for sustained performance in the demanding field of security consultancy.

Practice Guide

Mindset is what elevates technical competence into lasting professional value. Yet consultants often fall into predictable traps: clinging to the comfort of technical detail rather than stepping into the broader role of trusted adviser; abandoning structure when faced with ambiguity; or allowing bottom-up communication to bury recommendations beneath data. Others neglect resilience, leading to burnout, or underestimate political and cultural dynamics, treating them as secondary to technical findings. Each of these pitfalls erodes credibility and prevents consultants from influencing decisions at the level where it matters most.

To counter these risks, consultants must consciously adopt the mindset of the trusted adviser, framing work in terms of outcomes rather than deliverables. Structured methods such as hypothesis-driven analysis and the MECE principle bring clarity to complex problems, while the Pyramid Principle ensures that recommendations are delivered with impact and acted upon. Building resilience across mental, physical, and professional dimensions sustains long-term effectiveness, while reflective practice – through performance audits and learning loops – turns experience into growth. Above all, credible consultants combine technical accuracy with sensitivity to political, cultural, and organisational realities, ensuring that advice is both robust and workable.

You should now be able to distinguish between technical expert and trusted adviser, apply structured analysis and communication methods, manage ambiguity with confidence, and embed resilience and reflection into your practice. These are not abstract ideals but practical habits that sustain influence, trust, and credibility. The consultant's mindset provides the foundation for the detailed methods and processes that follow in later chapters, ensuring they are applied with judgement, adaptability, and professional integrity.

Chapter 3 – Core Skills That Cannot Be Outsourced

Technical expertise is essential in security consultancy, but alone, it is not sufficient. What distinguishes a professional consultant from a technical specialist is the mastery of a set of personal skills that cannot be automated, outsourced, or delegated. These skills determine whether analysis is trusted, whether recommendations are acted upon, and whether the consultant is valued as more than a supplier of technical outputs.

By the end of this chapter, you will be able to:

- Apply structured observation and note-taking techniques to capture details accurately and convert them into usable insights.
- Communicate effectively across diverse audiences, adapting language and emphasis to ensure clarity and influence.
- Use influencing and negotiation skills to secure buy-in, manage expectations, and resolve conflict constructively.
- Build trust through authentic communication and establish clear mutual expectations at the start of engagements.
- Assemble and maintain a consultant's toolkit that integrates physical preparedness with mental discipline to sustain long-term performance.

Introduction

Some of the most important skills in consultancy cannot be reduced to checklists or replicated by software. They are rooted in human perception, communication, and judgement. They determine whether a client believes your recommendations, whether colleagues respect your role, and whether projects succeed in real conditions rather than theory. These skills are not secondary to technical knowledge; they are what allow technical knowledge to be applied effectively.

Observation is one example. A consultant who notices a propped-open fire door, a distracted guard, or a pattern of staff behaviour may uncover the real vulnerability that a specification document never reveals. Note-taking transforms fleeting impressions into a structured record that can withstand scrutiny months later. Communication is another. A consultant who can explain a complex security concept to a board in terms of risk and reputation and then explain the same issue to an operator in terms of daily procedures, adds far more value than one who delivers a technically correct but inaccessible report.

Influencing and negotiation sit at the heart of consultancy. Security recommendations often challenge budgets, habits, or politics, and the consultant must be able to persuade, reframe, and compromise without losing sight of the core objective. Trust underpins all of this. From the earliest conversations, clients must believe that the consultant's advice is independent, credible, and aligned with their interests. Without trust, even the most carefully crafted analysis is disregarded.

Consultants need a toolkit – not only the physical essentials of site work, but also the mental disciplines that sustain performance under pressure. Checklists, structured methods, and resilience practices are as important as laptops and measuring tools. These elements are rarely glamorous, but they form the foundation of professional practice.

This chapter explores these core skills in detail, showing how they are developed, applied, and sustained in practice. They are the skills that cannot be outsourced – the consultant's enduring value when technology, markets, and threats are constantly changing.

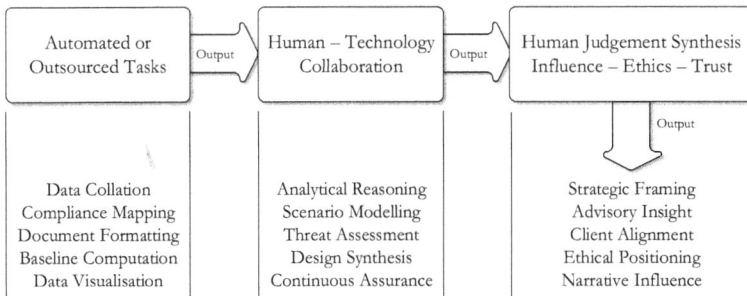

Automated or Outsourced Tasks	Human – Technology Collaboration	Human Judgement Synthesis Influence – Ethics – Trust
Data Collation	Analytical Reasoning	Strategic Framing
Compliance Mapping	Scenario Modelling	Advisory Insight
Document Formatting	Threat Assessment	Client Alignment
Baseline Computation	Design Synthesis	Ethical Positioning
Data Visualisation	Continuous Assurance	Narrative Influence

Figure 3 From Automation to Judgement

Observation and Note-Taking in the Field

Observation is one of the most valuable contributions a consultant can make to a project. Technical knowledge provides the framework for understanding systems, but it is direct observation that reveals how those systems function. A facility may appear compliant on paper, yet the living environment often tells a different story: barriers propped open for convenience, staff developing informal shortcuts, or technology used in ways that undermine its intended resilience. The consultant who cultivates disciplined observation can see beyond specifications and uncover how security is experienced on the ground.

Effective observation begins with an open mind. Checklists are useful for ensuring coverage, but they should not narrow attention to expected findings. The most significant insights often come from noticing what does not fit – a guard who waves colleagues through without checking credentials, a service door left open at shift change, or a camera repositioned to face a wall. These details may seem minor, yet they often indicate systemic weaknesses. The skilled consultant resists the temptation to confirm expectations and instead asks, "What is really happening here?"

One way to structure observations is to think in three categories: physical, procedural, and behavioural. Physical observations concern the built environment and technology – fences, locks, cameras, barriers, and lighting. Procedural observations focus on how processes are carried out, such as the management of access control, logging of incidents, or handling of keys. Behavioural observations look at how people engage with systems: whether staff follow rules consistently, how guards apply discretion, and whether organisational culture supports or undermines formal measures. Using such a framework ensures balance and prevents findings from being dominated by a single perspective.

Notes are how these observations are captured and preserved. Relying on memory after a long site visit is unreliable; details fade quickly, and impressions become blurred. Field notes should be clear, structured, and capable of standing up to later scrutiny. Recording not only what was seen, but also the context, adds weight to analysis. For example, "turnstile unstaffed at 10:15 during morning shift change; three staff entered without swiping cards" conveys far more than a vague comment such as "turnstile poorly controlled." Detail makes patterns easier to identify, allows comparison with procedures, and provides evidence if findings are questioned.

Different consultants favour different recording methods. Some use digital tablets that combine sketches, photographs, and annotations; others prefer notebooks that are discreet and reliable. The format matters less than the discipline: notes must be legible, organised, and backed up securely. A scanned copy of handwritten notes or immediate transfer of digital files helps protect against loss in demanding environments where information may otherwise be mislaid.

Observation also requires interpretation. A door repeatedly left ajar may reflect more than staff negligence. It may indicate that the access system is too slow, that staff are carrying loads that make the door difficult to close, or that organisational culture places convenience over compliance. Turning observation into analysis means asking why behaviours occur, not simply recording that they exist. This is where consultants provide real value: identifying the underlying causes that clients can address rather than producing a catalogue of surface faults.

Conversations with staff often extend and enrich what is seen. A receptionist who remarks that visitors are regularly waved through without checks may point to a wider cultural issue. A guard who admits that alarms are ignored because they trigger too frequently may reveal flaws in system configuration. Such insights emerge from attentive listening and discreet questioning. However, care is required in how notes from interviews are taken, since stakeholders may be sensitive about attribution. Many consultants record themes rather than verbatim quotations unless explicit permission is given, ensuring that analysis is accurate without undermining trust.

Consultants must be aware of bias. It is easy to give undue weight to observations that confirm expectations or to focus on dramatic failures while overlooking quieter but equally important deficiencies. Asking deliberately what is working well, or reviewing notes with a colleague, helps correct this tendency and ensures a more balanced picture. Over time, experience teaches consultants how to strike a balance: enough detail to be accurate and defensible, but concise enough to reveal patterns without being overwhelmed by minutiae.

Observation and note-taking may appear routine compared with advanced modelling or strategic planning, yet they underpin all other aspects of consultancy. Without reliable observation, analysis lacks a foundation. Without disciplined notes, insights are easily contested or forgotten. Developing these skills ensures that recommendations are grounded in reality, defensible under scrutiny, and responsive to the client's true needs. They are the first of the core skills that cannot be outsourced, and they remain essential to the profession.

Observation reveals truth that data hides. What you notice – and how you note it – defines your credibility.

Communicating Effectively Across Audiences

In security consultancy, the quality of advice is judged not only on technical accuracy but on the ability to communicate it clearly and persuasively. A sound recommendation has little value if decision-makers cannot understand it, or if operational staff do not see how to apply it in practice. Communication is therefore not a soft skill but a professional discipline that underpins every aspect of consultancy.

Consultants operate across varied audiences: a site engineer may need detailed specifications, a finance director may want a cost–benefit justification, and a regulator may seek assurance of compliance. Using the same message for all is ineffective. The task is to adapt without distorting the substance, ensuring that information is accessible and meaningful to each recipient. This begins with clarity. Security is a technical field, but acronyms and specialist terms (CCTV, ACS, IDS, VMS) often confuse those outside of it. The consultant must translate these into plain English while preserving accuracy: instead of describing "inadequate delay times on the perimeter fence," explain that "an intruder could enter within seconds, leaving staff little chance to respond." The meaning is intact, but the risk is tangible.

Beyond clarity, effective communication depends on framing. For senior executives, the priority is often business continuity, reputation, and regulatory compliance. The same issue that an engineer understands as a technical deficiency can be presented to a board as a risk to operations, an exposure to penalties, or a threat to customer confidence. For operational staff, the same recommendation may be framed in terms of reducing false alarms or improving safety during peak shifts. By connecting advice to the priorities of each audience, the consultant increases the likelihood that it will be accepted and acted upon.

The structure of communication is equally important. Many reports are written chronologically, presenting methods, then data, and only later the conclusion. By the time the recommendation appears, attention has waned. More effective is a top–down structure, long established in management consulting: state the conclusion first, then present supporting evidence. This respects the limited time of senior leaders and ensures that the central point is not lost. The same principle applies to presentations and briefings, where beginning with a clear recommendation baseline the discussion and gives context to the detail that follows.

Storytelling adds further impact. While consultancy is rooted in evidence, people respond strongly to narrative. A consultant who explains that "an intruder could pass through the unmonitored loading bay, enter the warehouse floor, and reach valuable stock before any alarm is raised" creates a vivid mental image that a technical phrase like "loading bay vulnerability" cannot achieve. When supported by data, such storytelling turns abstract risk into a scenario that demands attention.

Listening is as much a part of communication as speaking or writing. Clients' reactions often reveal where a message has failed to land: hesitation, defensiveness, or repeated questions may indicate the need to reframe or clarify. Active listening also signals respect. A client who feels heard is more likely to trust and act on advice, even when the message is difficult. Communication should be treated as a two-way process, where client feedback shapes how the message is delivered just as analysis shapes what is being said.

Medium also shapes message. Written reports require precision and structure; presentations call for brevity, confidence, and visual clarity; informal conversations on site demand sensitivity and adaptability. Each form of communication can enhance credibility, but each also carries risk if mishandled. A confused report undermines confidence in technical expertise, while an unfocused briefing may weaken influence. Professional consultants prepare carefully for all formats, recognising that every interaction conveys competence.

Visuals are often underestimated, yet a simple diagram can convey relationships more effectively than pages of text. A coverage map showing blind spots in camera placement may persuade decision-makers more quickly than a technical description. The key is discipline: visuals must illuminate the main point, not overwhelm with complexity. Used sparingly and with clarity, they can turn analysis into something grasped at a glance.

Cultural context also shapes how communication is received. In some regions, direct statements are valued; in others, an indirect and cautious style is expected. A message that is persuasive in one setting may appear aggressive, or alternatively indecisive, in another. Consultants working internationally must therefore adapt not only language but tone, balancing firmness with diplomacy in ways that align with local norms.

Examples from practice show the consequences of communication choices. In one project, a technically accurate but lengthy report failed to influence executives because the recommendation was buried in detail. When reframed into a short executive summary using a top–down structure, the same findings were accepted and implemented within weeks. In another case, a consultant initially emphasised technical compliance when presenting to a regulator. Resistance followed until the recommendation was repositioned as a measure to protect public trust and align with international standards. The technical evidence remained unchanged, but the reframing secured approval.

Good communication is what turns technical analysis into something clients can use. Observation and analysis count for little if they cannot be conveyed in ways that clients understand, believe, and act upon. Mastering clarity, framing, structure, and listening ensures that recommendations achieve their purpose: influencing decisions and creating lasting value for the client.

Influencing and Negotiation Skills

Unlike managers, consultants do not have authority over the client's staff, budgets, or operations. Their ability to effect change depends on persuasion rather than command. A consultant may present evidence, propose solutions, and highlight risks, but ultimately it is the client who decides whether to act. This dynamic makes influencing and negotiation indispensable skills that cannot be delegated or replaced by technology.

Influence begins with credibility. Clients are more likely to be persuaded by consultants who demonstrate independence, integrity, and competence. Technical expertise establishes the baseline, but credibility is reinforced through behaviour: consistency in messages, transparency about limitations, and honesty when challenges arise. Consultants who overstate certainty or promise results that cannot be guaranteed undermine their influence when outcomes fail to match assurances. In contrast, a consultant who explains both the strengths and limitations of their findings builds trust that makes their recommendations harder to dismiss.

Persuasion relies on more than facts. Data, risk assessments, and compliance requirements are important, but they rarely speak for themselves. Decision-makers interpret evidence through the lens of their own priorities, whether financial, operational, or political. Effective consultants frame their recommendations in ways that connect directly to those priorities. A proposal to strengthen perimeter security may be presented as a cost-saving measure by reducing theft, as a regulatory safeguard to avoid penalties, or as a reputational issue that protects customer confidence. The underlying recommendation remains the same, but the framing ensures that it resonates with the decision-maker's concerns.

Negotiation is closely tied to influence, because consultants frequently operate in environments where interests conflict. Budgets may be tight, departments may compete for resources, and senior leaders may have differing views of acceptable risk. In such situations, negotiation is about finding workable solutions that protect security objectives while respecting the realities of the organisation. This requires balance: pushing too hard may alienate stakeholders, while conceding too much may render recommendations ineffective.

A useful approach is interest-based negotiation, which focuses on underlying needs rather than fixed positions. For example, a client may reject the installation of additional barriers because of cost. If the consultant treats this as an absolute refusal, progress may stall. But by exploring the underlying concern – budgetary constraints in the current financial year – the consultant may identify alternatives, such as phasing the installation, using interim procedural measures, or reassigning funds from less critical areas. By addressing the client's true interests rather than their stated position, the consultant can often secure agreement without compromising core objectives.

Reframing is another powerful influencing tool. Clients may present problems in narrow technical terms, expecting equally narrow solutions. A client may insist that the issue is "failing CCTV" and that the solution must be new cameras. The consultant who simply agrees to this framing limits their ability to add value. Instead, by reframing the issue as a question of "situational awareness and monitoring effectiveness," the consultant can broaden the scope to include guard deployment, lighting, or control room practices. This not only addresses the underlying vulnerability more effectively but also positions the consultant as a strategic thinker rather than a technician.

Influence often depends on timing. A recommendation delivered when a client is distracted by other priorities, or when budgets are already allocated, may be ignored regardless of its merit. Consultants must therefore be sensitive to organisational rhythms, decision-making cycles, and political climates. Sometimes the most effective approach is to introduce an idea early and allow it to mature. Patience, persistence, and careful timing can make the difference between a proposal that is rejected and one that is adopted enthusiastically.

Sometimes conflict arises and managing it constructively is a vital skill. Recommendations may challenge existing practices, highlight failures, or imply criticism of staff. Clients may resist because they feel threatened, embarrassed, or defensive. In such situations, the consultant must separate criticism of systems from criticism of people. Phrases such as "the procedure is not working as intended" are less confrontational than "staff are failing to follow the rules." When individuals feel respected, they are more likely to accept recommendations that still require them to change.

It is also important to recognise the limits of influence. Consultants who push relentlessly risk damaging relationships and being excluded from future discussions. Sometimes the most effective form of influence is to step back, provide clear documentation of advice, and allow the client to make their own decision. While this may mean that recommendations are not adopted immediately, it preserves credibility and leaves the door open for future engagement. Clients often return when circumstances change, remembering the consultant who provided sound advice without applying undue pressure.

Influencing and negotiation are not about winning arguments or forcing compliance. They are about enabling clients to make informed decisions that balance security with other organisational needs. Consultants who master these skills become trusted advisers whose recommendations carry weight even in the most complex or contested environments. They demonstrate that influence is not a matter of authority but of credibility, empathy, and the ability to align solutions with client priorities.

Building Trust and Setting Expectations

Without trust, even the most carefully researched recommendations are unlikely to be acted upon. Clients value more than expertise; they seek confidence in the person providing the advice. When trust is absent, reports are shelved, conversations become defensive, and projects stall. When trust is present, clients are willing to share sensitive information, accept difficult messages, and make changes that may be politically or financially uncomfortable. Building and sustaining trust is therefore one of the most important skills a consultant must develop.

Trust begins at the first interaction. Before any analysis or site visit takes place, clients form impressions based on tone, transparency, and authenticity. Consultants who listen carefully, ask clarifying questions, and show genuine interest in the client's concerns establish credibility more quickly than those who focus immediately on showcasing technical expertise. Clients want to feel that their problems are understood before they want to hear solutions. A consultant who jumps to premature conclusions risks appearing arrogant or detached, whereas one who takes time to frame the problem in the client's own terms signals respect and alignment.

One of the most practical ways to establish trust early is through what *Flawless Consulting*[3] describes as "contracting conversations." These are not legal contracts but discussions that set out mutual expectations for how the engagement will proceed. They cover scope, responsibilities, timelines, and communication preferences. By clarifying these issues at the outset, the consultant prevents misunderstandings and demonstrates professionalism. For example, agreeing in advance how often progress updates will be provided, who will attend review meetings, and how feedback will be handled reassures the client that the process will be orderly and predictable.

Setting expectations also involves being honest about limitations. Consultants who pretend to know more than they do, or who promise results they cannot guarantee, may gain short-term approval but will quickly lose credibility when the reality does not match their assurances. A consultant who openly acknowledges uncertainties, explains assumptions, and sets realistic boundaries of responsibility builds a stronger foundation of trust. Clients are more willing to accept unwelcome findings when they come from someone who has consistently been candid about both strengths and limits.

Delivering difficult messages is a key test of trust. Security consultancy often requires pointing out vulnerabilities, failings, or cultural problems that clients may prefer to ignore. When presented clumsily, such messages can cause defensiveness and resistance. When presented with respect and balance, they can prompt constructive change. One useful technique is to frame issues in terms of systems rather than individuals. Saying "the access control system does not encourage consistent enforcement" is less confrontational than "guards are failing to do their jobs." Another is to balance critique with recognition, highlighting what is working well alongside areas of weakness. This approach reassures clients that the consultant's perspective is fair and objective rather than one-sided.

Trust is reinforced by consistency. Clients quickly notice discrepancies between what consultants say and what they do. Promising to deliver a report by a certain date but missing the deadline without explanation erodes credibility, even if the analysis itself is excellent. Conversely, meeting commitments reliably, however small, builds a reputation for dependability that supports influence in larger matters. Consultants should therefore treat every commitment as important, recognising that reliability is remembered long after technical details are forgotten.

Trust is cumulative. Each successful interaction adds to a reservoir of credibility that supports the consultant in future engagements. Consultants who establish trust in one project are often invited back for others, and clients who feel respected and understood become advocates within their organisations. This cumulative effect cannot be achieved quickly but must be built steadily through authenticity, transparency, and consistent delivery.

Trust and expectations are inseparable. Trust is strengthened when expectations are set clearly and then met consistently. Expectations are easier to set when trust exists, because clients believe that the consultant is acting in their best interest. Together, they create a relationship in which advice is not only heard but acted upon. Consultants who master this dynamic ensure that their work has lasting impact, because their recommendations are implemented rather than ignored.

The Consultant's Toolkit – Physical and Mental

Every profession has its tools, and consultancy is no different. While security consultants are rarely expected to carry extensive technical equipment, they do require a personal toolkit that combines practical field resources with mental disciplines. This toolkit does not just support daily tasks; it underpins credibility, efficiency, and resilience. A consultant who arrives unprepared appears unprofessional, while one who relies solely on intellect risks missing details that proper preparation would have revealed. The most effective consultants balance physical readiness with a mental framework that ensures consistent performance in any environment.

The physical toolkit begins with the basics required for fieldwork. A reliable notebook and pen may seem trivial, yet they remain indispensable in environments where electronic devices are restricted or unreliable. Digital tablets and secure laptops are equally important for analysis, but they should never replace traditional methods entirely. Measuring tools, flashlights, and simple items such as spare batteries and adapters can prevent small obstacles from derailing site visits. Identification, safety gear, and personal protective equipment are sometimes overlooked but are essential when visiting industrial sites or construction projects. The principle is not to carry every conceivable tool, but to assemble a compact kit that ensures the consultant can function independently and adapt to a wide range of site conditions.

Preparation is part of the toolkit. Experienced consultants rarely arrive at a site without prior research. Reviewing architectural drawings, studying aerial imagery, and checking regulatory requirements before stepping on site makes fieldwork more efficient and professional. Carrying copies of relevant standards, regulations, or client documents in digital or printed form ensures that findings can be compared immediately against benchmarks rather than left for later. Templates for checklists, observation logs, and interview notes provide structure that speeds up work and reduces the risk of omissions. Together, these elements form a toolkit that allows the consultant to collect data accurately, interpret it in real time, and respond to unexpected questions with confidence.

The mental toolkit is less visible but equally important. It begins with critical thinking. Consultants must habitually question assumptions, test evidence, and seek alternative explanations. The Five Whys, red team perspectives, and structured hypothesis testing are not optional extras but part of the everyday toolkit that separates rigorous analysis from superficial opinion. These methods prevent consultants from jumping to easy conclusions and equip them to defend their recommendations when challenged.

Resilience also belongs in the mental toolkit. Consultancy often involves long hours, demanding travel schedules, and high-stakes environments. The ability to manage fatigue, maintain focus under pressure, and recover quickly from setbacks is essential. Techniques such as mindfulness, deliberate rest, and physical exercise are not luxuries but professional tools that sustain performance. A consultant who neglects physical and mental resilience may deliver one strong project but struggle to maintain effectiveness over time. The mental toolkit therefore includes deliberate habits for managing stress, protecting energy, and maintaining balance.

Adaptability is another component. Consultants regularly enter environments that are unfamiliar, politically sensitive, or resistant to change. No toolkit can anticipate every scenario, but a mental framework that emphasises curiosity, humility, and flexibility ensures that the consultant can respond constructively. Being willing to adjust methods, ask for clarification, or acknowledge gaps in knowledge is not a weakness but a strength that builds credibility. Adaptability is supported by preparation but depends ultimately on mindset.

Reflection closes the loop of the mental toolkit. Consultants who take time after projects to review what went well, what could have been improved, and how they responded under pressure steadily improve their practice. Keeping a personal learning log, seeking feedback from colleagues, or replaying difficult conversations to consider alternative approaches turns experience into expertise. This reflective habit ensures that the toolkit is not static but evolves with each project, making the consultant more effective over time.

The consultant's toolkit is therefore more than a collection of items or techniques. It represents a professional posture: being ready for the expected, resilient against the unexpected, and reflective enough to learn from both. Consultants who cultivate this balance demonstrate reliability to clients, sustain their own performance, and build the habits that define long-term success. The physical items provide the means to gather and record information effectively, while the mental disciplines ensure that information is interpreted wisely and communicated persuasively. Together, they form a core skill set that cannot be outsourced and that distinguishes professional consultancy from casual advice. These habits ensure that performance remains consistent even as clients, technologies, and risks evolve – the ultimate test of a consultant's preparedness.

Practice Guide

The real value of a consultant lies in skills that cannot be automated or outsourced. Yet common pitfalls remain: treating observation as a checklist exercise rather than a search for meaning, relying on memory instead of disciplined notetaking, or failing to adapt communication for different audiences. Some consultants approach negotiation as a contest rather than a search for shared outcomes, while others compromise credibility by overpromising or by presenting conclusions as certain when evidence is incomplete. Professional presence can also be undermined by arriving unprepared for site work or by neglecting the mental disciplines that sustain judgement under pressure.

To avoid these hazards, consultants should record observations systematically and interpret them in context, recognising that small details often reveal deeper vulnerabilities. Communication must be adapted to the audience, ensuring clarity without loss of technical accuracy. Negotiation should be framed as alignment of interests, not a battle of wills, and credibility must be protected through candour, realistic commitments, and consistency in delivery. Preparing both a physical toolkit – notebooks, templates, and essential field equipment – and a mental toolkit of critical thinking, resilience, and reflection ensures that consultants remain effective across varied and demanding environments. Trust is built incrementally, through reliability, transparency, and meeting even small commitments.

You should now be able to observe systematically and capture insights accurately, communicate across diverse audiences, influence and negotiate to secure buy-in, build trust through authenticity and clear expectations, and maintain a balanced toolkit of skills and resources. These are the habits that transform technical outputs into lasting professional impact. These core skills underpin the ethical frameworks, professional standards, and global perspectives that follow, ensuring that consultancy remains not only technically sound but also effective in practice and trusted in the real world.

Chapter 4 – Professional Ethics and Standards

Ethical conduct is at the heart of professional consultancy. Technical expertise may open the door, but it is integrity, transparency, and adherence to recognised standards that sustain trust and credibility over the long term. Clients engage consultants not only for their knowledge but also for their independence, their ability to provide objective advice, and their willingness to highlight uncomfortable truths. In a field where recommendations often have significant safety, financial, and reputational consequences, the ethical stance of the consultant can matter as much as the technical analysis.

By the end of this chapter, you will be able to:

- Define the principles of professional ethics in consultancy.
- Identify ethical dilemmas and apply structured reasoning to resolve them responsibly.
- Maintain professionalism, independence, transparency, and credibility by managing conflicts of interest.
- Apply relevant professional codes of practice and international standards to consulting assignments.
- Use systematic frameworks to make ethical decisions under commercial or political pressure.
- Embed ethical awareness into personal conduct as well as organisational culture to sustain long-term credibility.

Introduction

Professional ethics and standards provide the foundation for consultancy. They establish the boundaries within which technical advice can be trusted, and they distinguish the consultant from the contractor or vendor. While technical accuracy may demonstrate competence, it is ethical conduct that signals independence and reliability. Clients who suspect bias, hidden interests, or a lack of transparency will hesitate to act on advice, no matter how well reasoned it may appear.

Security consultancy is especially challenging because advisers must balance technology, legal rules, and workplace politics. In this environment, money and personal agendas can sometimes influence decisions and make it harder to give truly independent advice. The temptation to recommend a favoured supplier, to downplay findings for fear of damaging relationships, or to exaggerate risks to win work is real and recurring. Such situations demand not only technical knowledge but ethical discipline.

Standards and codes of practice provide a framework to guide consultants through such dilemmas. International frameworks such as ISO 31000:2018[13] for risk management, ISO/IEC 27001:2022[15] for information security, and ASIS International's code of ethics[2] establish benchmarks of conduct and accountability. Regional requirements, from the Security Industry Regulatory Agency (SIRA[4]) in Dubai to the Security Industry Authority (SIA) in the UK, reinforce these obligations with legal and professional weight. By adhering to these frameworks, consultants protect not only their clients but also their own professional reputations.

Ethics in security consultancy are not just theory. They show up in everyday choices – deciding what work to take on, how to present results, how to protect private information, and how to stay professional, even when money pressures push the other way. Consultants who embed ethics into every stage of their practice build resilience against these pressures and strengthen their long-term credibility. In doing so, they contribute to a culture where ethical standards are not an afterthought but an integral part of consultancy.

This chapter explores what professional ethics means in real life conditions, how standards provide structure, and how consultants can navigate real-world dilemmas. It argues that ethics and standards are not constraints but enablers: they provide the consultant with the authority and credibility to influence decisions, protect independence, and ensure that advice leads to outcomes that are not only effective but also principled.

Defining Professional Ethics in Consultancy

Ethics in consultancy is often spoken of in abstract terms, but for the practising consultant it has a very specific and practical meaning. It refers to the consistent application of principles such as integrity, independence, and objectivity in every aspect of professional conduct. Ethics is not confined to avoiding corruption or malpractice; it is about maintaining credibility through fairness, honesty, and transparency, even under pressure from clients, colleagues, or commercial circumstances.

At its simplest, professional ethics can be thought of as the framework that governs how consultants behave when no one is watching. Clients cannot observe every decision made during an engagement, nor can they scrutinise every detail of analysis. Instead, they must trust that the consultant has acted in good faith, reported findings honestly, and prioritised the client's best interests. This reliance on trust means that consultants are held to higher expectations than many other roles in a project ecosystem.

Independence is at the centre of this definition. A consultant is valued precisely because they are not tied to the sale of a product, the installation of a system, or the operation of a facility. Their advice is meant to be impartial, based solely on the evidence observed and the client's stated objectives. If independence is compromised, so too is the consultant's usefulness. For instance, a consultant who accepts commissions from a vendor while recommending that vendor's products is no longer providing impartial advice. Even if the recommendation is technically sound, the perception of bias is enough to damage credibility.

Objectivity follows closely behind independence. Consultants are expected to base their advice on verifiable evidence rather than personal preference, organisational politics, or commercial incentives. Objectivity means testing assumptions, questioning data sources, and being prepared to revise conclusions when new evidence arises. A consultant who defends a predetermined solution regardless of evidence has abandoned objectivity, and by doing so they undermine both the profession and the client's trust.

Integrity provides the broader ethical compass. It is demonstrated through honesty in communication, consistency between words and actions, and the courage to highlight uncomfortable truths. Integrity requires that consultants avoid exaggerating risks to secure work, resist the temptation to conceal findings that may embarrass a client, and remain willing to speak openly even when the message is unwelcome. Having integrity does not mean being inflexible, but it does mean holding firm to core principles and not trading them away for quick gains.

Confidentiality is equally central to professional ethics. Consultants often gain access to sensitive data, proprietary systems, and vulnerabilities that, if disclosed, could cause real harm. Respecting confidentiality agreements, storing information securely, and resisting the temptation to use client information for competitive advantage are all ethical requirements. Breaches of confidentiality can have legal consequences, but even without legal action, they destroy the trust on which consultancy depends.

Ethical Pillar	Everyday Behaviours That Demonstrate It	Common Red Flags or Breaches	Corrective Actions or Safeguards
Integrity	States the truth even when inconvenient; discloses conflicts early; keeps promises and deliverables transparent.	Selective disclosure; "massaging" findings to please a client; hiding uncertainty or errors.	Formal conflict-of-interest declaration; independent peer review; transparent revision log.
Independence	Bases advice on evidence and not influence; resists client or supplier pressure; documents reasoning objectively.	Allowing commercial bias to steer conclusions; accepting gifts or favours; letting convenience dictate advice.	Separation of consultancy and sales functions; written independence statement in proposals; senior review before submission.
Objectivity	Uses structured analysis; tests assumptions; invites challenge from peers; welcomes data that contradicts own view.	Cherry-picking data; unverified opinions presented as fact; personal preference overriding evidence.	Use standard assessment templates; include dissenting notes in reports; maintain an audit trail of decisions.
Confidentiality	Protects sensitive client and system information; limits disclosure to authorised parties; anonymises examples in later work.	Discussing projects casually; re-using client material without permission; poor data handling or cloud hygiene.	Non-disclosure agreements; controlled document sharing; encryption and secure disposal procedures.

Table 2 The Four Pillars of Ethics

Ethics in consultancy also means recognising the boundary between advising and deciding. Consultants provide recommendations; it is the client who must ultimately choose a course of action. Ethical consultants respect this distinction, ensuring that they do not overstep by trying to control decisions or usurp client authority. Equally, they do not evade responsibility by hiding behind vague statements or withholding critical information. Clear, evidence-based advice delivered with respect for the client's decision-making authority strikes the correct balance.

Defining ethics in consultancy, then, is about more than codes and standards. It is about living out independence, objectivity, and integrity in a way that ensures clients can trust the advice they receive. It means resisting pressures to compromise principles, even when those pressures come from the very people who pay the bills. It requires courage to speak truthfully, humility to acknowledge limitations, and discipline to ensure that practice aligns consistently with professional values.

When ethics is understood in this way, it ceases to be an abstract or optional aspect of consultancy. It becomes the very core of professional identity. Consultants who internalise these principles differentiate themselves in the market, not only because of their technical expertise but because of the confidence they inspire. In a field where trust is the currency of influence, defining and living by professional ethics is what enables consultants to deliver real value.

Illustrative Example: Ethical Choices in Practice

Ethical challenges in consultancy rarely arrive as clear-cut dilemmas. More often they emerge in everyday decisions that determine whether advice remains credible. One consultant was asked by a government agency to reduce the scope of a threat and vulnerability assessment to save costs. On paper, the narrower scope appeared to meet the requirement, but in real conditions it would have excluded critical assets, leaving decision-makers with an incomplete picture of risk. The consultant faced two options: decline the work altogether or proceed with the reduced scope while making the limitations fully transparent in the report, clearly highlighting the deficiencies and unmapped risks so that the client could not mistake the partial assessment for a complete one. Either path involved commercial sacrifice: declining meant walking away from the contract entirely, while proceeding with full transparency demanded extra effort to document caveats and risked straining the client relationship by confronting them with gaps they preferred not to see. What the consultant refused to do was accept the reduced scope in silence, since that would have amounted to knowingly providing advice that misrepresented reality.

In another project, a review of a corporate headquarters uncovered weaknesses in the way senior executives accessed secure areas, but management were uncomfortable addressing the problem. The consultant was encouraged to soften the report, burying uncomfortable conclusions in appendices where they would attract little attention. Instead, the findings were presented clearly but respectfully, supported by evidence and phrased in a way that made action unavoidable without being needlessly confrontational. While politically difficult at the time, the approach safeguarded the consultant's credibility and ensured that the report drove meaningful change rather than being quietly shelved.

Commercial pressures can test ethics just as sharply. In one engagement, a large infrastructure client queried billing practices and implied that future work would depend on the consultant's flexibility. The temptation to inflate hours, assign unnecessary tasks, or recommend additional services was real. The consultant resisted, introducing detailed time-tracking linked to specific outputs and ensuring all charges were transparent. The outcome was not lower fees but stronger trust, as the client came to view the consultant as fair and dependable, prepared to justify every cost rather than exploit ambiguity.

Across these scenarios the same pattern emerges: ethical practice often carries a short-term cost, whether in lost revenue, strained relationships, or uncomfortable conversations. Yet those same choices reinforce long-term trust, the currency on which consultancy depends. Ethics in this sense is not abstract theory but a lived discipline, expressed in how consultants scope projects, report findings, and handle commercial relationships. Those who treat ethics as integral to their practice protect their own reputation and demonstrate that consultancy is a profession grounded in independence, honesty, and accountability.

Integrity is doing the right thing when no one can see you — and writing it down so everyone can trust you.

Independence, Transparency, and Conflicts of Interest

Independence is one of the defining characteristics of consultancy. Unlike contractors, suppliers, or integrators, consultants are valued precisely because they are not tied to specific products or delivery outcomes. Clients expect advice that is free from commercial bias and based solely on their needs. Independence must be demonstrated in practice through the choices consultants make, the relationships they form, and the way they present their findings.

The clearest threat to independence comes from conflicts of interest. These occur when a consultant's personal, financial, or professional interests have the potential to influence – or appear to influence – their judgement. In consultancy, perception can be as damaging as reality. A consultant who accepts referral fees from a security systems vendor while recommending that vendor's products may still believe their advice is objective, but the perception of bias can undermine credibility. Clients who suspect that recommendations are motivated by hidden incentives lose confidence in the advice, regardless of its technical validity.

Conflicts of interest can arise in more subtle ways. A consultant who previously worked for a client's preferred supplier may be perceived as biased even if they act objectively. Similarly, consultants who rely heavily on repeat business from a single client may face pressure to produce favourable findings, consciously or not. Even personal relationships – friendships with integrators, family connections to contractors, or shared professional networks – can create situations where independence is called into question. Ethical practice requires not only avoiding actual conflicts but also recognising and managing perceived ones.

Independence is protected by transparency. Consultants must be open about their relationships, financial interests, and limitations. Disclosing any potential conflict at the outset of an engagement allows the client to make an informed decision about whether and how to proceed. In some cases, the conflict may be minor and manageable – for instance, when a consultant has previously worked with a vendor but no longer has any financial ties. Sometimes being open means the consultant must step back from part, or even all, of the job. But being upfront always helps protect their credibility.

Independence also requires a clear boundary between consultancy and delivery. Some firms blur the line by offering both design and installation services, or by acting as consultants while also selling products. While such models may be commercially attractive, they risk compromising objectivity. A consultant who designs a system and then profits from installing it may face an inherent conflict between what is best for the client and what is most profitable for the firm. The ethical consultant must carefully consider how to structure services so that advice remains impartial and trusted.

Conflicts can also emerge during procurement. Consultants often assist clients in developing tender specifications, evaluating bids, or overseeing vendor selection. If consultants have existing relationships with bidders, or if they allow vendors to influence specifications in their favour, the procurement process is compromised. Ethical consultants avoid this by maintaining strict separation from vendors, refusing inducements, and ensuring that evaluation criteria are transparent and defensible. Any deviation from this risks undermining both the project and the consultant's professional reputation.

The principle of independence extends to reporting as well. Consultants may sometimes feel pressure to soften findings to maintain client relationships, particularly when results reflect poorly on senior management decisions. Yet independence requires that findings be reported honestly, even when inconvenient. This does not mean being unnecessarily confrontational but rather ensuring that reports reflect evidence without distortion. A consultant who shapes findings to suit client preferences may preserve short-term harmony but will ultimately erode trust once realities are discovered.

Transparency also applies to limitations of competence. Consultants who accept work outside their expertise without disclosure risk misleading clients. Independence requires being clear about what services can be delivered with confidence and what requires specialist support. Bringing in qualified partners or subconsultants is not a weakness but a demonstration of integrity. Pretending expertise where it does not exist is both unethical and professionally reckless.

Managing independence and conflicts of interest therefore requires a deliberate approach. Many consultants adopt formal conflict-of-interest policies, documenting relationships and disclosing them to clients. Some firms rotate staff assignments to avoid over-familiarity with specific vendors or clients. Others establish strict internal boundaries between consulting and delivery functions. Whatever the approach, the principle remains the same: independence must not only be maintained but must be seen to be maintained.

Independence, transparency, and conflict management are about safeguarding the consultant's most valuable asset – credibility. Clients may forgive mistakes, delays, or even occasional errors of judgement, but they rarely forgive perceived dishonesty or hidden motives. Consultants who protect their independence and act with transparency ensure that their advice is trusted, their reputation endures, and their influence remains strong.

Standards and Professional Codes

Ethics are supported and reinforced by external standards and professional codes that establish a shared framework for practice. These frameworks provide consultants with benchmarks against which to measure their conduct, and they offer clients assurance that work is being undertaken in line with recognised norms. Standards and codes are therefore more than compliance requirements; they are instruments of credibility and protection for both consultant and client.

International standards are among the most important reference points. ISO 31000:2018[13], the global standard for risk management, defines principles and processes that are directly applicable to security consultancy. It emphasises systematic identification, assessment, and treatment of risks, and it underlines the need for transparency and accountability throughout the process. For consultants, adopting ISO 31000:2018[13] ensures that recommendations are not simply subjective opinions but are grounded in internationally recognised methodology.

ISO/IEC 27001:2022[15], the standard for information security management, is equally relevant. Although traditionally applied to IT and data systems, its principles increasingly shape physical security, where cyber and physical risks converge. A consultant referencing ISO/IEC 27001:2022[15] signals awareness of this integration and demonstrates alignment with best practice. Similarly, ISO 18788, which governs management systems for private security operations, provides a framework that is particularly valuable in contexts where consultants must advise clients operating in complex or high-risk environments. It emphasises governance, accountability, and respect for human rights, linking consultancy practice not only to operational standards but also to ethical ones.

Beyond ISO, industry associations play a central role in establishing professional codes of conduct. ASIS International, one of the most widely recognised security bodies, has a Code of Ethics that requires members to perform duties with integrity, competence, and respect for the law. It explicitly obliges professionals to protect confidential information, avoid conflicts of interest, and act in a way that upholds the honour of the profession. For consultants, adherence to these codes is not optional; it is a condition of credibility within a global professional community.

Other professional frameworks reinforce these obligations. The Security Institute in the United Kingdom has its own code of ethics, centred on integrity, accountability, and respect for others. In the United States, the International Association of Professional Security Consultants (IAPSC) requires members to maintain independence from product and service providers to ensure unbiased advice. Each of these codes has different emphases, but all converge on the same fundamental principles: honesty, independence, and the prioritisation of the client's best interest.

National and regional regulations add another layer. In the United Arab Emirates, the Security Industry Regulatory Agency (SIRA[4]) establishes standards for security consultants, requiring compliance with local codes that govern design, risk assessment, and reporting. In the UK, the Security Industry Authority (SIA) regulates aspects of professional conduct, including licensing, training, and adherence to established practices. The European Union's Directive 2022/2557[7] on the resilience of critical entities also sets ethical and operational expectations for consultants advising operators of essential services. These frameworks remind consultants that ethics is not only a matter of professional pride but, in many jurisdictions, a legal obligation.

The value of standards lies not only in the content but also in the discipline they enforce. Consultants who align their methods with ISO or ASIS frameworks can demonstrate consistency and defensibility in their work. When challenged by clients, regulators, or courts, the ability to reference a recognised standard provides protection. It shows that recommendations were not arbitrary but derived from structured, widely accepted practice. This defensibility is particularly important in environments where decisions may later be scrutinised in investigations or legal proceedings.

Professional codes also help consultants navigate difficult situations. For example, when pressured by a client to alter findings, a consultant can point to the ASIS Code of Ethics[2] or the IAPSC independence requirement as external anchors that justify refusal. This shifts the argument from a personal stance to a professional obligation, reducing the perception of confrontation. In this way, codes act as shields that protect consultants from undue pressure while reinforcing credibility.

Adherence to standards is also a mark of professionalism in the eyes of clients. Organisations seeking consultancy support increasingly demand evidence of compliance with ISO certifications or professional memberships. Consultants who can demonstrate alignment with these frameworks differentiate themselves in the market, signalling not only technical competence but also ethical discipline. In an industry where trust is central, this differentiation often determines which consultants are engaged and which are overlooked.

At the same time, standards are not static. ISO documents are periodically revised, professional codes are updated, and regulatory frameworks evolve. Consultants have an obligation to remain current, ensuring that their practice reflects the latest requirements. This requires continuous learning, active participation in professional associations, and engagement with industry discussions. Failure to stay up to date risks not only professional obsolescence but also ethical lapse, as advice based on outdated standards may mislead clients.

Standards and professional codes provide consultants with both guidance and authority. They set down the principles of independence, transparency, and integrity, and they provide practical frameworks for applying those principles in diverse contexts. Consultants who embrace these frameworks demonstrate that ethics is not simply a personal preference, but a professional requirement anchored in shared international practice. In doing so, they strengthen their credibility, protect their clients, and reinforce the integrity of the profession as a whole.

Ethical Decision-Making in Practice

Understanding the principles of ethics and the guidance offered by professional standards is only the beginning. The real test comes in practice, when consultants are faced with dilemmas that require judgement under pressure. Ethical decision-making in consultancy is rarely about choosing between obvious right and wrong; it is more often about navigating competing pressures where the correct path is less clear. Commercial demands, political sensitivities, and client expectations can all create conflict with professional obligations. In such circumstances, the consultant must have both a framework for decision-making and the courage to apply it.

Several approaches to ethical reasoning can help guide these decisions. The utilitarian perspective emphasises outcomes, asking which course of action produces the greatest benefit or the least harm. A consultant using this lens might argue for a solution that, while not perfect, provides the most practical protection across an organisation By contrast, a duty-based view says some rules – like being honest, staying independent, and keeping information confidential – must always be followed, no matter what the result might be. In real conditions, consultants must weigh both perspectives, ensuring that advice delivers workable results without sacrificing the principles that uphold credibility.

There are some practical tools that can help consultants navigate ethical dilemmas. One widely used method is the "newspaper test": would you be comfortable if your decision were reported publicly, with your name attached? If the answer is no, the decision may be ethically unsound. Another tool is peer consultation, where discussing a dilemma with a trusted colleague, mentor, or professional body brings fresh perspectives and helps guard against blind spots or self-justification. Escalation pathways, such as raising concerns with senior leadership or ethics committees, provide further options when dilemmas exceed an individual's authority.

Confidentiality presents another frequent ethical dilemma. Consultants often encounter sensitive information – from security vulnerabilities to financial data – that clients expect to remain private. A situation may arise where sharing this information could benefit another project or strengthen the consultant's competitive position. Ethical decision-making requires resisting this temptation and respecting confidentiality agreements. Breaches may not only have legal consequences but also erode trust across the profession. The principle is simple: information obtained in one engagement is not to be reused without explicit consent.

Balancing transparency and discretion can also be difficult. For example, a consultant may uncover evidence of non-compliance with regulatory standards that the client is reluctant to disclose. The consultant must weigh loyalty to the client against obligations to regulators, stakeholders, or even the public. In such cases, ethical decision-making is aided by standards and codes that clarify duties of disclosure. While approaches differ across jurisdictions, the principle remains that consultants cannot collude in concealing breaches that may endanger safety or breach the law.

The most effective consultants embed ethical decision-making into their daily practice rather than treating it as an occasional challenge. This means creating personal habits of reflection, questioning assumptions, and seeking external validation of choices. It also means building an organisational culture where ethics are openly discussed, dilemmas are shared, and difficult conversations are encouraged rather than avoided. Firms that create such cultures reduce the likelihood of ethical lapses and strengthen the resilience of their staff.

Ethical decision-making in consultancy is not about perfection but about discipline. Consultants cannot eliminate dilemmas, but they can develop the tools and habits needed to navigate them responsibly. By applying structured reasoning, seeking peer input, and aligning with recognised codes, consultants ensure that their decisions are defensible and principled. In doing so, they protect their credibility, serve their clients with integrity, and reinforce the values that distinguish professional consultancy from mere technical advice.

Embedding Ethics into Security Practice

The challenge is to embed ethical principles into the daily practice of security consultancy so that they guide behaviour naturally rather than being treated as afterthoughts. Ethical practice is most effective when it is embedded in daily work – shaping methods, relationships, and decisions – rather than being limited to compliance routines or high-level statements with little practical impact.

The first step in embedding ethics is to make it visible in professional behaviour. Consultants lead by example, demonstrating independence, transparency, and integrity in every interaction. When consultants are candid about their limitations, open about potential conflicts, and consistent in meeting commitments, clients learn to expect and respect ethical conduct. In this way, ethics ceases to be something that needs constant explanation and becomes part of the consultant's reputation.

Consultancy firms also play a critical role. Organisational culture can either reinforce or undermine ethical practice. Firms that reward only revenue growth or short-term wins risk creating pressures that encourage staff to cut corners or overlook conflicts of interest. In contrast, firms that recognise and reward integrity, thoroughness, and client trustworthiness foster an environment where ethical practice is sustained. Embedding ethics into firm culture requires leadership commitment, clear internal policies, and mechanisms for staff to raise concerns without fear of reprisal.

Training and development help sustain this culture. While technical training is essential, ethics should also be addressed explicitly in professional development programmes. Role-playing dilemmas, discussing real-world case studies, and using structured frameworks for decision-making equip consultants with the confidence to handle ethical challenges. By making ethics a regular part of training, firms reinforce the idea that it is as central to consultancy as risk assessment or project management.

Embedding ethics also means integrating it into processes and deliverables. For example, reporting templates can include sections that highlight assumptions, limitations, and potential conflicts. Proposals can include clear statements of independence. Site visit protocols can specify how sensitive information will be handled and protected. By building ethics into the mechanics of consultancy work, consultants reduce the risk of oversight and signal to clients that ethical awareness is a deliberate part of practice.

Another aspect of embedding ethics is encouraging clients to adopt similar standards. Consultants are not only advisers but also influencers of organisational culture. When consultants model ethical practice and encourage clients to adopt transparent procurement processes, clear reporting, and open discussions of conflicts, they extend the impact of ethical principles beyond their own work. In this way, consultancy serves not just individual projects but the broader development of ethical awareness in the security industry.

Reflection is an additional mechanism for embedding ethics. Consultants who regularly review their decisions, analyse how dilemmas were handled, and consider what could have been done differently steadily improve their ethical judgement. Reflection can take many forms, from personal journals to structured debriefs within project teams. Over time, these habits create a feedback loop where ethical lessons become embedded in practice rather than remaining abstract principles.

A consultancy that consistently discloses conflicts, trains its staff to handle dilemmas, and builds ethics into its deliverables earns a reputation for integrity, often resulting in repeat business and long-term client relationships. Conversely, firms that neglect these practices may find themselves in reputational crises when questionable decisions are exposed, even if no formal rules were broken. In the security sector, where trust is paramount, reputational damage can be fatal to a firm's viability.

Technology also plays a growing role in consultancy, and with it come new ethical challenges. The rise of artificial intelligence and digital tools raises questions not only about data integrity, client confidentiality, and transparency of methods, but also about the privacy of information uploaded to third-party systems. Consultants must ensure that sensitive client data is never exposed to platforms without explicit consent, clear safeguards, and compliance with applicable data protection laws. Embedding ethics in this area means remaining vigilant about how such tools are applied, making sure they enhance analysis without eroding accountability. If AI-generated findings are included in reports, consultants must disclose their use, validate the outputs, and clarify where human judgement has shaped conclusions. Ethical practice must therefore evolve in step with technology, requiring ongoing review and adjustment rather than assuming that a single policy or decision will remain sufficient.

Embedding ethics into security practice means turning values into action. Independence, transparency, and integrity cannot remain aspirations on paper; they must be visible in daily decisions, client interactions, and project outcomes. Consultants who live by these standards safeguard their own credibility and build trust that endures beyond individual assignments. More than that, they set the benchmark for the profession itself, showing that security consultancy is not only the design of technical solutions but the delivery of a principled service in environments where complexity, pressure, and competing interests are the norm. Embedding ethics must be deliberate and measurable; incorporating ethical checkpoints in project reviews and client feedback loops ensures that values remain visible in daily consultancy operations.

Practice Guide

Ethics and standards are not constraints on consultancy but the foundation of credibility. Yet consultants often stumble when they underestimate the importance of perception in conflicts of interest, soften findings to preserve relationships, exaggerate risks to win additional work, or treat ethics as a theoretical subject rather than a daily discipline. Others fail to embed integrity into scoping, reporting, billing, and confidentiality, or allow knowledge of standards and regulations to lapse, leaving their advice outdated and their reputation vulnerable.

To avoid these pitfalls, consultants must treat ethics as a visible part of everyday work. Conflicts of interest, whether actual or perceived, should be disclosed openly, since suspicion alone can erode trust. Findings must be reported honestly and respectfully, neither concealed nor overstated. Independence requires resisting commercial pressure to compromise, while competence requires staying current with ISO frameworks, professional codes, and regional regulations. By embedding ethical awareness into every stage of practice, consultants not only protect their credibility but also demonstrate professionalism that clients recognise and respect.

You should now be able to define the principles of professional ethics in consultancy, recognise and address dilemmas responsibly, maintain independence and transparency, apply relevant standards and codes, make principled decisions under pressure, and embed ethics into both personal and organisational practice. These are not abstract ideals but practical habits that safeguard credibility and sustain influence. Ethics provides the bridge between the consultant's mindset and the wider professional and global contexts explored in later chapters, ensuring that consultancy is not only technically competent but also principled and trusted.

Chapter 5 – Global Perspectives on Security Consulting

This chapter aims to equip the reader with the skills and awareness necessary to operate effectively as a security consultant across international contexts.

By the end of this chapter, you will be able to:

- Recognise the differences in regulation, governance structures, and professional practice that characterise security consulting across regions.

- Interpret and apply key legal and regulatory frameworks, including GDPR[5] in Europe, NCEMA[18] in the United Arab Emirates, SIRA[4] requirements in Dubai, NIST guidelines in the United States, and ISO international standards.

- Adapt consulting methodologies to align with cultural expectations, legal obligations, and business practices in diverse environments.

- Compare and contrast approaches to risk assessment, compliance, and implementation in regions such as the UAE, European Union, United States, Africa, and Asia.

- Identify transferable principles that allow consultants to deliver consistent quality while respecting local variations.

- Develop an informed global perspective that supports multinational clients and projects operating across multiple jurisdictions.

Introduction

Security consulting is increasingly a global profession, yet it is never a uniform one. The principles of risk assessment, threat analysis, and protective design may be universal, but the way they are applied is profoundly shaped by context. Each region brings its own combination of regulatory frameworks, cultural expectations, and market maturity, meaning that consultants cannot assume that methods successful in one jurisdiction will be directly transferable to another.

Regulation is the most visible factor. In the European Union, the General Data Protection Regulation (GDPR[5]) has reshaped security practice by placing privacy and data protection at the centre of both technical and organisational measures. In the United States, the National Institute of Standards and Technology (NIST) frameworks dominate, but compliance often relies on voluntary adoption and industry self-regulation rather than statutory mandates. In the United Arab Emirates, centralised authorities such as the National Emergency Crisis and Disaster Management Authority (NCEMA[18]) and the Security Industry Regulatory Agency (SIRA[4]) define standards that consultants must follow with precision, particularly for projects involving critical national infrastructure. Elsewhere, as in many African and Asian states, international standards such as those produced by the International Organization for Standardization (ISO) often fill the gaps where local regulation is incomplete or emerging.

Cultural dimensions are equally important. European clients may expect extended consultation and consensus-building, reflecting traditions of legal tradition and due process. In the Gulf region, clients may anticipate firm guidance from consultants and close adherence to state-mandated frameworks. In Africa, consultants may need to navigate informal governance structures, political instability, or limited institutional capacity. Across Asia, approaches can vary widely, from Japan's highly structured and technical standards to India's rapidly evolving but sometimes fragmented regulatory landscape.

The maturity of regional security consulting markets also creates significant variation. In North America and Western Europe, consulting is an established profession with deep links to legal, engineering, and risk management disciplines. In contrast, in emerging markets, consultants may be expected to cover a wider scope of work, providing not only strategic advice but also design, implementation, and training functions.

This chapter examines these global perspectives through comparative examples from the United Arab Emirates (as a representative of the Gulf Region), the European Union, the United States, Africa, Asia, and Oceania. It considers how regulation, culture, and market maturity interact to shape consulting practice, and it highlights transferable principles that allow consultants to maintain professional standards while adapting to local realities. The objective is to equip practitioners with the awareness and flexibility required to operate confidently across jurisdictions, recognising that security is simultaneously a global discipline and a highly localised practice.

The United Arab Emirates

The United Arab Emirates provides one of the clearest examples of how regulation and governance define the role of the security consultant, and it also illustrates broader trends across the Middle East, especially the Gulf Region. The region as a whole is marked by rapid infrastructure development, the expansion of critical national infrastructure such as energy and aviation, and a strong emphasis on centralised governance. Yet the UAE stands out for the maturity and detail of its regulatory frameworks, which are more formalised than those of many neighbouring states. Where some Middle Eastern countries rely on imported standards or sector-specific mandates, the UAE has built a layered and prescriptive system that makes compliance central to the consultant's role. This contrasts sharply with regions such as Europe, where principle-based laws dominate, or the United States, where voluntary frameworks and market forces often shape practice.

At the federal level, the National Emergency Crisis and Disaster Management Authority (NCEMA[18]) sets the framework for resilience and continuity across the UAE. Its standards require organisations to demonstrate readiness for a wide spectrum of risks, from natural hazards to terrorism, and to integrate crisis management into planning and operations. These requirements shape how consultants conduct risk assessments, design protective measures, and frame recommendations to clients. Within Dubai, the Security Industry Regulatory Agency (SIRA[4]) provides an additional layer of prescription. SIRA's rules are among the most detailed in the world, stipulating technical specifications for surveillance, access control, alarm systems, and monitoring facilities. Consultants must be licensed by SIRA[4] and are expected to deliver solutions that align exactly with its requirements. Non-compliance is not tolerated, and audits and inspections are used to enforce adherence.

The coexistence of NCEMA[18] at the federal level and SIRA[4] at the emirate level produces a regulatory environment that is both comprehensive and complex. Consultants working outside of Dubai must comply with the regulations of the relevant emirate authority, in addition to national frameworks such as NCEMA[18]. Unlike ISO standards, which are widely recognised internationally but voluntary, NCEMA[18] and SIRA[4] are binding and backed by law. Nonetheless, ISO plays a complementary role, especially in multinational projects where clients seek alignment between local requirements and global benchmarks. The UAE is therefore representative of a broader Middle Eastern pattern, in which state authorities set the rules, but international frameworks are often used to give projects credibility and compatibility with global operations.

Cultural expectations reinforce this regulatory environment. Clients, many of whom are state-owned entities or large private developers, expect consultants to provide authoritative guidance rather than open-ended discussion. Decision-making processes are hierarchical, and demonstrating respect for authority is essential to establishing credibility. Consultants are often expatriates from Europe, North America, and Asia, but their success depends on adapting their methods to the governance style and cultural norms of Emirati institutions. Across the Middle East more broadly, similar expectations are common: deference to authority, reliance on government approval, and a preference for practical compliance over exploratory debate. In the UAE, however, these expectations are coupled with formal systems of enforcement that give consultants little scope for deviation from mandated standards.

Compared with other regions, the UAE highlights the difference between a state-driven compliance model and systems based on principle or voluntary adoption. In the European Union, frameworks such as GDPR[5] emphasise privacy rights and organisational accountability; in the United States, NIST standards provide guidance but rely on market adoption; in Africa, ISO often fills the gaps left by underdeveloped regulation. By contrast, the UAE and much of the Middle East demand compliance with detailed government standards, enforced through licensing and inspection. This gives clarity and consistency but restricts flexibility. For international consultants, the lesson is that credibility in this environment depends not only on technical competence but also on fluency in local regulation, sensitivity to cultural expectations, and alignment with the region's wider emphasis on resilience and state-led oversight.

Yet it is important to recognise that compliance alone does not equate to security. Meeting NCEMA[18] or SIRA[4] requirements demonstrates adherence to minimum expectations, but regulatory checklists cannot capture every risk or account for every organisational context. True security demands that compliance serve as the benchmark – the starting point from which consultants design measures that are appropriate, proportionate, and tailored to the specific circumstances of each client. By moving beyond compliance to apply judgement, creativity, and risk-based thinking, consultants ensure that protective measures are not only lawful but also effective in practice.

The European Union

The European Union provides a striking contrast to the prescriptive and state-driven model found in the United Arab Emirates and much of the wider Middle East. Where the Gulf states rely on centralised authorities to enforce detailed compliance frameworks, the European approach is grounded in law but expressed through principles rather than technical prescriptions. For consultants, this means that success depends less on meeting exact technical specifications and more on demonstrating that solutions respect rights, meet obligations, and can withstand legal and regulatory scrutiny. It is a system that prioritises accountability, transparency, and due process, reflecting the EU's broader political culture and traditions of governance.

At the heart of this environment lies the General Data Protection Regulation (GDPR[5]), which has reshaped the way organisations handle personal data and, by extension, the way security systems are designed. GDPR does not prescribe camera placements or access control specifications but requires consultants to justify why such measures are used, how they respect privacy rights, and how collected data will be safeguarded. This principle-based approach leaves consultants with scope to innovate, but it also imposes significant responsibility: every design choice must be proportionate, documented, and defensible under law. The regulation has also influenced regions far beyond Europe, including parts of the Middle East where multinational clients operating under GDPR seek to harmonise practices across their global portfolios.

The EU's security landscape extends far beyond GDPR. The Network and Information Security Directive, now evolving into NIS2[6], requires essential service operators and digital providers to maintain robust cybersecurity frameworks and incident-reporting capabilities. National governments also impose their own measures. Germany's IT Security Act, France's Loi de Programmation Militaire (military programming law), and the UK's Network and Information Systems Regulations exemplify how national obligations coexist with European-level directives. For consultants, this produces a multi-layered regulatory environment where compliance must be achieved on several levels simultaneously. Unlike in the UAE, where SIRA[4] and NCEMA[18] provide definitive standards with little variation, the European model requires constant interpretation and reconciliation of overlapping rules.

ISO standards play a particularly important role in this context. While GDPR[5] and NIS2[6] create the legal framework, ISO standards such as ISO/IEC 27001:2022[15] for information security provide the practical mechanisms through which compliance can be demonstrated. Many consultants rely on ISO to structure their recommendations, giving them credibility not only in Europe but also across global operations. This layering of legal obligations and international standards stands in contrast to the Middle Eastern model, where ISO is used as a complementary reference but is always subordinate to national mandates. In Europe, ISO often acts as the operational bridge between legal principle and technical implementation.

Cultural expectations in Europe reinforce this emphasis on process and accountability. Clients expect consultation, workshops, and dialogue, and decision-making typically involves multiple stakeholders. Transparency and consensus are valued, and consultants are often required to provide extensive documentation before approval is granted. This contrasts with the Gulf region, where clients often seek clear, directive advice and where government approval carries more weight than stakeholder consensus. In Europe, credibility lies in demonstrating not only technical expertise but also the ability to justify decisions in a way that aligns with law, culture, and procedure.

Compared with the United States, the European Union appears more rigid because regulations are binding and backed by penalties, while in the US frameworks such as NIST are often voluntary. Compared with the Middle East, Europe allows more flexibility in how systems are designed but far less tolerance for vague or undocumented decision-making. For consultants, the European Union demonstrates the importance of mastering principle-based compliance: it is not enough to deliver a system that works; it must also be proportionate, legally defensible, and respectful of rights. The broader lesson is clear: approaches that succeed in one region cannot be transplanted wholesale to another, and effective practice requires sensitivity to the political and cultural character of each jurisdiction.

The United States

The United States represents a markedly different environment for security consulting when compared with both the European Union and the Middle East. Where Europe enforces binding obligations through legal frameworks such as GDPR[5] and NIS2[6], and the UAE dictates prescriptive technical standards through NCEMA[18] and SIRA[4], the American model relies far more on voluntary adoption of frameworks and sector-specific guidance. This market-driven approach gives consultants significant flexibility but also requires them to demonstrate tangible business value to clients who often view security in terms of cost efficiency and return on investment rather than as a purely regulatory requirement.

The National Institute of Standards and Technology (NIST[19]) provides the most widely recognised frameworks, with its Cybersecurity Framework serving as the cornerstone of American practice. It sets out categories of functions – identify, protect, detect, respond, and recover – that guide organisations in building resilience. Alongside this, the NIST[19] Special Publication 800 series covers specific domains such as risk assessment, cryptography, and access control. Unlike in Europe or the Middle East, these frameworks are not universally mandatory; rather, they are widely adopted because they represent industry best practice and are often written into contracts. This creates an environment where consultants must be fluent in NIST standards, not because the law requires it, but because the market expects it.

Sector-specific regulation adds another dimension. The Federal Energy Regulatory Commission enforces Critical Infrastructure Protection standards for the energy sector, while the Department of Homeland Security issues directives for ports and transportation. The Federal Information Security Modernization Act imposes specific obligations on government agencies and contractors. These measures demonstrate that while there is no single unifying statute comparable to Europe's GDPR[5] or the UAE's NCEMA[18], consultants may face stringent requirements within particular industries. The result is a fragmented regulatory landscape where expertise must often be tailored to the client's sector.

ISO standards are also relevant in the United States, though their role is different from that in Europe. While ISO provides a bridge between principle-based law and practice in the EU, in the US it functions more as a way to align with global expectations, particularly for multinationals. American organisations often look to ISO certification when they operate internationally, and consultants must therefore be able to integrate ISO into NIST-based solutions. This reinforces the point that while American regulation is less centralised, consultants working for global clients must still balance local flexibility with international standards.

The consulting culture in the United States reflects the broader business environment, where directness, pragmatism, and competitiveness are highly valued. Clients expect consultants to provide clear and actionable advice, often supported by cost-benefit analysis and performance metrics. Unlike in Europe, where process and consensus are often prioritised, or in the Middle East, where compliance with state authority is paramount, American clients seek solutions that demonstrate measurable value and operational impact. This creates both freedom and pressure: consultants are less constrained by regulation but must constantly prove that their recommendations deliver tangible benefits.

In comparative perspective, the United States illustrates the opposite end of the spectrum from the UAE and the wider Middle East. Where those environments restrict flexibility by enforcing precise standards, the American model encourages diversity of practice but risks inconsistency and uneven coverage when organisations adopt frameworks selectively. Against Europe, the contrast is one of legal enforceability versus voluntary adoption: the EU obliges compliance with penalties for failure, while the US relies on market mechanisms to drive uptake. For consultants, the lesson is that credibility in the United States depends not only on knowledge of frameworks such as NIST and ISO, but also on the ability to frame security as an enabler of business performance. It is a system that offers scope for innovation and tailored solutions, but one that requires constant alignment between technical recommendations and commercial imperatives.

Africa

Africa presents one of the most diverse landscapes for security consulting, reflecting its wide variation in governance, economic maturity, and institutional capacity. In contrast to the prescriptive systems of the Middle East or the principle-based frameworks of Europe, many African states lack unified or consistently enforced security regulation. For consultants, this creates both challenges and opportunities. The challenge lies in the absence of binding national standards in much of the continent, which can lead to fragmented approaches. The opportunity lies in the ability to introduce and adapt international best practice, often with a degree of influence and flexibility not available in regions where compliance is rigidly enforced.

Regulatory development across Africa is uneven. South Africa has introduced one of the most comprehensive frameworks through the Protection of Personal Information Act (POPIA), which broadly aligns with Europe's GDPR[5] in protecting data rights and regulating information handling. In Nigeria, the Nigerian Data Protection Regulation has laid down baseline requirements for organisations, though enforcement capacity remains limited. Elsewhere, consultants frequently rely on international standards such as the ISO 27000 and 31000[13] series to structure security management and risk frameworks. ISO provides a valuable benchmark in contexts where local laws are incomplete or inconsistently applied, offering credibility to projects that must withstand scrutiny from international investors or multinational partners. Yet reliance on external frameworks can create gaps if local institutions lack the resources or expertise to sustain compliance once consultants depart.

Cultural and operational realities exert as much influence as regulation. In some African contexts, decision-making is shaped by informal governance structures or personal relationships rather than written standards. Trust, reputation, and long-term presence can carry more weight than technical specifications. Consultants must therefore invest in building relationships, demonstrating cultural sensitivity, and adapting recommendations to the local political and economic environment. In resource-constrained settings, clients often prioritise cost-effective solutions that deliver immediate resilience over complex, long-term systems. The consultant's role may extend beyond providing strategic advice to include capacity-building, training, and mentoring, helping local organisations develop the skills needed to maintain systems independently.

This emphasis on adaptability distinguishes Africa from regions with more mature frameworks. In the UAE and wider Middle East, consultants work under strict government authority. In Europe, consultants must carefully balance national and European-level directives, with compliance enforced through legal penalties. In the United States, clients expect consultants to demonstrate business value while aligning with voluntary frameworks such as NIST. Africa, by contrast, requires consultants to act as bridge-builders, introducing international standards like ISO while tailoring them to environments where enforcement mechanisms are weak and institutional capacity may be limited.

The diversity of Africa is therefore both a strength and a complexity. Consultants may work in advanced markets such as South Africa, where regulation mirrors global norms, or in emerging markets where projects are shaped by donor funding, international partnerships, or local political realities. Across the continent, the ability to combine technical knowledge with cultural adaptability and pragmatic problem solving is often more important than rigid adherence to external models. For international practitioners, Africa illustrates the importance of flexibility: success lies in creating solutions that are sustainable in local conditions while still aligning with global standards and expectations.

Asia

Asia presents one of the broadest spectrums of security consulting environments in the world, ranging from highly mature regulatory systems to markets where standards are still developing or unevenly enforced. Unlike the prescriptive state-driven regimes of the Middle East, or the principle-based frameworks of Europe, Asia embodies a hybrid model: in some countries the state sets detailed standards with precision, while in others, consultants must navigate fragmented regulations, diverse cultural expectations, and rapid economic transformation. For the international consultant, this diversity requires flexibility, regional awareness, and the ability to shift between compliance-driven practice and adaptive problem solving depending on the context.

In Japan, security regulation is deeply embedded within national governance. The Basic Act on Cybersecurity and related sector-specific rules impose detailed requirements, particularly in areas of critical national infrastructure. Consultants are expected to demonstrate meticulous compliance, backed by documentation and verification, with little tolerance for approximation. Singapore has developed a similarly advanced system under the Cybersecurity Act, with oversight by the Infocomm Media Development Authority. Here, cyber and physical security are tightly integrated, reflecting the city-state's role as a global financial and logistics hub. South Korea also follows a structured path, with strong emphasis on technology-driven security standards and state coordination.

In contrast, India presents a more fluid environment. The Computer Emergency Response Team (CERT-In[8]) issues national guidelines, and proposed data protection legislation has drawn on elements of Europe's GDPR[5]. Yet enforcement is often inconsistent, and consultants may find themselves bridging the gap between emerging national requirements and international standards such as ISO/IEC 27001:2022[15]. Southeast Asia adds further variety. Vietnam and Indonesia have introduced national cybersecurity strategies, while other states rely heavily on imported frameworks or multinational corporate policies. Across the region, ISO standards frequently serve as the operational backbone, enabling consultants to deliver solutions that align with global expectations even when local legislation is incomplete or unevenly applied.

Cultural context plays a critical role across Asia. In Japan and Singapore, deference to authority and respect for process reinforce compliance, much like the state-led model in the Middle East, though expressed in a more procedural rather than prescriptive form. In India and parts of Southeast Asia, personal relationships and trust can be as important as formal regulation, echoing some of the dynamics found in African markets. In China, where the state exerts tight control over both cyber and physical domains, consultants often work under close government scrutiny, with little space for independent interpretation. Across the region, building relationships and demonstrating cultural sensitivity are as essential as technical expertise, since client expectations often extend beyond compliance to encompass long-term trust and partnership.

Compared with Europe, which offers harmonised frameworks, Asia presents regulatory fragmentation that obliges consultants to treat each jurisdiction as unique. Unlike the US, voluntary adoption plays a smaller role, while approaches vary more widely than in the Middle East, where prescriptive state-led systems dominate. Success in Asia depends on flexibility and regional literacy. Precision and compliance are essential in structured environments such as Japan or Singapore, while projects in India, Vietnam, or Indonesia demand adaptability and capacity-building. Across the continent, effective practice is defined not only by technical knowledge but by the ability to balance a patchwork of regulations, cultural expectations, and international frameworks with cultural sensitivity and professional credibility.

Oceania

Oceania, and in particular Australia and New Zealand, offers a distinctive perspective within the global security consulting landscape. Both countries combine the traditions of Anglo-American governance with the realities of the Asia-Pacific region, where proximity to emerging markets and exposure to regional risk shape their security priorities. Compared with the prescriptive state-driven models of the Middle East or the principle-based frameworks of Europe, Oceania represents a middle ground. It embeds security within clear statutory obligations but retains enough flexibility for consultants to innovate, provided they can demonstrate proportionality, accountability, and alignment with national frameworks.

Australia has developed a strong regulatory environment anchored by the Security of Critical Infrastructure Act, which places obligations on operators in energy, telecommunications, and transport to implement protective measures against both physical and cyber threats. The Australian Cyber Security Centre provides detailed guidance and advisories that, while not always legally binding, strongly influence industry practice and procurement. New Zealand has adopted the Protective Security Requirements (PSR [20]) as its national baseline, integrating physical, personnel, and information security into a coherent set of expectations for organisations handling sensitive information. Unlike the highly prescriptive standards of Dubai's SIRA[4], the PSR[20] is principle-based, placing responsibility on organisations and their consultants to justify and evidence the effectiveness of their protective measures.

ISO standards play an important role in both countries, not as substitutes for national frameworks but as complementary benchmarks that align local practice with international expectations. Consultants frequently deploy ISO/IEC 27001:2022[15] or ISO 31000:2018[13] as part of their toolkit, particularly when working with multinational clients or when projects need to demonstrate global compatibility. This is a significant difference from the Middle East, where ISO is often secondary to government-mandated frameworks, and from the United States, where ISO is applied largely to support international operations rather than domestic compliance.

Cultural expectations further distinguish Oceania. In Australia, consulting practice is practical and outcome-driven, with clients seeking solutions that are efficient, resilient, and commercially viable. In New Zealand, by contrast, a strong culture of consensus and community shapes expectations: stakeholders anticipate consultation, transparency, and shared responsibility in decision-making. For consultants, this requires adaptability in style – delivering authoritative, efficiency-focused guidance in one context, while facilitating inclusive, consensus-based dialogue in another. These cultural dimensions echo some elements of Europe's procedural accountability and Africa's emphasis on relationship-building, while maintaining the Anglo-American focus on demonstrable results.

Oceania also exerts influence beyond its borders. Australian guidance and standards are frequently adopted in Pacific Island nations that lack the resources to develop comprehensive frameworks of their own, while New Zealand's PSR[20] has been cited as a model of integrated security practice. Consultants working in the region may therefore find their expertise extending into less mature markets, where they must adapt established frameworks to contexts with limited institutional capacity. The geography of Oceania introduces additional factors, including the importance of supply chain resilience, preparedness for natural disasters, and the challenges of operating across vast distances with relatively small populations.

When compared with other regions, Oceania occupies a position that blends statutory oversight with flexibility. It is more structured than many African and Asian markets, yet less prescriptive than the Middle East. It resembles Europe in its principle-based orientation yet places greater emphasis on practical outcomes and efficiency. It shares with the United States a strong commercial focus, but without the same reliance on voluntary frameworks. For the consultant, Australia and New Zealand demonstrate how security can be embedded into law and culture without eliminating innovation, and how global standards such as ISO can be woven into national frameworks to create solutions that are both accountable and adaptable.

Transferable Principles and Global Awareness

Transferable Principles Across Regions

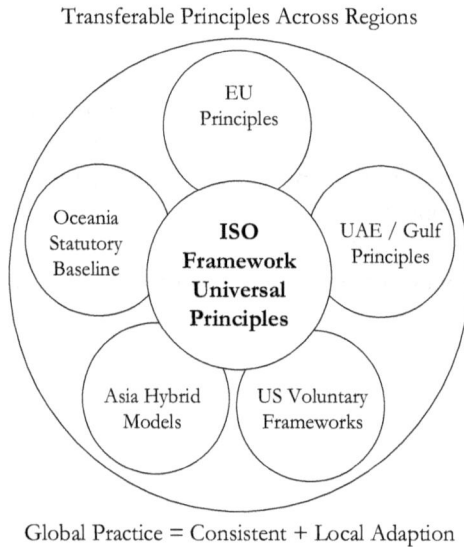

Global Practice = Consistent + Local Adaption

Figure 4 Global Standards, Local Adaptations

Across all the regions explored in this chapter, a common principle emerges: security consulting is global in scope but local in practice. The foundational ideas of risk management, resilience, and protective design are consistent across jurisdictions, yet the way they are applied is shaped by the specific regulatory, cultural, and market conditions of each environment. Consultants who assume a one-size-fits-all model quickly encounter resistance, while those who adapt too narrowly risk losing the benefits of global best practice. The true skill lies in finding the balance – applying universal principles while tailoring delivery to the realities of place.

International standards such as ISO provide an essential thread of continuity across jurisdictions. In Africa, ISO often compensates for incomplete or weak national regulation, giving projects legitimacy and structure. In Asia, where national laws can be fragmented and unevenly enforced, ISO acts as a stabilising reference point for multinational clients who require consistency. In Oceania, ISO integrates smoothly with domestic frameworks such as Australia's Security of Critical Infrastructure Act and New Zealand's Protective Security Requirements, reinforcing accountability while ensuring global compatibility. Even in regions with strong internal regimes, ISO is valuable. In Europe it provides the operational bridge between principle-based laws such as GDPR[5] and practical implementation. In the United States it supports international alignment, particularly for companies with global operations. In the Middle East, however, ISO remains subordinate to state-led frameworks such as NCEMA[18] and SIRA[4], demonstrating how prescriptive regulation can overshadow voluntary global standards. Consultants who are fluent in ISO gain not only technical credibility but also the ability to connect projects across borders.

Cultural adaptability is equally crucial. In Europe, clients expect consultation, consensus, and procedural transparency, reflecting a political culture that values process. In the United States, clients emphasise directness, efficiency, and measurable return on investment. In the Middle East, authority, deference, and precise compliance with government standards dominate expectations. In Africa, relationships, trust, and pragmatic solutions often outweigh rigid adherence to formal rules. Asia illustrates the full range, with Japan and Singapore requiring well-documented compliance while India and parts of Southeast Asia rely more on relationship-building and adaptable solutions. Oceania adds yet another dimension, blending Australia's pragmatic, outcome-focused approach with New Zealand's consensus-driven culture. Consultants who cannot adjust their style to these varying expectations risk delivering technically correct solutions that fail in real life, while those who adapt strengthen both trust and effectiveness.

Measures of value also differ between regions. In the United States, security is often justified in terms of liability reduction, operational efficiency, and financial return. In Europe, value is framed through compliance and accountability, with penalties acting as a major driver of investment. In the Middle East, the key measure is adherence to mandated standards, with success defined by alignment with government oversight. In Africa, value is measured by sustainability and practicality – solutions must be resilient but also achievable within resource constraints. Asia reflects this diversity, with some jurisdictions emphasising compliance and others innovation or cost-effectiveness, while Oceania combines accountability with practicality, expecting solutions that are both defensible and efficient.

From these variations, transferable principles can be distilled. Risk management, resilience, and protective design are universal, but their expression must shift to align with local expectations. Consultants need a toolkit that combines technical competence, regulatory literacy, and cultural intelligence. More than anything, they must act as translators – linking global frameworks such as ISO to local regimes such as GDPR[5], NIST, NCEMA[18], SIRA[4], or the PSR[20], while turning technical solutions into outcomes that are both culturally credible and commercially meaningful. No single region 'gets it right' in all contexts; the gold standard is a hybrid: the UAE's clarity and enforcement, the EU's proportionality and rights, the US's outcome-driven innovation, and Oceania's balanced statutory baselines – applied through a risk-based, ISO-aligned method and tailored to local law and culture. In a world where risks, clients, and projects cross national borders, it is this blend of consistency and adaptability that defines the successful international security consultant.

Methods travel poorly; principles travel well. Adapt form to culture – never compromise integrity.

Practice Guide

Global consultancy requires balancing universal principles with local realities. A recurring pitfall is assuming that methods proven in one jurisdiction can be transplanted unchanged into another. What works in the Middle East may fail in Europe, where principle-based accountability demands justification and documentation, or in Africa, where enforcement capacity may be weak. The UAE illustrates why prescriptive regulation dominates in the Gulf: detailed frameworks under NCEMA[18] and SIRA[4] reflect both the demographic reality of a workforce drawn from diverse educational and cultural backgrounds and a governance philosophy that prizes clarity, fairness, and national reputation. Such prescription provides certainty, limits interpretation, and helps align a varied population to consistent standards. Underestimating cultural expectations elsewhere can also be a problem: direct American-style delivery may alienate consensus-driven New Zealand stakeholders, while overlooking deference to authority in the Gulf risks undermining credibility. Other hazards include neglecting the unifying role of ISO standards, focusing narrowly on compliance without regard for sustainability, and producing recommendations that collapse when local resources cannot support them.

To avoid these errors, consultants must adapt methods to each jurisdiction's regulatory and cultural context while holding fast to universal standards of independence and professionalism. Cultural intelligence is as essential as technical skill: understanding whether clients expect directive advice, inclusive dialogue, or pragmatic solutions determines whether recommendations are accepted. Where enforcement is limited, consultants must design solutions that remain practical without external oversight, building capacity as well as compliance. International standards such as ISO provide the thread of continuity, offering credibility to multinational projects and ensuring that advice aligns with global best practice. Above all, consultants should seek balance: meeting legal requirements while ensuring that solutions are achievable, sustainable, and tailored to local capability.

You should now be able to recognise regional differences in regulation and practice, interpret and apply frameworks such as GDPR[5], NCEMA[18], SIRA[4], NIST, and ISO, adapt methodologies to cultural and legal contexts, compare approaches across jurisdictions, identify transferable principles, and develop a global perspective. These abilities allow consultants to deliver consistent, credible value across diverse markets. This grounding in global awareness prepares you to integrate technical expertise with cultural intelligence, enabling you to act as a translator between international standards and local realities – the hallmark of the successful international security consultant.

Reflections – Foundations of the Security Consultant

Part One has laid the groundwork for understanding what it means to be a security consultant. It has defined the profession, clarified its value, examined the mindset and resilience required, and established the ethical and cultural context within which consultants operate. These chapters have not attempted to provide methods or frameworks in detail – that comes later – but instead have built the essential foundations of identity, thinking, and integrity. Without these, no toolkit or methodology will be applied effectively.

The journey began by addressing the central question: what does a security consultant really do? Chapter 1 made clear that consultancy is distinct from design, integration, or operation. It is not about selling equipment or assuming management roles but about providing independent advice that delivers value to clients beyond technical fixes. By exploring common misconceptions, the chapter clarified that the consultant's role is to frame problems, test assumptions, and create options. The *Parking Garage Problem* Illustrative Example illustrated how clients often present symptoms rather than causes, and how consultants must uncover hidden objectives to identify what is truly needed. This theme – distinguishing surface requests from underlying issues and clarifying real value – runs throughout the book.

Chapter 2 turned inward, focusing on mindset and resilience. Consultancy is not simply an external activity but a discipline that begins with the consultant themselves. Mental resilience is required to handle rejection, complexity, and ambiguity. Physical resilience is needed to endure demanding schedules and environments. Professional resilience underpins the consultant's credibility, allowing them to maintain objectivity in the face of pressure. The chapter also emphasised the discipline of structured thinking – approaching problems with hypotheses, testing assumptions, and prioritising analysis. These are the habits that distinguish consultants from technicians, enabling them to provide clarity where others see confusion.

The discussion then moved into more practical intellectual tools. Chapter 3 presented structured frameworks such as SWOT, PESTLE, and hypothesis-driven analysis, showing how they provide order in the face of complexity. It also emphasised research discipline: gathering data from reliable sources, validating information, and being wary of assumptions or unverified claims. A critical point was that information is only as valuable as its interpretation. Consultants must use frameworks to make sense of data but always remain aware of their limitations. The use of AI and new technologies was introduced cautiously, stressing that while machines can analyse data, human consultants bring the intuition and contextual judgement that algorithms lack. This principle 'that technology can support but not replace human insight' was reinforced across later chapters.

Ethics and professionalism were the focus of Chapter 4. Here the consultant's independence, objectivity, and integrity were shown to be non-negotiable. Clients do not only buy knowledge; they buy trust. If a consultant is compromised by conflicts of interest or driven by hidden incentives, their advice becomes tainted, and their value evaporates. This chapter highlighted the importance of transparency, honesty, and the courage to provide unwelcome truths when they are necessary. Consultants often operate in politically charged environments, and their ability to maintain credibility depends on adhering to ethical standards even under pressure. The consultant's reputation is their most valuable asset, and it is built not on technical expertise alone but on the consistency of their professional conduct.

Chapter 5 widened the lens to the global stage. Security consultancy does not exist in a vacuum; it is shaped by the jurisdiction, regulatory context, and cultural environment in which it is practised. What is normal in one country may be illegal in another. The consultant must therefore be adaptable, culturally sensitive, and globally aware. This is not only about legal compliance but about credibility with clients and stakeholders. Understanding regional differences in governance, risk appetite, and social attitudes is essential for building trust and providing advice that is both relevant and respectful. The chapter reminded us that consultants are not only technical specialists but also interpreters of context, able to navigate diverse expectations and align them with universal principles of resilience.

Taken together, the chapters in Part One build a composite picture of the consultant's foundations. The role is defined not by technology or systems but by thinking, integrity, and adaptability. The consultant is a problem solver, a critical thinker, and an independent adviser. They must be resilient enough to withstand the pressures of the profession, disciplined enough to think clearly, ethical enough to retain credibility, and worldly enough to operate across borders and cultures. Without these qualities, technical knowledge will not be trusted or applied effectively.

It is important to reflect here on the learning objectives of Part One as a whole. You should now be able to distinguish between consultants, designers, integrators, and operators; understand how consultants create value beyond technical fixes; recognise common misconceptions about the profession; and appreciate the importance of resilience, ethics, and cultural adaptability. These objectives have been addressed across the five chapters, ensuring that the reader not only understands what consultancy is but also what it requires of those who practise it.

The conclusion of Part One is that consultancy begins with identity and mindset. Tools, methods, and models are important, but they rest on this foundation. A consultant who lacks resilience will burn out; one who lacks ethics will lose credibility; one who lacks cultural awareness will misstep in unfamiliar environments. By contrast, a consultant who possesses these qualities will be able to adapt to different challenges, earn trust, and apply tools effectively. These are the qualities that separate a trusted adviser from a vendor, and they must be established before moving into the practical toolkit of the profession.

Part Two builds directly on these foundations. Having established who the consultant is and how they must think and behave, the next step is to explore what they actually use in real life. Part Two introduces the consultant's toolkit – the principles, models, analytical techniques, and cultural insights that shape their assessments and recommendations. Here we move from identity and mindset to method and application. The aim is not to provide rigid formulas but to present structured approaches that consultants can adapt to context, ensuring their advice is both rigorous and relevant.

The transition is deliberate. Part One emphasised that consultancy is not about selling equipment or following checklists; it is about independent, structured thinking applied ethically and globally. Part Two now equips the consultant with the tools to do this work. Risk assessment principles, security models, analytical methods, human factors, and compliance frameworks will all be examined. Just as the consultant themselves must be resilient, ethical, and adaptable, so too must their toolkit. These tools must not be treated as universal solutions but as resources to be applied judiciously, always with an understanding of context and culture.

In this way, the book moves from the foundation of consultancy – identity, mindset, and integrity – into the practice of consultancy – the tools, frameworks, and methods through which value is delivered. The reader is now prepared to explore these tools, not as recipes to be followed blindly, but as instruments to be applied with professional judgement. The consultant's foundation has been laid; the toolkit is the next step.

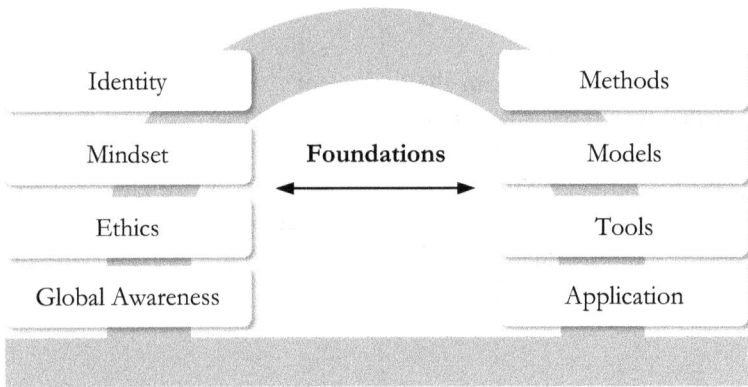

Identity	Methods
Mindset	**Foundations**	Models
Ethics	Tools
Global Awareness	Application

Foundations shape practice: Identity, Mindset, Ethics, and Awareness lead to Tools, Methods, and Models

Figure 5 Part 1 Reflections Bridge

Part 2 – The Security Toolkit

Foundations alone are not enough. To turn professional judgement into effective practice, consultants need a toolkit of methods, standards, and approaches that can be applied in diverse contexts.

The chapters that follow move from assessing risks to shaping physical protection, bridging electronic and cyber-physical systems, embedding people and culture, and evaluating the role of technology. The part concludes with a study of compliance, showing how formal requirements can either support or distort resilience depending on how they are applied.

Together, these tools form the consultant's working repertoire. They provide a common language for engaging with clients, regulators, and project teams, while also offering structured ways of diagnosing problems and designing proportionate solutions. By the end of Part 2, you will be equipped with the practical methods needed to apply the principles introduced in Part 1 and ready to explore how consultants put them into action in Part 3.

Chapter 6 – Risk Assessment Made Practical

Risk assessment is at the heart of effective security consultancy, yet it is often overcomplicated or reduced to a box-ticking exercise. This chapter is designed to show how consultants can make risk assessment practical, clear, and decision-focused. The objectives below outline the skills and understanding the reader will develop.

By the end of this chapter, you will be able to:

- Apply the Threat, Vulnerability, and Risk Assessment (TVRA) process in plain English, avoiding unnecessary jargon.
- Apply and explain the threat, vulnerability, and impact model across different client contexts.
- Convert risk assessment findings into prioritised, actionable steps that align with client objectives.
- Recognise and avoid "spreadsheet theatre" where complex matrices create the illusion of control without driving decisions.
- Use structured consulting tools such as issue trees, hypothesis-driven analysis, and the MECE principle to structure risk assessments effectively.
- Conduct risk assessments under real-world constraints, including limited data and time, while still producing useful outputs.
- Present clear, concise, and actionable recommendations that decision-makers can act on with confidence.

Introduction

Risk assessment sits at the core of security consultancy because it provides the foundation upon which all other recommendations rest. Without a clear understanding of the risks facing an organisation, even the most sophisticated technical design or security investment may fail to deliver value. Yet risk assessment is also one of the most misunderstood activities in the profession. Too often it becomes an exercise in producing complex matrices and colourful charts that impress on paper but offer little practical guidance. Consultants must therefore approach risk assessment with a mindset that prioritises clarity, relevance, and action.

The purpose of this chapter is to make risk assessment practical. It sets out how consultants can apply the threat, vulnerability, and impact model in a way that is easy to explain and easy for clients to act on. Rather than aiming for false precision, the emphasis is on producing a reasoned view of the most important risks and on structuring findings so that decisions can be made confidently. This is where the consultant adds value: by translating technical observations into business consequences and by ensuring that recommendations are prioritised according to what matters most to the client.

A risk assessment is not a document – it's a decision engine. If it doesn't guide action, it hasn't done its job.

Risk assessment also benefits from the structured thinking approaches used in wider management consulting. Tools such as issue trees, hypothesis-driven analysis, and the MECE principle allow consultants to break down complex scenarios into manageable parts, avoid duplication, and ensure nothing essential is missed. These techniques help to move risk assessment away from being a descriptive exercise and towards being a decision-support tool.

This chapter highlights the importance of critical thinking in avoiding what might be called "spreadsheet theatre" – the tendency to mistake the production of detailed registers for meaningful analysis. By working through a practical example of a small retail store, the reader will see how even with limited data it is possible to conduct a useful assessment and provide actionable outcomes. In this way, risk assessment becomes less about bureaucracy and more about delivering clarity, insight, and value to the client.

The Threat, Vulnerability, Impact Model

The foundation of any risk assessment is the relationship between threats, vulnerabilities, and impacts. This logic must be explained clearly, because it shapes every recommendation that follows. Done well, it helps clients see not only what risks exist, but why they matter and how to respond.

- **Threats** are potential sources of harm. They may be intentional, such as hostile insiders or organised criminals; accidental, such as human error; or environmental, such as floods or power failures. Threats are external to the consultant's control, but what can be influenced is how the organisation prepares to deter or withstand them. The task is not to predict every possible threat, but to identify those credible in the client's specific context.

- **Vulnerabilities** are weaknesses that threats can exploit. These may be technical, procedural, or cultural. A propped-open door, for example, becomes significant only when linked to a credible threat such as unauthorised entry. Consultants should avoid cataloguing weaknesses in isolation; vulnerabilities matter only when connected to realistic threats and relevant impacts.

- **Impacts** are the consequences if a threat exploits a vulnerability. These range from financial loss and reputational harm to safety risks and operational downtime. The same vulnerability may produce very different impacts depending on context: a hospital system outage affects patient safety, a data centre faces contractual penalties, and an airport may trigger national security concerns.

A simple chain makes this logic tangible:

- *Threat* – a robbery attempt.
- *Vulnerability* – lack of secure doors and weak staff training.
- *Impact* – financial loss, harm to staff, reputational damage.

By articulating risks in this way, the consultant links cause to consequence and shows why specific controls should be prioritised.

Asset / Function	Identified Vulnerability	Exploiting Threat	Likely Impact if Realised	Risk Priority / Action Owner
Perimeter fence and gates	Manual gates left unsecured out of hours	Opportunistic intrusion	Minor breach; delayed detection	Medium – FM to enforce lock-up procedure
Access control system	Outdated firmware and default passwords	Cyber compromise of access logs	Unauthorised access; loss of audit trail	High – IT to patch and reset credentials
Security control room	Over-reliance on one trained operator	Fatigue, procedural lapse	Missed alarm; delayed response	Medium – HR/Security to rotate staff and retrain
Server racks in data hall	Inadequate physical segregation.	Insider threat.	Equipment tampering; data loss.	High – Design to install cages and audit access.
Visitor management	Manual paper log only.	Social engineering.	Unverified entry; identity misuse.	Medium – Security to digitise process.
Utility supply	No redundancy for key transformer.	Power outage.	Loss of critical systems.	High – Engineering to plan backup feed.

Table 3 Threat–Vulnerability–Impact Traceability Matrix

The model is versatile but must never be applied mechanically. Overstating threats (e.g. nation-state attacks on a small logistics firm) or listing vulnerabilities without context creates noise and undermines credibility. Equally, inflating every risk as "critical" paralyses decision-making. The value lies in anchoring the model to the client's operating reality, filtering out the trivial, and highlighting the chains that matter most.

Used consistently, the threat–vulnerability–impact model enforces discipline and clarity. It provides a structured narrative that decision-makers can grasp: *if this happens, here is where we are exposed, and here is what it could mean for us.* This keeps the assessment practical, relevant, and focused on enabling action.

From Assessment to Action – Risk Scoring and Prioritisation

Once threats, vulnerabilities, and impacts have been identified, the next step is to turn that understanding into an actionable set of priorities. This is where many risk assessments fail. They often stop at description, producing pages of entries without giving the client any sense of what matters most. A consultant's responsibility is not just to capture risks but to make them manageable, ranking them in a way that allows decisions to be made confidently.

The first challenge is avoiding false precision. Risk assessments are often presented as numerical scores, suggesting a level of accuracy that is not truly achievable. Multiplying probabilities by impacts to generate risk values may look scientific, but in practice these numbers are usually based on subjective judgement. Two consultants may score the same risk differently, and clients may place too much weight on the apparent objectivity of the numbers. This does not mean that scoring should be abandoned, but rather that it must be approached with humility and transparency. The numbers are not the truth – they are tools to help prioritise.

Different methods of scoring exist, and consultants must choose the one that best suits the client's maturity and needs. Qualitative scoring is the simplest, often using categories such as low, medium, and high to describe likelihood and impact. While less precise, this approach can be easily understood and is less likely to mislead clients with spurious accuracy. Quantitative scoring, where risks are given numeric values, may be more persuasive in certain contexts but demands discipline. If used, it should be supported by clear definitions, ranges, and assumptions. Otherwise, it risks becoming an exercise in "spreadsheet theatre", where the complexity of the scoring obscures rather than clarifies.

A practical way forward is to treat scoring as a means of structuring discussion rather than as an end in itself. The consultant can use scales and values to guide debate with stakeholders, helping them to explore what they see as most critical. This shifts the focus from arguing about numbers to agreeing on priorities. The output should not be a perfect calculation but a reasoned consensus about which risks require immediate attention and which can be tolerated or monitored.

Prioritisation also requires distinguishing between what is urgent and what is important. Urgent risks are those that demand immediate action because they are either highly credible or could cause significant harm in the near term. Important risks are those that may be less immediate but could have major long-term consequences if neglected. Consultants must help clients balance the two. For example, a faulty fire alarm system may be urgent, while a lack of cyber awareness training may be important but less pressing. Both must be addressed, but the sequencing will differ.

Budget constraints make prioritisation even more essential. Most organisations cannot address every identified risk simultaneously. Consultants must therefore provide a clear rationale for recommending that one set of controls is implemented before another. This may involve simple matrices that plot likelihood against impact, but it should always be framed in terms of business value. The key is to answer the client's real question: given our limited resources, where will we get the greatest reduction in risk for the effort and money spent?

The consultant's greatest contribution is in cutting through the noise. Risk registers can quickly balloon to dozens or even hundreds of entries. Left unfiltered, they overwhelm clients and undermine decision-making. A consultant must apply discipline, narrowing the focus to the ten or fewer risks that truly matter. This does not mean discarding the rest – lower ranked risks can still be tracked – but it does mean that leadership attention is directed towards the issues that, if left unaddressed, could have the most serious consequences.

Risk scoring and prioritisation are about translation. The consultant translates raw observations into structured insights that point directly to action. This process bridges the gap between technical analysis and executive decision-making. A risk assessment that merely describes is incomplete. A risk assessment that prioritises, explains, and guides action is the one that delivers value.

Using Consulting Frameworks to Structure Risk Analysis

Risk assessment is not only technical; it is also a consulting exercise. The consultant's value lies in structuring complex problems so they can be understood and acted upon. Management consulting tools are useful here, provided they are applied with discipline.

An issue tree breaks a broad question into its component parts. Asking "What are the security risks to this airport?" might branch into perimeter, insider, cyber, and supply chain categories. This prevents vague debate and ensures that each area is examined systematically. The MECE principle (Mutually Exclusive, Collectively Exhaustive) reinforces this discipline: categories must not overlap, and together they must cover the whole picture. Applied correctly, this avoids both duplication and blind spots.

Hypothesis-driven analysis adds further focus. Rather than collecting data indiscriminately, the consultant begins with working assumptions about the most significant risks, then tests these against evidence. For example, assuming perimeter intrusion is the dominant risk at a port may be confirmed – or disproved – by surveys and incident records. This approach keeps the assessment purposeful and prevents data hoarding.

These frameworks also help guard against bias. Confirmation bias and availability bias can skew judgement; structured methods force consultants to test assumptions and examine all categories, not just the obvious. At the same time, frameworks must remain flexible. Poorly designed issue trees or untested hypotheses can channel thinking in the wrong direction. Consultants should use them as reference points rather than rigid prescriptions.

Using such frameworks also aligns the consultant's work with how executives are accustomed to receiving analysis. Business leaders are familiar with structured problem solving; when security risks are presented in the same way, credibility increases. Instead of lengthy lists of observations, the consultant provides a logical narrative: starting assumptions, tested evidence, and validated priorities.

In short, issue trees, MECE structures, and hypothesis-driven analysis bring order to risk assessments. They make the process transparent, reduce wasted effort, and sharpen communication. By applying these methods thoughtfully, consultants elevate risk assessments from descriptive registers to persuasive, decision-ready tools.

Critical Thinking Toolkit – Spotting "Spreadsheet Theatre"

Risk assessments are often judged by their appearance rather than their substance. A colourful heat map, a long register of risks, or a spreadsheet filled with scores and multipliers can create the illusion of rigour. Yet beneath the surface, many such documents are little more than "spreadsheet theatre" – a performance of analysis that looks impressive but provides little practical value. A consultant must be able to recognise this trap and, more importantly, help clients avoid falling into it.

Spreadsheet theatre occurs when presentation is confused with genuine insight. A typical example is the risk matrix that assigns numbers for likelihood and impact, multiplies them together, and produces a neat grid of coloured boxes. While this can be a useful visual tool, it can also mislead. The numbers often lack solid grounding, being based on subjective estimates rather than reliable data. Assigning a likelihood of "0.6" instead of "medium" does not make the assessment more accurate – it simply disguises subjectivity with a veneer of mathematics. Clients may then assume that the resulting rankings are objective truth rather than informed opinion.

Another common manifestation is the over-engineered risk register. Consultants sometimes produce registers that run to hundreds of entries, each coded, scored, and cross-referenced. At first glance, this appears thorough. In reality, such registers often overwhelm the client and obscure the handful of risks that genuinely require attention. Leaders cannot act on a list that long; instead, they become paralysed or default to treating all risks as equal, which defeats the point of prioritisation. The consultant's task is not to create a compendium of every conceivable risk but to filter, interpret, and present the few that matter most.

Critical thinking is the antidote to spreadsheet theatre. The consultant must constantly ask: what decisions will this assessment inform? If a table, chart, or register does not contribute to clearer decision-making, it risks becoming decoration rather than substance. A well-designed risk assessment may in fact be shorter, with fewer visuals, but sharper in its conclusions. The measure of success is not how polished the report looks but how effectively it guides action.

One way to guard against spreadsheet theatre is to stress-test the assessment by asking "so what?" after each entry. For example, if the assessment identifies "unsecured windows" as a vulnerability, the consultant should ask: so what? What threat does this connect to, and what impact would it have? If the answer is minor or irrelevant, the entry may not deserve prominence. This discipline strips away superficial observations and keeps the assessment focused on risks that have meaningful consequences.

Another safeguard is to involve stakeholders in the scoring and prioritisation process. Rather than producing scores in isolation, the consultant can facilitate workshops where managers and staff debate likelihoods, impacts, and priorities. This turns the risk assessment into a shared process of reasoning rather than a black box calculation. It also builds ownership, ensuring that the final rankings reflect the organisation's own view of what matters, not just the consultant's view. When people see their reasoning reflected in the outcome, they are more likely to act on the recommendations.

A useful exercise is to compare an elaborate risk register with a distilled top ten list of risks. If the top ten cannot be explained clearly in plain language, the register has failed. A chief executive does not need to know that risk number 127 scored 3.6 out of 5 on the likelihood scale. They need to know whether the business is exposed to data loss, insider fraud, regulatory penalties, or safety incidents. By translating the detail into a handful of high-impact risks expressed in everyday terms, the consultant delivers something that drives board-level discussion.

Spreadsheet theatre also thrives when consultants focus on the mechanics of scoring instead of the logic of risk. For example, debating whether the probability of a threat is 30 per cent or 40 per cent is less useful than discussing what factors make the threat more or less likely and what could be done to influence them. Numbers should serve as prompts for discussion, not as substitutes for it. Critical thinking means keeping the focus on underlying reasoning rather than the superficial appearance of precision.

There are times when detailed scoring and registers are necessary – for instance, in highly regulated environments where documentation is required for compliance. Even in such cases, however, the consultant must separate compliance outputs from decision-support outputs. One document may satisfy regulators, but another, simpler narrative may be required to guide executives. When compliance and decision-support are blurred, the result is assessments that satisfy auditors but fail to improve security. A disciplined consultant therefore provides two outputs: a formal record to meet regulatory demands and a clear narrative to guide leadership decisions.

The danger of spreadsheet theatre is not only wasted effort but also misplaced confidence. An organisation that sees a polished heat map may assume its risks are under control, even if critical vulnerabilities remain unaddressed. This false sense of security can be more dangerous than having no assessment at all because it lulls decision-makers into complacency. Consultants must therefore challenge assumptions, even if it means questioning the very tools and templates their own profession has popularised.

Spotting and avoiding spreadsheet theatre is about keeping risk assessment anchored in purpose. The purpose is to inform decisions and drive action, not to produce documents that look professional but lack substance. By applying critical thinking, asking "so what?", engaging stakeholders, and distilling findings into plain language, the consultant ensures that the assessment remains practical and credible. In doing so, they replace theatre with analysis and produce outputs that genuinely enhance the client's ability to manage risk.

Illustrative Example: Small Retail Store Assessment

One of the most effective ways to understand how a risk assessment should work in real conditions is to apply the principles to a simple, recognisable scenario. A small retail store provides an ideal case because it highlights the consultant's challenge of working with limited inputs, constrained budgets, and non-technical decision-makers. Unlike a major infrastructure facility, a small store rarely has detailed risk data, specialist staff, or sophisticated systems. Yet the consultant must still deliver an assessment that is clear, prioritised, and actionable.

Imagine being engaged by the owner of a clothing shop located on a busy high street. The owner has noticed minor thefts, occasional vandalism, and worries about staff safety during late trading hours. The engagement is limited in scope: there is no appetite for extensive surveys or complex modelling, only a request for a straightforward assessment that can inform practical improvements. This scenario captures the essence of consultancy – providing value under real-world constraints.

The first step is to frame the exercise using the threat, vulnerability, and impact model. Threats include shoplifting, burglary after hours, abusive customers, and accidental incidents such as fire. Vulnerabilities include the lack of CCTV coverage, poorly lit entrances, absence of staff training in conflict management, and weak locks on the rear service door. Impacts range from financial loss through theft, to reputational harm if customers feel unsafe, to regulatory penalties if fire safety provisions are inadequate.

Working systematically, the consultant links these elements into risk chains. For example, the threat of burglary after hours is linked to the vulnerability of inadequate locks, with an impact of significant stock loss and disruption to trading. Another chain connects the threat of customer aggression to the vulnerability of untrained staff, with impacts on staff wellbeing, potential legal claims, and customer trust. Each chain is described in plain language, ensuring that the store owner can immediately see the logic.

The next stage is scoring and prioritisation. Given the limited data, a qualitative scale is most appropriate. Likelihood is assessed as low, medium, or high based on observable patterns and local crime statistics. Impact is judged in terms of financial, safety, and reputational consequences. By applying this method, the consultant identifies that while minor shoplifting is frequent, the impact is low, so it should not dominate. By contrast, the risk of fire – although less likely – carries catastrophic potential and therefore deserves high priority. The consultant can now explain that resources should not be exhausted chasing small losses when greater threats remain unaddressed.

With the prioritisation clear, the consultant develops practical recommendations. For burglary risk, upgrading locks on rear doors and installing a basic monitored alarm system provides significant improvement at relatively low cost. For staff safety, introducing simple conflict management training and a discreet panic button at the counter builds confidence without major expense. For fire safety, ensuring that extinguishers are maintained, escape routes are clear, and staff know how to respond in an emergency is critical. These measures do not require advanced technology or heavy investment, but they directly address the most significant risks identified in the assessment.

An important part of the exercise is presentation. The store owner is unlikely to read a fifty-page report. Instead, the consultant produces a short summary that outlines the top five risks, explains the reasoning behind their prioritisation, and lists clear, achievable actions. This may be supported by a simple table or diagram showing how the threats, vulnerabilities, and impacts connect. The emphasis is on clarity, not on overwhelming the client with detail.

The consultant must also anticipate objections and constraints. The owner may argue that investing in fire safety yields no visible benefit, while installing cameras feels more tangible. Here the consultant's role is to explain the trade-offs. A single fire could destroy the business, whereas shoplifting is a manageable cost of trading. By reframing the discussion in terms of survival and continuity rather than convenience, the consultant helps the client make rational choices.

This exercise also illustrates the broader value of consultancy skills. Technical expertise alone is not enough; the consultant must communicate persuasively, adapt recommendations to budget realities, and tailor outputs to the client's understanding. The ability to distil complex analysis into simple, business-relevant terms is what differentiates a useful consultant from one who merely compiles observations.

The exercise highlights the scalability of the risk assessment process. The same logic applied to a small store can be extended to larger, more complex organisations. The threats may change, the vulnerabilities may be more numerous, and the impacts may be broader, but the underlying chain of threat, vulnerability, and impact remains constant. By practising with small-scale scenarios, consultants build the discipline to apply the model consistently in high-stakes environments.

The small retail store assessment shows how consultants can create value even with minimal data and modest budgets. It demonstrates that risk assessment is not about producing exhaustive registers or impressive graphics, but about clarifying priorities and providing actionable steps. By focusing on what truly matters, and by communicating this in plain language, the consultant ensures that even the smallest client receives advice that improves their resilience and protects their business.

Global Perspectives and Regulatory Foundations

Although the logic of threat, vulnerability, and impact is universal, expectations around risk assessment differ across regions. Consultants must therefore show not only that their method is robust, but that it aligns with the frameworks and cultural context in which the client operates.

In Europe, ISO 31000:2018[13] remains the core reference point, stressing integration with business processes rather than stand-alone risk exercises. A security consultant working with a European data centre should therefore demonstrate not just physical and cyber assessment, but also how findings link to executive decision-making and compliance obligations under measures such as the EU Network and Information Security Directive or the General Data Protection Regulation.

In the United States, NIST[19] provides more prescriptive models such as the Cybersecurity Framework and Special Publication 800-30. These expect structured scoring, documentation, and auditable outputs. For consultants, the challenge is balancing completeness with clarity: meeting regulatory expectations while avoiding the trap of producing detail that overwhelms decision-makers.

In the Middle East, authorities such as the UAE's NCEMA[18] and Dubai's SIRA[4] blend international standards with national resilience priorities. Risk assessments here often serve dual purposes: supporting operational decisions while also satisfying licensing or certification requirements. Consultants must be sensitive to geopolitical context and demonstrate how their approach supports both compliance and resilience.

Asia and Africa present a mixed picture. Developed economies such as Singapore and Japan follow ISO-aligned frameworks, while developing markets may lack formal regulation. Yet international investors frequently demand compliance with global standards. Consultants must therefore balance best practice with local realities, often taking an educational role to explain why particular methods matter.

Across all regions, a recurring risk is that assessments become mere compliance exercises. When this happens, the goal of informing decisions is overshadowed by the pressure to complete checklists. The effective consultant acknowledges regulatory foundations, produces outputs that withstand audit, but ensures the final product still delivers clarity, prioritisation, and business value.

This means framing risk assessments so that they are both compliant and useful. A European client may need a register formatted for auditors; an American client may expect detailed scoring; a Middle Eastern client may require alignment with licensing conditions. But in each case, the consultant should still distil the findings into a clear set of priorities that management can act on. Regulations provide structure, but it is the consultant's discipline that makes them decision-support tools rather than bureaucratic burdens.

Practice Guide

Risk assessment is only valuable when it enables decisions. The Threat–Vulnerability–Impact model, when applied in plain English, provides a disciplined way of identifying what matters most and why. Each of the learning objectives has been met: the use of TVRA has been demonstrated in practical terms; the importance of structuring findings into prioritised, actionable steps has been reinforced; the pitfalls of "spreadsheet theatre" have been examined; and the value of consulting frameworks such as issue trees, hypothesis-driven analysis, and the MECE principle has been illustrated. The global perspectives discussion confirmed that these principles apply universally, while regulatory foundations showed how assessments must adapt to local contexts without slipping into compliance-only exercises.

A recurring pitfall to avoid is the temptation to over-engineer registers and matrices, mistaking volume and colour for insight. False precision, long lists of unconnected vulnerabilities, or exaggerated threats create noise that confuses rather than clarifies. Equally dangerous is allowing compliance requirements to dominate the exercise, reducing risk assessment to paperwork designed to satisfy auditors rather than to improve resilience. Consultants must resist these traps by keeping their focus on clarity, credibility, and business value.

Best practice lies in translating assessments into decisions that clients can act on with confidence. This means presenting the logic of risks as clear chains of cause and consequence, linking threats, vulnerabilities, and impacts in ways that make sense to non-technical stakeholders. It requires prioritising ruthlessly, narrowing focus to the few risks that truly matter, and explaining why certain measures should come before others. It also involves engaging stakeholders in the reasoning process so that ownership is shared, and the assessment becomes a tool for consensus rather than a consultant's private calculation.

Above all, the consultant's task is to keep risk assessment practical. This is achieved by combining technical knowledge with consulting discipline, ensuring that findings are structured, decisions are informed, and actions are proportionate to context. By doing so, risk assessments move beyond compliance outputs and become instruments of real resilience. The ability to structure and communicate risk assessments in this way forms the foundation for the consultant's wider toolkit, preparing the ground for the integration of people, procedures, culture, and technology in the chapters that follow.

Chapter 7 – Physical Security Fundamentals

Physical security remains the bedrock of protection, even in an era where cyber risks dominate much of the discussion. Without effective physical measures, electronic systems and procedural controls are easily undermined. This chapter is designed to provide a practical foundation in physical security, enabling consultants to apply layered defence concepts, identify design flaws, and recommend solutions that balance resilience with usability.

By the end of this chapter, you will be able to:

- Apply the principles of perimeter-to-core layered defence, linking deterrence, detection, delay, and response.

- Evaluate the effectiveness of barriers, access control, and detection measures, and explain how they interact as part of a system.

- Identify common failures in physical security design, including operational workarounds, and describe their consequences.

- Conduct and interpret site walk-throughs and red team style assessments that reveal overlooked vulnerabilities.

- Translate technical concepts into clear, business-relevant advice, distinguishing between over-engineered solutions and proportionate measures that add value.

- Adapt physical security advice to different global contexts, recognising the influence of regulatory frameworks and cultural factors.

Introduction

Physical security remains the foundation on which every other protective measure depends. Without control of space, no cyber defence, procedural safeguard, or cultural initiative can function properly. A facility that permits unauthorised entry at its perimeter, or fails to physically protect its core assets, cannot be secured by technology alone.

Physical security works best when built up in layers, each adding protection: deterrence, detection, delay, and response. Each function plays a distinct role, and when integrated, they provide a level of protection that no single measure can achieve in isolation. A fence discourages intruders and shows that the site is controlled, access systems identify and block unauthorised attempts, barriers slow down progress, and security staff or responders deal with incidents when they occur. The consultant's task is to evaluate how these layers combine in real life, ensuring that they create a system that is proportionate, effective, and sustainable.

Because physical measures are highly visible, they shape how people experience a facility as much as how they protect it. Systems that obstruct daily operations are likely to be bypassed; however strong they appear on drawings. When security feels excessive or overbearing, it can damage culture by creating frustration or resentment, leading people to see it as a barrier rather than support. Consultants must therefore balance resilience with usability and perception, considering not only whether measures should exist but how they function in real conditions, and how they are received by those who use them. Measures that integrate smoothly into daily life build trust and reinforce security culture; those that impose unnecessary burdens risk undermining it.

Few sites begin with a blank canvas. Most have grown through piecemeal additions, regulatory changes, or responses to incidents, leaving overlaps and gaps. Consultants must assess both the adequacy of individual elements and their integration into a functioning whole. They must also recognise that physical protection cannot stand apart from procedural and technological measures: a secure server hall is meaningless if staff can enter unchallenged through a side door, and a strong visitor policy is worthless if emergency exits are left unsecured.

This chapter explores how consultants apply the fundamentals of physical security in practice. It begins with the principle of perimeter-to-core layered defence, before examining the tools of barriers, access control, and detection. It then considers common design failures, the use of red team walk-throughs, the balance between security, usability, and cost, and global variations shaped by regulation and culture. Together, these perspectives demonstrate how physical measures remain the non-negotiable base upon which resilience is built.

Perimeter-to-Core Layered Defence

Layered defence is one of the most enduring principles in physical security. It recognises that no single measure is sufficient, and that resilience is achieved through successive layers, each performing a distinct role. At the heart of this approach are four functions: deterrence, which discourages hostile acts by making them appear difficult or unprofitable; detection, which ensures that any attempt is noticed; delay, which slows progress and buys time; and response, which interrupts the attack and resolves the incident. For consultants, the task is not simply to confirm that measures exist, but to assess whether these four functions are achieved across the facility in a coherent sequence.

The outer boundary is the first point of contact between the facility and the outside world, where deterrence and early detection are most important. Fences, walls, lighting, and signage mark clear boundaries and establish authority, while sensors and cameras provide detection, alert responders, and supply video verification as event intelligence. These measures should be judged not only by appearance but by how well they perform in real life and how they are experienced by those who use them. A fence that looks imposing but can be climbed in seconds, or a camera positioned with blind spots, fails to meet its purpose.

Attention then shifts to the points of entry. Gates, doors, and vehicle barriers are where detection and delay become critical. Access control systems, guards, and screening procedures establish legitimacy, while physical barriers slow or prevent forced entry. Vehicle bollards provide a clear example: they can halt hostile vehicles long enough for a response to be mobilised. The challenge for consultants is to judge whether the measures are proportionate to the risk and to the environment. A staffed reception and turnstiles may be sufficient for a commercial tower, while critical infrastructure facilities may demand reinforced mantraps, vehicle barriers to recognised Hostile Vehicle Mitigation (HVM) standards, and baggage or parcel screening.

Beyond the entry points, circulation spaces such as lobbies, corridors, and service routes form a middle layer that is often neglected. These areas determine whether an unauthorised individual can move freely once inside. Effective zoning, separation of public and staff-only areas, and controlled access to sensitive zones prevent such movement. The principle applies in many contexts: hospitals must clearly separate waiting areas from clinical spaces, and data centres must prevent access from shared offices to server halls, except through successive controlled points. Even if an intruder breaches the perimeter, these internal layers ensure that they encounter further resistance.

The assets of greatest value reside at the core, whether they are data halls, control rooms, vaults, or hazardous stores. Here, the emphasis falls on delay and response. Reinforced construction, secure doors, and biometric access control are intended to ensure that even if an adversary reaches this stage, they cannot succeed before responders intervene. What matters most to the consultant is the relationship between barriers and response time. A vault door that resists attack for ten minutes is worthless if the response takes twenty, yet if intervention is guaranteed within two minutes, lighter measures may suffice. This reinforces the principle that no layer should be judged in isolation, but only in relation to the others.

The effectiveness of layered defence depends on integration. A site with a strong perimeter but weak internal zoning still allows intruders to move unchallenged once inside. Another may have a fortified core but an outer boundary so porous that adversaries can disrupt operations before defenders can react. Consultants must identify these disconnects and emphasise that resilience arises from how layers work together.

Insider risk complicates the picture further. A staff member with legitimate credentials may bypass several layers, moving straight to the core. To mitigate this, consultants should recommend additional controls such as access audits, continuous monitoring, and reinforcement of security culture. This demonstrates that layered defence is not purely a physical model but one that must include procedural and human elements.

The model must also evolve. Threats change, facilities expand, and technology advances. Measures that once deterred opportunistic trespass may be inadequate against adversaries using hostile reconnaissance or drones. Regular review and testing are essential to ensure that deterrence, detection, delay, and response remain aligned with the current risk profile.

Security Layer	Primary Objective	Typical Measures / Controls	Verification or Test Method	Common Weaknesses Found
Perimeter	Deter and delay unauthorised approach.	Fencing, gates, barriers, lighting, signage, intrusion detection.	Physical inspection, gate audit, CCTV review, intrusion sensor test.	Gaps under fences, unmonitored gates, poor illumination.
Building Shell	Prevent unauthorised entry to facility envelope.	Walls, doors, windows, locks, glazing, access control.	Door/lock inspection, forced-entry test, access log review.	Propped-open doors, weak hinges, poor hardware maintenance.
Internal Zoning	Separate secure areas by criticality.	Access zones, airlocks, turnstiles, mantraps, partition walls.	Access control test by credential, tailgate observation.	Zoning not enforced, unlabelled areas, inconsistent card rights.
Asset Enclosure	Protect high-value assets and data.	Cages, server racks, vaults, safes, tamper seals.	Access attempt simulation, seal integrity check.	Shared keys, missing audit trail, unlocked racks.
Control Room / Operations Centre	Maintain command, control, and situational awareness.	Operator workstations, alarm management, redundancy.	System redundancy test, alarm-response drill, log review.	Single point of failure, alarm fatigue, no backup comms.
People and Procedures	Ensure human reliability and behavioural compliance.	Training, SOPs, role separation, supervision.	Training record audit, procedural walk-through, observation.	Complacency, poor induction, over-delegation.
Maintenance and Assurance	Sustain performance of protective measures.	Preventive maintenance, audits, re-testing.	Schedule compliance review, re-certification.	Deferred maintenance, outdated documentation.

Table 4 Layered Defence Summary and Verification Tests

However, layered security should not be understood as a simple sequence of concentric circles through which an adversary must pass. That traditional model is increasingly outdated, because modern threats rarely follow a predictable or linear path. Instead, the consultant must view deterrence, detection, delay, and response as interdependent principles that operate in parallel, linked by technology, people, and processes. A sensor does not trigger delay before a guard reacts; it should connect directly to the responders, providing real-time intelligence that shapes their actions. Barriers are not just passive obstacles; they can be instrumented to signal intrusion and accelerate intervention. In other words, each measure must be integrated with the others in a three-dimensional network of overlapping functions rather than arranged as sequential rings.

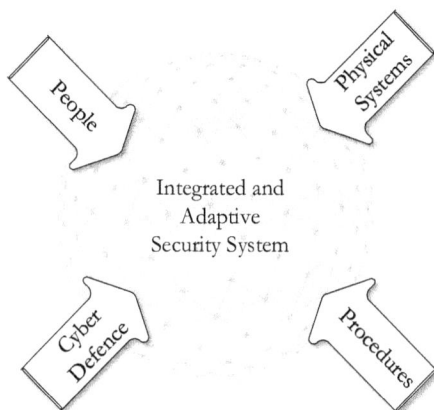

Figure 6 Integrated and Adaptive Systems

The Grigg Evolved Equilibrium Resilience Model (GEERM) provides a structured way to understand how security principles, systems, and behaviours interconnect in real life. It recognises that protection depends not only on the strength of individual controls, but on the coherence of the entire ecosystem – how physical, digital, human, and procedural domains interact through governance and feedback over time. As in other resilient systems, effectiveness arises from networks rather than chains: deterrence reinforces detection, detection accelerates response, response stabilises recovery, and every layer informs the others. By applying this model, consultants move beyond static diagrams of concentric circles to a living architecture of defences that overlap, integrate, and evolve with changing conditions.

Barriers, Access Control, and Detection

Barriers, access control, and detection are the most visible elements of physical security. They shape how people and vehicles interact with a facility, and for many clients they represent the tangible face of protection. For consultants, the task is not to catalogue their presence but to judge whether they perform their intended role in practice and whether they function together as part of a coherent system.

Barriers are the fundamental element of physical protection. They may be fences, walls, bollards, glazing, or landscaping features, and their purpose is to channel movement and resist forced entry. The essential point is that barriers provide resistance measured in time rather than in absolutes. A fence may delay an intruder by seconds, a reinforced door by minutes, and a crash-rated bollard by the amount of energy it can absorb. Consultants must therefore assess whether barriers are appropriate for the likely threats and whether they provide enough delay for a response to be effective. A chain-link fence might deter casual trespassers, but it will not stop a determined intruder; a shallow-mounted bollard might stop a car but not a heavy truck. The evaluation is always relative to the threat profile and the time available for response and intervention.

Access control systems regulate who may pass through barriers. At their simplest they consist of locks and keys; at their most complex, they employ electronic credentials, biometrics, or airlock-style mantraps. Their value depends as much on human behaviour as on technical performance. A card reader is useless if tailgating is common, and even the most advanced mantrap fails if throughput is mismatched to daily traffic, creating pressure for workarounds. Consultants must therefore assess access control both for reliability and for usability, anticipating how people will interact with the system under real conditions. Over-engineered solutions may frustrate staff, leading to circumvention, while under-engineered systems may appear convenient but leave the facility exposed.

Detection provides the eyes and ears of the security system. It includes cameras, intruder alarms, motion sensors, and more advanced technologies such as radar or thermal imaging. The critical issue is not simply whether detection is possible but whether it is timely and actionable. A camera system that produces hours of footage without active monitoring does not contribute to real-time protection, and a motion sensor that generates constant false alarms quickly leads to complacency. Consultants must therefore assess detection alongside the procedures and staffing that support it, ensuring that alerts are meaningful and linked to an effective response.

These elements must be judged together, not in isolation. A barrier without detection can be breached unnoticed, while detection without delay gives no time for response. Access control may stop authorised staff but not an intruder forcing entry. The consultant's task is to examine how measures integrate so that deterrence, detection, delay, and response are delivered as a single outcome. A vehicle gate illustrates the point: barriers halt vehicles, access control verifies drivers, and cameras record incidents – if any one element fails, the integrity of the whole system is weakened.

Sustainability is equally important. Security measures degrade over time, and without structured maintenance, even the most robust system becomes ineffective. Barriers corrode, locks wear out, and detection equipment loses reliability. Consultants must therefore assess not only current performance but also the capacity of the organisation to maintain and operate the system in the long term. This includes the funding of maintenance contracts, the availability of spare parts, and the training of staff who administer the technology. A sophisticated access control platform is of little value if no one on site knows how to manage user credentials.

Another dimension is the temptation to adopt advanced technology for its own sake. Clients may be drawn to biometric systems or AI-driven surveillance without considering whether these address the most pressing risks. Often, modest improvements in discipline, training, or physical reinforcement can achieve more than expensive innovations. The consultant must therefore be prepared to test vendor claims against the client's actual risk profile and operational context, ensuring that every measure is proportionate and adds tangible value.

The interaction between physical measures and culture should not be overlooked. Barriers, access control, and detection depend on staff following procedures and guards enforcing rules. A propped-open door or an operator ignoring alarms undermines even the strongest system. Observing how people interact with physical measures during a site walk-through often reveals more than technical specifications. Consultants must therefore consider cultural factors alongside engineering and technology, recognising that effective security is as much about behaviours as it is about hardware.

Barriers, access control, and detection represent the core toolkit of physical security, but their value lies not in their presence but in their deployment, integration, usability, and sustainability. Consultants must look beyond technical specifications to ask whether each measure fulfils its intended role, whether they work together as a coherent system, and whether they will continue to do so over time. By keeping evaluation proportionate and grounded in real-world behaviour, consultants help clients avoid ineffective investments and achieve resilience that is practical, credible, and enduring.

Common Design Failures and Lessons Learned

Physical security design often falls short in practice, even where principles are well understood and significant investment has been made. Consultants regularly encounter facilities where barriers, access control, and detection are all present, yet vulnerabilities remain. These failures usually arise not from lack of resources but from poor integration, flawed assumptions, or neglect once systems are installed. Recognising these recurring patterns is one of the consultant's most valuable contributions.

Typical failures include neglected details, overreliance on technology, inadequate maintenance, conflicts between architectural intent and security requirements, weak integration between layers, and operational behaviours that undermine design intent. Each exposes how resilience can be compromised by simple oversights.

Neglected details often prove decisive. A single unsecured side gate or overlooked emergency exit can render an otherwise robust perimeter ineffective. Overreliance on technology is another common issue, where organisations invest heavily in cameras or biometric readers but fail to enforce basic practices such as closing doors or supervising entry. Maintenance lapses quickly erode protection: corroded fences, broken locks, damaged bollards, or alarm systems ignored due to false alerts are all signs of a system that once worked but has not been sustained.

Conflicts with architectural priorities add further risk. Designs that prioritise aesthetics or openness can unintentionally weaken security. Glass façades may look impressive but compromise blast resistance unless laminated or treated; open atriums may create inviting spaces but also offer clear sight lines for intruders. Without consultant oversight, such decisions often leave vulnerabilities hidden behind architectural intent.

Weak integration between layers is a common failure. Some sites secure the perimeter but leave internal circulation open, while others reinforce the core yet neglect the outer boundary. Operational behaviours also reveal flaws that design alone cannot anticipate. Staff may hold open turnstiles during busy periods, prop fire doors for ventilation, or wave vehicles through screening points to avoid congestion. In each case, the system is technically sound but undermined by the realities of daily routine.

Post-incident reviews frequently show that breaches occur not because measures are absent but because they are misaligned, poorly maintained, or bypassed in practice. This shows that the real test of physical security lies in how well it operates day-to-day, not in the scale of investment.

Design failures show how quickly systems unravel when details are missed, maintenance is neglected, integration is weak, or operations override intent. For consultants, the value lies in turning these patterns into foresight, using lessons from past projects to identify risks before they cause loss. By doing so, they help clients build systems that are not only technically strong but also sustainable, proportionate, and resilient in practice.

Illustrative Example: When Barriers Exist but Systems Fail

A global financial services headquarters in a major city had invested heavily in its physical security programme. The site featured perimeter fencing with electronic detection, full-height turnstiles in the main lobby, extensive CCTV coverage, and a delivery bay equipped with vehicle screening systems. On paper, the facility met the regulatory requirements for a critical site and appeared resilient.

A red team style walk-through, however, revealed that the measures were not functioning as intended. The perimeter fence was robust but easily bypassed through a fire exit door routinely propped open for ventilation. The turnstiles created long queues during shift changes, leading staff to hold them open for colleagues – defeating its purpose of stopping more than one person getting through at a time. At the delivery bay, guards frequently waved trucks through without screening to avoid bottlenecks, undermining the barrier and detection systems. Even at the vehicle gate, an earlier incident had shown how a delivery gate left unlocked for convenience allowed intruders to drive directly into the site, bypassing electronic access controls entirely.

The common theme across these lapses was not the absence of security measures but their misalignment with daily operations. Staff and contractors, under pressure to maintain efficiency, developed workarounds that compromised the systems. Guards, tasked with avoiding congestion, prioritised throughput over procedure. The result was a layered defence that looked impressive on paper but failed when tested against real behaviours.

This case demonstrates a recurring lesson: physical security cannot be judged solely by the presence of hardware. Barriers, access control, and detection systems must fit the pace and routines of daily operations, be maintained consistently, and supported by user discipline. Consultants assessing facilities of this type should look beyond technical specifications to observe how people interact with measures under routine conditions. A fence, turnstile, or scanner only works if people use it properly.

Red Team Walk-Through as a Consulting Tool

One of the most effective ways for consultants to evaluate physical security is through a red team walk-through. This approach adopts the perspective of an adversary and tests how a facility's measures function in practice. Unlike desk-based reviews, which focus on design intent, a walk-through reveals what actually happens when people interact with the environment. Vulnerabilities that appear minor on drawings – such as a poorly lit corner or an unattended side door – often become glaringly obvious when experienced first-hand.

A red team walk-through begins with reconnaissance. Consultants ask: how would an intruder approach the site, where are the natural hiding places, and which entrances are least visible? Observations outside the boundary can identify weaknesses such as insufficient lighting or fences that can be climbed. Once inside, attention shifts to how barriers and access controls are really used. Can the consultant follow staff through a turnstile without challenge, or enter through an emergency exit left open for convenience? These small tests expose weaknesses in training, design, or culture.

Balanced against the red team view is the blue-team perspective, which represents the defenders – the guards, staff, and systems responsible for protecting the facility. For consultants, this means assessing guard training, monitoring procedures, escalation protocols, and the ability of responders to act decisively. Combining the two perspectives provides a full picture of how security works: the red team highlights vulnerabilities, while the blue team demonstrates whether defences are capable of detecting and responding to them.

Central to this analysis is the concept of competing timelines. The adversary has a finite period in which to act before their objective is achieved. The responders have their own timeline, beginning with detection and ending with threat neutralisation. Security succeeds when the responders can act quickly enough to interrupt and prevent the adversary's progress. This principle connects the red- and blue-team perspectives and provides a clear framework for evaluation.

Detection is the first element shaping the timeline. The earlier hostile activity is identified, the more time responders gain. Perimeter cameras, patrols, or sensors extend detection outward, giving responders a head start. Delay then stretches the adversary's timeline. Barriers, locks, and reinforced doors force intruders to expend time and effort, increasing the chances of interruption. Response completes the sequence, requiring staff or external forces to act decisively before the adversary achieves their goal. The consultant's task is to judge whether these three elements – detection, delay, and response – are aligned so that the protective timeline outpaces the attacker's.

Consultants must also ensure that delay mechanisms do not obstruct defenders themselves. Heavy doors or cumbersome locks may slow intruders, but if they also hinder guard movement or emergency access, the protective timeline is compromised. Testing both attacker and responder movement is therefore essential.

Cultural issues are often exposed through this process. A red team perspective may show staff ignoring strangers in restricted areas, while a blue-team assessment reveals gaps in guard training or supervision. Both translate into delayed detection or inadequate response, eroding the responder's advantage. These examples show why consultants must consider human behaviour as part of the security system, not as an external factor.

The combination of red and blue-team approaches, structured around competing timelines, gives consultants a persuasive narrative for clients: will our responders act before an adversary succeeds?

Balancing Security, Usability, and Cost

Designing effective physical security is not a matter of adding as many barriers, locks, or sensors as possible. The challenge is to balance three more dimensions: protection, usability, and cost. Measures must be proportionate to the threats faced and workable within the environment in which they are deployed. Achieving this balance is one of the most difficult aspects of consultancy because it requires not only technical understanding but also sensitivity to human behaviour, operational needs, and financial constraints.

Usability is often the first test of whether a system will succeed. A measure that interferes with daily operations is likely to be ignored or worked around, not because staff lack discipline but because the design conflicts with the realities of work. The consultant's role is to anticipate these pressures and recommend measures that integrate with routine operations. Security that works with people rather than against them has a far greater chance of being effective.

Cost is an equally important factor. Resources are finite, and clients must decide where to invest. A common mistake is to pursue sophisticated or fashionable technologies on the assumption that complexity equals resilience. Yet a biometric access system adds little if staff prop open side doors, and advanced camera analytics may not be cost-effective if the true vulnerability lies in perimeter fencing. Consultants must help clients distinguish between essential and peripheral measures, identifying where investment genuinely reduces risk. This includes considering not only the upfront price but also the lifecycle costs of maintenance, licensing, and staffing. A system that appears affordable at procurement may impose unsustainable burdens once operational.

Proportionality unites these considerations. The aim is neither minimalism nor excess, but alignment of measures with the assessed risk profile. Over-engineered solutions may waste resources, alienate users, and encourage circumvention, while under-engineered ones may provide convenience at the cost of exposure. A critical infrastructure site may justify reinforced mantraps and vehicle barriers built to international standards, whereas a regional office may only require well-managed access control and clear zoning. The principle is not maximum strength everywhere, but appropriate and proportionate strength where it matters most.

The role of the consultant is to frame these trade-offs in business terms. Clients respond more readily to explanations of value – reduced risk, preserved operations, regulatory compliance, or reputational protection – than to technical specifications alone. By articulating how security, usability, and cost can be balanced through proportionality, consultants provide guidance that is both practical and persuasive.

Effective physical security depends on alignment between design, operation, and behaviour. A system that performs on paper but conflicts with daily use will fail in practice.

Security measures succeed when they are proportionate to the threat, sustainable over time, and aligned with how people use the facility. By anticipating behaviours, considering lifecycle costs, and ensuring that operations remain viable, consultants prevent both under-protection and over-engineering. This balance, consistently applied, is what transforms physical security from a set of controls into a living system that enables organisations to function with confidence.

Global Perspectives on Physical Security

While the principles of deterrence, detection, delay, and response apply universally, the way they are implemented varies widely across regions. These differences reflect regulatory frameworks, cultural expectations, and the types of threats considered most credible. Consultants advising multinational clients must understand these variations and be able to explain why solutions differ across contexts.

In Europe, physical security has long been shaped by the risk of terrorism and political violence. Facilities in cities such as London, Madrid, and Paris incorporate blast-resistant glazing, vehicle barriers designed to stop truck-borne improvised explosive devices (IEDs), and zoning that separates public and restricted areas. Guidance from national authorities, such as the National Protective Security Authority (NPSA) in the United

Kingdom, has established best practice by integrating security into design stages rather than adding it as an afterthought.

In the United States, regulation combines with a strong culture of litigation to influence design. Federal standards issued by the Department of Homeland Security and the Federal Emergency Management Agency set benchmarks for critical infrastructure, while the Occupational Safety and Health Administration addresses workplace safety. Visible deterrence is often prioritised, with prominent guard forces and extensive CCTV used not only for security but also to reassure stakeholders. Consultants working in this environment must balance a client's desire for demonstrable security with the need to avoid redundant or excessive measures that increase liability without improving resilience.

In the Middle East, the presence of critical national infrastructure and the influence of government regulators drive a robust approach. Authorities such as the National Emergency Crisis and Disaster Management Authority in Abu Dhabi specify detailed requirements for perimeter protection, access control, and surveillance. Projects in this region frequently demand high levels of resilience, including blast resistance, hostile vehicle mitigation, and in some cases integration with armed response. Compliance is not optional, and consultants must adapt their advice to environments where oversight is strong, and security culture prioritises robustness over convenience.

In Japan and Singapore, physical security is closely integrated with broader resilience planning. Designs must account for natural hazards such as earthquakes and typhoons alongside malicious threats, leading to an emphasis on redundancy and structural resistance as much as on access control or surveillance.

In Africa, physical security priorities are strongly shaped by local crime rates, political instability, and resource constraints. Facilities often rely on guard forces, basic fencing, and simple access control, with limited budgets for advanced systems. Consultants must therefore focus on practical and sustainable measures, emphasising improvements such as lighting, reinforced doors, or reliable locks, which can deliver more long-term value than complex technologies that cannot be maintained.

Although each region has distinctive drivers, common themes are clear. Regulations set the baseline, but cultural expectations determine whether measures are accepted or circumvented. Visible deterrence may be effective in one society but counterproductive in another. Proportionality is vital everywhere, as over-engineering wastes resources and under-engineering leaves organisations exposed. The consultant's role is to interpret international standards flexibly, ensuring that they are applied in principle but adapted to local conditions. By doing so, security advice remains credible, usable, and sustainable across diverse environments.

Practice Guide

Physical security is the foundation upon which all other protective measures depend. This chapter has shown how consultants must approach it as both a technical discipline and as a practical enabler, applying layered defence principles, evaluating barriers, access control, and detection, and adapting advice to different regulatory and cultural environments.

The pitfalls to avoid are well established. Overreliance on technology is common: cameras, biometrics, or AI-driven analytics are often treated as substitutes for good practice, yet without discipline and integration into response they add little value. Neglected maintenance is another recurring failure, as barriers corrode, locks wear down, and alarms become background noise unless lifecycle funding and training are secured from the outset. Operational workarounds undermine many systems, whether through fire doors propped open, turnstiles held during peak flows, or vehicles waved through screening points. Conflicts between architectural intent and resilience are equally damaging, as aesthetic choices can create vulnerabilities if not discreetly mitigated. Over-engineering is as harmful as under-protection: measures that are disproportionate to the threat waste resources, frustrate users, and erode compliance.

Best practice flows directly from these lessons. Consultants should interpret deterrence, detection, delay, and response not as abstract categories but as outcomes that must operate together under real conditions. Site walk-throughs and red team assessments reveal vulnerabilities that drawings cannot, while blue-team perspectives test whether detection, delay, and response timelines are strong enough to outpace adversaries. Maintenance and operational continuity must be embedded into every recommendation, ensuring measures are sustainable over time. Equally, technical design must be translated into business-relevant language so that clients understand value – reduced risk, preserved operations, and compliance – rather than just specifications or cost. Above all, proportionality is the guiding principle: recommending solutions that are credible, usable, and sustainable in their context, rather than fashionable or excessive.

The consultant's role is to ensure that physical measures enable resilience in practice. This requires designing systems that integrate seamlessly into operations, that clients can afford to maintain, and that adapt both to evolving threats and to diverse regulatory and cultural contexts. By avoiding recurring pitfalls and reinforcing good practice, physical security advice becomes not just a technical specification but a living system – the non-negotiable base upon which procedural, cultural, and technological measures can be built. Ultimately, the consultant's value lies in acting as the integrator by bringing together physical and cyber measures, people, and culture into a system that delivers resilience in practice.

Chapter 8 – Electronic and Cyber-Physical Convergence

The boundary between physical and digital security has become increasingly blurred. Modern access control, CCTV, and building management systems are all networked devices, meaning that a weakness in cyber protection can directly undermine physical safeguards, and vice versa. Consultants are not expected to be deep technical experts in IT or OT, but they must understand how convergence changes the risk landscape and be able to guide clients towards proportionate, practical measures. This chapter provides the foundation needed to recognise vulnerabilities at the intersection of physical and cyber systems and to explain them clearly to non-technical stakeholders.

By the end of this chapter, you will be able to:

- Understand the fundamentals of IT (Information Technology) and OT (Operational Technology) as they apply to physical security systems.

- Recognise how cyber weaknesses can compromise physical security measures, and how physical risks can in turn affect digital resilience.

- Identify secure integration points between physical systems such as CCTV, access control, and intrusion detection, and the IT infrastructure on which they depend.

- Apply minimum cyber hygiene practices when reviewing or advising on physical security projects.

- Evaluate common failure points in electronic and cyber-physical integration, including poor configuration, lack of patching, and cultural gaps between IT, OT, and security teams.

- Translate complex technical risks into plain business language so that boards and executives can make informed decisions.

- Recommend proportionate and appropriate risk mitigation measures that strengthen convergence without over-engineering solutions.

Introduction

The convergence of physical and digital security is one of the defining features of modern practice. Where once physical security systems such as locks, CCTV cameras, and alarms operated independently of information technology, today almost every significant measure is connected to a network. Cameras transmit images using IP protocols, access control systems run on servers that also host corporate applications and building management systems are integrated into cloud platforms. This shift has created new opportunities for efficiency and integration, but it has also opened new vulnerabilities that consultants must be able to recognise and explain.

Convergence matters because it means that weaknesses in one domain can compromise the other. A poorly configured firewall may allow a hacker to access the video management system, turning off cameras at critical moments. An insider who gains control of a physical access server may be able to disable alarms or create fraudulent access credentials. Equally, a physical intrusion can give an adversary access to network cabinets, servers, or power systems that support digital resilience. The old distinction between cyber and physical is therefore increasingly incorrect. In reality, security must be seen as a single system with overlapping layers.

For consultants, the challenge lies not in becoming cyber specialists but in acting as interpreters between technical experts and business leaders. Most clients want to understand the risks in terms of business impact, not in terms of technical jargon. A consultant who can explain that "a vulnerability in the CCTV system could expose the company to reputational damage if footage is leaked" will be more effective than one who describes port numbers and encryption protocols. This ability to translate is what allows the consultant to add value in an area where the technical details can easily overwhelm the discussion.

In one documented case, attackers gained access to a casino's high-roller database through a smart fish tank thermometer connected to the network. In another, a breach of a building management system allowed attackers to disable alarms and heating controls in a commercial complex. These incidents show that vulnerabilities often arise at the points where physical and cyber systems overlap, and that adversaries are quick to exploit overlooked devices. Consultants must therefore approach every assignment with the assumption that if a system is connected, it can be attacked.

Convergence also shifts the consultant's focus from isolated measures to integration points. It is no longer enough to ask whether cameras exist or whether doors have electronic locks. The critical questions are how those devices are connected, who administers them, and what happens if they are compromised. A simple default password on a networked camera can provide an entry point into the wider corporate network. A building access control system connected to human resources databases may be exploited to create fraudulent credentials. These are not purely technical failures; they are systemic vulnerabilities that can undermine entire security programmes.

The consultant must also be aware of cultural divides. IT and physical security teams often work separately, with different priorities and vocabularies. IT departments focus on confidentiality, integrity, and availability of data, while physical security teams focus on access, safety, and incident response. When systems converge, these differences can create blind spots. An IT team may apply patching policies that conflict with operational uptime, or a physical security team may install devices without consulting network administrators. Consultants play a key role in bridging these silos, ensuring that integration is planned and that both sides understand the risks and dependencies involved.

The introduction to convergence sets the stage for the rest of the chapter. It highlights that the consultant's role is not to master every technical detail but to recognise that convergence changes the risk landscape fundamentally. Security is no longer a matter of physical barriers on one side and digital defences on the other, but of a unified system in which weaknesses cross boundaries. By approaching convergence with clarity, proportionality, and the ability to translate technical issues into business relevance, consultants ensure that their advice remains practical, credible, and aligned with client needs.

IT and OT Fundamentals

A central challenge in advising on cyber-physical convergence is that consultants often come from physical security backgrounds, while the issues increasingly involve information technology (IT) and operational technology (OT). It is therefore essential to establish a clear, plain-

English understanding of these domains, not at the level of technical engineering but at the level needed to evaluate risks and explain them to clients. Consultants do not need to be network architects, but they must know enough to ask the right questions, recognise red flags, and connect technical findings to business consequences.

Information Technology (IT) refers broadly to the systems that handle data. This includes corporate networks, email servers, cloud platforms, databases, and user devices. IT is characterised by a strong emphasis on data confidentiality, integrity, and availability. In practical terms, IT is about protecting information from unauthorised access, preventing tampering, and ensuring that systems remain online and usable. For security consultants, IT matters because many physical systems now rely on IT infrastructure to function. Access control servers may run on the same networks as office applications. CCTV management software may be hosted in cloud environments. If IT systems fail, physical security can fail with them.

Operational Technology (OT), by contrast, refers to the systems that monitor and control physical processes. These include Supervisory Control and Data Acquisition (SCADA) platforms, Building Management Systems (BMS), and Industrial Control Systems (ICS). OT has historically been separate from IT, designed to ensure the safe and reliable operation of machinery, utilities, and infrastructure. The priorities are slightly different: availability and safety come first, with confidentiality often a secondary concern. In OT environments, even a brief outage can have significant consequences – shutting down a production line, halting a power plant, or disabling life-safety systems. For consultants, OT matters because many physical security systems are embedded in these environments. Fire alarms, environmental controls, and even elevator systems may be part of a wider OT network.

The convergence of IT and OT introduces vulnerabilities. Historically, OT systems were isolated, operating on proprietary protocols with little or no connection to the internet. As they have become integrated with IT networks for efficiency and monitoring, they have inherited the vulnerabilities of those networks. Default passwords, unpatched devices, and poorly configured connections have allowed attackers to move from IT systems into OT environments. For example, a breach of a corporate email server may provide credentials that also allow access to a building management system. Once inside, an attacker may disable alarms, manipulate environmental controls, or disrupt physical operations.

Consultants must also understand how physical security devices themselves straddle IT and OT. Modern cameras are essentially specialised computers, running operating systems, connecting via internet protocols, and storing data on servers. Access control systems manage both physical doors and digital credentials, often linked to HR databases. Intrusion detection systems may connect to monitoring centres through the internet. Each of these devices is a node on a network, vulnerable to the same types of attack as any IT system. A camera with a default password can become a gateway for intruders to access the wider corporate network.

For consultants, the value lies in understanding enough of these fundamentals to bridge conversations between IT staff, OT operators, and business leaders. When an IT manager speaks of patching cycles, the consultant must understand that delaying updates may leave physical security systems exposed. When an OT operator insists that a system cannot be restarted without disrupting operations, the consultant must balance the need for continuity with the risks of leaving vulnerabilities unaddressed. This requires not technical mastery but clarity of perspective – knowing that both IT and OT have legitimate priorities, and that security solutions must reconcile them rather than favour one at the expense of the other.

Another important concept is segmentation. IT and OT environments should be separated by clear boundaries, such as firewalls and access controls, to prevent attackers from moving freely across networks. Consultants should look for evidence of such segmentation and question clients when systems appear to be on flat networks with no separation. A single compromised device on a flat network can give an adversary lateral movement across the entire environment. Similarly, role-based access controls should restrict who can administer security systems. Consultants should ask whether the same account that logs into office email can also reconfigure the CCTV server – a red flag for convergence risk.

IT and OT fundamentals provide consultants with a vocabulary and perspective. Knowing the difference between a corporate network and an industrial control system, recognising that availability may be prioritised over confidentiality in certain contexts, and understanding that modern security devices are essentially computers, allows consultants to approach assessments with confidence. They can then ensure that convergence issues are considered not as an afterthought but as an integral part of risk management.

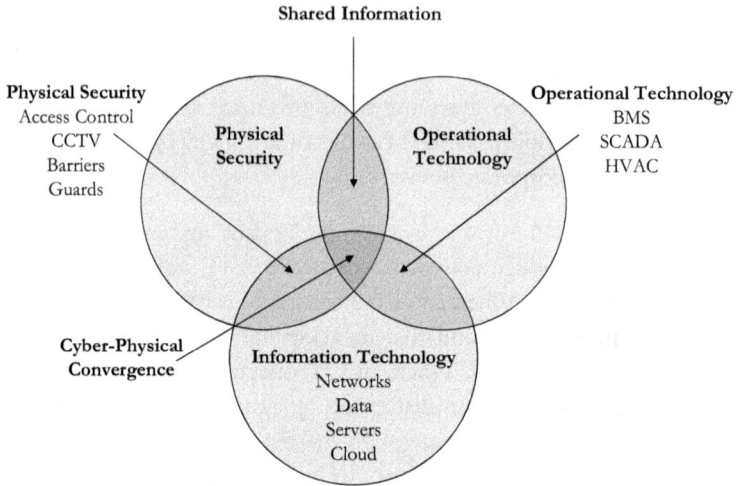

Shared Information

Physical Security
Access Control
CCTV
Barriers
Guards

Physical Security

Operational Technology

Operational Technology
BMS
SCADA
HVAC

Cyber-Physical Convergence

Information Technology
Networks
Data
Servers
Cloud

Figure 7 Where Physical Meets Digital

Secure Integration Points

In converged environments, the greatest vulnerabilities are rarely within the devices themselves but at the points where systems connect. These integration points are where data, control signals, and user access flow between domains. They are also the places most often neglected, with IT assuming integrators will secure devices, integrators assuming IT will enforce controls, and operators assuming defaults are safe. For consultants, examining these junctions is one of the most valuable contributions that they can make.

CCTV is a clear example. Cameras connected via IP transmit footage to central servers, and if connections are insecure, attackers can intercept or manipulate video. Many breaches have stemmed from cameras being left on factory default credentials or that they are made accessible directly from the internet. Consultants should confirm that authentication and encryption are enabled, that access is restricted, and that the consequences of server compromise have been considered. The risk is not only lost images but loss of trust in the system itself.

Access control creates similar exposure. These systems are often linked to HR or time-and-attendance databases, creating opportunities for fraud if integration is insecure. Common failures include shared administrative accounts and controllers placed on flat networks. Consultants should recommend segmentation, role-based access, and regular privilege reviews.

Intrusion detection and alarm systems also cross into IT networks, often through cloud dashboards or IP-based monitoring. Poorly configured, these can expose sensitive alarm data or allow suppression of signals. Consultants should establish how messages are transmitted, whether encryption and redundancy are applied, and whether portals use strong authentication.

Building management and industrial control systems raise further concerns. Heating, Ventilation, and Air Conditioning (HVAC), power, and life-safety functions are increasingly connected for efficiency and remote support. Without secure gateways and structured patching, they provide adversaries with routes into core functions. Consultants should always confirm that corporate IT and OT environments are segmented and that updates are managed without leaving systems indefinitely exposed.

Certain misconfigurations appear again and again. Default settings left unchanged, open network ports, unnecessary services, and weak encryption are all common. Asking basic questions – who has administrator rights, are default accounts still active, how is traffic segmented – often reveals overlooked weaknesses.

The principle remains consistent: networks should be divided so compromise in one system does not spread across others, and privileges should be limited to those who need them. Consultants add value by identifying where these principles have not been applied and by translating the implications into business terms. Saying "the access control server is on the same network as finance" is clearer when reframed as "an attacker could both unlock doors and alter payroll in one move."

Integration points are where weaknesses can undermine entire programmes, yet most vulnerabilities found there arise from routine oversights rather than advanced attacks. Default accounts, weak passwords, and flat networks are hygiene failures, not technical mysteries.

The corrective measures – password control, segmentation, authentication, least privilege, patching, monitoring, and staff awareness – are simple in concept but decisive in effect. When explained in proportionate business language, these practices give executives the clarity and confidence to act on convergence risks, while providing the foundation on which more sophisticated measures can be built.

Converged environments require consultants to evaluate not just devices but relationships – between IT, OT, and physical systems – where vulnerabilities and responsibilities intersect.

Minimum Cyber Hygiene for Physical Projects

When physical systems converge with IT and OT environments, resilience often depends less on advanced tools than on simple, routine discipline. Basic practices form the first line of defence. Their absence is one of the most common findings during assessments, yet clients often assume vendors or integrators will have taken care of them.

Password management is the most obvious example. Many devices are still deployed with factory defaults that are widely known and searchable online. Consultants should confirm that these have been changed, that policies enforce complexity and renewal, and that administrators use individual accounts rather than shared logins. Weak credentials in a single CCTV camera or controller can open a pathway into the wider network.

Equally important is patching. Cameras, controllers, and servers all run on software that requires updates, but these devices are often excluded from IT patch cycles for fear of downtime. This leaves them exposed long after vulnerabilities are published. Consultants should ask how updates are tested, how downtime is managed, and whether there is a documented process. The risks of exploitation and disruption usually outweigh the inconvenience of controlled outages.

Remote access presents another frequent weakness. Integrators or vendors may connect via insecure channels such as open Virtual Privat Networks (VPNs), remote desktop tools, or cloud portals with weak credentials. Consultants should check who has access, how it is controlled, and what logs are kept. Multi-factor authentication, time-limited credentials, and clear contractual responsibilities are proportionate safeguards.

Logging and monitoring are often overlooked, even though they provide one of the most valuable sources of security intelligence. Access control systems, CCTV servers, and alarm panels all produce event records such as door openings, alarm activations, and administrator logins. Too often, these logs are retained only for compliance purposes, stored without review, or automatically overwritten after a short period. Without structured analysis, this information becomes wasted data that fails to detect patterns of misuse or attempted compromise. Consultants should determine whether logging is enabled by default, how long data is retained, and whether alerts are generated for unusual activity such as repeated failed logins, out-of-hours access, or attempts to disable cameras. They should also ask who is responsible for reviewing these logs, how often reviews take place, and whether findings are acted upon. Logging is not only about forensics after an incident; when used proactively, it provides early warning of attacks before they escalate.

Network hygiene also matters. Flat networks, where every workstation can see security devices, create opportunities for lateral movement. Segmentation, firewalls, and least privilege should be expected. Consultants should always ask whether CCTV servers or access control controllers sit on isolated networks and whether only authorised administrators can reach them.

Hygiene extends to people. Guards, operators, and facilities staff often manage day-to-day systems and should be included in awareness programmes. Understanding password policies, patching needs, and monitoring responsibilities helps prevent escalation from simple mistakes.

These practices are neither costly nor technically complex. Simple steps such as changing passwords, keeping systems updated, separating networks, and checking logs cost little but make a major difference to resilience. When explained in business terms – such as avoiding downtime, protecting reputation, and staying compliant – they provide clients with a straightforward justification for taking action.

Common Failures and Lessons Learned

Despite the increasing awareness of cyber-physical convergence, many organisations continue to repeat the same mistakes when deploying or maintaining electronic security systems. These failures are rarely caused by sophisticated adversaries exploiting unknown vulnerabilities. More often, they result from oversights, complacency, or a lack of coordination between the teams responsible for physical security, IT, and OT. By recognising these recurring problems, consultants can highlight them early, explain their consequences, and prevent clients from repeating costly errors.

One of the most widespread failures is reliance on "security by obscurity". Many organisations assume that because a system uses proprietary protocols or specialised equipment, it is unlikely to be attacked. This assumption has been disproven time and again. Attackers routinely research and exploit niche systems, particularly when they are exposed to the internet. Physical security devices such as cameras and access controllers are often overlooked by IT teams precisely because they are seen as obscure. Consultants must challenge this assumption directly, reminding clients that obscurity is not security and that adversaries are often highly motivated to study specialised systems.

Vendor lock-in represents another recurring weakness. Organisations frequently rely on proprietary systems that cannot be updated, patched, or integrated without returning to the original vendor. This dependency creates long-term vulnerabilities, as outdated software remains in place long after it is known to be insecure. Consultants should encourage clients to demand open standards, contractual commitments to provide updates, and exit strategies in case vendors fail to deliver. By doing so, they prevent systems from becoming unmaintained liabilities.

Poor integration practices are also a major source of vulnerability. Integrators may connect physical systems to corporate IT networks without applying basic security measures such as segmentation or access control. In many cases, devices are connected directly to the internet for convenience, bypassing firewalls altogether. Consultants must be alert to these shortcuts and stress the importance of secure integration points, as discussed earlier. A device connected for remote monitoring without proper controls can quickly become the weakest link in an otherwise strong security system.

Another recurring failure is cultural misalignment between teams. IT, OT, and physical security professionals often operate in silos, each with different priorities and assumptions. IT staff may be focused on protecting data, OT staff on ensuring operational uptime, and physical security staff on preventing intrusions. When these priorities clash, vulnerabilities are created. For example, IT may insist on regular patching, while OT resists downtime for fear of disrupting processes. Physical security may install devices without consulting IT, leading to conflicts over network use. Consultants must act as translators between these groups, highlighting the need for cooperation and explaining that convergence risks cannot be managed in isolation.

Maintenance failures are another consistent theme. Devices that were secure at the time of installation become vulnerable as software ages, credentials are forgotten, and logs are ignored. In some cases, security measures actively degrade over time: cameras with dirty lenses, sensors that generate false alarms, or servers that run out of storage capacity. The absence of a structured maintenance plan means that vulnerabilities accumulate until they are exploited. Consultants should stress that cyber-physical systems are not "fit and forget" assets but require continuous upkeep to remain effective.

A lack of incident reporting and learning also contributes to repeated failures. When systems are compromised, many organisations treat the event as isolated rather than systemic. They may replace a breached device but fail to review whether similar vulnerabilities exist elsewhere. Lessons are not captured, and the same mistakes recur. Consultants should encourage post-incident reviews and the creation of feedback loops. Each incident should be used as an opportunity to improve processes across the organisation, not just at the point of failure.

Examples from past incidents reinforce these lessons. Breaches of CCTV systems due to unchanged default passwords have occurred across multiple sectors, from retail to critical infrastructure. Access control servers have been compromised because administrators reused credentials across networks. Building management systems have been exploited because they were connected directly to the internet for remote access. Each of these failures was avoidable with basic hygiene, better integration, and improved collaboration between teams.

For consultants, the key lesson is that most convergence failures are not technical mysteries but predictable consequences of poor practice. By focusing attention on the recurring issues – obscurity, vendor dependency, poor integration, siloed cultures, weak maintenance, and absent learning – consultants can add significant value. They prevent clients from repeating mistakes that others have already paid for and help embed a culture of continual improvement.

Common failures in cyber-physical convergence are avoidable. They result less from the ingenuity of adversaries and more from the failure of organisations to apply consistent discipline. Consultants must draw on these lessons, not only to critique but also to guide. By anticipating where systems will fail, they help clients design, maintain, and operate integrated security environments that are resilient, sustainable, and resistant to exploitation.

Explaining Convergence to Clients

The most challenging aspect of cyber-physical convergence is often not technical but communicative. Consultants may understand the risks of insecure integration, weak cyber hygiene, or poorly configured systems, but unless these issues are explained in terms that clients can grasp and act upon, the assessment will fail to achieve its purpose. Boards and executives rarely want to hear about encryption protocols, port numbers, or network segmentation. What they need is a clear explanation of how vulnerabilities in converged systems translate into business risks and which proportionate measures can reduce them.

The first step is to frame convergence in plain English. Instead of describing a vulnerability as "an open port on a network device", the consultant might explain that "the CCTV system can be reached from outside the building without permission". Rather than discussing patching cycles in abstract terms, it is better to say that "if this server is not updated, an intruder could shut down alarms or unlock doors remotely". The focus should always be on consequences – downtime, financial loss, reputational harm, or regulatory penalties – because these are the terms in which business leaders make decisions.

Clients also need to understand that convergence is not a theoretical risk but a reality. The example of a casino database compromised through a smart thermometer in a fish tank is more memorable than a technical lecture on IoT (Internet of Things) vulnerabilities. A building management system exploited to disable alarms makes the risk tangible.

These examples demonstrate that the threats are real, relevant, and increasingly exploited by adversaries. By connecting convergence risks to real incidents, consultants create urgency without resorting to fearmongering.

Another important part of explanation is proportionality. Executives may fear that convergence requires massive investment or wholesale replacement of systems. The consultant must reassure them that most improvements involve simple, balanced measures. Changing default passwords, segmenting networks, enforcing multi-factor authentication, and monitoring logs are not radical steps, but they greatly reduce risk. By emphasising practicality and proportionality, the consultant builds trust and avoids being seen as a scaremonger.

It is also vital to explain convergence as both a risk and an opportunity. On the risk side, integration increases the attack surface; on the opportunity side, it allows for greater efficiency, better monitoring, and improved resilience when done correctly. By framing convergence as something to be managed rather than feared, consultants help clients see investment as an enabler of confidence rather than as a burden. For example, integrating access control with HR systems may create risks if done insecurely, but if secured properly it can reduce insider threats by automatically revoking access when staff leave the organisation.

Consultants should also act as translators between technical specialists. IT staff, OT operators, and physical security managers often speak different languages. When these groups meet, misunderstandings can stall progress. The consultant's role is to bridge these divides, rephrasing IT concerns about "flat networks" into physical security terms such as "all devices are connected together with no barriers, meaning that if one is compromised, all are compromised". Likewise, when OT operators worry about downtime, the consultant can reframe this as "patching needs to be managed without shutting down life-safety systems". By ensuring that each group understands the other's priorities, the consultant prevents convergence risks from being ignored due to cultural silos.

Communication must be action-oriented. It is not enough to highlight risks; the consultant must present clear, prioritised recommendations that clients can implement. This means avoiding vague statements such as "improve cyber hygiene" and instead offering practical steps such as "change all default passwords within one week" or "implement network segmentation between access control and finance servers within six months". Clear recommendations give clients a roadmap and demonstrate that convergence risks can be managed in a structured way.

Explaining convergence to clients is about translation, proportionality, and action. Consultants must turn technical vulnerabilities into business-relevant consequences, use real examples to create urgency, and propose practical steps that can be implemented without overwhelming operations. By doing so, they ensure that clients not only understand the risks but are motivated and empowered to address them. Convergence is a reality of modern security – and with the right explanation, it becomes an opportunity to build systems that are both resilient and trusted.

Global Perspectives and Regulatory Foundations

Convergence is not only a technical issue but also a regulatory one. Different regions frame the integration of IT, OT, and physical security through distinct standards and obligations. In Europe, the EU NIS2[6] Directive requires operators of essential services to secure both physical and digital systems, with convergence risks explicitly included in resilience planning. The ISO/IEC 27001:2022[15] family of standards provides a global baseline for information security, while ISO 22301:2019[12] links these requirements to continuity of operations. In the United States, the NIST[19] Cybersecurity Framework and Special Publication 800-82 (for Industrial Control Systems) set expectations for how IT and OT should be protected, often mandating structured approaches to segmentation and patching.

In the Middle East, regulators such as NCEMA[18] in the UAE combine international standards with national resilience priorities, with requirements for integrated physical and cyber measures often forming part of the expectations for critical sites. Compliance with standards such as NCEMA 7000[18] and the UAE's Information Assurance Regulation is typically tied to licensing or approval processes for critical entities, reinforcing that convergence controls are not optional but a condition of operation. Elsewhere in Asia, Singapore's Cybersecurity Code of Practice for Critical Information Infrastructure integrates physical and cyber requirements, while Japan's guidance on smart infrastructure stresses resilience against both natural hazards and cyber-physical attack.

For consultants, the task is not to memorise every regulation but to show that their advice aligns with whichever framework governs the client's environment. By referencing recognised standards, they reassure boards and regulators that convergence has been addressed systematically, while ensuring that recommendations remain practical and proportionate.

Practice Guide

Convergence has redefined the security landscape, making the separation between physical and digital protections increasingly hard to justify. This chapter has addressed each of the learning objectives: IT and OT fundamentals have been explained in clear terms; the vulnerabilities that arise at integration points have been highlighted; minimum cyber hygiene practices have been established as non-negotiable; recurring failures such as reliance on obscurity, vendor lock-in, and siloed working have been exposed; and methods for explaining convergence to clients in business-relevant language have been illustrated.

The pitfalls to avoid are consistent and predictable. Default passwords, unpatched devices, insecure remote access, and poorly segmented networks leave systems open to compromise. Equally damaging are cultural divides where IT, OT, and physical security teams work in isolation, each assuming the other will address vulnerabilities. These failures show that convergence risks often stem less from technical sophistication and more from complacency and poor communication. Consultants must be wary of treating integration as purely a technical task or of assuming that vendor solutions remove the need for oversight.

Best practice lies in applying simple, proportionate measures before considering more advanced solutions. Enforcing password discipline, patch management, segmentation, and log monitoring provides a strong baseline at little cost. Consultants should ensure that integration points – such as CCTV servers linked to IT networks or access control tied to HR systems – are reviewed not only for functionality but for security implications. Each recommendation must remain proportionate to context, ensuring that convergence controls strengthen resilience without imposing unnecessary complexity. The ability to translate technical issues into business consequences, such as reputational harm or operational downtime, ensures that executives engage with and act on convergence risks.

For consultants, the opportunity is to act as interpreters and integrators, bridging silos and reframing convergence from a source of anxiety into an enabler of resilience. By combining technical awareness with plain-English communication, they can help clients adopt measures that are both effective and sustainable. Convergence will only deepen as systems become more interconnected; consultants who can keep recommendations practical, proportionate, and clearly linked to business outcomes will ensure that their clients remain resilient in this evolving environment. The next chapter turns from systems to people, exploring how culture and behaviour shape security outcomes and how consultants can embed resilience through the human dimension.

Chapter 9 – People, Procedures, and Culture

Security measures succeed or fail largely because of people. Technology and procedures provide the framework, but it is human behaviour and organisational culture that determine whether those measures work in practice. Consultants must therefore be able to evaluate not only technical designs but also the procedures and cultural attitudes that shape daily security performance. This chapter provides the foundation for recognising how people, processes, and culture interact, and how consultants can guide clients towards proportionate and sustainable improvements.

By the end of this chapter, you will be able to:

- Recognise how people and organisational culture influence security outcomes in both positive and negative ways.
- Assess security procedures for clarity, relevance, and enforceability, identifying where they enable consistent behaviour and where they fail.
- Identify cultural behaviours that undermine security, such as propping open doors, ignoring alarms, or tailgating.
- Apply lessons from the Illustrative Example to understand the real-world consequences of cultural weaknesses in security.
- Advise on building and sustaining a positive security culture that aligns with business objectives and daily operations.
- Integrate human factors into technical designs so that systems are usable, credible, and effective over time.
- Recommend proportionate, practical measures that embed secure behaviours without overburdening staff or creating resistance.

Introduction

Security is often thought of in terms of barriers, technology, and regulations, but the decisive factor is almost always people. A facility may invest in state-of-the-art cameras, biometric readers, or reinforced barriers, yet the effectiveness of these measures is determined by how people use them. A guard who ignores an alarm, an employee who props open a door, or a manager who treats security as an afterthought can render the entire system ineffective. For consultants, recognising this truth is fundamental. Security measures are only as strong as the people and culture that surround them.

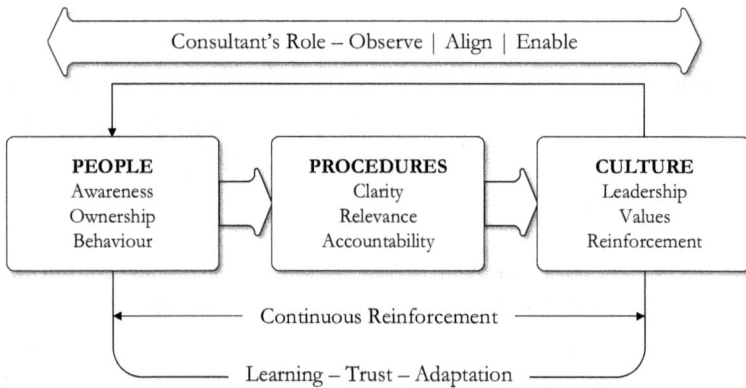

Figure 8 The Human Core of Security

Procedures provide the first link between technology and people. They translate technical capability into expected behaviour – who checks visitor credentials, how alarms are escalated, or when doors must be locked. Yet procedures are often written in ways that are too complex, impractical, or disconnected from reality. Staff quickly learn to ignore rules that obstruct their work, creating gaps between the documented system and actual practice. Consultants must therefore evaluate not just whether procedures exist, but whether they are understood, realistic, and followed.

Culture magnifies this effect. A strong security culture means that staff take ownership of resilience, noticing when something is wrong and acting to correct it. In organisations with weak culture, security is seen as someone else's responsibility – often the security department or contractors – and lapses go unchallenged. The same technology can perform very differently in two organisations simply because of cultural attitudes. Consultants must therefore pay close attention to culture, even if it is less tangible than physical or electronic measures.

Examples show why people matter. A global bank may have invested heavily in access control and surveillance, yet if its staff routinely hold open secure doors for convenience, adversaries can walk straight in. A hospital may have robust procedures for protecting medical records, but if staff share login credentials to save time, those protections are meaningless. These scenarios illustrate that human behaviour is not a side issue but the critical determinant of whether security succeeds or fails.

The focus on people, procedures, and culture shows that assessments must extend beyond technical design to include human factors. It defines the consultant's role as both analyst and interpreter – as someone who can identify weaknesses in procedure and culture, explain their significance in business terms, and recommend improvements that are proportionate and sustainable.

In modern practice, this perspective is more important than ever. As systems become more complex and interconnected, the points of failure increasingly lie in how people interact with technology. Security culture, once seen as a soft issue, is now recognised as a strategic enabler of resilience. Consultants who can assess and improve this dimension add real value to clients, bridging the gap between technical potential and operational reality.

Security Procedures

Procedures are the bridge between design and behaviour. They take the intent of security systems and translate it into instructions for people – when to lock doors, how to handle visitors, who responds to alarms, and what steps to take during an emergency. In principle, they provide consistency and predictability, ensuring that staff act in line with established standards rather than improvising in the moment. In practice, however, procedures are often where the gap between policy and reality emerges, and this gap is where consultants must focus their attention.

When well designed, security procedures provide several strengths. They create clarity by setting out expectations in writing, leaving little room for misunderstanding. They provide accountability, making it clear who is responsible for particular actions. They also act as training tools, allowing new staff to learn consistent practices. In regulated environments, procedures provide evidence of compliance, demonstrating to auditors and regulators that controls are not only installed but formally managed.

Consultants reviewing procedures should acknowledge these strengths, because they explain why written policies remain an important part of security management.

Different regions embed this expectation in distinct ways. In Europe, regular drills and training are part of business continuity compliance. In the United States, there are controls for awareness and accountability, requiring evidence that staff understand and follow documented procedures. In the UAE, rehearsal of roles and clarity of responsibilities are often a condition for licensing critical entities. Consultants should be alert to these frameworks, because they shape how procedures are designed, tested, and enforced.

Yet weaknesses are just as common, and in some organisations they dominate. One of the most frequent problems is excessive complexity. Procedures that run to dozens of pages, filled with technical jargon and unrealistic instructions, are rarely read or followed. Staff under time pressure find shortcuts, either ignoring steps or creating informal workarounds. For example, a visitor sign-in process that requires multiple forms may look thorough on paper but will collapse under the weight of daily traffic. Consultants must look not only at what the document says but also at how staff actually behave.

Another weakness lies in procedures that are disconnected from operational reality. A fire evacuation plan may assume that staff will use designated escape routes, but in practice those routes may be difficult to access or overlooked during an emergency. An alarm escalation procedure may assume that security staff are always available, even at peak demand. These disconnects create false confidence. Consultants should compare documented procedures with site walk-throughs and interviews, highlighting where the written system diverges from what actually happens on the ground.

Enforcement is another challenge. Even well-written procedures can fail if there is no accountability for following them. Staff may prop open doors in violation of policy because no one enforces the rule, or guards may skip bag checks because supervisors do not monitor compliance. A consultant should always ask how adherence is measured, whether audits are conducted, and whether non-compliance carries consequences. In many cases, a lack of enforcement reflects cultural attitudes – a sign that security is not prioritised by leadership.

A further weakness comes from rigidity. Procedures that are too prescriptive may fail in dynamic situations. If staff are required to follow exact scripts, they may be unable to adapt to circumstances not covered in the document. For example, a procedure that dictates exact steps for responding to one type of alarm may leave staff paralysed when confronted with a different scenario. Effective procedures strike a balance – detailed enough to provide guidance, but flexible enough to allow professional judgement. Consultants must assess whether procedures encourage compliance without stifling adaptability.

Training and communication also determine the effectiveness of procedures. Policies that exist only in binders or on intranets are of little value if staff are unaware of them. Regular drills, refresher training, and visible reinforcement are needed to embed procedures into daily practice. Consultants should look for evidence of this: do staff know where to find instructions, have they been trained, and do they demonstrate knowledge in practice? If procedures are unknown or ignored, they are functionally absent.

The consultant's role in assessing procedures is therefore both analytical and observational. Reviewing documents is important, but it must be complemented by interviews, site tours, and scenario testing. Asking staff simple questions such as "what do you do if this alarm sounds?" often reveals whether procedures exist only on paper or are genuinely embedded. Consultants should be alert for signs of workarounds, such as taped-over door locks, informal visitor badges, or staff who describe "how things are really done" as distinct from written instructions. These are indicators of procedural weakness that must be addressed.

In highlighting weaknesses, consultants must also frame their recommendations constructively. Simply criticising procedures as inadequate may alienate staff and managers. Instead, the consultant should explain how weaknesses create risk and offer proportionate improvements. For example, suggesting that a complex sign-in process be streamlined to reduce delays while still capturing essential data shows respect for operational realities. Linking recommendations to business benefits, such as smoother operations or reduced liability, helps gain acceptance.

Procedures are both a strength and a vulnerability. They provide the structure that connects people with systems, but when poorly designed, unrealistic, or unenforced, they become points of failure. Consultants must therefore evaluate not only the existence of procedures but their clarity, relevance, and application. In doing so, they help clients bridge the gap between intent and reality, ensuring that security measures are supported by behaviours that are practical, consistent, and resilient.

Security Culture

Security culture is the invisible element that determines whether people follow procedures and use systems as intended. It is the set of shared values, attitudes, and behaviours that shape how individuals approach security in their daily work. Unlike physical barriers or written policies, culture cannot be bought, installed, or mandated overnight. Yet it is one of the most powerful forces in determining security outcomes. Where culture is strong and positive, it acts as a force multiplier, amplifying the effectiveness of technology and procedures. Where culture is weak or negative, it undermines even the most sophisticated systems and leaves organisations vulnerable.

Positive security culture is characterised by ownership, vigilance, and pride. Staff see security as part of their role rather than a burden imposed on them. They understand not just the rules but the reasons behind them, and they act accordingly. Examples include employees challenging unrecognised or unauthorised people, promptly reporting suspicious incidents, and showing respect for procedures such as logging visitors or securing documents. In organisations with positive culture, compliance becomes the norm not because people are forced, but because they believe it protects their colleagues, their workplace, and their mission.

Negative security culture, by contrast, is marked by indifference, avoidance, and cynicism. Some staff go through daily routines without ever thinking about security, acting with an unconscious or deliberate *"it won't happen to me"* attitude. This mindset reflects a deeper disengagement – whether through complacency, distraction, or a belief that risk is somebody else's problem. In such environments, security is often seen as the sole responsibility of guards, facilities teams, or management. Common signs include ignoring alarms, routinely propping open secure doors, or treating training as a box-ticking exercise. Workarounds become normal practice, such as sharing access cards or disabling "annoying" alarms. In extreme cases, negative culture results in open defiance of rules, often tolerated by supervisors who regard enforcement as disruptive or unpopular.

Leadership has a decisive influence on which culture prevails. Positive culture is cultivated when leaders model secure behaviours themselves – wearing badges, complying with checks, taking part in drills, and speaking openly about the value of vigilance. Conversely, leaders who disregard procedures or mock security requirements signal to staff that compliance is optional. Consultants should therefore evaluate leadership attitudes carefully, because the tone from the top often shapes the day-to-day culture more than any written policy.

Training and awareness are also central. Positive culture thrives when training is not only instructional but engaging, explaining the "why" as well as the "what". Campaigns that use real examples, storytelling, and reinforcement create an emotional connection that drives behaviour. Negative culture often emerges where training is perfunctory, poorly communicated, or disconnected from the realities of staff roles. In such cases, people disengage and see rules as irrelevant bureaucracy.

The presence or absence of fear also distinguishes cultures. Negative cultures sometimes rely on punishment to enforce compliance, which may achieve short-term results but fosters resentment and avoidance. Staff comply when watched but cut corners when unobserved. Positive culture, in contrast, is built on ownership, pride, and accountability. Staff feel trusted and valued, and lapses are treated as opportunities for improvement rather than only grounds for punishment. Consultants should encourage organisations to reward positive behaviours and avoid over-reliance on deterrence.

Technology interacts closely with culture. Positive culture emerges when systems are user-friendly and support staff in doing their jobs. A fast, reliable access control system reinforces good habits, while an obstructive or error-prone system drives workarounds. In a negative culture, frustration with technology quickly translates into shortcuts and indifference. Consultants must therefore consider how staff perceive systems as much as how they perform technically.

It is important to note that culture varies across regions and industries. In some settings, visible security presence is seen as reassuring; in others, it may be perceived as intrusive or a sign of mistrust. National culture influences attitudes towards authority, rules, and privacy. Consultants working internationally must recognise these differences and adapt their recommendations to fit the local context while still achieving resilience.

Regulatory environments reinforce these cultural dimensions. In the UAE, NCEMA[18] highlights the role of leadership in sustaining resilience and promotes continuity responsibilities that extend beyond senior management. While the standard does not explicitly mandate staff involvement at every level, its guidance and associated training encourage organisations to embed resilience across the workforce rather than confining it to a single department. European regulators often treat culture as part of occupational safety, aligning with ISO 45001:2018, which stresses leadership engagement and worker participation. Singapore's Cybersecurity Code of Practice requires operators of essential services to run awareness programmes and sustain vigilance, recognising that culture is central to resilience. Consultants should therefore adapt cultural advice not only to national attitudes but also to the regulatory expectations that formalise them.

Assessing culture requires careful observation and sensitivity. It is not enough to read policy documents or attend formal briefings. Culture is revealed in how people talk about security, whether supervisors reinforce rules, and how staff behave in practice. A consultant who notices staff joking dismissively about training, ignoring alarms, or inventing shortcuts has uncovered signals of negative culture. Conversely, staff who correct one another constructively, take drills seriously, and ask thoughtful questions about procedures demonstrate a positive culture at work.

Security culture can be a decisive advantage or a crippling weakness. Positive culture magnifies the impact of systems and procedures, embedding resilience into daily operations. Negative culture undermines investment, creating vulnerabilities that no amount of technology can fully mitigate. Consultants must be able to distinguish between the two, explain their implications to clients, and recommend measures that shift culture in the right direction. By doing so, they provide insights that go beyond technical fixes, helping organisations build security that is credible, sustainable, and lived in practice.

Procedure / Policy Intent	Critical Frontline Behaviour Required	Typical Failure Mode	Underlying Cause	Corrective Measure / Reinforcement
Access control and visitor management	Challenge unknown persons; ensure passes are displayed and logged.	Tailgating; unchallenged visitors.	Social discomfort; poor role modelling.	Empower staff to question politely; reinforce in training and briefings.
Key and asset control	Secure issue, return, and record of keys and portable assets.	Shared or unrecorded use.	Time pressure; weak supervision.	Automate logging; designate key custodian; audit randomly.
Alarm acknowledgement and escalation	Act promptly and according to SOP hierarchy.	Alarm fatigue; assumption others are responding.	Overload; unclear roles.	Rotate duties; simplify screens; clear escalation chart.
Incident reporting	Record all security events, not only major ones.	Informal resolution; under-reporting.	"Nothing happened" culture; fear of blame.	Simplify report form; emphasise learning not blame.
Access to restricted zones	Comply with zoning, even for short tasks.	"Quick access" shortcuts.	Production pressure; unclear boundaries.	Visual zoning cues; supervisor enforcement.
Maintenance and housekeeping	Keep doors, exits, and detection equipment unobstructed.	Equipment blocked; sensors taped over.	Competing operational priorities.	Joint inspection with FM; positive reinforcement for compliance.

Table 5 From Procedure to Frontline Behaviour

Illustrative Example: The Propped-Open Door

Few examples illustrate the impact of culture on security as clearly as the case of the propped-open door. It is a scenario that consultants encounter repeatedly across sectors, from offices and hospitals to industrial plants and data centres. The door itself may be protected by an expensive electronic access control system, reinforced locks, and integrated alarms. Yet despite these investments, staff habitually wedge it open for convenience, defeating the entire system. This Illustrative Example shows how cultural behaviours can undermine technology, how the consequences can escalate, and what lessons consultants must draw.

The background is straightforward. A medium-sized corporate facility had invested heavily in security upgrades, including a modern access control system with proximity cards and electronic logging of every entry. The main entrances were well designed, but a side door near the staff car park became the weak point. Staff frequently propped it open to avoid the inconvenience of badging in and out, particularly when carrying equipment or returning from breaks. Over time, this behaviour became normalised. Even though signage prohibited it and alarms sometimes sounded, the practice continued.

The consequences were significant. First, the access control system's audit function was compromised. Because people bypassed the system, management could no longer rely on logs to determine who was inside the building at a given time. This had safety as well as security implications, particularly during evacuations. Second, the open door provided opportunities for unauthorised access. Cleaners, contractors, and eventually unknown individuals were observed entering without checks. On one occasion, a theft occurred, with equipment taken from an office close to the side door.

The incident revealed deeper cultural issues. Interviews with staff showed that many did not view security as their responsibility. They saw the access control system as an obstacle rather than a safeguard. Supervisors were aware of the practice but tolerated it, believing that convenience and productivity outweighed the risks. The security team logged repeated alarms from the door but treated them as nuisances rather than warnings. The system had become background noise, with cultural apathy undermining its purpose.

From a consultant's perspective, the case highlights several lessons. First, security technology must be matched with behaviour. A system that creates frustration will inevitably be bypassed. In this case, the door was located in a high-traffic area where people naturally sought shortcuts. No amount of signage or alarms could counteract the daily incentive to prop it open. Consultants should always consider whether design encourages or discourages compliance, and whether procedures align with the way people actually use a facility.

Second, culture requires leadership reinforcement. The acceptance of propped-open doors reflected a lack of priority from managers. Had supervisors consistently reinforced the rule and explained its importance, behaviour might have changed. Instead, their tolerance signalled to staff that security was optional. Consultants must stress that leadership attitudes are decisive – staff follow the behaviours they see modelled.

Third, small lapses can create large vulnerabilities. What seemed to staff like a harmless convenience created opportunities for intrusion and theft, undermining the credibility of the entire security programme. The lesson for consultants is to highlight how minor cultural behaviours can cascade into serious risks, making the invisible visible for clients.

Solutions must be proportionate and practical. In this case, the consultant recommended a combination of physical and cultural measures. On the physical side, adding self-closing mechanisms, and adjusting alarm escalation reduced opportunities for misuse. On the cultural side, staff were briefed on why the door mattered, and supervisors were tasked with reinforcing compliance. By combining these approaches, the client was able to change behaviour without alienating staff.

The case of the propped-open door demonstrates how culture can defeat technology, how leadership attitudes shape behaviour, and how consultants can intervene with practical solutions. It reinforces the broader message of this chapter: that security is not just about systems and procedures but about the daily choices people make. By recognising and addressing these cultural vulnerabilities, consultants help clients turn investments into resilience rather than wasted effort.

Building and Sustaining a Security Culture

Improving security culture is not achieved by installing new barriers or drafting new procedures alone. Culture is built gradually through leadership, reinforcement, and shared responsibility. It is sustained when staff understand why security matters, see their leaders model the right behaviours, and feel that vigilance is both valued and expected. Advising on culture requires not only technical knowledge but also insight into human behaviour and organisational dynamics.

The starting point is leadership commitment. A culture of security cannot thrive if leaders treat it as secondary to productivity or convenience. Executives, managers, and supervisors must demonstrate that security is non-negotiable and integral to business resilience. This is less about issuing memos and more about visible behaviour. When leaders consistently comply with badge checks, participate in evacuation drills, and challenge lapses respectfully, they set a standard that filters throughout the organisation. Consultants must assess whether leadership commitment is genuine and recommend ways to strengthen it if absent.

Training and awareness programmes are the next building block. Staff need to know not just what to do but why it matters. Explaining the rationale behind security measures turns them from arbitrary rules into shared responsibilities. For example, teaching staff that failing to log out of a workstation could lead to data theft makes the rule relevant to their daily roles. Campaigns that use storytelling, case studies, or incident examples are more effective than dry presentations. Consultants should recommend training that is engaging, context-specific, and refreshed regularly so that awareness does not fade.

Reinforcement through incentives and accountability is also critical. Positive reinforcement – recognising staff who demonstrate good security behaviours – helps normalise vigilance. Equally, there must be accountability for repeated non-compliance. A culture in which staff believe there are no consequences for ignoring security rules will inevitably slide into apathy. Consultants can advise on systems of recognition and accountability that balance encouragement with firmness, ensuring that compliance becomes part of professional identity.

Communication is another essential element. Security culture is undermined when messages are inconsistent, contradictory, or drowned out by operational demands. Clear, consistent communication from leadership about expectations and priorities reinforces the message that security matters. This communication should extend to feedback loops: staff should be encouraged to report problems and suggestions without fear of reprisal. A culture of openness allows vulnerabilities to be identified early and demonstrates that security is a collective effort rather than a top-down imposition.

Integration with daily operations sustains culture over time. Security measures must be embedded in routine workflows so that compliance becomes second nature. For instance, visitor management should be designed to align with reception practices, not as an extra burden. Access control should be integrated with HR processes so that staff changes are reflected automatically. When measures fit smoothly into work, staff are more likely to accept them. Consultants must examine how security procedures intersect with daily operations and recommend adjustments that reduce friction.

Leadership modelling, training, reinforcement, communication, and integration together create the conditions for positive culture to flourish. Yet sustaining culture requires continual effort. Over time, staff turnover, organisational change, and evolving threats can erode vigilance. Consultants should therefore encourage clients to adopt cycles of assessment and improvement. Culture should be reviewed periodically through staff surveys, interviews, and audits, with adjustments made as necessary. A culture that is not actively maintained will gradually weaken.

It is also important to frame culture as an enabler, not a burden. When staff see security as protecting their safety, reputation, and livelihoods, they are more likely to embrace it. When they see it as bureaucracy imposed from above, they will resist. Consultants can help reframe culture by linking it to values staff care about, whether that is protecting patient safety in a hospital, safeguarding intellectual property in a research facility, or ensuring customer trust in a retail environment.

Building and sustaining a positive security culture requires commitment at every level of the organisation. Consultants must guide clients in creating conditions where leadership models good behaviour, staff understand why security matters, procedures are integrated with daily operations, and reinforcement ensures accountability. By embedding culture in this way, organisations move beyond compliance and towards resilience. Security becomes not something imposed but something lived – a force that strengthens every system, every procedure, and every person.

Culture translates policy into practice. Without behavioural alignment, even the most advanced systems degrade into procedure without performance.

Integrating Human Factors into Security Design

Security designs that fail to consider human factors almost always fail in practice. A system that looks flawless on paper may collapse when people interact with it under the pressures of daily work. Consultants must therefore ensure that human behaviour, usability, psychology, and organisational dynamics are integrated into every design and assessment.

This does not mean diluting resilience but aligning protective measures with the way people actually operate.

People bring unique insight to security that technology alone cannot provide. Artificial Intelligence (AI), including large language models and generative AI, can analyse data at scale and predict events with impressive speed, but human intuition is different. A guard may get a gut feeling that something is wrong – perhaps from a tone of voice, a glance, or behaviour that does not quite fit the data. That feeling may occasionally be wrong, but at other times it sees beyond what electronic analysis alone reveals. Consultants must stress to clients that resilience comes from combining both capabilities: predictive technology for scale and speed, and human intuition for context and nuance.

A major focus for consultants is the social-technical interface – the point where people and systems meet. These interfaces must be designed to work with, rather than against, the operator. Several considerations are critical here.

Ease of use and intuitive navigation are paramount. Operators should not waste valuable seconds searching for functions, especially under stress. A control room display that requires multiple clicks to access a camera feed may look efficient to a designer but will fail an operator responding to a fast-moving incident. Interfaces should be designed so that the correct action is the natural, almost automatic, choice.

Ergonomics also play a vital role. Poorly designed desks, screens, or control panels can create fatigue, discomfort, and errors. Operators required to twist awkwardly to monitor displays or respond to alarms are more likely to miss critical details. A socio-technical interface must be physically comfortable and arranged in a way that supports attention and sustained vigilance. Consultants observing control rooms should look for signs of poor ergonomics and highlight how these increase the likelihood of mistakes.

Standards increasingly reflect these human dimensions. ISO/IEC 27001:2022[15] requires information security controls to be maintained and continually improved so that they remain effective and sustainable. ISO 45001:2018 addresses inclusivity, worker participation, and ergonomics as part of occupational safety. FEMA guidance on emergency operations centres in the United States emphasises ergonomic layouts and clear command-centre workflows. In Japan, resilience policies and human-factors research highlight the importance of human-centred approaches, though formal standards on control room design are less explicit. Such frameworks give consultants reference points to judge whether designs genuinely support operators or inadvertently obstruct them.

Clear and concise information is another essential factor for good design and for promoting a positive security culture. Systems that bombard operators with irrelevant alerts or present cluttered displays create confusion. The operator's mental workload must be carefully managed: too much information leads to overload, while too little leaves them blind to unfolding risks. Good design supports the operator's mental model of the system – their internal understanding of how the environment works, how alerts fit together, and what actions they should take. Consultants should assess whether displays and alarms are helping operators build and maintain this model or whether they are adding complexity that undermines performance.

The psychology of people plays a central role in efficiency. Operators are not passive recipients of information but active participants in interpretation and decision-making. Fatigue, stress, and workload directly affect how quickly and accurately they respond. A system that supports the operator's mental state – by reducing unnecessary workload, simplifying navigation, and providing clarity – will perform far better than one that treats the operator as an afterthought. Consultants must be alert to these psychological dimensions, recognising that the efficiency of people is inseparable from the efficiency of the system itself.

Procedures must be clear and concise. In emergencies, staff cannot be expected to read long instructions or interpret complex flowcharts. They need short, direct guidance that they can remember and act upon quickly. For example, fire evacuation procedures should be stated in plain language and reinforced with drills so that people know instinctively what to do. Consultants should evaluate whether procedures support staff in moments of pressure or whether they add confusion when clarity is most needed.

Physical elements of a security scheme should assist people rather than hinder them. Design flaws that obstruct staff responses can turn protective measures into liabilities. Barriers that block lines of sight, for instance, may slow down security officers trying to assess a situation. Bollards or gates that create bottlenecks may impede evacuation as much as they prevent intrusion. Consultants must examine whether physical features are enhancing or obstructing human response and recommend redesigns where necessary. The goal is to build an environment that enables operators, guards, and responders to act swiftly and effectively.

Integration with workflows is another key consideration. Security measures should be embedded into normal routines rather than imposed as extra burdens. For example, visitor management should align with reception practices so that it becomes part of the natural flow of welcoming guests rather than a disruptive add-on. Access control should integrate with HR systems so that permissions update automatically when staff join or leave. Alarm escalation should follow the same paths as other incident management processes. When security is seamless, compliance becomes natural. When it is disjointed, staff see it as an obstacle to be bypassed.

Inclusivity is also essential. A system that works for most staff but excludes others cannot deliver consistent resilience. Access points should be designed for wheelchair users as well as able-bodied staff. Training should consider language diversity to ensure that instructions are understood by everyone. Consultants should view inclusivity not only as a moral obligation but as a security requirement: a system that excludes is a system that fails.

Observation during site visits often reveals the gaps between design and human factors. Consultants may see guards improvising alarm responses because panels are confusing, staff struggling with heavy security doors, or operators distracted by cluttered screens. These details are not trivial – they are where resilience is won or lost. Consultants should document these findings and explain to clients that addressing them will reduce errors, increase efficiency, and make security more credible in daily use.

Integrating human factors into security design means recognising that people are central to resilience. Systems must be designed for usability, clarity, ergonomics, and inclusivity. Social-technical interfaces should reduce workload and support the operator's mental model. Procedures should be concise and actionable, and physical elements should assist rather than hinder staff. Technology, including artificial intelligence, brings speed and predictive power, but human intuition adds depth and context. By balancing these strengths and aligning systems with people, consultants help clients create security environments that are not only technically robust but also operationally effective and psychologically sustainable.

Practice Guide

Security succeeds or fails through people. This chapter has demonstrated how procedures, culture, and human factors shape the effectiveness of every system, and the learning objectives have been addressed: the influence of people and culture has been explored, procedures have been assessed for clarity and enforceability, cultural behaviours such as tailgating and propped-open doors have been examined, the Illustrative Example has shown their real-world impact, strategies for building and sustaining a security culture have been provided, and the integration of human factors into technical design has been explained.

Common failures in this area follow recognisable patterns, and consultants must be able to spot them early. Procedures often collapse under the weight of complexity, leaving staff to improvise or ignore them. Culture drifts into indifference when leadership fails to model secure behaviour, when supervisors tolerate workarounds, or when training is reduced to box-ticking. In many organisations, some staff do not even think about security, moving through daily routines with an unconscious or deliberate *"it won't happen to me"* attitude. Technology is undermined when staff see it as an obstacle rather than a support. Each of these failures shows that human factors are not a soft add-on but a critical determinant of resilience.

Good practice lies in embedding ownership, clarity, and usability into every aspect of security. Procedures should be written in plain, concise language, tested against real operational conditions, and reinforced by training that explains the "why" as well as the "what." Culture must be shaped by leaders who demonstrate secure behaviour themselves and who encourage staff to take pride in vigilance rather than treating it as an imposition. Reinforcement should combine recognition of positive behaviours with accountability for repeated lapses. Systems and environments should be designed to work with people – ergonomically, intuitively, and inclusively – so that secure behaviour is the natural choice rather than the difficult one.

The consultant's task is to highlight cultural weaknesses as rigorously as technical ones, to explain how small behaviours can create large vulnerabilities, and to recommend practical measures that align people, procedures, and technology. When culture is strong, procedures credible, and human factors considered in design, security becomes a lived practice rather than a set of rules. Across all regions, regulators and standards bodies are converging on the same expectation: that security is sustained through credible procedures, positive culture, and designs shaped around people. These lessons prepare the ground for the next chapter, which turns to technology as an enabler rather than a substitute, examining how consultants can consolidate these people-centred principles into an integrated technical toolkit.

Chapter 10 – Technology as Enabler, Not Substitute

Technology plays a critical role in modern security, but it is not a substitute for people, procedures, and good culture. This chapter will explore how consultants should frame technology as an enabler that amplifies human capability rather than a solution that can stand alone.

By the end of this chapter, you will be able to:

- Understand the role of technology as one layer of defence rather than the entirety of security.
- Recognise how technology can multiply human capability by enhancing detection, monitoring, and response.
- Identify the risks of over-reliance on technology, including false confidence, system failure, and user workarounds.
- Analyse how technology must be integrated with procedures and culture to function effectively.
- Evaluate the impact of emerging technologies such as AI, robotics, and IoT while avoiding hype and overselling.
- Apply lessons from case studies to distinguish between technology that supports resilience and technology that distracts from it.
- Develop the ability to advise clients proportionately, ensuring that investments in technology are sustainable, credible, and embedded into wider security frameworks.

Introduction

Technology has long been the most visible part of security. Cameras, card readers, barriers, and alarms give organisations a tangible sense of protection, something that can be purchased, installed, and demonstrated to stakeholders. This visibility often leads clients to see technology as the solution in itself – a way to buy resilience without addressing the harder questions of behaviour, procedures, and culture. Consultants must challenge this assumption, showing that while technology is essential, it is only one element of a layered approach.

The history of security demonstrates this tendency towards technological optimism. As new systems became available – from early CCTV in the 1960s to integrated digital platforms today – each was hailed as a potential substitute for people. The promise was always that fewer guards would be needed, human error would be eliminated, and costs would be reduced. Yet incidents across industries continue to show that without effective oversight, maintenance, and cultural alignment, technology fails. Cameras may record incidents, but if no one is watching or responding, their value is retrospective. Biometric readers may offer robust access control, but if staff allow others to tailgate or prop doors open, the system is defeated.

The task is not to reject technology but to position it correctly. Technology should be framed as an enabler – a means of amplifying human capability, improving efficiency, and reducing risk – but never as a replacement for people or sound processes. When integrated thoughtfully, technology allows staff to detect incidents earlier, respond more effectively, and maintain situational awareness across complex sites. When treated as a substitute, it creates false confidence, leaving organisations exposed to both predictable failures and unpredictable events.

The role of the consultant is also to cut through the hype that surrounds emerging tools. Vendors frequently present new products as game-changers, emphasising automation, predictive capability, or artificial intelligence as substitutes for human judgement. While these developments are valuable, they come with limitations. Machine learning algorithms may identify unusual behaviour patterns, but they cannot interpret context in the way an experienced operator can. Large language models may process data quickly, but they cannot apply intuition – the gut feeling that something is wrong even when the indicators are subtle or ambiguous. Consultants must remind clients that technology augments human awareness; it does not replace it.

Another reason for careful framing is cost. Security budgets are often tight, and technology investments compete with staffing and training. Organisations may be tempted to invest heavily in systems while neglecting the people who use them. This imbalance undermines resilience. A state-of-the-art control room staffed by undertrained operators will fail in practice. Conversely, modest but reliable technology, integrated with strong procedures and supported by trained staff, can provide excellent results. Consultants therefore need to guide clients in making proportionate investments, ensuring that technology is embedded in a wider framework that includes people and culture.

The introduction of this chapter must also address the dangers of dependency. As systems become more complex, organisations often find themselves vulnerable to outages, cyberattacks, or simple human error in configuration. Over-reliance on technology can lead to complacency, where staff assume that the system will detect or stop everything. In reality, resilience comes from recognising that technology is a tool, not a guarantee. Consultants must encourage clients to build redundancy, maintain manual fallbacks, and ensure that people remain trained and alert even in highly automated environments.

The place of technology in security is that of a multiplier, not a substitute. It is a layer within a larger framework that includes design, procedures, and culture. Its value is greatest when it works with people, not in place of them. For consultants, this perspective is essential: clients need to be shown that resilience is built on integration and proportion, not on technology alone. This chapter will develop these themes, exploring how technology enhances capability, where it introduces risks, how it can be integrated with procedures, and how consultants should assess the promises of emerging tools.

Technology as a Multiplier of Human Capability

When deployed well, technology does not replace people but multiplies what they can achieve. It enables small teams to monitor large areas, enhances the speed and accuracy of decision-making, and provides tools that extend human senses beyond their natural limits. Consultants must understand this principle in order to help clients position technology correctly – not as an end in itself, but as a means of giving people more reach, more insight, and more efficiency.

The concept of "force multiplication" is central here. In the military, a force multiplier is any factor that makes a unit significantly more effective without increasing its size. In security, technology serves this role. A single guard equipped with radios, surveillance cameras, and access to alarm feeds can cover a facility that would otherwise require dozens of staff. Technology extends the range of detection, reduces the time needed to verify events, and allows one person to manage risks that would otherwise overwhelm them.

CCTV is one of the clearest examples. Without cameras, a security officer can only observe what is directly in front of them. With cameras, the same officer can oversee dozens of locations simultaneously. Motion detection and video analytics can further enhance this, highlighting areas of concern and allowing the operator to focus attention where it is most needed. Yet the value is not in the cameras alone – it is in the ability of the operator to interpret the feed, respond appropriately, and direct resources quickly. The technology multiplies human vision, but it is the human who turns vision into action.

Access control is another example. Manual checks at every door would be slow and labour-intensive. Electronic systems allow one guard to monitor hundreds of entries at once, flagging only those that require attention. Biometric systems, in particular, strengthen identity assurance, making it harder for credentials to be borrowed or forged. For the consultant, the lesson is that these technologies reduce the burden on staff while increasing accuracy. But they must be carefully managed; if users share credentials or prop open doors, the multiplier effect is lost.

Analytics and automation also demonstrate the enabling role of technology. Intrusion detection systems, for example, can filter out environmental noise and focus alerts on real threats, saving operators from fatigue. Predictive analytics can identify patterns in access or behaviour that may indicate insider threats. These tools allow people to focus their efforts where they are most valuable – investigating anomalies and making decisions – rather than wasting time on routine checks.

Yet it is vital to stress that technology does not multiply capability in a vacuum. It must be integrated with procedures and supported by training. A powerful CCTV system is wasted if operators are not trained to interpret incidents, just as biometric systems are undermined if staff are not educated about credential security. Consultants should emphasise that the multiplier effect arises from alignment – technology plus people plus procedures. Without this integration, technology can create new vulnerabilities instead of reducing them.

An often-overlooked aspect is morale and perception. Staff who feel supported by reliable tools are more confident and effective. Conversely, poorly performing systems can frustrate and demotivate. For example, unreliable alarms that constantly generate false positives cause operators to tune out, reducing vigilance. Reliable systems, by contrast, reinforce a sense of professionalism and pride. Consultants should therefore assess not only technical performance but also how systems affect the attitudes and efficiency of those who use them.

Technology also allows organisations to extend protection into areas where people cannot easily go. Thermal imaging cameras can see in darkness, drones can patrol large perimeters, and sensors can monitor environments that are dangerous for humans. These capabilities enhance resilience by covering blind spots and reducing risk to personnel. Again, the human role remains central: people must interpret, decide, and act on the data provided.

Technology should be seen as a multiplier of human capability. It enables staff to cover more ground, make better decisions, and maintain vigilance across complex environments. It enhances efficiency, accuracy, and reach, but only when integrated with procedures and operated by trained staff. For consultants, the message to clients is clear: technology does not replace people, but it allows people to achieve far more than they could alone.

Risks of Over-Reliance on Technology

While technology can multiply human capability, it can also create new risks if organisations come to depend on it as a substitute for people, procedures, or good security culture. Over-reliance on technology is one of the most common weaknesses observed in security consultancy. Clients often assume that investment in advanced systems is a guarantee of resilience. In reality, technology is vulnerable to failure, exploitation, and misuse, and it cannot compensate for poor behaviour or weak culture. Consultants must therefore guide clients to see technology as a tool, not a solution in itself.

One of the most common dangers is the false sense of security. Organisations frequently treat technology as infallible, not giving it a second though after it has been installed. A facility with hundreds of cameras may assume that it is well protected, even though no one is actively monitoring the feeds. A site with biometric access control may believe it is immune to intrusion, yet staff can still undermine it by holding doors open for others or by allowing tailgating. Over-reliance creates complacency: staff assume the system will do the work for them, and vigilance declines. Consultants should emphasise that a system is only as effective as the people who operate it.

System failure is another key risk. Technology is vulnerable to power outages, cyberattacks, hardware faults, and software errors. A surveillance system may fail during a storm, leaving blind spots. An access control system may be disrupted by a network outage, forcing staff to prop doors open. These events are not rare; they are inevitable over time. Organisations that rely entirely on technology without contingency measures are left exposed when failure occurs. Consultants must therefore encourage redundancy, manual fallback processes, and regular drills that prepare staff for operating without technology.

False alarms present another challenge. In practice, many of these are better described as nuisance alarms – alerts triggered by external but unwanted factors such as weather, wildlife, or passing traffic. The industry often calls them "false," but the system is functioning as designed; the problem is that the trigger is not relevant to security. Intrusion detection systems, video analytics, and access control can generate high volumes of such alarms, which creates fatigue. Operators become desensitised and may fail to act on genuine incidents. Over-reliance on automation without effective filtering and human oversight leads to missed events. Consultants should therefore advise on how to reduce nuisance triggers, balance automation with operator judgement, and ensure that systems assist rather than overwhelm.

User workarounds also weaken technology. Systems that are poorly designed or inconvenient to use are quickly bypassed. Staff may share access badges if card systems are used, or they may circumvent biometric readers altogether if those are slow or unreliable. Operators may disable alarms that trigger too often. These behaviours undermine the system and highlight that technology alone does not enforce compliance – it must be supported by usable design and cultural reinforcement. Consultants observing these behaviours should recognise them as signals of over-reliance: the assumption that technology will work even when staff are actively undermining it.

Cybersecurity is another area of risk. Modern security systems are increasingly integrated with IT networks, creating vulnerabilities to hacking and malware. CCTV cameras, access control servers, and IoT sensors can all be exploited if not properly secured. Over-reliance on technology without adequate cyber protection exposes organisations to attacks that may disable or manipulate systems. A consultant must highlight that resilience requires not only physical security but also robust cyber hygiene, particularly where critical infrastructure is concerned.

Complacency in training is a further problem. Organisations that invest heavily in technology often neglect training, assuming that systems will "take care of security." This creates skill erosion among staff. Operators become passive, waiting for systems to tell them what to do rather than maintaining situational awareness. In incidents where systems fail, untrained staff are left unable to respond effectively. Consultants should emphasise that training must continue regardless of how advanced the technology is, and that drills should simulate both normal and abnormal conditions.

Another subtle risk of over-reliance is strategic distraction. Organisations may focus so much on acquiring and upgrading technology that they neglect other aspects of security. Large sums are spent on new platforms while basic procedural weaknesses remain unaddressed. Consultants must help clients resist the lure of technological "silver bullets" and instead pursue a balanced approach that invests in people, culture, and procedures alongside systems.

Over-reliance can erode accountability. When organisations believe that systems are responsible for security, individual responsibility weakens. Staff may excuse lapses by pointing to "system error" rather than recognising their own role in prevention. This shift in mindset undermines ownership, which is essential for resilience. Consultants should be alert to this cultural signal and work to reframe technology as a support for people, not a replacement for their responsibility.

The risks of over-reliance on technology are clear. It creates false confidence, leaves organisations vulnerable to outages and attacks, generates alarm fatigue, encourages workarounds, undermines training, and erodes accountability. Consultants must consistently remind clients that technology alone cannot deliver security. True resilience comes from integrating systems with people, procedures, and culture, ensuring that when technology fails – as it inevitably will at times – the organisation remains protected.

Integrating Technology with People and Procedures

Technology achieves little in isolation. Its value lies in how it is integrated with the people who operate it and the procedures that give it context. Without this integration, even the most advanced systems can become expensive failures. For consultants, the central task is to ensure that technology aligns with organisational workflows, supports operators rather than overwhelming them, and reinforces procedures instead of replacing them.

The first principle of integration is usability. Systems must be intuitive and convenient for staff, or they will quickly be bypassed. A well-designed access control system, for example, speeds up entry while maintaining strong verification. A poorly designed system that rejects authorised users or creates long queues will encourage workarounds, such as sharing badges or propping doors open. Consultants must assess whether technology works with the rhythm of operations or against it, and whether its design promotes compliance or circumvention.

Training is another essential element. Technology cannot deliver value unless people know how to use it effectively. A CCTV system with advanced analytics requires operators who understand what the alerts mean, how to interpret them, and when to escalate. An access control system that integrates with HR databases requires administrators who know how to maintain permissions accurately. Consultants should evaluate training programmes and recommend improvements, ensuring that systems are supported by knowledgeable users who remain confident in both routine and emergency conditions.

Procedures provide the framework that connects technology with behaviour. For instance, an alarm system is only effective if there are clear procedures for who responds, how escalation occurs, and what steps are taken after confirmation. Without this, alarms become background noise rather than triggers for action. Similarly, visitor management technology is only effective when procedures define who checks identification, how access is recorded, and what happens if anomalies are detected. Consultants must ensure that procedures are written to integrate technology into real practice, not merely to describe it in theory.

The way people interact with systems is especially important. Operators under stress must be able to act quickly and confidently. This requires systems that reduce mental workload rather than increase it. Interfaces should present information clearly, highlight priorities, and guide operators towards correct actions. Social-technical design – ease of use, ergonomics, and intuitive navigation – plays a decisive role. Consultants should observe operators in real conditions, noting where confusion, delay, or frustration occur, and recommend redesigns that simplify rather than complicate.

Integration also requires alignment with wider workflows. Security should not be treated as an add-on but as part of the organisation's daily operations. For example, integrating access control with HR ensures that staff departures immediately remove credentials, reducing insider risk. Linking alarm systems with incident management platforms ensures that responses are managed through established procedures. Embedding security into routine processes makes it more natural and less likely to be bypassed. Consultants should look for opportunities to tie security into existing systems rather than creating isolated procedures.

Another factor is inclusivity. Systems that exclude certain groups – for example, turnstiles that are inaccessible to wheelchair users or procedures that assume fluency in one language – undermine resilience. Integration means ensuring that all staff can participate in security equally. Consultants should examine whether technology and procedures accommodate diversity and accessibility, recognising that gaps in inclusivity create exploitable weaknesses.

Integration also extends to crisis conditions. During incidents, systems must support staff rather than obstruct them. A fire alarm should not only sound but also trigger procedures for evacuation, with technology guiding safe routes and verifying roll calls. An intrusion detection system should escalate to designated responders with clarity about roles and next steps. Consultants must ensure that technology contributes to resilience under stress, not just efficiency in routine conditions.

Integration is about building credibility. Staff will only respect systems that are usable, procedures that are realistic, and processes that are reinforced by leadership. If any element is out of alignment, security will be seen as obstructive or irrelevant. Consultants play a crucial role in identifying misalignments and recommending adjustments that ensure technology enhances rather than hinders.

Technology delivers value only when integrated with people and procedures. Resilience arises from coordination, not automation.

Technology delivers value only when it is aligned with people and procedures. Usability, training, procedural clarity, workflow integration, inclusivity, and crisis readiness are all essential. Consultants must observe, analyse, and advise on how these elements fit together, ensuring that technology is an enabler embedded within daily operations. Security that integrates systems with human behaviour is resilient, credible, and sustainable – security that relies on systems alone is fragile and short-lived.

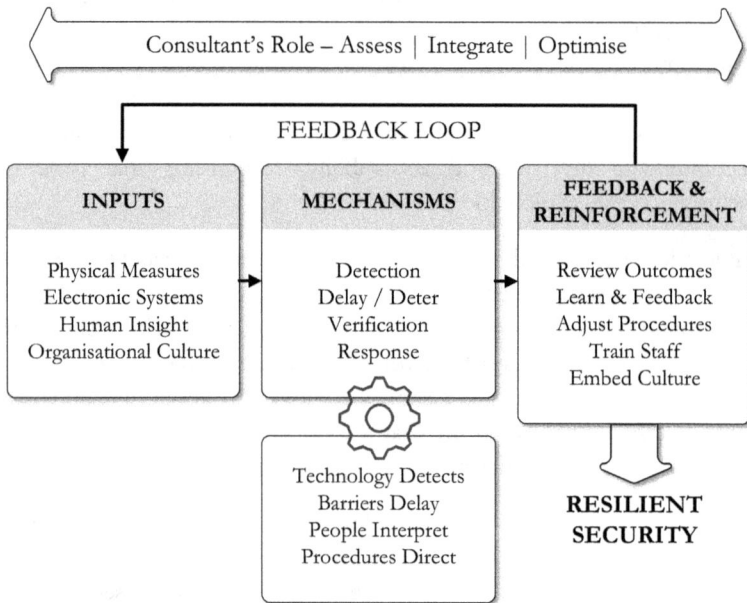

Figure 9 The Integrated Human Security System

Emerging Technologies and Their Implications

The pace of technological change in security is accelerating. Artificial intelligence, machine learning, robotics, drones, and cloud-based platforms are rapidly transforming what organisations can deploy to protect people and assets. These developments hold enormous potential, but they also bring complexity, cost, and new forms of vulnerability. Consultants have a vital role in separating promise from reality, ensuring that emerging technologies are used as enablers of resilience rather than expensive distractions or hidden liabilities.

At the time of writing, Artificial intelligence (AI) and machine learning are perhaps the most widely promoted developments in security. AI promises to process vast amounts of data quickly, detecting anomalies that humans might miss. Video analytics powered by machine learning can identify unusual patterns of movement, flag abandoned objects, or track individuals across multiple cameras. Predictive analytics can forecast potential risks by identifying correlations in data streams. These capabilities extend human capacity by focusing attention on the most relevant events. However, they also create risks of false positives and false negatives. AI may misclassify normal behaviour as suspicious, creating wasted responses, or it may miss genuinely dangerous actions. Consultants must help clients calibrate expectations, ensuring AI is framed as an aid to human decision-making rather than a substitute for human judgement.

Large language models (LLMs) represent another area of development, offering natural language interfaces for querying data or generating reports. While useful for simplifying access to complex datasets, they are not infallible. LLMs can produce outputs that are plausible but incorrect, and they lack the intuition that humans bring – the gut feeling that something is wrong even when data appears normal. Consultants must caution clients against treating LLMs as authoritative, stressing that they are tools for efficiency, not sources of absolute truth.

Robotics and drones are increasingly deployed for patrols, inspection, and monitoring. Drones can survey large perimeters quickly, inspect hard-to-reach infrastructure, or provide aerial situational awareness during incidents. Ground robots can patrol sites, detect anomalies, and act as mobile sensor platforms. These systems expand coverage while reducing risk to personnel. Yet they also raise operational challenges. Drones may be grounded by weather, require regulatory clearance, or be vulnerable to interference. Robots may struggle in complex environments or fail without human oversight. Consultants should advise clients to view these technologies as supplements to existing patrols and monitoring, not replacements for human presence.

Cloud-based platforms and the Internet of Things (IoT) are reshaping integration. Security management systems hosted in the cloud offer scalability, remote access, and centralised control across multiple sites.

IoT devices such as smart locks, wireless sensors, and connected cameras provide flexibility and lower installation costs. However, these innovations also introduce cyber risks. Cloud services are dependent on network connectivity, and IoT devices are often vulnerable to hacking if poorly secured. A compromise in one device can cascade across the network, creating systemic vulnerabilities. Consultants must therefore emphasise the need for robust cyber hygiene, encryption, and segmentation to prevent exploitation.

Automation is another growing trend. Automated access systems, self-monitoring sensors, and AI-driven triage platforms are designed to reduce manual intervention. When reliable, they reduce workload and increase efficiency. Yet automation can also reduce vigilance if staff come to trust the system blindly. An automated system that classifies an incident as benign may be accepted without question, even when context suggests otherwise. Consultants should advise clients to build in mechanisms for human review, maintaining a balance between efficiency and accountability.

The risks of hype are ever-present. Vendors often market emerging technologies as transformative, promising cost savings, reduced staffing, and foolproof protection. History shows that such promises are rarely delivered without significant caveats. Fingerprint scanners once promised perfect access control but were often defeated by environmental conditions. Early video analytics claimed to detect loitering or aggression reliably but proved inaccurate in real-world use. Consultants must help clients distinguish between marketing claims and operational reality, emphasising trial deployments, pilot testing, and proportionate investment.

Another implication of emerging technologies is dependency. Organisations may become locked into proprietary ecosystems, where one vendor's platform requires specific hardware, software, or service contracts. This reduces flexibility and can increase long-term costs. Consultants should encourage clients to prioritise open standards and interoperability, ensuring that systems remain adaptable as needs change.

Privacy and ethics are also important. Emerging technologies often collect and process personal data on an unprecedented scale. Facial recognition, behavioural analytics, and biometric systems raise legal and ethical questions about consent, proportionality, and oversight. Consultants must ensure that clients understand regulatory frameworks, from GDPR[5] in Europe to local data protection laws elsewhere and advise on privacy-by-design principles. Failure to address these issues not only creates legal exposure but also risks eroding trust among staff and the public.

The responsibility is twofold. First, to remain informed about technological developments so that advice is current and credible. Second, to frame emerging technologies realistically, highlighting both their enabling potential and their risks. The consultant's role is not to dismiss innovation but to ensure that it serves resilience, aligns with procedures and culture, and avoids creating dependencies or vulnerabilities that outweigh its benefits.

Emerging technologies present extraordinary opportunities to extend human capability and improve security outcomes. But they must be approached critically, tested thoroughly, and integrated carefully. Consultants should position them as enablers – tools that amplify human capacity, reinforce procedures, and fit within cultural frameworks – rather than as substitutes for human judgement or professional responsibility. By doing so, they help clients harness innovation responsibly, achieving resilience that is both technologically advanced and operationally credible.

Illustrative Example: The Unwatched Camera Wall

One of the most common examples of misplaced faith in technology is the over-reliance on CCTV. Organisations often assume that installing more cameras directly equates to stronger security. In practice, however, the effectiveness of surveillance depends not on the number of devices but on how information is processed, interpreted, and acted upon. This example – the unwatched camera wall – illustrates how investment in technology without attention to people and procedures can create a dangerous illusion of resilience.

A major transportation hub invested heavily in surveillance infrastructure. Hundreds of high-definition cameras were installed, all feeding into a central control room equipped with large video walls. At first glance, the facility appeared highly secure. Visitors were impressed by the scale of the system, and management assumed that every corner of the site was under continuous observation. Yet during a consultant's assessment, a critical weakness emerged: although the cameras functioned as intended, there were far too many feeds for the operators to monitor effectively.

Operators were faced with walls of screens, each displaying multiple video streams. Human attention is limited, and studies consistently show that people monitoring CCTV lose concentration after just 20 minutes. In this case, the workload was overwhelming. Important events went unnoticed, suspicious behaviour was missed, and operators reported feeling fatigued and demoralised. The organisation had invested millions in equipment but had neglected the human factors that make surveillance viable.

The consultant's review revealed several specific problems. First, there was no prioritisation of feeds. All cameras were displayed equally, regardless of risk profile. An unoccupied storage corridor received the same attention as a crowded passenger concourse. Second, there were no clear procedures for how operators should divide their attention, escalate incidents, or rotate tasks to avoid fatigue. Third, training was limited; operators had been shown how to use the software but had not been prepared for the realities of sustained observation.

The result was predictable: when a minor incident occurred, such as unauthorised access to a restricted area, it was often not detected until long after the fact. The system provided excellent retrospective evidence – recordings were used to review what had happened – but it failed to deliver real-time security. Technology had been treated as a substitute for vigilance rather than an enabler of it.

The consultant recommended several corrective measures. First, the system should be reconfigured to use intelligent video analytics, flagging anomalies for operator review rather than expecting staff to watch every feed continuously. This shifted the burden from passive monitoring to active assessment. Second, cameras were categorised by risk level, with high-priority areas given prominence on the display wall while low-priority feeds were relegated to secondary screens. Third, staffing levels were adjusted to ensure sufficient operators were available during peak times, and shifts were redesigned to reduce fatigue. Fourth, procedures were rewritten to guide how alerts were handled, including escalation steps and communication protocols.

Training was also overhauled. Operators were taught not only the technical features of the system but also the psychology of vigilance, the dangers of fatigue, and techniques for maintaining focus. Regular drills were introduced to simulate incidents, ensuring that operators practised decision-making under realistic conditions. These measures transformed the control room from a passive display centre into an active decision-making hub.

The illustrative example highlights several lessons for consultants. Technology that is impressive in scale can still fail in practice if it is not aligned with human capacity. More cameras do not automatically mean better security; without integration, they can overwhelm rather than assist. Procedures and training are as important as the hardware itself, and cultural attitudes towards vigilance shape whether systems are used effectively.

It also highlights the importance of perception versus reality. To senior management and visitors, the camera wall symbolised security – a visible demonstration of investment. Yet the consultant's assessment revealed that the system was delivering little real-time protection. This disconnect between appearance and reality is common in organisations that prioritise technological visibility over operational effectiveness. Consultants must therefore be willing to challenge assumptions, even when it means questioning high-profile investments.

The case illustrates the broader principle of this chapter: technology should be positioned as an enabler, not a substitute. The camera wall could have been a powerful tool for situational awareness, but only when integrated with procedures, training, and cultural reinforcement. Without those elements, it became a costly illusion. By reframing technology as part of a wider system – one that supports people rather than attempting to replace them – consultants help clients achieve resilience that is credible, sustainable, and genuinely effective.

Practice Guide

Technology remains indispensable to modern security, but it is effective only when understood as one layer within a broader framework. This chapter has hit its learning objectives: the role of technology as an enabler rather than a substitute has been established; its ability to multiply human capability has been demonstrated; the risks of over-reliance, including false confidence, failure, and workarounds, have been analysed; integration with procedures and culture has been shown to be essential;

the impact of emerging technologies has been evaluated critically; and case studies have illustrated the difference between credible resilience and costly illusion.

Consultants will recognise the recurring weaknesses that undermine performance. Organisations frequently mistake visibility for effectiveness, assuming that more cameras, sensors, or systems automatically equate to greater protection. Over-reliance fosters complacency, erodes staff skills, and creates vulnerabilities when systems fail. Vendors often amplify this risk by promoting new technologies as silver bullets, promising automation and elimination of human error. Consultants must resist this narrative and warn against investments that create dependency without adding proportionate value.

Good practice lies in reframing technology as a multiplier of human capability. When aligned with people and procedures, technology extends reach, accelerates response, and enhances decision-making. Integration is the decisive factor: systems must be usable, intuitive, and inclusive, supported by clear procedures and continuous training. Emerging technologies should be adopted selectively, tested in real contexts, and positioned as tools that support resilience rather than as replacements for human judgement. The consultant's role is to challenge hype, promote proportionate adoption, and ensure that technological investment remains credible, sustainable, and embedded in daily practice.

Technology is most powerful when it amplifies people, not when it seeks to replace them. Consultants who guide clients towards proportionate, integrated, and realistic use of technology ensure that resilience is achieved in practice rather than projected in appearance. This approach positions technology not as the foundation of security, but as an enabler that strengthens the enduring pillars of people, procedures, and culture. With these four pillars in place, the consultant's task shifts from understanding the toolkit to applying it – engaging with clients, shaping projects, and navigating the consulting process explored in the next part of the book.

Chapter 11 – Compliance, Standards, and Certification

Compliance, standards, and certification sit at the intersection of governance, assurance, and practice. For some organisations, they represent a burden of bureaucracy; for others, they provide a framework for trust and accountability. For consultants, the challenge is to interpret and apply these requirements in a way that builds resilience rather than stifling it. This chapter will equip readers to critically assess compliance demands, align them with operational realities, and guide clients towards credible, proportionate, and sustainable approaches.

By the end of this chapter, readers will be able to:

- Understand the role of compliance, standards, and certification in shaping modern security practice.
- Recognise the difference between compliance-driven and risk-driven security and identify where each approach succeeds or fails.
- Evaluate key international standards and frameworks, including ISO, IEC, NIST, and regional requirements, and interpret their practical relevance.
- Analyse the strengths and limitations of certification schemes, including ISO certification, SOC 2, and PCI DSS.
- Advise clients on how to prepare for audits, gather evidence, and demonstrate compliance credibly.
- Guide organisations in embedding compliance into daily practice so that standards become routine rather than paperwork exercises.
- Balance regulatory obligations with proportional, risk-based measures that deliver resilience while avoiding unnecessary bureaucracy.

Introduction

Compliance has become a central feature of modern security management. From international standards such as ISO 27001:2022[15] to sector-specific frameworks such as PCI DSS or NERC CIP[21], organisations measure their maturity by the number of certificates displayed on office walls or the strength of their audit reports. Compliance can provide reassurance to executives, regulators, and customers that a recognised benchmark has been achieved. It offers consistency, a shared language, and evidence that the organisation is making a formal effort to manage its risks responsibly. However, consultants must make one point clear: compliance is not the same as security.

This distinction is critical. Compliance requirements are designed to be broadly applicable, covering a wide range of industries and environments. They provide general rules, not tailored solutions. A single standard may apply equally to a hospital, a shipping terminal, and a financial trading floor, even though the threats to each are entirely different. The codes, standards, and regulations themselves do not know the site, its vulnerabilities, or its operational context. They cannot reflect the unique risks of a specific facility. Compliance confirms only that minimum requirements have been met according to a framework. It does not guarantee that an organisation is resilient against the threats it actually faces.

The danger is that compliance can create a false sense of security. Certificates and audit reports provide visible assurance that can be presented to boards, regulators, and clients. This reassurance, however, is often legal rather than practical. Compliance offers legal cover by showing that an organisation has followed prescribed processes and met recognised benchmarks. But it cannot cover the full spectrum of threats that are specific to a site or an operation. When organisations equate compliance with security, they risk assuming that a paper framework will protect them against a real-world adversary. In reality, compliance protects reputations and legal liability far more effectively than it protects assets and people.

This gap between compliance and actual security performance is where consultants must focus their attention. An organisation may achieve ISO certification and still suffer a breach, not because the standard was flawed, but because it was never designed to anticipate every risk. Compliance frameworks are by necessity generic and sometimes slow to adapt to emerging threats. A standard written five years ago cannot reflect today's evolving attack methods in detail. For this reason, consultants should present compliance as the starting point – a basic level of assurance – not the final measure of resilience.

The cultural impact of compliance also deserves scrutiny. In many organisations, the pursuit of compliance degenerates into a bureaucratic exercise. Staff complete forms, produce audit evidence, and follow prescriptive checklists because they must satisfy auditors, not because they believe it improves security. This "tick-box mentality" can become dangerous. It shifts focus away from outcomes and towards appearances. Managers may feel reassured that because procedures exist on paper, risks are under control, even though those procedures may not be followed in practice. Compliance without genuine integration creates hollow security.

Yet it would be wrong to dismiss compliance entirely as a burden. When approached critically, compliance offers real benefits. Standards capture decades of lessons learned and provide a structured foundation that organisations can build upon. They make security more transparent to outsiders, reassuring regulators and customers that baseline requirements are being addressed. They create a benchmark that consultants can use to measure maturity and identify gaps. And they provide a reference point that can be communicated across industries and national borders. The problem lies not in the existence of compliance, but in how organisations interpret and apply it.

For consultants, the challenge is to reframe compliance for their clients. Compliance is a tool – a baseline that provides assurance and reduces liability – but it is never a complete solution. True resilience requires tailoring measures to the specific threats, vulnerabilities, and contexts of the site. Consultants must help clients navigate the tension between satisfying regulatory demands and building security that genuinely works in practice. Compliance should not be abandoned or ignored, but it must be placed in its proper role: a foundation upon which to build, not the finished structure.

This chapter will explore the role of compliance, standards, and certification in depth. It will distinguish between compliance-driven and risk-driven approaches, analyse key frameworks and their relevance, evaluate certification processes, and consider how standards can be embedded into daily practice. It will also examine failures where organisations appeared secure on paper but were exposed. Throughout, the focus will remain on the consultant's task: guiding clients to see compliance not as the end goal but as a step towards genuine, site-specific resilience.

Compliance-Driven vs Risk-Driven Security

The distinction between compliance-driven and risk-driven approaches is one of the most important lessons for both consultants and their clients. Compliance-driven security focuses on meeting external requirements – standards, laws, and certification schemes. Risk-driven security focuses on the actual threats and vulnerabilities of the organisation and seeks to mitigate them proportionately. Both approaches have value, but they are not the same, and confusing one for the other can undermine resilience.

Compliance-driven security is attractive to organisations because it is measurable and demonstrable. Audits, checklists, and certificates provide tangible evidence that requirements have been met. Boards and regulators find this reassuring, and it often provides a degree of legal protection. If an incident occurs, an organisation can show that it met industry standards and passed recognised audits, reducing exposure to liability. For this reason, compliance-driven approaches are widely adopted, particularly in regulated sectors such as finance, energy, and healthcare.

However, compliance-driven approaches also create significant weaknesses. First, they are inherently backward-looking. Standards and codes of practice are based on accumulated experience, setting out what has gone wrong in the past. They are updated periodically but always lag behind new methods of attack. An organisation that focuses solely on compliance may be blind to emerging threats that have not yet been written into the frameworks. For example, early ISO information security standards did not anticipate the scale of ransomware or supply chain cyberattacks, leaving compliant organisations exposed despite their certificates.

Second, compliance-driven approaches are often rigid. Auditors require documented processes, written policies, and formal evidence. This encourages organisations to create detailed procedures that look convincing on paper but may not reflect how people behave in practice. As explored earlier, this creates a tick-box mentality where success is measured by documents rather than outcomes. Consultants often find organisations with multiple certifications but glaring practical weaknesses, such as doors left unsecured, staff unfamiliar with procedures, or poorly trained operators. In these cases, compliance has created a veneer of security that collapses under real-world pressure.

Risk-driven security begins from a different premise. Instead of asking "what does the standard require?" it asks, "what risks does this organisation face, and how can they be mitigated proportionately?" This approach starts with a thorough assessment of threats, vulnerabilities, and impacts. It recognises that every site is unique, and that measures must be tailored to context. A port facility facing risks from smuggling and sabotage will require different controls than a hospital facing risks from insider theft and data breaches.

The strength of a risk-driven approach is that it is forward-looking and adaptive. It seeks to anticipate emerging threats and align protective measures with the specific vulnerabilities of the organisation. Risk-driven security may go beyond compliance, introducing measures that exceed minimum standards when justified by the threat environment. For example, a compliant organisation may have standard access control in place, but a risk-driven organisation operating in a high-threat region may add anti-tailgating mantraps and hostile vehicle mitigation because the specific risks demand them.

Another strength of risk-driven security is proportionality. Compliance frameworks are designed to apply universally, which can make them either too light or too heavy for a particular site. A small business may struggle with the administrative weight of ISO certification, while a critical infrastructure site may find that minimum standards are insufficient. A risk-driven approach calibrates controls so that they are neither excessive nor inadequate, aligning investment with the actual risk profile. Consultants play a key role in ensuring that proportionality is maintained, helping clients avoid both under-protection and wasteful over-engineering.

Yet risk-driven security also has its challenges. It is harder to measure and demonstrate than compliance. Boards may struggle to accept recommendations that go beyond regulatory requirements, especially when they involve additional cost. Regulators may still penalise organisations that have adopted risk-driven measures if they do not meet prescribed standards. For this reason, consultants must help clients balance the two approaches: satisfying compliance obligations while also addressing site-specific risks.

For consultants, the task is not to dismiss compliance but to contextualise it. Compliance provides a necessary baseline – a minimum assurance that key controls are in place – but it must never be mistaken for a guarantee of resilience. Consultants should guide clients to treat compliance as one layer of defence, useful for legal, reputational, and governance purposes, but always supplemented by risk-driven measures tailored to their operations.

A practical method is to align compliance frameworks with the outputs of risk assessments. Instead of treating compliance as the final objective, consultants can map standards onto the risk profile of the site, identifying where compliance requirements overlap with actual risks and where additional measures are required. This ensures that compliance is achieved while also addressing the gaps that frameworks cannot anticipate. It also helps organisations demonstrate to regulators and auditors that their security is not only compliant but also risk-based, which strengthens credibility.

Compliance-driven and risk-driven security represent two different approaches to resilience. Compliance-driven approaches provide legal cover, consistency, and demonstrable assurance but risk creating rigidity and false confidence. Risk-driven approaches provide adaptability, proportionality, and alignment with actual threats but are harder to formalise and prove. The consultant's role is to bridge these approaches, ensuring that clients meet their obligations while also building resilience that is credible, proportionate, and tailored to their unique environment. This helps organisations avoid confusing compliance with real security and instead use it as one tool within a wider, risk-based approach.

Compliance provides assurance, not immunity. Consultants must translate regulatory frameworks into risk-based actions that withstand real-world conditions.

Key International Standards and Frameworks

Security consultancy operates within a landscape shaped by international standards and frameworks. These documents provide structure, benchmarks, and shared terminology, but they also introduce complexity and the risk of misapplication. For consultants, the task is not simply to list or memorise standards, but to interpret their relevance, explain their implications, and integrate them into proportionate resilience strategies. Each framework brings strengths and limitations, and none can be applied in isolation without regard for the site-specific risks of the organisation.

Among the most widely recognised frameworks is ISO 27001:2022[15], the standard for information security management systems (ISMS). It provides a systematic approach to managing sensitive information, ensuring confidentiality, integrity, and availability. Certification to ISO 27001:2022[15] demonstrates that an organisation has defined policies, controls, and risk management processes. For consultants, the strength of ISO 27001 lies in its adaptability – it requires organisations to conduct risk assessments and apply controls proportionately. However, its weakness is that certification can become an end in itself, with organisations focusing on producing documentation for auditors rather than embedding security into operations. Consultants must stress that ISO 27001 is a tool, not a guarantee, and that its value depends on how well it is integrated into daily practice.

Closely linked is ISO 22301:2019[12], the standard for business continuity management. This framework ensures that organisations can continue operating during and after disruptive incidents. It covers business impact assessments, continuity planning, and recovery strategies. For clients, ISO 22301 certification signals to stakeholders that resilience has been formally addressed. Yet, as with other standards, certification does not necessarily mean that real resilience exists. A company may pass an audit by documenting contingency plans but still fail to recover effectively because those plans were never tested. Consultants should ensure that continuity frameworks are not only compliant but also practical, rehearsed, and adaptable to evolving threats.

Another cornerstone is ISO 31000:2018[13], which provides principles and guidelines for risk management. Unlike the more prescriptive standards, ISO 31000 is conceptual, offering a framework rather than a set of certifiable requirements. Its strength lies in its broad applicability – it can be adapted across industries and disciplines. For consultants, ISO 31000 is particularly useful because it bridges security with wider enterprise risk management, aligning protective measures with organisational strategy. The limitation, however, is that its flexibility can lead to inconsistent application. Without careful interpretation, organisations may claim to follow ISO 31000 without adopting rigorous risk practices.

For industrial environments, IEC 62443 is a critical standard. It addresses cybersecurity for operational technology (OT) and industrial control systems (ICS), recognising that these environments face unique threats distinct from traditional IT. Energy utilities, manufacturing plants, and transport systems increasingly rely on ICS that were not originally designed with security in mind. IEC 62443 provides a framework for securing these systems, including requirements for component suppliers, integrators, and asset owners. Consultants working in critical national infrastructure must be familiar with IEC 62443, as it is one of the few international standards specifically addressing the convergence of cyber and physical domains.

In the United States, the NIST Cybersecurity Framework (CSF) has become highly influential. Developed by the National Institute of Standards and Technology, it provides a set of functions – Identify, Protect, Detect, Respond, and Recover – that organisations can use to structure their cybersecurity practices. While not mandatory, it is widely adopted because of its clarity and flexibility. For consultants, the NIST CSF is valuable not only for U.S. clients but also as a reference point globally. Its limitation, however, is similar to other frameworks: it provides structure, not assurance. An organisation may align with NIST CSF in theory but remain vulnerable in practice if implementation is superficial.

In Europe, EN standards developed by the European Committee for Standardisation (CEN) and the European Committee for Electrotechnical Standardisation (CENELEC) provide benchmarks for physical security products such as locks, safes, doors, and barriers. These standards are particularly relevant when specifying equipment, as they provide measurable criteria for resistance levels. Consultants can use EN classifications to compare products objectively and ensure that procurement decisions meet required specifications. Yet even here, certification should not be mistaken for suitability. A door certified to a high EN standard may perform well in laboratory conditions but fail in a real-world installation if fitted poorly or used inappropriately. Consultants must remind clients that product certification is not the same as system-level resilience.

Regional and sector-specific frameworks add further layers. In the European Union, the NIS Directive and its successor NIS2[6] Directive impose obligations on operators of essential services and digital service providers to implement security measures and report incidents. NIS2[6] expands the scope and strengthens enforcement, reflecting the increasing importance of cyber resilience across sectors. Consultants supporting clients in Europe must therefore ensure that compliance obligations are understood and embedded, while also reminding organisations that these directives provide minimum legal baselines, not comprehensive protection.

In the United States, the NERC Critical Infrastructure Protection (CIP) standards apply to the energy sector, requiring utilities to secure their bulk power systems. These standards are prescriptive and mandatory, and failure to comply can result in significant penalties. While they raise the baseline for critical infrastructure, they also demonstrate the challenge of prescriptive compliance: organisations sometimes focus on passing audits rather than addressing operational vulnerabilities. Consultants must help clients navigate the balance between meeting regulatory requirements and sustaining practical resilience.

In the Middle East, frameworks such as the UAE National Emergency Crisis and Disaster Management Authority (NCEMA) standards provide a regional layer of requirements. NCEMA[18] issues detailed guidance on business continuity, crisis management, and critical infrastructure protection, tailored to the UAE context. Similarly, local security regulators such as the Security Industry Regulatory Agency (SIRA) in Dubai impose specific requirements for surveillance and access control systems. Consultants working in the region must understand both the international frameworks and the regional overlays, ensuring that clients achieve compliance without losing sight of operational realities.

Across all these frameworks, the consultant's role is interpretation and alignment. Standards are only as valuable as the way they are applied. A compliant organisation is not automatically a secure one. The consultant must therefore ensure that standards and frameworks are used as tools within a broader resilience strategy. This means mapping requirements against site-specific risks, identifying where compliance suffices and where additional measures are needed, and ensuring that certification efforts do not become ends in themselves.

It is also essential to communicate to clients that no single framework covers everything. Each addresses a different aspect of resilience – information security, business continuity, risk management, industrial control, or product assurance. Consultants must weave these elements into a coherent whole, avoiding duplication while filling gaps. This requires judgement, experience, and the ability to translate abstract requirements into practical measures that align with operations.

International standards and frameworks provide the scaffolding of modern security practice. They create consistency, enable benchmarking, and give regulators and customers confidence. But they also risk being misinterpreted as complete solutions when they are only partial tools. The consultant's task is to help clients navigate this landscape, ensuring that compliance obligations are met while resilience is achieved. Standards are a foundation, not a finished structure – and it is the consultant's role to ensure that foundation supports a security strategy that is proportionate, site-specific, and sustainable.

Certification and Audit Processes

Certification and audit processes are the mechanisms through which compliance is tested, demonstrated, and validated. For many organisations, achieving certification is the ultimate goal: proof that they have met a recognised standard, evidence that can be shown to regulators, customers, and shareholders. The process provides external assurance, signalling that security measures are not only in place but also formally recognised. Yet the reality is more complex. Certification and audits can add real value when used properly, but they can also create distortions, with organisations focusing more on appearances than outcomes. Consultants must therefore guide clients through these processes carefully, ensuring that certification supports, rather than undermines, resilience.

At their core, certifications exist to provide assurance. Standards such as ISO 27001:2022[15], ISO 22301:2019[12], or ISO 9001 are accompanied by certification schemes run by accredited bodies. These schemes require organisations to document their policies and procedures, demonstrate implementation, and submit to external audits. The certification process is cyclical, typically involving initial assessments, surveillance audits, and recertification every few years. For organisations, this creates a discipline of regular review and evidence gathering. For consultants, the value lies in how this discipline can drive continuous improvement – provided it is not reduced to a box-ticking exercise.

The audit is the central mechanism in certification. Auditors review documentation, interview staff, and conduct spot checks to verify that the organisation is meeting the requirements of the standard. Audits can be internal, conducted by the organisation itself, or external, carried out by independent certification bodies. Both have value. Internal audits help organisations identify gaps before they become liabilities, while external audits provide credibility and third-party assurance. The consultant's role is often to prepare clients for both – ensuring that documentation is complete, processes are demonstrable, and staff are ready to respond confidently to auditor questions.

The strengths of certification are clear. It creates accountability by requiring organisations to prove, not just claim, that they follow standards. It enables benchmarking, allowing organisations to compare themselves with peers. It reassures customers, partners, and regulators that controls are in place. In some industries, certification is effectively a licence to operate: for example, PCI DSS compliance is a requirement for any organisation that handles payment card data. Without certification, participation in the market may not be possible. Consultants must therefore treat certification as both a business necessity and a governance tool.

Yet weaknesses are equally apparent. Certification can foster a culture of compliance for its own sake. Organisations often focus narrowly on passing the audit rather than embedding resilience. This is particularly evident in the production of documentation. In some cases, organisations prepare detailed manuals and procedures purely for auditors, while staff on the ground remain unaware of them. The result is a parallel system: one that exists on paper to satisfy certification, and another that governs daily operations. Consultants must be alert to these disconnects and emphasise that certification has little value if the certified processes do not match reality.

Another weakness lies in the uneven quality of audits. While many certification bodies apply rigorous standards, others take a more superficial approach. Organisations may "shop around" for auditors they perceive as less demanding, undermining the credibility of the entire system. In some regions, certification has become a transactional process – a stamp purchased rather than earned. Consultants must advise clients to select reputable, accredited certification bodies and should caution against approaches that prioritise speed and convenience over integrity.

Certification also has limits in scope. By definition, standards cannot anticipate every risk or context. An organisation may be certified under

ISO 27001:2022[15] but still lack adequate physical security, or it may hold ISO 22301:2019[12] certification while failing to prepare for specific regional hazards such as flooding or civil unrest. Certification provides assurance against a defined framework, not a guarantee of comprehensive security. Consultants must therefore help clients understand what certification does and does not cover.

The audit process itself can create challenges. Audits are episodic, taking snapshots at particular moments in time. Organisations may focus their efforts on preparing for audits, creating a burst of activity to ensure compliance during the inspection, only to relax afterwards. This "audit spike" undermines continuous improvement and creates cycles of frantic preparation followed by complacency. Consultants should encourage clients to treat audits as checkpoints within an ongoing process, embedding compliance into daily practice so that readiness is sustained year-round.

Preparation for audits is one of the most valuable services consultants can provide. This includes reviewing documentation, conducting mock audits, training staff on likely auditor questions, and identifying gaps that need to be addressed. More importantly, it includes ensuring that processes are genuinely implemented and not simply documented. Staff interviews are a critical part of audits, and auditors will quickly detect if employees are unfamiliar with the procedures they are supposed to follow. Consultants should therefore focus on embedding practices in reality rather than rehearsing staff to recite policies.

Certification also has strategic implications. For some organisations, certification is primarily about external reassurance – a way to demonstrate credibility to partners and regulators. For others, it is about internal discipline, creating structured frameworks that guide behaviour. Consultants must understand which drivers are most important for the client and tailor their approach accordingly. In regulated industries, the consequences of failing certification can be severe, ranging from fines to loss of operating licences. In competitive markets, certification can be a differentiator, signalling trustworthiness to customers.

Despite the weaknesses, certification retains enduring value when approached with the right mindset. It provides a structured framework that, if integrated properly, helps organisations identify gaps, formalise processes, and sustain improvement. It creates external accountability, ensuring that security is not left entirely to internal judgement. The consultant's role is to ensure that certification does not become a hollow exercise. This means guiding clients to view audits as opportunities for improvement, aligning certification efforts with risk assessments, and using standards as tools to embed resilience.

Certification and audit processes are double-edged. They provide external assurance and accountability, but they can also create distortions if treated as ends in themselves. For consultants, the task is to ensure that certification supports rather than substitutes for real security. This requires honest assessment of gaps, insistence on practical implementation, and advice that positions certification within a broader risk-driven strategy. By reframing certification as a means rather than an end, consultants can help organisations achieve not only compliance but also resilience that is meaningful, credible, and sustainable.

Embedding Standards into Daily Practice

The ultimate test of compliance and standards is not the possession of a certificate or the outcome of an audit, but whether the principles are embedded into the daily life of the organisation. A policy locked in a filing cabinet or an ISO manual uploaded to an intranet is of little value if staff are unaware of it, unable to use it, or unwilling to follow it. Consultants must therefore focus not only on whether standards have been formally adopted, but on whether they have been translated into practices that guide behaviour and strengthen resilience.

Embedding standards begins with usability. Policies and procedures must be written in clear and accessible language, avoiding excessive jargon or legalistic phrasing. Frontline staff cannot be expected to interpret dense manuals under pressure. Instead, they need concise, actionable instructions that fit their role and environment. A well-drafted policy is not one that satisfies auditors alone, but one that can be understood and applied in the moment by the people it is designed to guide. Consultants reviewing documentation should test for this usability, asking whether staff can grasp and apply the instructions without confusion.

Training is another essential element. Standards and compliance frameworks often require training programmes, but their effectiveness varies widely. Too often, training is delivered as a one-off event, perhaps during induction, and then forgotten. Embedding standards requires ongoing, engaging training that connects with staff in meaningful ways.

Scenario-based exercises, drills, and simulations are particularly valuable because they turn abstract policies into lived experiences. For example, a business continuity plan should not remain theoretical; it must be rehearsed through table-top exercises and live drills so that staff gain confidence in applying it under stress. Consultants should assess whether training is not only delivered but also reinforced and evaluated.

Awareness campaigns help reinforce the cultural dimension of compliance. Posters, reminders, intranet updates, and leadership messages can keep standards visible in daily operations. The tone of these campaigns matters. They should not present compliance as a burden, but as part of professional pride and responsibility. Staff are more likely to adopt standards when they see them as aligned with organisational values and their own sense of responsibility, rather than as arbitrary rules imposed from above. Consultants can recommend creative awareness programmes that highlight the "why" as much as the "what," linking standards to safety, resilience, and reputation.

Integration into workflows is equally important. Security measures that sit apart from normal operations are likely to be bypassed. For example, if visitor management processes are cumbersome and delay business meetings, staff will be tempted to circumvent them. If access controls do not integrate with HR systems, permissions may remain active long after employees leave. Consultants should look for ways to embed compliance requirements into existing business processes so that they become seamless. Automation often plays a role here, with digital systems ensuring that compliance checks happen automatically rather than relying on manual intervention.

Leadership commitment is a critical success factor. Embedding standards into daily practice requires leaders at every level to model the behaviour they expect from staff. When executives visibly follow access protocols, participate in training, and speak positively about compliance, they send a clear signal that standards matter. Conversely, if leaders disregard procedures, staff quickly learn that compliance is optional. Consultants should therefore evaluate leadership behaviours and provide guidance on how managers can actively support embedding efforts.

Auditing and monitoring must also shift focus. Instead of treating audits as episodic events designed only to pass certification checks, organisations should build internal monitoring processes that track compliance continuously. Spot checks, internal audits, and feedback mechanisms can ensure that standards are followed in practice, not just in documentation. Consultants can help design these mechanisms, ensuring they are proportionate and constructive rather than punitive. Feedback loops are especially valuable: when staff see that reporting non-compliance or suggesting improvements leads to positive change, they are more likely to engage with the process.

Technology can support embedding efforts, but it must be used wisely. Digital platforms for training, compliance tracking, and workflow integration can help make standards visible and manageable. For example, dashboards can provide real-time information on compliance performance, highlighting areas of strength and weakness. However, consultants must caution against over-reliance on technology, which can reproduce the same pitfalls seen in certification more broadly. Systems that are cumbersome, poorly integrated, or opaque can frustrate staff and encourage workarounds. The guiding principle should always be that technology supports people, rather than the other way around.

Cultural reinforcement is the final and perhaps most important dimension. Standards will only embed successfully if they become part of the organisational culture. This requires more than training and awareness campaigns; it requires staff to believe that compliance is part of doing the job properly. Positive reinforcement, recognition of good practice, and peer accountability all play a role. For example, staff who consistently follow procedures can be recognised formally, while teams that perform well in exercises can be commended. Consultants should highlight examples of positive reinforcement as a way to shift culture from compliance as obligation to compliance as ownership.

For consultants, the central lesson is clear: embedding standards into daily practice is the bridge between paper compliance and lived resilience. Certification may satisfy external requirements, but only embedded practice creates real security. Consultants must therefore evaluate not only whether standards have been adopted, but whether they are operationalised, understood, and owned by staff at every level. This requires a holistic approach, addressing documentation, training, workflows, leadership, monitoring, technology, and culture.

Embedding standards into daily practice ensures that compliance is more than a bureaucratic exercise. It transforms abstract requirements into behaviours and processes that protect the organisation in reality. Consultants play a vital role in guiding this transformation, helping clients move beyond certificates and audits towards resilience that is lived every day. By focusing on embedding, consultants can ensure that standards fulfil their purpose – not as paperwork, but as practical enablers of security.

Illustrative Example – The Certified but Unsecure Organisation

The following example – a composite drawn from multiple real-world scenarios – shows how certification can create the illusion of resilience while leaving an organisation dangerously exposed. It highlights the consultant's role in identifying gaps between paper compliance and operational reality, and it demonstrates why compliance should always be treated as a foundation rather than a complete solution.

The organisation in question was a mid-sized financial services provider operating across several regions. It prided itself on its reputation for professionalism and its ability to reassure clients with internationally recognised certifications. Prominently displayed in the reception area were plaques showing ISO 27001:2022[15] certification for information security management and ISO 22301:2019[12] certification for business continuity management. These achievements were central to the organisation's marketing strategy, emphasised in sales pitches and regulatory filings. At first glance, the company appeared highly mature in its security posture.

When consultants were engaged to conduct a broader assessment, however, a more complex picture emerged. On paper, the organisation had comprehensive policies covering access control, incident management, data protection, and continuity planning. The documentation was extensive, and during the initial audit reviews, everything appeared compliant. The problems only became visible when consultants moved beyond documents and began observing day-to-day operations.

The first issue was with physical security. Although the ISO 27001:2022[15] documentation described strict access protocols, consultants observed staff propping open secure doors for convenience. Tailgating was common, with employees holding doors open for visitors and colleagues without verifying credentials. When questioned, staff admitted that the formal process was "too much hassle" and that "everyone knows everyone here anyway." The certified procedures existed, but they were not applied.

Information security presented a similar problem. The organisation had detailed policies for password management and multi-factor authentication. Yet consultants discovered that shared accounts were still in use in several departments, and sensitive passwords were written on sticky notes attached to monitors. Staff explained that the formal processes slowed them down and interfered with client service. In practice, business priorities had trumped compliance requirements.

Business continuity planning was also revealed to be superficial. The organisation had passed ISO 22301:2019[12] audits by presenting comprehensive continuity plans and evidence of periodic reviews. But when consultants asked staff about their roles during a simulated disruption, confusion quickly became apparent. Many employees had never seen the continuity plan, and those who had were unsure of how to implement it. The plan had been written to satisfy auditors, not to guide real operations.

The weaknesses extended to culture. Interviews revealed that many employees viewed certification as a "box to tick" for regulators and clients rather than as part of their responsibility. The plaques in reception were seen as marketing tools, not as reflections of daily practice. Leadership reinforced this perception, focusing more on achieving certifications than on embedding security into workflows. Staff compliance was measured by audit outcomes, not by lived behaviours.

This case shows how certification can create a false sense of security, masking weaknesses behind documents and audits while daily practice falls short. The consultant's role was to bridge this gap by embedding standards into training, culture, leadership, and design, turning compliance from an end goal into a baseline. Over time, the organisation shifted towards risk-driven security, retaining certificates but treating them as part of a wider resilience strategy. The lesson is clear: certification may reassure regulators and clients but only lived behaviours and risk-driven measures deliver real resilience.

Practice Guide

Compliance, standards, and certification are central to modern security practice but are never the same as resilience. This chapter clarified that compliance forms a baseline rather than a complete solution. It distinguished compliance-driven from risk-driven approaches, reviewed the strengths and weaknesses of major frameworks, assessed the value and limits of certification and audits, and showed how standards can be embedded into daily operations. It also examined the cultural and operational consequences of treating compliance as an end in itself.

However, some common pitfalls remain. Organisations often equate certificates with security, assuming that passing an audit proves resilience when it offers only legal or reputational assurance. This fosters a tick-box mentality in which documented systems exist on paper but fail in practice. Over-focus on audits encourages superficial documentation, parallel processes, and misplaced confidence. Consultants must challenge this mindset, reminding clients that standards cannot predict every risk and that certification alone cannot protect against local vulnerabilities.

Good practice lies in repositioning compliance as a foundation. Frameworks such as ISO 27001:2022[15], ISO 22301:2019[12], ISO 31000:2018[13], NIST CSF, IEC 62443, NCEMA[18], and NIS2[6] all offer useful lessons but must be adapted to the organisation's threat environment. Certification and audits should serve as catalysts for improvement, not as final goals. Embedding standards through accessible policies, scenario-based training, integration with workflows, leadership example, and constructive monitoring turns compliance into lived behaviour rather than bureaucracy. Consultants should help organisations map compliance duties against their risk assessments to align obligations with proportionate, risk-driven controls.

The consultant's task is to help clients view compliance as one layer within a resilient strategy. Standards and certification provide confidence to regulators and customers, but true resilience is achieved only when they are internalised within organisational culture and daily practice. By embedding frameworks into behaviour and aligning them with dynamic, risk-driven measures, consultants transform compliance from a paper exercise into a meaningful contributor to security – not a ceiling that limits ambition, but a floor on which genuine resilience is built.

Reflections – From Tools to Application

Part 2 has explored the consultant's toolkit: the structured principles, analytical frameworks, and cultural insights that underpin professional security consultancy. If Part 1 established the mindset of the consultant, Part 2 has shown the instruments through which that mindset is applied. It has emphasised that tools are not sufficient in themselves, but must be applied with skill, judgement, and a clear understanding of human and organisational realities.

The first chapter of this part introduced the fundamentals of risk assessment. It emphasised that security decisions are always about balancing probabilities and consequences, recognising that resources are finite and risks cannot be eliminated entirely. By examining the principles of likelihood, consequence, and proportionality, this chapter established the logic that underpins all security consultancy. It also introduced the crucial idea of competing timelines: the delay imposed on an adversary versus the response time of the defender. This principle captures the essence of physical security and shows why detection, delay, and response must be treated as an integrated system rather than isolated measures. Consultants must always be alert to this interplay when recommending controls, ensuring that defences slow the adversary without obstructing the responder.

The next chapter examined established models and methodologies. These frameworks – defence in depth, concentric layers, and blue team adversary models – provide ways of structuring thought and communicating complex ideas. The key message was that models are useful but incomplete. They simplify reality, offering consultants and clients a way to conceptualise protection, but they must not be mistaken for reality itself. Consultants who apply models mechanically risk producing designs that look logical on paper but fail in practice. The point is that models are guides, not rules, and their value lies in how they are adapted to specific contexts.

Chapter 8 moved into analytical techniques. Here the focus was on structured tools such as SWOT, PESTLE, bow-tie analysis, and event and fault tree methods. These techniques add rigour to consultancy by making assumptions explicit and showing how risks interconnect. Importantly, they also provide a language for communicating with clients. Complex risks can be difficult to convey, but visual tools and structured analysis help decision-makers understand both threats and options. The caution, however, is that these tools must not be applied for their own sake. Consultants must avoid the temptation to produce diagrams and matrices that look impressive but add little insight. The true value lies in using analysis to test assumptions, expose blind spots, and focus attention where it matters most.

From there, the part turned to human factors and organisational behaviour. This chapter underscored that people are the decisive element in security. Procedures that are too complex are bypassed; cultures that are indifferent undermine even the best systems. The chapter distinguished between positive and negative security cultures, showing that attitudes, leadership behaviours, and staff engagement determine whether protective measures are followed consistently. It also examined socio-technical interfaces: the ergonomics, clarity, and usability of systems that shape how operators respond under pressure. Human psychology, workload, and intuition all influence outcomes. Consultants must therefore assess not only whether procedures exist but whether they are understood, followed, and supported by design. This reinforced the broader theme that security is as much about behaviour as it is about barriers.

Chapter 10 expanded this idea by looking at technology and automation. It acknowledged the growing role of sensors, analytics, and artificial intelligence, but cautioned against the belief that technology can replace human oversight. Automation brings speed and efficiency but also new vulnerabilities, especially if it fails in unexpected ways. Human oversight provides context, adaptability, and ethical judgement – qualities machines cannot replicate. Consultants must therefore recommend systems that blend automation with human control, ensuring that technology supports rather than supplants professional decision-making. This chapter also highlighted the dangers of over-reliance on emerging tools, such as predictive analytics based on large language models. These can identify patterns, but they cannot replace the human "gut feeling" that sometimes sees beyond the data.

The final chapter in this part addressed compliance, standards, and certification. It highlighted the double-edged nature of compliance: essential for legal and reputational assurance, but dangerous if mistaken for security itself. The key message was that compliance can create a false sense of security, as codes and standards are generalised and cannot account for site-specific risks. Certification is valuable but incomplete, and consultants must help clients move beyond a compliance-driven mindset to a risk-driven one. Embedding standards into daily practice, rather than treating them as paperwork exercises, is the consultant's responsibility. The example of the certified but unsecure organisation illustrated this vividly, showing how documentation and plaques can mask cultural weaknesses and operational shortcuts. Resilience is created not by certificates but by behaviours.

Taken together, these chapters demonstrate that the consultant's toolkit is not a checklist of methods to be applied mechanically. It is a repertoire of approaches to be selected, adapted, and integrated according to context. Consultants must exercise judgement, recognising that every tool has limitations and that resilience is achieved through a blend of systems, processes, and culture. The danger is not in using the wrong tool, but in mistaking the tool for the solution. The true craft of consultancy lies in knowing which tools to use, how far to trust them, and when to look beyond them.

The learning objectives for this part emphasised understanding risk assessment, applying models critically, using analytical techniques, integrating human factors, evaluating technology, and distinguishing between compliance and real security. Each chapter has addressed these objectives, reinforcing that the consultant must be both analytical and adaptive. Knowledge of tools is necessary but not sufficient; the ability to apply them in context is what creates professional value.

As we move into Part 3, the emphasis shifts from tools to application. The consultant does not operate in isolation but within a project ecosystem of clients, contractors, regulators, and integrators. The next part examines how consultants navigate these environments, when to lead and when to advise, and how to manage the political and contractual complexities that shape outcomes. It shows how the toolkit developed in Part 2 is applied in practice – not in abstract analysis, but in live projects with competing priorities, constrained budgets, and diverse stakeholders.

This transition mirrors the consultant's professional journey. Mastery of tools is the foundation, but mastery of application defines the practice. Part 2 has equipped the reader with principles and methods; Part 3 shows how those methods are used to create impact. The consultant's role is not only to know but to do, and it is this translation from knowledge to application that we now explore.

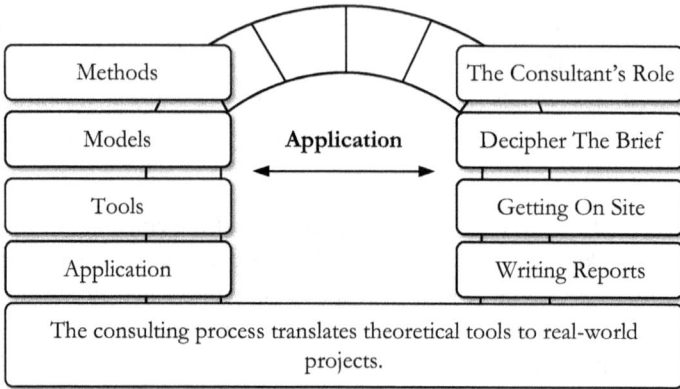

Figure 10 Part 2 Reflections Bridge

Part 3 – The Consulting Process

Consultancy is judged not by knowledge alone but by how that knowledge is applied. Having explored the consultant's foundations in Part 1 and the technical toolkit in Part 2, this part turns to the process of delivery. It follows the consultant through each stage of engagement: finding a place in the project ecosystem, securing work, clarifying briefs, gathering evidence, shaping designs, and presenting recommendations that influence decisions.

Projects are rarely neat or predictable. Deadlines slip, assumptions clash, and politics shape outcomes as much as technical factors. Consultants rarely hold authority; their influence depends on credibility, clarity, and the ability to balance independence with alignment to client goals. The consulting process is therefore the discipline of translating ideas into action under imperfect conditions.

Part 3 serves as the bridge between the consultant's foundations and their tools, and the advanced practices that will be explored in Part 4.

Chapter 12 – The Consultant's Role in the Project Ecosystem

Security consultants rarely work on a blank canvas. More often, they enter projects already in motion – shaped by architectural deadlines, procurement constraints, regulatory requirements, and client expectations. Understanding how to position oneself within this fast-moving ecosystem is critical. A technically excellent consultant who does not understand their place in the wider delivery structure risks being sidelined, misused, or ignored. This chapter prepares consultants to operate effectively within complex project environments, to collaborate without losing independence, and to influence outcomes without formal authority.

By the end of this chapter, you will be able to:

- Map the project lifecycle and identify how consulting inputs align with each phase – from strategy and design to implementation and operation.

- Recognise when to lead, when to support, and when to step back across different project stages.

- Interface effectively with clients, regulators, contractors, integrators, and operations teams.

- Apply principles from Flawless Consulting[3] and the PMI/PRINCE2 frameworks to manage role clarity and influence without authority.

- Navigate political, contractual, and delivery tensions without compromising ethics or objectivity.

- Identify practical points of integration where consultants can add value and avoid friction.

- Prevent scope creep and misalignment by understanding how consultants fit into procurement and delivery structures.

Introduction

Every project is an ecosystem of moving parts, shaped by clients with strategic objectives, contractors with commercial pressures, regulators with compliance mandates, and integrators responsible for translating design into operational systems. Within this environment, the consultant must find a role that is influential but not intrusive, authoritative yet not controlling. This balance is what often distinguishes effective consultants from those who undermine projects through overreach or poor stakeholder engagement.

The role of the consultant is defined as much by relationships as by technical skill. A consultant may bring deep expertise in security risk assessment, system design, or project governance, but if that knowledge cannot be placed into the context of design teams, procurement frameworks, or operational realities, its value diminishes. The most effective consultants are therefore those who understand how to map their contribution across the lifecycle of a project, from early design through procurement and implementation to ongoing operation.

It is also important to recognise that the consultant's authority is rarely formal. Unlike a contractor, the consultant does not usually hold delivery responsibility for physical assets or construction packages. Instead, their influence is exercised through advice, persuasion, and the credibility they bring to discussions. This makes the consultant highly sensitive to political and contractual complexities. Misjudging when to push a point or when to step back can create conflict, alienate stakeholders, or expose the consultant to risks that lie outside their scope of engagement.

The purpose of this chapter is to define that role clearly and to provide the reader with practical guidance on how to navigate it. The discussion will move through the project lifecycle, identifying the points at which a consultant adds the greatest value. It will then examine the management of stakeholders, the critical role of integration between disciplines, and the contractual limits that define professional boundaries. An example will demonstrate how these themes converge in a real-world scenario, while a set of best professional disciplines will provide a practical toolkit for avoiding common pitfalls.

By the end of this chapter, the reader should not only understand the theoretical role of the consultant but also have the insight needed to apply it in practice, positioning themselves as trusted and credible contributors within the project ecosystem.

Project Lifecycle Mapping

Every project moves through a sequence of stages that together form its lifecycle. While terminology may differ between industries, the underlying pattern is consistent: concept, design, procurement, implementation, and operation. Each of these stages creates different demands on the consultant and calls for a shifting balance between leadership, advisory, and observational roles. Understanding this lifecycle is essential for a consultant to know where they fit, where they can add value, and where they risk stepping beyond their remit.

At the concept stage, the project is little more than an idea, often driven by strategic needs such as expanding capacity, improving resilience, or complying with regulation. This is the stage where consultants are typically engaged to provide feasibility assessments, threat and vulnerability studies, or high-level design advice. The consultant's value lies in framing the problem correctly, helping the client articulate objectives, and translating broad ambitions into clear technical and operational requirements. For example, a client may state that they want a secure data centre, but without guidance this ambition is meaningless. The consultant can clarify whether the priority is resilience against hostile intrusion, protection from insider threats, or compliance with a specific regulatory framework. At this stage, the consultant's influence is strongest, since early advice can shape the direction of the project.

As the project moves into the design stage, the consultant's role shifts from problem framing to solution definition. Here the consultant works with architects, engineers, and specialist designers to translate requirements into practical layouts and specifications. It is during this phase that conflicts often arise between security and other design priorities, such as aesthetics, circulation, or cost efficiency. The consultant must learn to operate as a translator, ensuring that security requirements are understood in terms that other professionals can act upon. For example, specifying a mantrap at the entrance to a critical facility is a security need, but the architect may view it as a disruption to the intended flow of people through the building. The consultant's role is not only to insist on the requirement but also to explain the rationale in ways that align with the architect's perspective, perhaps by showing how security features can be integrated into the overall design language. The consultant's effectiveness at this stage depends heavily on their credibility and the trust that they establish with other design disciplines.

The procurement stage presents a very different set of challenges. Here, consultants are often asked to prepare technical specifications, assist in tender evaluations, or provide impartial advice on vendor proposals. The consultant's neutrality is critical. Unlike contractors or suppliers, the consultant must not have a commercial interest in the outcome of procurement, as this would undermine their independence. Clients rely on consultants to ensure that specifications are robust, performance requirements are measurable, and evaluation criteria are transparent. At the same time, consultants must recognise the political pressures that often surround procurement. Large contracts attract lobbying from vendors and integrators, and clients may have preferences shaped by existing relationships. The consultant's role is to protect the integrity of the process, ensuring that security requirements are not diluted by commercial considerations and that all bidders are treated fairly.

Implementation is the stage most people associate with construction or system deployment. For the consultant, this is not about managing trades or installing equipment but about design assurance. The consultant ensures that contractors are building to specification, that changes are governed properly, and that shortcuts are not taken under the pressure of time or budget. Typical tasks include reviewing shop drawings, attending site inspections, and witnessing testing and commissioning. Authority at this stage is limited. Consultants do not usually hold contractual power over contractors and must work through the client's project manager or contract administrator. They must be especially careful not to give direct instructions to contractors without the authority to do so, as this can expose them to liability for costs or delays arising from such actions. Effectiveness therefore depends on a careful balance: asserting technical standards firmly while respecting contractual boundaries. Overstepping risks liability, while underplaying the role risks defects being missed.

The last stage is operation, which is often overlooked by consultants who disengage once the construction phase is complete. In reality, operation is where the consultant's earlier work is tested in practice. Post-occupancy evaluations, audits, and optimisation exercises are invaluable for both the client and the consultant. For the client, they provide assurance that the systems delivered are performing as intended and that operational staff are using them effectively. For the consultant, they provide feedback that can inform future projects and strengthen credibility. This stage is also where consultants can demonstrate long-term value, positioning themselves not only as designers but as partners in the continuous improvement of security. For example, conducting a review six months after handover may reveal that staff are bypassing certain security features because they interfere with daily routines. This insight allows the consultant to recommend adjustments, balancing security effectiveness with operational practicality.

Different industries formalise the project lifecycle in different ways. The RIBA Plan of Work in the UK, the PMI lifecycle promoted through the Project Management Institute, and ISO 21500:2021[14] on project management all provide structured frameworks for describing these phases. While the terminology varies, the principles are aligned: projects move from initiation to definition, from execution to closure, and consultants must adapt their role accordingly. The value of referencing such frameworks is that they provide a common language across disciplines. When a consultant explains their role using a recognised lifecycle framework, it reassures clients and collaborators that their approach is systematic, not improvised.

It is also worth noting that not every consultant is engaged across the full lifecycle. In some cases, the consultant may only be contracted for a specific stage, such as preparing a risk assessment during concept design or reviewing tender responses during procurement. While these engagements can be valuable, they limit the consultant's influence. Without continuity across stages, the consultant risks having their recommendations diluted or misinterpreted. For example, a consultant who produces a comprehensive threat assessment at the concept stage may find that their recommendations are watered down during procurement if they are not present to defend them. Conversely, being engaged across all stages allows the consultant to maintain consistency and integrity of intent, but it also exposes them to a wider range of political and contractual risks.

In practice, consultants must be flexible. In one project they may be the lead advisor throughout, guiding the client from feasibility to operation. In another they may be one of several advisors, stepping in only to provide specialist input at a key stage. The challenge is to understand the boundaries of each engagement, to maximise influence without overstepping contractual roles, and to adapt style and approach to the demands of the project lifecycle stage.

Mapping the consultant's role against the lifecycle is not simply an academic exercise. It is a practical framework that helps consultants answer three essential questions: Where am I adding value? Where do I risk overreach? Where must I step back? By revisiting these questions at each stage of the lifecycle, the consultant can remain aligned with both client expectations and professional boundaries, ensuring that their contribution strengthens the project rather than complicating it.

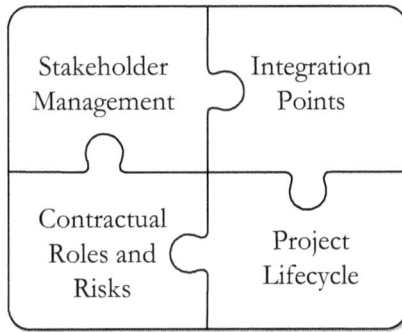

Figure 11 Elements of the Consultant's Role

Project Stage	Security Consultant	Designer / Engineer	Integrator / Contractor	Operator / Client Team
Concept / Feasibility	R – Lead risk assessment and concept definition.	C – Advise on design viability.	I – Provide budget/practical input.	C – Define operational intent.
Schematic Design	A – Approve security concept and requirements.	R – Develop coordinated layouts.	C – Advise on buildability.	I – Review functional alignment.
Detailed Design	C – Support specification and standards review.	R – Produce construction drawings, BoQs.	C – Verify integration feasibility.	I – Provide O&M perspective.
Tender / Procurement	R – Prepare evaluation criteria, technical clarifications.	C – Support tender documentation.	R – Submit proposals and compliance data.	A – Approve preferred bidder.
Construction / Implementation	C – Monitor compliance with design intent.	C – Respond to site queries.	R – Install, configure, test.	I – Witness progress and quality.

Project Stage	Security Consultant	Designer / Engineer	Integrator / Contractor	Operator / Client Team
Commissioning / Handover	R – Validate performance, witness FAT/SAT.	C – Confirm design acceptance.	R – Provide documentation, training.	A – Accept system and sign off.
Operation / Maintenance	C – Conduct post-occupancy reviews.	I – Advise on upgrades.	C – Provide technical support.	R / A – Operate and maintain systems.

Table 6 Project Lifecycle RACI for the Security Strand

Stakeholder Management

Every project involves a web of stakeholders, each with their own priorities and pressures. The consultant's ability to navigate these relationships is often the key factor in a project's success. Technical expertise may secure a seat at the table, but it is stakeholder management that ensures advice is acted upon.

The primary stakeholders in most security projects can be grouped into four categories: the client, contractors, regulators, and integrators. Secondary actors such as operations staff, finance teams, and end users may appear peripheral but often wield significant influence over how security measures are perceived and adopted.

The client relationship is fundamental. Clients engage consultants to provide expertise they lack, and they expect advice that is technically sound and aligned with organisational goals. Some clients are sophisticated project owners; others are embarking on a major development for the first time. In either case, clarity and transparency are vital. The principles of *Flawless Consulting*[3] emphasise the importance of an explicit contracting conversation at the outset – not the legal contract, but a discussion of mutual expectations. Defining what success looks like, what the consultant can and cannot deliver, and what support the client must provide helps prevent later disappointment and builds trust.

Trust is central because the consultant's authority is rarely formal. Unlike a contractor who can issue instructions, the consultant relies on influence built on competence, clear communication, and integrity. Credibility comes from expertise applied in context. Communication means making technical content accessible without diluting accuracy. Integrity requires honesty, even when pointing out uncomfortable truths such as underfunded budgets or unrealistic schedules.

Contractors represent a different dynamic. Their priority is delivery under commercial pressure, and they may see the consultant as an obstacle. The consultant must balance enforcing standards with being practical to avoid creating conflict. Explaining requirements in terms of protecting the contractor's reputation or avoiding costly rectification often proves more persuasive than abstract technical arguments.

Regulators bring another layer of complexity. Their role is to enforce codes and statutory requirements. Consultants frequently act as translators, aligning regulatory intent with practical design solutions. Proactive engagement builds credibility and can prevent costly redesigns later.

Integrators are often the most challenging group. They straddle design and delivery, and they may have commercial ties to particular technologies. The consultant must guard impartiality by articulating performance requirements, resisting pressure for proprietary solutions unless they genuinely add value, and keeping long-term client interests paramount.

Beyond these formal groups lie subtler politics. Departments may compete for influence, with IT resisting integration on its networks or facilities staff objecting to measures they see as disruptive. Here the consultant's role is to depersonalise conflict by reframing issues around shared outcomes such as resilience, compliance, or operational continuity.

Managing stakeholders requires adaptability. At times the consultant must lead, such as when presenting to a board or defending a design requirement. At other times they must step back, advise, or simply observe. Knowing which posture to adopt requires judgement and humility. Overreaching creates resentment, under-reaching risks irrelevance.

Cultural sensitivity is also essential. In some jurisdictions regulators expect consultants to adopt an authoritative stance; in others deference is the norm. Multinational corporations may expect alignment with internal governance, while family-owned businesses may rely more on personal trust. Recognising these differences prevents missteps and preserves credibility.

Stakeholder management is about balance. The consultant must be credible without arrogance, assertive without rigidity, and influential without dominating. Those who master this balance find their advice acted upon and their role valued well beyond their formal authority.

Influence in consultancy is achieved through structure, not authority. Mapping the lifecycle, managing stakeholders, and respecting contractual boundaries allow the consultant to lead through evidence, not control.

Integration Points

Security is one of many disciplines that must come together to create a functioning project. The consultant's role is not to impose security as a standalone element but to integrate it into the broader framework of design, technology, and operations. The quality of this integration often determines whether security measures are accepted, effective, and sustainable, or whether they are resisted, bypassed, or quietly undermined.

The most obvious point of integration is with architecture. Buildings are the physical containers of security measures, and every architectural decision affects how security can be delivered. Circulation routes, entrances, glazing, landscaping, and mechanical plant areas all have security implications. A consultant who fails to integrate with the architectural team risks producing recommendations that are impractical, unattractive, or prohibitively expensive. Conversely, early integration can transform security from an afterthought into a natural component of design. Crime Prevention Through Environmental Design (CPTED) is a clear example. Its principles show how the arrangement of spaces, lighting, and sightlines can reinforce natural surveillance and territorial reinforcement, reducing the need for intrusive technology. Consultants who can translate CPTED concepts into architectural language make security an enabler of design rather than an obstacle.

Integration with IT and operational technology is increasingly critical. Modern security systems rely on networks, servers, and software, blurring the boundary between physical and cyber domains. Access control platforms interface with human resources databases, video surveillance systems stream across corporate networks, and perimeter sensors feed into integrated monitoring platforms. For consultants, this means working alongside IT professionals who may have different priorities. Whereas the security consultant might prioritise resilience and redundancy, the IT manager may focus on minimising bandwidth consumption or enforcing corporate cybersecurity policies. Conflicts are common, such as when IT departments resist deploying video storage servers on their network due to capacity concerns, or when security teams specify proprietary systems that clash with enterprise IT strategies. The consultant's role is to bridge these divides, explaining to IT teams why certain security requirements are non-negotiable, while also encouraging security contractors to align with enterprise standards.

Operational teams are another essential integration point. No matter how advanced the systems or how refined the design, it is the operational staff who will live with the outcomes. Security officers, facilities managers, and end users often have practical insights that consultants overlook. For example, a consultant may specify biometric readers at all staff entrances for identity assurance, only to find that operational staff struggle to manage throughput during peak hours. Involving these teams early ensures that security solutions are workable in practice. Moreover, operational staff are the ones who either comply with or bypass systems. If a security design makes their jobs harder without adding perceived value, they may disable features or find workarounds. Consultants who engage operational stakeholders avoid these pitfalls and foster a culture where security is respected rather than resisted.

Integration also extends to business processes. Many organisations treat security as a technical system rather than a management function, but consultants who understand business integration add significant value. Linking access control databases with HR processes ensures that staff departures trigger immediate revocation of access rights. Aligning incident response procedures between the physical security operations centre and the IT security operations centre ensures that cyber and physical events are detected, correlated, and managed together. These are not technical details but strategic alignments that improve resilience across the organisation. Consultants who can position security as part of enterprise risk management find their advice more readily accepted at board level.

The practical reality of integration is that it often involves friction. Architects may resist visible security features that compromise their design vision. IT managers may object to security devices that do not conform to corporate standards. Contractors may prefer simpler, less integrated solutions that reduce their risk. The consultant's role is to mediate, translate, and align. This requires an ability to understand enough of each discipline to speak its language. With architects, this might mean showing how bollards can be integrated into landscaping as seating rather than appearing as hostile barriers. With IT teams, it might involve demonstrating how video compression standards reduce network load. With operations, it may require conducting walkthroughs to demonstrate how security features support their routines rather than hinder them.

When such friction is not managed, it leads to failed integration. Security added late or treated as a bolt-on often results in retrofits, cost overruns, or systems that do not function properly. For example, placing large cameras on a façade without consulting architects can create visual intrusion that the client later demands to remove. Likewise, failing to coordinate with IT may leave a surveillance system unable to connect to the enterprise network, forcing the installation of costly standalone infrastructure. These failures weaken client confidence and damage the consultant's credibility.

A consultant who masters integration gains a powerful advantage. They are no longer seen as a narrow specialist but as a collaborator who understands the bigger picture. This positions them as a trusted advisor at senior levels of the organisation. Integration therefore extends beyond technical necessity to professional identity. By demonstrating that security can coexist with design, technology, and operations, the consultant shows that they are not merely protecting assets but enabling projects to succeed holistically.

Integration points define the consultant's real contribution. Technical expertise provides the foundation, but it is integration that determines whether security is accepted and sustainable. By working effectively with architects, IT specialists, and operational teams, and by framing security as part of wider business processes, the consultant ensures that their advice is not only implemented but valued. Integration is not a technical add-on but a core part of the consultant's role in the project ecosystem.

Contractual Roles and Risks

The consultant's place in a project is defined not only by technical expertise and stakeholder relationships but also by contractual boundaries. A consultant who does not understand these boundaries risks liability exposure, reputational damage, and strained client relationships. Contractual awareness is therefore as important as technical competence, and consultants must learn to protect both themselves and their clients by respecting the limits of their role.

One of the most important contractual principles is that consultants are advisers, not deliverers. Unlike contractors, they do not supply or install equipment, nor do they direct subcontractors. Their obligation is to provide professional advice, documentation, and assurance. This distinction is critical because liability is interpreted according to role: courts judge responsibility against the consultant's contractual remit, insurers underwrite cover on the same basis, and clients set their expectations accordingly. Stepping outside these boundaries exposes the consultant to claims that properly belong elsewhere. For example, if a consultant instructs a contractor to change a cable route without authorisation from the project manager, and the change causes delay or non-compliance, the consultant may be held responsible for consequences that should have remained with the contractor.

Limits of liability are a standard feature of consultancy contracts and deserve careful attention. Consultants typically cap their liability to a multiple of their fees, often linked to professional indemnity insurance. This is reasonable because consultants do not control budgets, schedules, or contractors, yet their advice may influence all three. Without limits of liability, a consultant could be exposed to claims vastly exceeding their remuneration. Clients sometimes resist liability caps, arguing that consultants should stand behind their advice fully. Consultants must be prepared to explain that professional indemnity insurance exists to protect both parties, and that unlimited liability would either make consultancy unaffordable or drive qualified professionals out of the market.

Intellectual property rights are another area of frequent misunderstanding. Consultants produce reports, specifications, and designs that have intellectual property value. The default position in many jurisdictions is that the consultant retains ownership of intellectual property while granting the client a licence to use it for the project.

Clients, however, often expect outright ownership. Consultants must strike a balance: protecting their intellectual capital while allowing clients to use deliverables freely within the intended scope. Problems arise when clients attempt to use consultant designs on projects beyond the original commission without agreement. Equally, consultants must avoid recycling confidential client material for other projects. Clarity in contracts about ownership and permitted use is essential to avoid disputes.

Scope creep is a persistent risk in consultancy engagements. It occurs when the client's expectations expand beyond the agreed deliverables without a corresponding adjustment in fees or time. Scope creep is rarely malicious; more often it is the natural result of evolving projects. However, unmanaged scope creep undermines profitability and can create resentment. Consultants must learn to recognise when requests fall outside of scope and to manage them through change control. This does not mean refusing reasonable client requests but rather ensuring that all parties are aware of the implications. A clear scope of services at the outset, supported by a process for managing variations, is the best defence.

Change control and governance are closely related. Projects inevitably evolve, and consultants must be part of the mechanism that manages change. Good governance requires that changes are documented, evaluated for cost and risk impact, and approved at the right level. Consultants can add value by ensuring that security implications are considered in every change, from altering floor layouts to substituting equipment. However, consultants must resist the temptation to approve changes unilaterally. Approval belongs to the client and their appointed contract administrator. The consultant's role is to advise, to document, and to highlight risks, not to authorise on behalf of the client.

Commercial consulting practice outside of the security field reinforces these principles. Alan Weiss, in his work on management consulting, emphasises the importance of clear contracting and disciplined scope management. McKinsey consultants have long been trained to define governance structures that prevent scope drift. These general consulting practices translate directly into security consultancy. The consultant who behaves like a professional service provider rather than a technical hobbyist earns greater respect and avoids many common disputes.

Ethical boundaries also form part of contractual responsibility. Consultants must avoid conflicts of interest that compromise their independence. A consultant who specifies a particular product while receiving undisclosed commissions from the vendor is breaching professional integrity and exposing both themselves and their client to risk. Similarly, consultants should not allow contractors to blur lines by offering inducements in exchange for favourable recommendations. Transparency, independence, and integrity are essential, and contracts should reinforce them by prohibiting referral fees or undisclosed incentives.

The risks of ignoring contractual boundaries are significant. Consultants who assume authority they do not possess may be exposed to claims for delays, cost overruns, or system failures. Consultants who neglect intellectual property rights may find their work reused without recognition or remuneration. Consultants who fail to manage scope creep may undermine their own financial viability. Conversely, consultants who understand and respect contractual roles are better positioned to deliver value while protecting themselves.

Practical strategies help reinforce these boundaries. Clear documentation is one. Every piece of advice, every review, and every observation should be recorded and communicated formally. Informal conversations are useful for relationship building but dangerous if relied upon in disputes. Another strategy is professional indemnity insurance, which must be maintained at levels proportionate to the consultant's engagements. Consultants should cultivate the habit of saying no when requests fall outside of their remit, but in a way that remains constructive – not as rejection but as redirection into proper channels.

Contractual awareness does not diminish the consultant's influence; it strengthens it. Clients respect consultants who are clear about their boundaries and who operate professionally. Far from being an obstacle, contractual discipline demonstrates maturity and reliability. The consultant who respects contractual roles is more likely to be trusted with sensitive projects and long-term relationships.

The consultant's role is defined as much by what they do not do as by what they do. They are not contractors, project managers, or suppliers, and their liability, intellectual property, and scope must be managed accordingly. By maintaining clear contractual awareness, consultants protect their independence, their reputation, and their clients. This discipline allows them to focus on their true value: delivering independent advice, integrating security into the project ecosystem, and navigating complex stakeholder environments without being trapped by responsibilities that are not theirs to bear.

Illustrative Example: Physical–Cyber Integration with Conflicting Stakeholders

This example shows how the consultant's role in the project ecosystem plays out in practice. It follows the delivery of a data centre project requiring integration of physical and cyber security, illustrating how lifecycle awareness, stakeholder management, integration, and contractual discipline converge in a complex environment.

The project began with a client commissioning a new data centre to host sensitive government workloads. Concerned about both physical intrusion and cyber compromise, the board appointed a consultant to develop an integrated strategy. A threat and vulnerability assessment identified the need for layered barriers, robust access control, continuous surveillance, and alignment with the client's cyber monitoring systems. At this concept stage, the consultant's role was to lead, shaping objectives and setting the foundation for design.

As the design and procurement phases progressed, tensions emerged. The architect resisted perimeter measures that threatened the campus aesthetic, the IT integrator pressed for a proprietary platform, and the contractor promoted open-protocol devices. The consultant avoided rigidity, instead reframing each discussion around the client's overarching goal: a resilient and compliant facility. With the architect they explored design options that softened visual impact, with the IT integrator they insisted on interoperability testing, and with the contractor they supported the use of open standards while emphasising that integration would still require careful specification, configuration, and testing. Political pressures then surfaced during procurement, but the consultant maintained independence by documenting all advice, linking recommendations to performance requirements, and reinforcing governance so that final decisions rested with the client.

Implementation and operation created fresh challenges. During installation, the IT integrator tried to bypass certain physical controls, claiming that cyber measures made them unnecessary. The consultant resisted by recording the non-conformances and escalating them through the client's governance process rather than issuing instructions directly, which would have exceeded their authority. At handover, attention shifted to the operations teams. Cultural divides between physical and cyber staff threatened to undermine integration, with each group working to its own procedures. The consultant bridged this gap by running joint workshops and scenario exercises, helping the teams agree on shared protocols and establish a coordinated approach to incident response.

The lessons are clear. Consultants must adapt posture across the lifecycle: leading at concept stage, advising during design and procurement, and stepping back at implementation while safeguarding integrity through governance. Success rests on balancing stakeholder relationships, maintaining contractual discipline, and integrating not only systems but also organisational cultures. Above all, the case demonstrates that influence is more powerful than authority, and that the consultant's greatest contribution lies in enabling alignment across stakeholders towards a common objective.

Professional Disciplines

While frameworks and principles are valuable, consultants also need practical habits that guide daily work. Professional disciplines give consultants a framework for consistent practice. They are not rigid templates but reminders of behaviours that safeguard both consultant and client.

The first discipline is defining scope clearly. Consultants should ensure that their scope of services is unambiguous, documented, and confirmed with the client at the outset. This includes what is included, what is excluded, and what assumptions apply. Revisiting scope throughout the project helps to prevent creeping expectations and ensures additional work is agreed formally rather than absorbed informally.

The second discipline is maintaining change control. Projects inevitably evolve, but unmanaged changes undermine both security outcomes and consultant credibility. Every change should be documented, assessed for implications, and approved through the client's governance process. Consultants should avoid informal agreements, no matter how expedient, and use established procedures to reinforce transparency and fairness.

Governance itself forms the third discipline. Consultants should understand where they sit within project reporting lines and use these structures to protect their independence. Escalating disputes formally, rather than attempting informal resolution, prevents exposure to liability and strengthens credibility. Concise and timely reporting at governance meetings also builds trust and influence.

Independence is another essential practice. Consultants must avoid conflicts of interest, whether through vendor influence, referral fees, or personal relationships. By making independence explicit, and explaining that recommendations are based on objective analysis, consultants differentiate themselves from commercially driven parties and reassure clients of their neutrality.

Communication underpins all of these practices. Consultants should make technical advice accessible in plain English, respond promptly, and maintain transparency about progress and risks. Listening is as important as explaining. By engaging with stakeholder concerns, consultants frame security as a shared objective rather than an imposed requirement.

Disciplined record keeping provides continuity and protection. Advice, reviews, and observations should be documented systematically, creating an audit trail that supports accountability and builds a knowledge base for future work.

These practices may appear straightforward but are often neglected under pressure. Consultants who apply them consistently safeguard their independence, reduce risk, and demonstrate professionalism in every engagement.

Practice Guide

Security consultants rarely work in isolation; their value lies in understanding how to operate effectively within the wider project ecosystem. This chapter has shown how mapping the project lifecycle provides a framework for clarity, ensuring consultants know when to lead, when to advise, and when to step back. It has demonstrated that stakeholder management is as important as technical competence, requiring credibility, diplomacy, and adaptability across clients, regulators, contractors, integrators, and operational teams. It has emphasised that integration – with architecture, IT, operations, and business processes – is the difference between security measures being embedded and sustainable or resisted and bypassed. And it has reinforced that contractual discipline protects both consultants and clients, ensuring independence, proportionality, and professional credibility are not compromised.

Common errors present significant risks: overreaching into delivery roles, allowing scope to drift unchecked, neglecting to document advice, or failing to adapt style to the rhythms and politics of a project. These traps leave consultants exposed to liability, reputational damage, or irrelevance. Good practice comes in recognising and respecting professional boundaries, making expectations explicit from the outset, maintaining traceability of recommendations, and engaging governance processes rather than working around them. Consultants who communicate clearly, respect scope, and manage integration proactively are those who gain trust and repeat engagement.

The overarching lesson is that influence outweighs authority. Consultants succeed not by issuing instructions but by shaping decisions through evidence, reasoning, and trust. By aligning their role with lifecycle stages, adapting posture to stakeholder dynamics, and maintaining ethical independence, consultants ensure their advice is both credible and acted upon.

This ecosystem perspective sets the stage for the next chapters, where the consultant moves from positioning within projects to the skills of winning the work, defining scope, and building lasting professional relationships. Mastery of role, relationships, and boundaries is therefore not the end of consultancy practice – it is the foundation upon which all future engagements depend.

Chapter 13 – Winning The Work

Every consultancy project begins with the same challenge: securing the engagement. Winning work is not about aggressive selling but about establishing trust, demonstrating credibility, and setting the tone for the entire relationship. Success depends not on selling harder, but on demonstrating value, credibility, and clarity to potential clients. Consultants must avoid the twin dangers of overpromising and under-pricing, both of which can lead to disputes and damaged relationships. This chapter explores how to qualify opportunities, prepare compelling proposals, and set the foundations for trust.

By the end of this chapter, you will be able to:

- Recognise the difference between formal tenders and informal opportunities and position themselves effectively in both.
- Write proposals that emphasise outcomes and value rather than just deliverables.
- Apply value-based pricing approaches, linking fees to measurable benefits, return on investment, or avoided loss.
- Define scope clearly to prevent disputes and avoid the trap of scope creep.
- Use a client qualification checklist to decide which opportunities are worth pursuing.
- Reframe weak proposals into strong, winning documents through structured improvement.

Introduction

Winning consultancy work is not simply about sales techniques or aggressive pricing. It is about establishing trust and demonstrating that the consultant can deliver insight, clarity, and value. Unlike products, consultancy cannot be evaluated in advance; it is intangible until delivered. This means clients must make decisions based on confidence in the consultant's credibility, expertise, and integrity. For this reason, consultancy is often described as a business built on trust rather than transactions.

The process of securing work begins long before a proposal is submitted. Reputation, visibility, and networks play a significant role in shaping opportunities. Clients often prefer consultants they already know or who come recommended by trusted peers. This is because risk is inherent in buying consultancy. A poorly performing consultant can waste resources, derail projects, or expose the organisation to reputational damage. To reduce that risk, clients favour advisors who appear credible, reliable, and aligned with their values. The consultant's task is therefore to demonstrate expertise in ways that reassure decision-makers. This may involve publishing articles, presenting at conferences, or maintaining strong professional relationships that position the consultant as a trusted authority.

At the same time, consultants must be wary of overpromising. In the effort to win work, it can be tempting to assure clients that every objective can be met within tight budgets and timelines. Such commitments may secure the project initially, but they almost always lead to disputes later. Scope creep, missed deadlines, and budget overruns are often the consequence of proposals that prioritised winning the contract over delivering realistic value. Trust is eroded quickly when promises are not met, and reputations built over years can be lost in a single project. The disciplined consultant therefore approaches proposals with honesty and proportion, balancing the need to secure work with the need to protect credibility.

Pricing is another dimension where trust is central. Clients often lack a clear sense of what consultancy should cost, particularly when comparing firms of different sizes and structures. Some consultants respond by pricing low in order to undercut competitors, hoping to secure work by appearing cost-effective. In practice, this strategy often backfires. Low prices can signal inexperience or desperation, and they rarely sustain the resources needed to deliver quality outcomes. The result is dissatisfied clients and a consultant trapped in a cycle of undervaluing their expertise. A more effective approach is to link fees to value – showing clients how consultancy creates return on investment, prevents losses, or enables opportunities that outweigh the cost. This reframes consultancy from an expense to an enabler, strengthening the client's confidence that the engagement will be worthwhile.

Another critical aspect of trust lies in scoping. Ambiguous proposals, where deliverables and responsibilities are left vague, almost always create conflict. Clients may expect more than the consultant intended, while consultants may feel pressured to take on additional work without compensation. This damages relationships and undermines future opportunities. Clear scope definition, by contrast, provides a framework for accountability. It clarifies expectations on both sides, reduces the likelihood of disputes, and positions the consultant as a professional who values transparency.

We must also acknowledge the duality of opportunity: formal and informal. Formal tender processes, with their rigid structures and evaluation criteria, appear objective but are often influenced by prior relationships and reputations. Informal opportunities, arising from networks, recommendations, and chance conversations, may bypass formal processes entirely. Consultants must learn to operate effectively in both environments, recognising when to invest time in lengthy tender submissions and when to cultivate relationships that create opportunities before tenders are even released.

Winning consultancy work is about aligning expertise with trust. Proposals, pricing, and scoping are mechanisms for demonstrating credibility, but they are secondary to the consultant's reputation and integrity. Clients decide whom to engage based on a combination of rational evaluation and instinctive confidence. Consultants who are clear, honest, and consistent in their engagements build long-term relationships that extend beyond single projects. Those who chase work through overpromising or under-pricing may win in the short term but lose in the long run.

This chapter will therefore explore the practical dimensions of winning work: how to approach tenders and informal opportunities, how to write proposals that focus on outcomes, how to scope and price to avoid disputes, and how to qualify clients before committing effort. The focus is not on aggressive sales techniques but on sustaining credibility and trust – the currency on which consultancy depends.

Tender Processes and Informal Opportunities

Consultancy work is secured through two broad pathways: formal tenders and informal opportunities. Both demand different skills, and both carry risks as well as advantages. A consultant who understands how these channels operate, and how to position themselves effectively within them, is far more likely to secure meaningful projects than one who relies solely on chance or habit.

Formal tenders are structured procurement exercises, often mandated in government contracts and increasingly common in large corporations. They are designed to provide transparency and fairness by inviting multiple firms to submit proposals against a set of requirements. The process typically includes a request for proposal (RFP) or invitation to tender (ITT), detailed submission guidelines, evaluation criteria, and strict deadlines. From the client's perspective, tenders provide a way to demonstrate impartiality, achieve competitive pricing, and document compliance with procurement rules. For consultants, tenders represent access to significant projects, but they also require substantial investment of time and resources.

A strong tender submission begins with understanding the scoring criteria. Most RFPs break evaluation into weighted categories such as technical capability, methodology, past experience, and price. Consultants who simply recycle generic proposals rarely score well, because evaluators look for tailored responses that demonstrate alignment with the specific project objectives. This means consultants must read the tender carefully, analyse what the client values most, and structure their responses accordingly. For example, if innovation carries a high weighting, the proposal should emphasise novel approaches, whereas if experience is paramount, case histories must be prominent.

Another challenge in tendering is the sheer volume of competition. Larger firms may dominate shortlists due to brand recognition, while smaller consultancies can struggle to stand out. Yet smaller firms often succeed by focusing on niches, emphasising agility, and offering personalised service. Consultants must therefore position themselves clearly: rather than attempting to appear all things to all clients, they should highlight distinctive strengths that differentiate them from competitors.

Despite their structured appearance, tenders are rarely as objective as they seem. Pre-existing relationships often play a significant role in shaping outcomes. Clients are more likely to select firms they trust, even when evaluation appears numerical. This does not mean the process is corrupt, but rather that procurement teams are influenced by credibility and confidence as much as by written scores. Consultants must therefore recognise that reputation and visibility, cultivated before the tender is issued, strongly affect results. Networking, thought leadership, and past performance all help ensure that when a tender is released, the consultant is already seen as a credible contender.

In contrast, informal opportunities arise through relationships, networks, and reputation. They are not governed by rigid processes but by trust and timing. A chance conversation at a conference, a referral from a past client, or a reputation established through publications can all generate opportunities without an RFP. Informal channels are particularly important for boutique consultancies and independent practitioners, who may not have the resources to compete in large tender processes. These opportunities often allow greater scope for tailoring engagements to client needs, and they frequently lead to more collaborative and less adversarial relationships.

Cultivating informal opportunities requires a different set of skills from tendering. Consultants must invest in visibility, ensuring that potential clients are aware of their expertise before a need arises. This can involve writing articles, speaking at industry events, or sharing insights on professional networks. It also involves maintaining relationships with past clients, checking in periodically, and offering advice without always expecting immediate work. Trust is built over time, and informal opportunities often go to consultants who are already perceived as part of the client's trusted circle.

The danger with informal opportunities is over-familiarity. Consultants who rely too heavily on personal networks may fail to diversify their client base, leaving themselves vulnerable to changes in personnel or budget priorities. They may also face accusations of favouritism if engagements bypass competitive procurement. For this reason, even informal work must be documented with clear proposals, scopes, and contracts. Professional discipline should not be sacrificed for convenience.

Balancing formal and informal approaches is essential. Formal tenders can provide access to large, high-profile projects, but they are resource-intensive and often heavily weighted in favour of established players. Informal opportunities can be faster to secure and more tailored, but they require long-term relationship building and may be more vulnerable to changes in personal networks. Successful consultants operate in both spaces, recognising that opportunities are shaped by reputation as much as by paperwork.

A practical strategy is to treat every engagement, whether won formally or informally, as an investment in future opportunities. Delivering excellent work, maintaining integrity, and leaving clients with a positive impression increases the likelihood of repeat work and referrals. Similarly, publishing insights and contributing to professional debates builds a reputation that positions the consultant for informal approaches. Over time, these investments reduce reliance on resource-heavy tender processes, as clients begin to approach the consultant directly.

Tenders and informal opportunities represent two complementary paths to winning consultancy work. Formal processes require precision, tailoring, and significant investment of effort. Informal opportunities demand visibility, relationship-building, and trust cultivated over time. Both require professional discipline and integrity. Consultants who understand how to operate effectively in both contexts maximise their chances of securing meaningful projects, while those who rely solely on one approach risk being either commoditised in tenders or dependent on personal networks. Winning the work, therefore, is not about luck or aggressiveness, but about building credibility and trust across multiple channels.

Credibility
- Reputation
- Integrity
- Thought Leadership

Sustainable Consultancy Practice

Clarity
- Transparency
- Defined Deliverables
- Realistic Commitments

Value
- Value-based pricing
- Results Over Activity
- Aligned Expectations

Figure 12 Winning Values – Building Credibility

Proposals that Win

Proposals are the primary vehicle through which consultants translate their expertise into commitments that clients can evaluate. They are more than administrative documents; they are opportunities to demonstrate understanding, differentiate from competitors, and persuade clients that engaging the consultant will create tangible value. Winning proposals do not simply respond to requirements – they show insight into the client's challenges and present a credible pathway to outcomes that matter.

The first principle of strong proposals is clarity of problem definition. Many clients issue briefs or RFPs that are vague, contradictory, or incomplete. Simply restating the brief in a proposal does little to inspire confidence. Consultants must demonstrate that they have understood the underlying challenge, not just the surface request. This requires careful reading of the documents, but also critical interpretation. If a tender asks for a "review of security systems," for example, the consultant should frame this in terms of resilience, risk reduction, or compliance outcomes, showing the client that they see beyond the literal wording. Clarifying the real problem signals professionalism and reassures the client that the consultant will not only deliver tasks but solve problems.

The second principle is to focus on outcomes rather than activities. Many weak proposals focus on activities rather than outcomes – how many site visits, how many interviews, how many pages of report. While detail has its place, clients are less interested in how busy the consultant will be than in what will change as a result. A winning proposal articulates outcomes such as reduced risk, improved compliance, greater stakeholder confidence, or cost savings. The consultant must link deliverables to benefits, shifting the narrative from inputs to results. This approach frames the engagement as an investment with a return, rather than as a cost to be minimised.

Structure is also vital. Proposals that are confusing, overly technical, or poorly organised create doubt about the consultant's ability to deliver clear and structured advice. A strong proposal tells a coherent story: here is the challenge, here is why it matters, here is how we will address it, and here is what you will gain. Each section should flow logically, using clear language and avoiding jargon that alienates non-specialist readers. Even technical appendices should be written with clarity, ensuring that decision-makers of different backgrounds can understand the key messages. Consultants should remember that proposals are often read by mixed audiences – procurement teams, technical specialists, and executives – each of whom must find the document credible.

Differentiation is another key element. Clients may receive dozens of submissions, many of which look and sound similar. To stand out, a consultant must highlight what makes their approach distinctive. This may be deep sector experience, an innovative methodology, or a track record of delivering results in similar contexts. Differentiation should be credible and evidenced; vague claims of being "innovative" or "client-focused" mean little without concrete examples. Case studies and references provide powerful support, showing that the consultant has not only proposed but delivered.

Tone matters too. Proposals that are arrogant or dismissive of competitors can alienate clients, just as those that are defensive or apologetic undermine confidence. The most effective tone is confident but respectful, professional but approachable. Clients must feel that the consultant is a partner who understands their challenges, not a vendor trying to impress with jargon or grandiose claims. Clarity, humility, and a focus on the client's interests create trust.

Another important consideration is risk acknowledgement. Many proposals attempt to present engagements as risk-free, as though the consultant can guarantee flawless delivery regardless of circumstances. This is rarely credible. Clients know that projects face uncertainties, whether from access limitations, changing regulations, or stakeholder resistance. A winning proposal acknowledges risks openly and explains how they will be managed. This demonstrates realism and preparedness, qualities that clients value. It also distinguishes the consultant from competitors who overpromise.

Proposals should also demonstrate efficiency. Clients often worry about consultants producing lengthy reports that gather dust. By outlining how findings will be communicated concisely, in formats tailored to different audiences, the consultant can show that they respect the client's time and decision-making needs. Offering options such as executive summaries, presentations, or workshops helps reassure clients that outputs will be practical and usable.

Price presentation is part of the proposal's effectiveness. While the detailed discussion of pricing belongs to the next section, the way fees are framed in the proposal influences client perception. Linking fees explicitly to outcomes and value is more persuasive than presenting them as hourly rates or lump sums. A consultant who shows that their work will reduce losses, avoid regulatory penalties, or improve efficiency positions their fee as an investment rather than a cost.

A practical way to develop strong proposals is through storyboarding before writing. By mapping out the structure and key messages visually, consultants can ensure the proposal tells a coherent story before filling in details. This technique, borrowed from disciplines such as design and communication, prevents disjointed submissions and helps focus on outcomes. Storyboarding also enables team input, ensuring that subject matter experts, writers, and project managers align before drafting begins.

To illustrate the difference between weak and strong proposals, consider the following exercise. A weak proposal might state: "We will conduct ten site visits, hold fifteen interviews, and produce a 100-page report on your current security systems." While technically responsive, it offers little insight. A stronger version would read: "Our engagement will assess your current systems against international best practice, identify vulnerabilities that could expose your operations, and provide a prioritised action plan to strengthen resilience. We will conduct site visits and interviews to ensure recommendations reflect your operational reality, and we will present findings in both a concise executive briefing and a detailed technical report." The second version links activities to outcomes, demonstrates understanding, and reassures the client that outputs will be practical.

Proposals that win share several qualities: they define the problem clearly, focus on outcomes, differentiate credibly, maintain a confident but respectful tone, acknowledge risks, and demonstrate efficiency. They are structured coherently and tailored to the client's context. Consultants who approach proposals in this way build trust and stand out in competitive fields. Weak proposals, by contrast, recycle generic text, emphasise activities over outcomes, and create doubt about the consultant's ability to deliver. The proposal is often the client's first serious impression of the consultant's thinking. Getting it right is not just about winning the work but about establishing the credibility that underpins the entire engagement.

Winning consultancy work is not about persuasion through price but through clarity of value. Credibility, proportion, and transparency create trust long before any proposal is read.

Pricing Strategies

Few aspects of consultancy generate as much uncertainty as pricing. Clients often struggle to understand why consultancy fees vary so widely, while consultants themselves frequently wrestle with how to price services in ways that are both competitive and sustainable. Getting it wrong has serious consequences. Under-pricing undermines credibility and profitability, while overpricing can exclude the consultant from opportunities. Effective pricing strategies are therefore not simply about numbers but about positioning, trust, and the ability to demonstrate value.

The most common pricing model is time-and-materials, where clients pay for the hours worked plus any associated costs. This approach appears transparent: the client knows exactly what they are paying for, and the consultant is compensated for the time invested. However, it also creates drawbacks. Time-based billing encourages a focus on inputs rather than outcomes. Clients may resent bills that grow as hours accumulate, while consultants may feel pressured to demonstrate busyness rather than efficiency. In some cases, time-based billing also discourages innovation, as consultants receive no reward for completing work more quickly or producing disproportionate value.

A second model is the fixed-price contract, where the consultant agrees to deliver a defined scope for a set fee. This provides clarity for both sides and encourages efficiency. The client knows the cost in advance, and the consultant is incentivised to deliver within budget and time constraints. The risk lies in scope definition. If the project expands beyond the agreed deliverables, disputes often arise. Consultants can find themselves delivering significant additional work without additional compensation, while clients may feel frustrated when consultants attempt to renegotiate fees mid-project. For this reason, fixed-price contracts are only effective when scoping is rigorous and both sides are disciplined about change control.

An alternative approach is value-based pricing, a concept popularised in consulting by Alan Weiss. Instead of linking fees to hours or deliverables, this model ties them to the value the client derives from the engagement. If a consultant's work reduces risks that could cause multimillion-dollar losses, the fee is framed as a fraction of that avoided cost. If advice enables new business opportunities or increases efficiency, the consultant's fee is positioned relative to the resulting gains. Value-based pricing reframes consultancy from an expense to an investment. Clients are less concerned about how many hours are worked when they see a direct link between the consultant's advice and their own success.

Implementing value-based pricing requires confidence and skill. Consultants must be able to articulate the client's potential return on investment and have the courage to link fees to outcomes. This means asking searching questions during the initial conversations: What is the cost of the risk if left unaddressed? What revenue opportunities could this project unlock? What reputational damage could be avoided by proactive action? By quantifying the stakes, consultants can justify fees that reflect the value delivered. This approach also aligns incentives: the client wants the consultant to succeed, because the benefits outweigh the costs.

However, value-based pricing is not without challenges. Some clients, particularly in the public sector, are constrained by procurement rules that favour time-based or fixed-fee models. Others may resist outcome-linked pricing if they feel benefits are too intangible or uncertain to quantify. Consultants must therefore adapt their pricing model to the context while still framing discussions around value. Even if the final contract is fixed-price or time-based, demonstrating the link between the engagement and the client's objectives strengthens trust and reduces the temptation to compare bids solely on cost.

A further strategy is the retainer model, where the consultant is paid a regular fee for ongoing access to expertise. This is common in legal or advisory services, and it provides stability for both client and consultant. Retainers are particularly valuable when the client's needs are continuous but unpredictable, such as ongoing regulatory support or advisory input during long projects. The risk is that if usage is low, clients may question the value of the arrangement. Consultants must therefore ensure that retainers are framed as access to readiness and availability, not just to billable hours.

Hybrid models also exist. Some consultants use a combination of fixed fees for defined deliverables with time-based rates for additional services, or they set a base fee supplemented by performance-related bonuses. These arrangements can work well if structured clearly, but they must avoid becoming overly complex. Simplicity aids trust, while opacity breeds suspicion. Consultants should therefore ensure that clients understand how fees are calculated and what they cover.

Regardless of the pricing model chosen, transparency is critical. Clients must feel that pricing is fair, proportionate, and aligned with outcomes. Hidden charges, ambiguous terms, or unexplained variations erode trust quickly. Clear proposals that explain how fees are structured, what they include, and under what circumstances they may change are essential. Consultants should also be prepared to explain their value directly, linking expertise, track record, and outcomes to the fee requested. This is particularly important when competing with lower-cost providers. Rather than racing to the bottom, consultants should emphasise quality, reliability, and the cost of failure if the engagement is mishandled.

It is also important to know when to walk away. Not every opportunity is worth pursuing, and clients who demand unsustainably low fees often create more problems than they are worth. Consultants who undervalue themselves risk resentment, financial strain, and reputational damage when corners are cut to make projects viable. Walking away from unviable opportunities protects the consultant's brand and allows focus on clients who appreciate and are willing to pay for value. In the long run, this strengthens rather than weakens the practice.

Pricing strategies are not simply financial calculations but reflections of how consultancy is positioned. Time-based billing, fixed-price contracts, value-based pricing, retainers, and hybrids all have their place, but each carries strengths and risks. The consultant's task is to choose models that align with context, communicate value clearly, and maintain transparency. Above all, pricing should reinforce trust rather than undermine it. When clients see fees as investments in outcomes, consultants secure not only projects but also long-term credibility and relationships.

Illustrative Example: Winning on Value, Not Price

A government agency issued a tender for a major security assessment across several critical facilities. The evaluation criteria gave heavy weighting to price, and many bidders responded by cutting margins aggressively. One consultancy submitted a bid 30 percent lower than the market average, hoping that low cost would compensate for weaker experience. Another consultancy took a different approach. Rather than focusing on inputs and price, it framed its proposal around outcomes: reduced exposure to regulatory penalties, improved resilience of national infrastructure, and a clear action plan for prioritising investment.

In pricing, this second consultancy applied a value-based model. Instead of listing only hours and tasks, it linked its fee to the cost of avoided failures. It demonstrated that even a single regulatory breach could result in fines far exceeding the consultancy fee, and that early remediation of vulnerabilities would save millions in potential losses. The proposal explicitly tied recommendations to measurable benefits, positioning the fee as an investment rather than an expense.

During evaluation, the low-priced bidder scored well on cost but poorly on methodology and credibility. Procurement officials grew concerned about whether the firm could deliver at the proposed rate, and whether corners would be cut to remain viable. The value-focused proposal, though more expensive, scored highly on technical credibility and outcomes. When weighted scoring was applied, the agency selected the second consultancy, citing confidence in its approach and the sustainability of its pricing.

Competing on price alone is risky: it erodes credibility, undermines quality, and often leads to disputes when delivery fails to match promises. Consultants who define scope precisely, link fees to outcomes, and frame proposals as the first demonstration of value stand out even in competitive tender environments. By positioning cost within the context of avoided risk and delivered benefit, they turn procurement from a price contest into a decision about trust and long-term impact.

Scoping and Avoiding Disputes

If pricing sets the commercial framework for a consultancy engagement, scope defines its boundaries. Clear scoping is one of the most important safeguards for both consultant and client, yet it is frequently neglected in the rush to secure work. Ambiguity over scope is one of the most common causes of disputes, cost overruns, and relationship breakdowns. Consultants who master the discipline of defining, negotiating, and documenting scope protect not only their profitability but also their professional credibility.

Scope is the description of what will be delivered, under what conditions, and to what level of detail. It sets expectations for both sides. Without it, clients may assume that all related issues are included, while consultants may believe that only narrow tasks are covered. The result is misalignment, frustration, and often the sense that one side is being taken advantage of. Clear scope creates transparency. It tells the client exactly what to expect and gives the consultant a defensible position if additional requests arise.

The first principle of effective scoping is precision. Vague phrases such as "review security arrangements" or "support risk management" are invitations to conflict. Consultants must specify exactly what will be reviewed, which areas will be covered, what outputs will be delivered, and what exclusions apply. A scope statement should identify deliverables in measurable terms – for example, "a report of approximately 50 pages, including a prioritised risk register and three alternative design options" – rather than leaving details implicit. Where possible, scope should also clarify what is not included. Explicit exclusions can prevent disputes by ensuring clients do not assume services will be provided outside the agreed terms.

The second principle is proportionality. Scope must be realistic in relation to the budget, timeframe, and resources. Overpromising in scope is as damaging as under-pricing in fees. Consultants sometimes accept wide or ambitious scopes in order to secure the work, only to discover later that they cannot deliver within the agreed parameters. This leads to stress, disputes, and reputational harm. It is better to negotiate scope honestly at the outset, even if this means scaling down expectations, than to disappoint clients later. Professional credibility rests on delivering what is promised, not on agreeing to anything and everything.

Negotiation is central to scoping. Clients may initially present broad or vague requirements, expecting the consultant to define the detail. Consultants must use this as an opportunity to demonstrate value. Asking clarifying questions, reframing the brief in terms of outcomes, and proposing structured deliverables all show professionalism. For example, if a client requests "a review of site security," the consultant might propose "a TVRA-based assessment of physical security systems at three sites, resulting in a prioritised list of vulnerabilities and recommended mitigation options." This reframes a broad request into a precise, actionable scope. Clients often appreciate this clarity, as it shows the consultant has thought through the work carefully.

Another element of scoping is boundaries of responsibility. Consultants must be explicit about their role in relation to other parties. If a consultant is providing advisory input only, this must be stated clearly to avoid liability for implementation failures. If subcontractors are involved, their responsibilities should be defined. Consultants should also clarify dependencies: for example, timely access to documents, interviews, or site visits may be required for the consultant to deliver on time. These dependencies should be written into the scope so that delays caused by the client do not unfairly penalise the consultant.

Change control is another essential safeguard. No matter how carefully a scope is defined, projects evolve. New requirements emerge, priorities shift, and unforeseen challenges appear. Without a process for managing change, consultants risk being drawn into delivering significant additional work without compensation. A well-structured scope should include a clear statement that any work beyond the defined deliverables will require a formal change order, with associated adjustments to fees and timelines. This is not about being inflexible but about ensuring that changes are managed transparently and fairly.

A useful tool for scoping is the client qualification checklist. Before committing to work, consultants should ask themselves key questions:

- Is the client clear about their objectives?
- Is the budget proportionate to the scope?
- Are the deliverables realistic in the timeframe?
- Does the client have a history of scope creep or poor communication?
- Is there a clear process for change control?
- Is the consultant confident that value can be delivered?

If the answer to any of these questions is uncertain, the consultant should either negotiate scope more clearly or decline the work. Saying no to poorly scoped opportunities is not a failure; it is a sign of professional maturity.

It is also important to consider scope in relation to pricing. The two are inseparable. A fixed price contract is only fair if scope is tightly defined. Value-based pricing works best when outcomes are clear. Time-and-materials arrangements still require scope to avoid endless expansion of hours. Consultants should ensure that scope and pricing are always aligned; otherwise disputes are inevitable.

Scoping is about more than defining tasks; it is about setting the terms of trust. A clear scope shows professionalism, builds confidence, and reduces the likelihood of conflict. A vague scope undermines trust, creates disputes, and damages relationships. Consultants who take the time to scope carefully, negotiate honestly, and document clearly protect both themselves and their clients. They also signal that they value transparency and integrity, qualities that strengthen their reputation. Winning the work is not just about securing a signature; it is about establishing a framework for success. Clear scope is the foundation of that framework.

Practice Guide

Winning consultancy work is not achieved through aggressive selling but by demonstrating credibility, clarity, and value. This chapter has shown how consultants can position themselves effectively across both formal tenders and informal opportunities, how proposals should focus on outcomes rather than inputs, how pricing must be aligned with value, and how clear scoping prevents disputes. The learning objectives set at the start have been met: you can now distinguish between procurement channels, prepare proposals that persuade, apply value-based approaches to pricing, define scope with precision, and use client qualification as a safeguard against misaligned opportunities.

The pitfalls to avoid are well known. Overpromising in order to secure work almost guarantees disputes later, while under-pricing traps consultants in unsustainable cycles that damage both profitability and credibility. Ambiguous scoping leads to scope creep and conflict, and generic proposals fail to inspire confidence. Equally, chasing every opportunity without qualification wastes time and dilutes focus. Each of these missteps weakens trust, the very foundation on which consultancy depends.

Best practice comes in reframing proposals as the first deliverable – a demonstration of how the consultant thinks, communicates, and positions value. Proposals that define the real problem, link outcomes to measurable benefits, and present pricing as an investment rather than a cost set the tone for the entire relationship. Consultants who scope with precision, explain exclusions, and maintain transparency in pricing signal professionalism and reduce the likelihood of disputes. Saying no to unqualified or poorly structured opportunities is itself a mark of credibility, protecting both consultant and client from engagements that are destined to disappoint.

The point is that winning work is not about winning at any cost; it is about securing engagements that are viable, proportionate, and grounded in trust. Consultants who discipline themselves to align proposals, pricing, and scope with genuine client value build not only projects but enduring professional relationships. As the process moves from winning work to shaping it, the consultant's next task is to transform client briefs into structured plans that deliver clarity, direction, and results – the focus of the following chapter.

Chapter 14 – From Brief to Plan

Client briefs are rarely complete, clear, or aligned across stakeholders. They may be politically worded, technically vague, or missing key information. A skilled consultant must be able to interrogate, interpret, and reshape these briefs into a structured plan that reflects real needs, not just written requests. This chapter helps consultants master the early phase of engagement – the critical process of moving from ambiguity to clarity, from broad ambition to actionable scope.

By the end of this chapter, you will be able to:

- Identify and interpret the hidden assumptions, constraints, and omissions within client briefs.
- Engage early with stakeholders to surface risks, tensions, and success factors.
- Conduct a "contracting conversation" to define roles, responsibilities, and working dynamics.
- Translate vague or conflicting goals into clear deliverables that are feasible, and outcome focused.
- Build an initial project plan that balances structure with flexibility and prepares for change.
- Prevent misalignment, scope creep, and early project derailment through disciplined planning.

Introduction

No matter how carefully a client prepares their request for consultancy support, the brief is never enough. It may be structured and well written, but it is almost always incomplete. It may outline the scope of work, but it rarely reflects the full context, political tensions, or constraints shaping the project. Consultants who take briefs at face value often find themselves chasing objectives that were never agreed internally, delivering to criteria that remain undefined, or being blamed for failing to meet expectations that were never explicitly stated. The early moments of an engagement are critical, not because they offer clarity, but because they demand interpretation.

Consultants must learn to read a brief not just for what it says, but for what it does not say. Every word reflects assumptions about the client's internal alignment, resource availability, and risk appetite. A line requesting "a review of current security operations" could mean anything from a light-touch benchmarking exercise to a detailed root cause analysis of systemic failures. A phrase such as "assist with regulatory readiness" might conceal a looming deadline, unresolved stakeholder tensions, or past audit failures. The brief provides clues but not answers, and the consultant's job is to interrogate the gaps.

This interpretive mindset is not an act of cynicism; it is a professional discipline. Strong consultants assume that briefs are political documents, shaped by internal compromises, legacy thinking, or leadership agendas. They do not assume bad faith from the client, but they also do not assume clarity. Instead, they seek to uncover what the client really needs, which may not align with what has been written. This requires empathy, critical questioning, and the courage to challenge where necessary.

Clients are often unaware of their own internal misalignment. Different departments may have different expectations of what the consultant is meant to achieve. A brief drafted by one team may be delivered by another, and its reception by operational stakeholders may be lukewarm or hostile. Consultants who fail to diagnose this at the outset risk building plans that are technically sound but politically unworkable. Detecting this misalignment early can prevent weeks or months of wasted effort.

Interpreting the brief is not only about identifying risk. It is also about identifying opportunity. Clients may ask for a narrow piece of work without realising the broader value a consultant could deliver. A well-crafted initial conversation can turn a basic compliance request into a strategic engagement that addresses root causes, adds value, and strengthens long-term resilience. Consultants who simply answer the brief may miss the chance to shape it. Those who engage with the problem behind the problem often create deeper trust and longer-term partnerships.

The remainder of this chapter will explore how consultants move from ambiguous starting points to structured, deliverable plans. This involves diagnosing the real need, engaging stakeholders early, negotiating expectations and roles through the contracting conversation, and translating ambition into defined outcomes and project structure. It is a process that balances analysis and intuition, planning and adaptation, precision and empathy. Done well, it sets the foundation for the entire engagement.

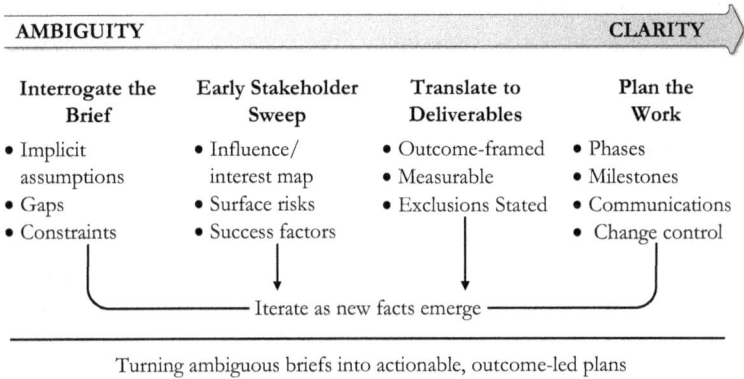

AMBIGUITY			CLARITY
Interrogate the Brief	**Early Stakeholder Sweep**	**Translate to Deliverables**	**Plan the Work**
• Implicit assumptions	• Influence/ interest map	• Outcome-framed	• Phases
• Gaps	• Surface risks	• Measurable	• Milestones
• Constraints	• Success factors	• Exclusions Stated	• Communications
			• Change control

Iterate as new facts emerge

Turning ambiguous briefs into actionable, outcome-led plans

Figure 13 From Brief to Plan: Clarification Map

Diagnosing the Real Need

Consultancy does not begin with the scope of work; it begins with a question: what is the client really trying to achieve? Behind every formal brief lies a complex mix of motivations, pressures, and expectations. These are rarely expressed in full. The written request may refer to a system upgrade, an audit, or a security design, but the real driver could be a regulatory concern, an internal power struggle, or a recent near-miss that has shaken senior confidence. Consultants who treat the brief as the full picture risk missing the underlying problem. The real work begins when consultants start asking questions, not about what the client says they want, but about what success really looks like.

Diagnosing the real need requires more than technical knowledge. It demands curiosity, emotional intelligence, and the willingness to pause before jumping to solutions. A consultant's instinct may be to respond immediately with a proposal or plan, especially when deadlines are tight or procurement processes are underway. But responding too early, before the true nature of the problem is understood, increases the risk of misalignment. The project may be delivered on time and to specifications yet still fail to deliver meaningful value. Consultants must therefore resist the urge to rush and instead adopt a diagnostic mindset.

A useful starting point is to distinguish between presenting problems and underlying issues. The presenting problem is what the client puts in the brief. For example, "we need a review of our access control system." The underlying issue might be a series of unauthorised access incidents that leadership has downplayed, or a loss of confidence in the system's integrity due to poor recordkeeping. The consultant's job is to explore both. This means asking early, open-ended questions that probe context: What triggered the request? What would success look like? Who is the ultimate sponsor? What has been tried already, and why did it not work?

Sometimes the client does not know the full answer. Briefs are often written by operational managers or procurement teams with limited strategic context. Senior stakeholders may have different expectations or conflicting priorities. By the time a brief is issued, political compromises may already have been baked into the wording. Consultants who accept the brief as definitive may inadvertently align with one camp in an internal conflict. By contrast, consultants who uncover different expectations and bring them together early can help the client team work towards common goals.

This diagnostic process also involves identifying constraints. Clients may ask for improvements without acknowledging limits on budget, time, access, or authority. The consultant must assess feasibility early. If a client wants to "enhance security culture" across a global organisation but only has a two-month window and minimal stakeholder access, the consultant must question whether the objective is realistic, or whether a more focused pilot approach might be a better starting point. These early discussions establish credibility. A consultant who asks tough but constructive questions is more likely to earn trust than one who promises too much too soon.

Cultural context also shapes the real need. In some organisations, security requests are thinly veiled attempts to satisfy regulators. In others, they are driven by internal reputation concerns. For example, a department trying to recover credibility after a security failure. Understanding the client's internal dynamics is critical. What is being said in the brief may be less important than what is being felt but not spoken. Consultants should look for cues – vague language, defensive wording, or sudden urgency – that suggest deeper drivers at play. Sometimes, what appears to be a technical request is actually a need for external validation or an independent recommendation.

One powerful technique for diagnosing need is to ask what will happen if nothing is done. This question shifts the conversation from deliverables to risk. If the client cannot articulate the consequence of inaction, the request may lack urgency, or it may be politically motivated. If the consequence is severe but unspoken, the consultant may be entering a highly sensitive environment. In either case, the insight is valuable. The role of diagnosis is not to uncover secrets, but to understand the real stakes, and ensure that the project is scoped and delivered accordingly.

Diagnosing the real need is a form of professional humility. It means acknowledging that no matter how experienced the consultant may be, they do not yet know the full picture. It means asking questions not to challenge the client's authority but to enhance the relevance and success of the engagement. And it means recognising that in consultancy, clarity is earned and not assumed.

Consultancy begins with interpretation, not instruction. The ability to question, reframe, and structure a client's brief defines professional value more than technical precision alone.

Engaging Stakeholders Early

Even the most carefully written client brief is only one voice among many. Successful consultants recognise that the formal request rarely represents a unified view. Different stakeholders bring different expectations, concerns, and levels of influence, and unless these are surfaced and reconciled early, they will derail the project later. Engaging stakeholders early is not a courtesy; it is a risk mitigation strategy.

Every organisation is a network of power, priorities, and personalities. A consultant may be hired by the security director, but implementation may depend on operations, IT, or facilities. Finance may control budget, legal may scrutinise outputs, and procurement may impose process constraints. Each of these functions may have different definitions of success. Some may welcome the consultant's arrival, others may see it as a threat, or as a source of additional work. If these expectations are not aligned at the outset, the project will suffer delays, passive resistance, or outright rejection, regardless of the quality of the work delivered.

Effective stakeholder engagement begins with stakeholder identification. This is not simply a list of people copied on emails; it is a structured effort to understand who has interest, influence, or veto power. A basic mapping exercise, identifying stakeholders as high or low in influence and interest, provides immediate insight into where effort must be concentrated. High-influence, high-interest stakeholders must be engaged directly. Low-influence but high-interest individuals may still be important allies. High-influence, low-interest figures, such as senior executives, may require briefings even if they are not involved day-to-day, to avoid surprises that could destabilise progress.

Once stakeholders are identified, the consultant's job is to engage them meaningfully. This does not mean overwhelming them with detail but rather asking targeted questions that reveal expectations and concerns. What outcomes do they want? What risks do they see? What past experiences shape their perception of this engagement? Consultants should listen actively, noting not just the content but the tone and context of responses. Resistance is not always verbal; it often shows in vagueness, deflection, or silence. These are signals that trust has not yet been established or that previous consultancy engagements have left a negative legacy.

Early engagement also helps to surface hidden risks. A stakeholder who feels excluded may later challenge recommendations. A department that feels blamed may withhold data or delay approvals. A senior sponsor who is unaware of internal tensions may overestimate the organisation's readiness for change. The consultant's job is not to solve internal politics, but to understand them, and to design an engagement approach that works with, rather than against, the organisation's reality.

Timing matters. Consultants who engage stakeholders too late often find that key decisions have already been made, or that unspoken resistance has hardened into opposition. The best time to engage is during the diagnostic phase, before the scope is finalised. This allows the consultant to refine the engagement approach in light of real-world complexity. It also creates space for informal conversations – over coffee, during walkarounds, or in small group meetings – where stakeholders may be more candid than in formal sessions.

When done well, early engagement creates a sense of shared ownership. Stakeholders begin to see the consultant not as an outsider delivering a fixed package, but as a partner helping to solve a shared problem. This shift in mindset can have a profound impact on project momentum. People support what they help to shape. Conversely, stakeholders who feel a solution is being imposed upon them – especially if it affects their workflows or exposes past failings – are far more likely to resist, even if they do so subtly.

Engagement also sets expectations. Stakeholders must understand what the consultant is doing, what input is needed from them, and how their contributions will be used. Clarity prevents misunderstanding. If people feel tricked or misrepresented, trust is quickly lost. Consultants should therefore explain their role openly, confirm how confidentiality will be handled, and keep stakeholders informed throughout. A short, well-timed briefing can prevent weeks of miscommunication later.

Early stakeholder engagement is an investment in long-term influence. Consultants rarely have formal authority. Their effectiveness depends on credibility, access, and relationships. Each early interaction builds or erodes that capital. Consultants who are seen as fair, competent, and respectful earn the right to ask difficult questions and recommend uncomfortable changes. Those who rush to deliver without first listening will find their proposals ignored or quietly undermined.

In complex projects, influence is built before analysis begins. Consultants who take the time to engage stakeholders early not only reduce the risk of failure, but they also increase the likelihood that their work will be understood, accepted, and implemented. And in consultancy, implementation is the ultimate test of value.

The Contracting Conversation

The moment a consultant agrees to take on a project, the nature of the relationship begins to define the outcome. That relationship is not formed by a purchase order or a signed contract alone, it is shaped by a deeper mutual understanding of roles, expectations, and responsibilities. Peter Block refers to this process as the *contracting conversation* – not in the legal sense, but in the interpersonal sense. It is the consultant's opportunity to clarify the working relationship before the real work begins. When done well, it prevents miscommunication, reduces tension, and lays the foundation for trust.

At its core, the contracting conversation is about alignment. Consultants enter environments shaped by existing workflows, personalities, and politics. Without clear alignment, even the most technically competent consultant will struggle to deliver value. The client may expect more than is feasible. The consultant may assume influence they do not have. Team members may hold back because they do not know how the consultant fits into the hierarchy. These are not just administrative concerns, they are operational risks. Clarifying roles at the outset avoids confusion later.

The conversation begins by defining the purpose of the engagement. What is the consultant being asked to achieve, and why now? Understanding this context ensures the consultant is not just filling a technical role but contributing to a strategic outcome. This should go beyond the wording of the brief and explore what success would actually look like for the client. A consultant who begins with "What does success look like for you in three months?" is already reframing the relationship as a collaborative partnership rather than a transactional exchange.

Next comes the discussion of roles. What is the consultant responsible for, and what remains with the client? Will the consultant lead meetings, or will the client? Is the consultant expected to challenge assumptions, or simply validate them? Will the consultant have access to frontline staff, or will information be filtered through management? These questions help avoid situations where consultants are later accused of overreach or of being too passive. They also clarify dependencies – what the consultant needs from the client in order to deliver effectively.

Block's model also includes a discussion of "wants" and "offers." The consultant must ask not only what the client wants but also state clearly what they are offering, and not offering, in return. For example, a consultant might offer to deliver a gap analysis and recommendations but clarify that implementation support is out of scope. This transparency prevents scope creep and protects the relationship from false assumptions. It also provides a natural moment to discuss budget, access, and potential constraints. Far from being uncomfortable, these discussions are often welcomed when handled with clarity and professionalism.

Another important aspect is addressing concerns. The contracting conversation creates a space where both parties can raise any anxieties about the work. The client may be worried about internal resistance or political sensitivities. The consultant may be concerned about access to data or clarity of objectives. Surfacing these concerns early, without judgement, allows them to be factored into the plan. Suppressed concerns often re-emerge at inopportune moments, undermining trust and derailing progress. When concerns are named and acknowledged at the outset, they can be managed collaboratively.

The tone of the conversation matters. It should be candid, respectful, and unhurried. This is not about negotiating every detail in a rigid way but about setting shared expectations. It is the moment when the consultant earns the right to challenge, question, and guide. Consultants who rush past this conversation, eager to demonstrate value or begin the technical work, may find that their position later becomes unstable. Conversely, those who establish boundaries early are more likely to be seen as professional, reliable, and trustworthy.

A written document may follow this conversation – typically a scope of work or proposal – but the relational contract is more than a document. It is an ongoing agreement about how the consultant and client will work together. It sets the tone for future disagreements, determines how challenges will be handled, and frames the level of candour that is possible throughout the engagement. A well-handled contracting conversation makes difficult conversations later not only possible but constructive.

In consultancy, the early moments shape everything. The contracting conversation is not just a checklist item; it is an act of leadership. It demonstrates to the client that the consultant takes the engagement seriously, values transparency, and is committed to a working relationship based on mutual respect and clearly defined roles. It is, in many ways, the first act of delivery.

Illustrative Example: Reframing a Security Operations Brief

A large airport issued a consultancy brief requesting "a review of current security operations." At first glance, the document appeared professional:

it contained a scope, listed key contacts, and specified a six-week timeframe. However, the wording was vague. It did not define what "review" meant, what outputs were expected, or how findings would be used.

The consultant began by engaging stakeholders across security, operations, and compliance. These conversations revealed that expectations were far from aligned. The security department expected benchmarking against international best practice. Operations wanted workflow improvements to reduce bottlenecks. Compliance expected evidence that regulatory gaps had been closed following a recent inspection. Finance, who controlled budget approval, had assumed the work would be limited to cost-neutral recommendations.

To prevent confusion, the consultant held a contracting conversation with the senior sponsor and department leads. This clarified roles, confirmed that the consultant would provide independent analysis rather than lead implementation, and surfaced a hidden driver: a civil aviation authority audit was scheduled for the end of the year. Without early diagnosis, this critical context would have been missed.

The broad ambition of "reviewing operations" was then converted into three clear deliverables:

1. Gap analysis of operations against International Civil Aviation Organization (ICAO[10]) Annex 17 and national aviation regulations, supported by structured interviews and document review.
2. Operational risk assessment, focused on staff deployment and access-control processes.
3. Improvement roadmap, prioritised into short-term actions for audit readiness and longer-term recommendations for efficiency gains.

A phased work plan with defined milestones was agreed, ensuring each deliverable was delivered to the right audience at the right time. The project concluded with the regulator recognising demonstrable improvements, while the client retained a clear plan for further enhancement.

The case highlights the risks of treating briefs at face value. By interrogating assumptions, engaging stakeholders early, and reframing ambition into defined outcomes, the consultant transformed a vague request into a structured plan that delivered both compliance assurance and operational value.

From Ambition to Deliverables

Once the consultant and client have established mutual understanding through diagnosis and contracting, the next challenge is to convert ambition into tangible deliverables. Clients often begin with broad aspirations – "improve security", "strengthen resilience", or "review risk exposure" – but these statements are too vague to guide effective work. The consultant's task is to shape these ambitions into specific outputs that are measurable, achievable, and valuable. This translation process is not just about narrowing the brief; it is about aligning expectations and ensuring clarity on what will be delivered, when, and to what standard.

Ambition is not the problem. Clients are right to aim high, but ambition without structure creates confusion. Without defined deliverables, progress is impossible to track and success impossible to measure. Consultants must use their professional judgement to interpret ambition through the lens of feasibility, context, and value. For example, a client's desire to "secure the site" might evolve into a set of phased deliverables: a threat vulnerability and risk assessment (TVRA), a prioritised list of recommendations, a concept design for layered protection, and a roadmap for implementation aligned to budget and regulatory deadlines. Each of these elements can be discussed, agreed, and costed, turning a general ambition into a focused engagement.

The most effective way to do this is through structured conversation. Consultants should take the client's stated objective and ask: what will this look like in practice? Who needs to be involved? What outputs are expected? How will we know when it is complete? These questions do more than clarify scope, they force both sides to be explicit. They also uncover hidden assumptions. A consultant may assume that "review site access" means observing entry points and assessing access control technology. The client may believe it includes policy review, visitor management workflows, and staff interviews. Only by interrogating the language can both sides avoid costly misunderstandings.

Deliverables should be framed in terms of outcomes, not just tasks. Clients are less interested in what consultants *do* than in what those actions will *achieve*. Instead of listing "conduct 10 stakeholder interviews", a better deliverable might be "identify operational barriers to implementing revised emergency response protocols." This approach links the consultant's effort directly to the client's goals and demonstrates that the work is both purposeful and actionable. Outcome-focused deliverables also create a more natural alignment with value-based pricing and help justify investment.

It is equally important to match deliverables to available resources. There is little value in promising a 100-page strategy document if the client has no capacity to read or implement it. Consultants should design deliverables that reflect the client's absorption capability. Sometimes, a short executive summary and a visual roadmap will do more good than a technically perfect report that sits unread. This is not a call to simplify content unnecessarily, but a reminder that value lies in usability. The best deliverables inform decisions, guide action, and build confidence.

Prioritisation is another key discipline. When faced with a long list of client ambitions, consultants must help decide what matters most now. This requires sensitivity to urgency, risk, and internal momentum. Not every issue needs to be solved at once. Consultants should work with the client to distinguish between high-impact, time-sensitive actions and longer-term recommendations. This prioritisation also supports phased delivery, which can be easier to manage both operationally and financially. Clients are more likely to approve a sequenced set of deliverables than a single, complex engagement.

Deliverables must be documented clearly. This includes scope, assumptions, format, and approval criteria. A simple table listing each deliverable, its description, and how success will be assessed can avoid a great deal of ambiguity. Consultants should avoid generic phrases and instead write in specific, practical terms. For example:

- **Ambition:** Improve control room effectiveness
- **Deliverable:** Conduct a gap analysis of current control room operations against *ISO 11064-1:2000 Ergonomic design of control centres – Part 1: Principles for the design of control centres*, supported by three days of on-site observation and stakeholder interviews. Produce a prioritised improvement plan with cost-banded recommendations.

In this way, the consultant helps the client see exactly what will be delivered, and why. This clarity sets the stage for successful planning and execution. It also becomes the reference point against which progress is measured, and changes are managed. Vague ambition, however well intentioned, cannot be delivered. But ambition that has been converted into structured, outcome-oriented deliverables becomes the foundation of project success.

Planning the Work

Once deliverables have been clearly defined, the next step is to plan the work. This does not mean creating a complex project management framework – although in some large or regulated engagements that may be necessary – but rather building a realistic, structured plan for how the consultant will achieve the agreed outcomes. Planning brings coherence to the engagement. It provides visibility for the client, focus for the consultant, and a reference point for adjusting course when the inevitable changes arise.

The starting point is to break down each deliverable into logical phases. These may include discovery, analysis, stakeholder engagement, development, and reporting. Mapping these phases helps both the consultant and client to understand how the work will progress over time. It also prompts important questions about dependencies. For example, whether certain tasks require client input or access to specific systems, and whether those elements are available when needed. Consultants should identify these early to avoid last-minute delays that could have been anticipated.

Timelines must be realistic. Consultants under pressure to win work may be tempted to agree to compressed schedules, but this often backfires. Rushed work creates quality risks, increases the likelihood of missing key details, and places undue strain on relationships. Consultants should propose timelines that reflect not just the time needed to complete tasks, but the time required to review, absorb, and act on them. Where work requires input or feedback from the client, this should be built into the schedule and not assumed to happen instantly.

Milestones provide structure within the plan. These are points where specific outputs are completed, reviewed, or approved. Milestones help manage expectations, reduce the risk of scope creep, and create moments to assess progress. They also offer a natural rhythm for client engagement, keeping stakeholders informed and involved. A good plan does not overwhelm the client with constant updates, but neither does it go silent for weeks. Milestones should be set at intervals that are meaningful without being disruptive.

Resourcing is another factor to consider. While many consultancy engagements are delivered by individuals or small teams, even solo consultants need to account for their own availability, competing commitments, and support needs. If travel is involved, this must be scheduled realistically. If specialised input is needed – for example, from technical experts or local partners – their availability and role should be planned in advance. Overcommitting resources can damage credibility; under resourcing can damage outcomes. A realistic resourcing plan builds trust and avoids operational gaps.

Planning must also address risk. Every engagement contains uncertainties, data may not be available, stakeholders may become unresponsive, organisational changes may shift priorities. Consultants should identify these risks and agree with the client on how to handle them. This does not require a formal risk register unless the project demands one, but it does require forethought. A simple "if-then" mapping – if access is delayed, then the reporting timeline moves; if key data is missing, then alternate sources will be used – can prevent disputes and support adaptive delivery.

Communication is a central part of planning. Consultants should agree early on how they will communicate progress, issues, and decisions. This may include regular calls, summary emails, milestone presentations, or shared project dashboards. The goal is to keep the client engaged and informed without consuming excessive time. Good communication builds confidence. Silence breeds concern, especially in high-pressure or politically sensitive environments. A basic communication plan, tailored to the client's culture and preferences, adds significant value.

Documentation matters. Even simple plans should be written down and not just held in the consultant's head. A short document or table that outlines phases, milestones, timelines, responsibilities, and risks helps everyone stay aligned. It also provides a baseline for managing change. If the client's needs evolve – as they often do – the consultant can refer back to the agreed plan and adjust it collaboratively, rather than appearing to move the goalposts. Written plans create accountability and reduce the chance of misinterpretation.

Planning is not a bureaucratic task; it is leadership. It shows that the consultant is taking the work seriously, is thinking ahead, and is committed to delivering not just outputs but outcomes. A well-structured plan, even if simple, signals professionalism. It reassures the client, focuses the consultant, and sets the conditions for effective delivery.

Practice Guide

Consultancy engagements rarely begin with clarity. The consultant's value lies in turning ambiguity into structure, transforming incomplete or politically shaped briefs into actionable, outcome-focused plans. The learning objectives have been addressed: we have examined how to diagnose the real need behind the stated request, how to engage stakeholders early to surface risks and expectations, how to conduct the contracting conversation to define roles and responsibilities, how to translate ambition into clear deliverables, and how to develop plans that are structured but flexible.

The pitfalls to avoid are consistent. Consultants who take briefs at face value risk building elegant solutions to the wrong problems. Those who fail to engage stakeholders early will discover resistance too late. Skipping the contracting conversation leaves expectations unspoken, breeding frustration when misunderstandings arise. Deliverables framed as tasks rather than outcomes become irrelevant, while rushed or unrealistic planning undermines both credibility and results. Each of these errors erodes trust at the very point when it should be built most strongly.

Good practice is rooted in disciplined curiosity and structured engagement. Consultants who interrogate briefs with respect uncover hidden drivers and constraints, allowing projects to be shaped to real needs rather than surface requests. By engaging stakeholders early, they build ownership and reduce resistance. By conducting the contracting conversation openly, they prevent disputes and establish professional boundaries. By shaping deliverables in terms of outcomes, they make their value visible and their work actionable. And by planning with realism – considering milestones, risks, dependencies, and communication – they reassure clients that the engagement is under control.

The forward lesson is clear: consultancy does not begin with solutions, but with questions. The transition from brief to plan is where trust is forged and success becomes possible. Consultants who treat this phase as an administrative hurdle will find their projects faltering; those who embrace it as a critical act of leadership will set the stage for credibility, clarity, and impact. As the book moves into how consultants work on site and in the field, planning provides the foundation for effective execution and delivery.

Chapter 15 – On-Site and In the Field

Fieldwork is where consultancy moves from theory to practice. However well a project is scoped, the reality of operations only becomes clear when observed directly. Site visits and interviews provide the raw material for meaningful recommendations, revealing strengths, weaknesses, and cultural dynamics that documents alone cannot capture. Done well, they generate insight; done poorly, they risk becoming stage-managed exercises that show only what the client wants seen.

Consultants must therefore prepare thoroughly, observe systematically, and engage constructively. Fieldwork is not just about technical data but about how systems, processes, and people interact in practice. It requires curiosity, impartiality, and the confidence to ask difficult questions while maintaining professional respect.

By the end of this chapter, you will be able to:

- Conduct effective site surveys and stakeholder interviews that gather reliable and actionable insights.
- Recognise and counter the risks of "stage-managed" visits, ensuring a more authentic picture of operational reality.
- Prepare systematically for fieldwork using structured checklists, tools, and pre-visit research.
- Apply disciplined observation techniques to identify physical, procedural, and cultural vulnerabilities.
- Manage the interpersonal and political dynamics that influence access, candour, and cooperation during site engagements.
- Record, validate, and protect sensitive observations in a way that supports later analysis while maintaining confidentiality and professional integrity.

Introduction

Fieldwork is where a consultant proves their worth. If it is done badly, later analysis will be based on weak information. If it is done well, it provides genuine insights that test assumptions and expose the real factors driving risk. This chapter sets out how to plan, carry out, and record site visits so they deliver accurate understanding, avoid being stage-managed, and create the solid evidence needed for reliable recommendations.

A site visit is not a tick-box exercise but the foundation of reliable insight. Consultants who rely only on documents risk missing the reality of how people work, and those who accept a guided walk-through at face value see only what has been curated.

Fieldwork is both technical and relational. It requires systematic observation of entrances, perimeters, and systems, while also engaging constructively with people at every level. The consultant must balance curiosity with diplomacy, probing weaknesses without alienating staff. Preparation and structure provide discipline, but flexibility is essential: no checklist can anticipate every anomaly, and unexpected opportunities often yield the most valuable insights.

Interpersonal dynamics must also be recognised. People behave differently when observed, often displaying stricter compliance than in normal operations. The consultant's task is to move beyond this surface performance to uncover candid perspectives and subtle cues that signal vulnerabilities.

Fieldwork is where credibility is built or lost. Done poorly, it creates weak foundations for later analysis. Done well, it produces authentic insights that validate or challenge assumptions and reveal the underlying dynamics of risk. This chapter explains how to prepare, conduct, and record site engagements in ways that generate real understanding, resist stage-management, and build the evidence base on which sound consultancy depends.

Preparing for a Site Visit

Fieldwork begins well before the consultant arrives at the gate. The success of a site survey depends on how thoroughly the consultant has prepared: what information has been gathered in advance, what tools and materials have been assembled, and how clearly the objectives of the visit have been defined. A site visit is not simply a tour; it is a structured investigative exercise, and like any investigation, preparation determines the quality of the outcome.

Effective preparation starts with research. Every facility exists in a particular operational, geographical, and regulatory context. Before setting foot onsite, the consultant should study available documentation such as site drawings, floor plans, operational manuals, and previous audit reports. Maps, satellite imagery, and local infrastructure data provide further insight into the surrounding environment and its impact on security. Public records, press reports, and regulatory filings may also yield valuable information on incidents, compliance history, or organisational priorities. This background research prevents the consultant from wasting time asking questions that could have been answered in advance, while also sharpening the focus on areas where gaps or contradictions are most likely to appear.

The consultant's personal toolkit is another vital element of preparation. Site visits can be demanding, requiring long periods of walking, standing, or observing in difficult environments. Appropriate clothing and personal protective equipment are essential, not only for safety but also for credibility. Turning up unprepared for site conditions sends a poor signal to both client and staff. Beyond basic attire, consultants should assemble a set of practical tools: a notebook or tablet for structured observations, a reliable camera where permitted, measurement devices such as laser distance finders, and copies of any checklists or survey forms that will guide the visit. Where electronic devices are restricted, the consultant should be ready to revert to analogue methods such as sketches, a tape measure, and written notes.

Preparation also requires clarity of scope. Consultants must enter the site with a clear understanding of what they are there to observe and why. A visit framed too broadly risks descending into aimless wandering, while one framed too narrowly may miss critical vulnerabilities outside the immediate area of focus. The consultant should review the agreed scope of work, extract the fieldwork elements, and translate them into specific objectives for the visit. For example, if the engagement involves assessing perimeter security, the consultant should plan a systematic inspection of fences, gates, and lighting, while also allowing time to observe how those features are actually used by staff and visitors.

Equally important is understanding what not to do. Consultants should resist the temptation to turn a site visit into a catch-all assessment of everything they notice. Not every observation is relevant to the engagement, and pursuing side issues can dilute credibility. Discipline in sticking to scope, while remaining alert to anomalies that could have significant impact, is a hallmark of professional fieldwork.

Safety and security protocols also demand attention. Many sites, particularly those in critical national infrastructure or high-security sectors, impose strict entry requirements. Consultants may need advance clearance, background checks, or special permits. They may be prohibited from carrying certain items or using cameras. Failure to prepare for these requirements can result in wasted travel, lost credibility, or even denied access. Consultants should confirm all entry procedures with the client beforehand and ensure that any documentation or identification needed is in place. They should also be prepared to respect the client's security rules without complaint, even if those rules appear inconvenient. Professionalism is demonstrated not by challenging such controls, but by complying while still conducting an effective survey within the permitted boundaries.

A key preparatory step is developing a survey plan. This is a structured outline of what will be done during the visit, when, and with whom. It should include an itinerary of which areas will be visited, which stakeholders will be interviewed, and how much time is allocated for each activity. A strong plan allows the consultant to balance the need for thoroughness with the practical constraints of the day. At the same time, it should not be so rigid that it prevents adaptation to unforeseen opportunities, such as impromptu conversations with frontline staff or access to areas not originally scheduled.

The survey plan should also anticipate interpersonal dynamics. Consultants should identify in advance who the key stakeholders are, what their roles involve, and what interests or biases they may bring to the visit. Understanding this context enables more effective questioning and prevents the consultant from being caught off guard. For example, a facilities manager showing the consultant around may promote the strengths of the maintenance programme but play down problems with staffing or budgets. Knowing this in advance helps the consultant ask balanced questions and confirm the details with other people on site.

Another consideration is time management. Site visits are often limited in duration, and consultants can easily lose valuable hours if they are not disciplined. A good rule is to prioritise the areas most critical to the engagement early in the visit, leaving less critical observations to later in the schedule. Consultants should also plan time for unstructured observation – moments to pause and watch how people use spaces, how systems interact, and how procedures are followed. These unscripted periods often yield insights more valuable than any checklist item.

Preparation must include consideration of data handling. Site visits often involve exposure to sensitive information, whether physical documents, access credentials, or operational details. Consultants should plan how they will record and store data securely, how confidentiality will be preserved, and how sensitive notes or photographs will be protected. Clients are reassured when consultants demonstrate forethought in this area, and credibility is easily undermined if notes are left unsecured or photographs shared carelessly.

All these elements together create the basis for a professional site survey. A consultant who arrives properly prepared, with research done, tools ready, a clear plan, and an understanding of both the scope and the sensitivities, is much more likely to produce reliable and useful insights. Preparation is not just paperwork; it is the beginning of analysis and the platform on which all later fieldwork relies.

To support this process, a structured checklist covering research, equipment, scope, safety, and data security can be adapted for use across different projects. Used consistently, this tool not only improves the quality of fieldwork but also builds the consultant's reputation for rigour, professionalism, and attention to detail.

1. Pre-Visit Research

☐ Review available documentation: site drawings, floor plans, policies, past audit reports.

☐ Study external context: maps, satellite imagery, surrounding infrastructure.

☐ Check for public domain information: incidents, regulatory actions, press reports.

☐ Clarify scope of the survey against agreed terms of reference.

2. Permissions and Access

☐ Confirm visitor clearance, passes, and any background checks required.

☐ Verify restrictions on electronic devices, photography, and data capture.

☐ Arrange escorts or access to specific zones in advance.

3. Personal Readiness

☐ Ensure appropriate clothing and PPE (Personal Protective Equipment – safety shoes, hard hat, high-visibility vest, etc.).

☐ Carry identification and any required permits.

☐ Prepare for environmental conditions (weather, noise, long periods on foot).

4. Tools and Equipment

☐ Notebook, pens, and backup recording options.

☐ Digital devices where permitted (tablet, laptop, voice recorder).

☐ Measuring tools (laser rangefinder, tape measure).

☐ Camera or phone (if authorised) for annotated photographs.

☐ Copies of observation forms or survey templates.

5. Survey Plan

☐ Define objectives: what must be observed, tested, or verified.

☐ Identify areas to be visited and order of inspection.

☐ Allocate time to each activity, prioritising critical zones first.

☐ Plan stakeholder interviews and informal conversations.

☐ Build in time for unstructured observation.

6. Stakeholder Mapping

☐ Identify key people to meet: managers, operators, guards, maintenance staff.

☐ Understand likely perspectives, biases, or incentives.

☐ Prepare tailored questions for each group.

7. Safety and Security Protocols

☐ Familiarise yourself with site safety procedures and emergency contacts.

☐ Ensure compliance with local regulations and client requirements.

☐ Avoid carrying prohibited items or sensitive materials.

☐ Carry your own PPE

8. Data Handling

☐ Decide how notes, drawings, and photos will be stored securely.

☐ Establish confidentiality protocols for sensitive observations.

☐ Prepare a chain of custody for any restricted information.

Always rehearse the visit in your mind before arrival. Imagine the order in which you will move through the site, who you will speak to, and how you will capture data. This mental run-through highlights gaps in preparation and ensures you arrive confident, structured, and ready to adapt.

Conducting Effective Surveys

Preparation sets the stage, but the real value of consultancy emerges onsite, where observation, questioning, and connection of detail generate insight. A survey is not a casual walk-through, but a structured process designed to reveal how a facility functions. It requires discipline, curiosity, and the ability to manage both the technical and human dimensions of the visit.

The first step is orientation. Even with prior study of drawings or imagery, the consultant should take a few minutes to absorb the environment. Initial impressions often reveal gaps between documented procedures and the reality on site. A site may claim strict access control, yet staff hold doors for one another. A facility may emphasise perimeter security, yet adjacent land use undermines it. Such cues are fleeting and easily missed.

From there, surveys should follow a logical sequence. A common method is to work from the perimeter inwards, examining each layer of defence in turn. At the perimeter, assess fences, gates, lighting, signage, and surveillance. Next, review vehicle controls, reception areas, and access points. Deeper inside, focus on restricted zones, sensitive equipment, and control rooms. This structure reduces the chance of oversight and reinforces the principle that effective security depends on layers of security working together.

Flexibility remains vital. Consultants should adjust when anomalies or opportunities appear: a malfunctioning gate, an unplanned conversation, or a chance to observe a procedure in action. The challenge is to maintain overall direction while pursuing valuable leads. Effective surveys balance structure with adaptability.

Observation must extend beyond infrastructure to include procedures and culture. How do guards interact with staff and visitors? Are protocols followed naturally, or only when observed? Are workarounds evident, such as doors propped open, improvised signage, shared credentials? These details reveal security culture as much as the quality of formal systems.

Capturing evidence reliably is essential. Memory is fallible, so notes should be clear, structured, and timestamped. Annotated sketches are often more useful than photographs, especially where cameras are restricted. Where photographs are permitted, they should be taken discreetly and always linked to context. The details of how to organise and interpret notes are covered further in the section on recording and validation.

Time management is critical. Consultants often face pressure to cover a large site in limited time. One technique is to triage findings as high, medium, or low significance during the visit. This ensures urgent issues receive focus and prevents minor points from dominating.

Engagement with people adds depth. Informal conversations with guards, operators, or maintenance staff often yield more than formal briefings. These individuals understand weaknesses, workarounds, and recent incidents. Open questions such as *"What happens when this system fails?"* invite candid responses. Contradictions between frontline accounts and management reports provide valuable lines of enquiry.

Checking information from more than one source is key to being credible. You should almost never take a single answer as the full truth. Compare what you see with what is written down and what people tell you. For example, if managers say access logs are checked every day, look at a few logs yourself and ask staff how they do it. If everything matches, you can trust it more. If it does not, you have found a gap.

Using your senses can also reveal useful clues. Loud noise in a control room might point to poor design. Strong smells could mean maintenance problems. The way staff behave can show something about the workplace culture. These are not scientific measurements, but they help build a fuller understanding.

Surveys must always follow ethical standards. Consultants should not mislead or pressure staff. Secret recording, testing controls without permission, or forcing answers damages trust and breaks professional standards. The consultant's job is to highlight risks, not to catch staff out. Acting ethically protects reputation and makes sure the findings are seen as fair.

Before leaving, time should be set aside for a rapid debrief. Notes should be reviewed, ambiguities clarified, and key findings captured while fresh. If working in a team, members should compare impressions to reconcile differences. This immediate consolidation reduces gaps later and strengthens the evidence base.

Conducting effective surveys is a multidimensional task. It requires technical competence, structure, flexibility, interpersonal skill, and ethical conduct. Consultants who master these elements move beyond surface impressions to build a reliable, evidence-based picture of the site. This credibility strengthens later recommendations, ensuring they reflect not only theory but the realities of operations.

Fieldwork converts theory into evidence. Observation must be systematic, ethical, and traceable – turning what is seen into knowledge that can withstand professional scrutiny.

Avoiding Stage-Managed Visits

One of the greatest risks in consultancy fieldwork is mistaking a choreographed performance for reality. Many site visits are managed, consciously or not, to present the facility in its best light. Managers want to impress, staff want to appear compliant, and escorts often steer consultants towards strong areas while avoiding weak ones. If this theatre is accepted uncritically, the resulting analysis will be distorted, leaving vulnerabilities unrecognised and recommendations incomplete.

The signs of stage-management are usually clear. Visits that follow rigid, predetermined routes suggest limits on what the consultant is meant to see. Facilities that look unusually tidy, freshly painted, or quiet on the day of inspection may have been prepared. Staff giving rehearsed answers or deferring to a manager rather than speaking directly often indicates coaching. None of these signals prove deception, but they do show that the consultant may be seeing a curated version of reality.

The first countermeasure is to vary the routine. Consultants should request small deviations from the planned route, such as inspecting a secondary entrance, a storage area, or a less visible perimeter section. Even a short detour can reveal inconsistencies. Where possible, ask to see systems in use rather than simply described. Watching an access control point in operation, for example, often shows whether guards follow protocol or only recite it.

Engaging informally with staff is equally valuable. Formal interviews have their place, but casual conversations during a walk-through often provide more candid insight. Open questions like, *"What challenges do you face when it gets busy?"* or *"What happens if this system goes down?"* encourage staff to describe reality rather than rehearsed scripts. Consultants must listen for hesitation, contradiction, or discomfort – cues that practice differs from policy.

Timing is another tool. Visits scheduled for convenient hours rarely reflect true conditions. A control room may appear calm mid-morning but chaotic during shift change. Where possible, consultants should request to visit at varied times, including evenings, weekends, or high-traffic periods. If this cannot be arranged, staff should at least be asked how conditions differ outside normal hours.

Cross-checking information makes findings more reliable. What people say should be compared with what is seen and what records show. For example, if managers claim CCTV is monitored continuously, this can be checked by asking operators how they handle alerts, watching the system in use, and reviewing sample footage. Consistency across these sources builds confidence; differences point to useful questions. The same principle applies to the areas often overlooked. Back gates, temporary offices, and service corridors may reveal more about daily practice than the main entrances. Watching how contractors, cleaners, or delivery staff use security controls can show whether good practice runs across the site or is limited to showcase areas.

Tact is essential. Escorts may believe they are helping by guiding the consultant to areas of strength. Staff may want to demonstrate professionalism by giving rehearsed answers. These behaviours are cultural rather than malicious. The consultant's task is not to accuse but to create opportunities for a fuller picture. Requests framed as professional diligence rather than suspicion – *"It would be useful to see how the delivery process works, could we look at the loading bay?"* – maintain trust while probing beyond the script.

Documentation provides a final safeguard. Consultants should note what was shown, who was present, and under what conditions. Recording that *"escort directed us away from restricted zone X"* is not an accusation; it is an objective fact that may later prove significant if the zone emerges as critical. Clear records protect the consultant and support defensible analysis.

After the visit, critical reflection helps. If everything appeared flawless, that itself is suspicious – no facility is without weakness. Consultants should ask: *What was I not shown? Whose voice did I not hear? What questions went unanswered?* These reflections highlight gaps for follow-up.

Avoiding stage-managed visits does not mean distrusting the client. It means recognising that every organisation presents itself positively under scrutiny. The consultant's responsibility is to look beyond performance to underlying reality. With persistence, tact, and structured methods, fieldwork can produce authentic insights that support reliable recommendations, rather than conclusions built on a stage set – impressive from the front but hollow behind the scenes.

Illustrative Example: Behind the Stage Set

A consultancy team was engaged to review security operations at a regional distribution hub. On arrival, they were greeted by senior managers who had organised a tightly scripted tour. The route moved smoothly from the main entrance to the control room and finally to a showcase warehouse. Everywhere appeared immaculate: guards in pressed uniforms, access control procedures followed to the letter, and a spotless control room with monitors aligned and staff attentive.

At first glance, the facility seemed exemplary. Yet several cues suggested the performance had been carefully staged. The tour avoided side entrances and outbuildings. Staff gave rehearsed answers, often glancing at their manager before speaking. The atmosphere felt unnatural, more like a demonstration than daily operation.

Rather than challenge the managers directly, the consultants varied their approach. They asked if they could briefly see a delivery in progress at the loading bay, framed as part of routine diligence. Reluctantly, the escort agreed. The short detour revealed a more authentic picture: contractors entered through a rear gate where guards checked vehicles hurriedly, sometimes waving them through without full inspection. Pallets were stacked near the perimeter fence, creating blind spots and potential climbing points. None of this had featured in the official tour.

The consultants also struck up informal conversations with staff. A guard at the loading bay explained that checks were rushed during peak hours to keep traffic moving. A warehouse worker mentioned that doors were often propped open for airflow in the summer heat, despite official policy to the contrary. These candid remarks painted a picture very different from the rehearsed compliance on display earlier.

Cross-referencing evidence confirmed the gap between performance and practice. Visitor logs showed entries that did not match CCTV footage. Rosters suggested the control room was sometimes staffed by only one operator, contrary to policy. When asked discreetly, a junior technician admitted that overtime shortages often left equipment faults unreported. None of these issues had been mentioned by management during the official briefing.

The team documented each finding carefully. Rather than presenting accusations, they noted objectively what was observed and under what conditions: *"escort diverted tour away from rear gate," "loading bay door propped open at 14:35," "guard reported vehicle checks inconsistent at peak times."* This evidence was later cross-checked against logs and maintenance records.

The final report concluded that while the facility had strong policies on paper, its practical execution was uneven. The official tour had highlighted strengths but masked vulnerabilities that could have gone unnoticed if the consultants had accepted the performance at face value. By probing respectfully, varying the route, and engaging directly with frontline staff, they built a more accurate picture.

The lesson from this case is that stage-managed visits are rarely malicious; they reflect a natural desire to impress outsiders. But they can create dangerous blind spots if consultants rely solely on curated evidence. In this case, the ability to read subtle cues, deviate tactfully from the script, and validate findings across multiple sources turned what could have been a superficial exercise into a meaningful assessment.

Interviews and Stakeholder Engagement in the Field

While structured observation of the physical environment is essential, much of the most valuable intelligence comes from people. Interviews and informal conversations reveal how systems are used, what challenges staff face, and how culture shapes day-to-day practice. A facility may have robust policies, but unless they are understood and followed by people, they remain ineffective. For the consultant, engaging stakeholders is therefore a critical component of understanding operational reality.

Preparation begins with mapping who to speak with. This should cover senior management, frontline operators such as guards and control room staff, facilities and maintenance personnel, IT or operations staff where convergence issues arise, and external contractors. Each group holds different pieces of the puzzle; no single perspective is sufficient.

Questions should be tailored. Managers can be asked about policy, budget, or compliance drivers. Guards may reveal procedural workarounds. Maintenance staff often know system weaknesses and spare-part shortages. Contractors may highlight gaps in access control or supervision. Asking the same generic questions often leads to shallow answers. Tailored questions that fit the person's role show respect and make people more likely to speak openly.

The manner of engagement strongly shapes the quality of information. Consultants must establish rapport quickly by listening actively and asking open questions. A leading prompt such as *"You always follow procedure, don't you?"* invites rehearsed answers, whereas *"Can you walk me through what happens when a visitor arrives unexpectedly?"* encourages authenticity.

Trust is essential but fragile. Many staff have experienced audits that left them feeling exposed. Consultants should reassure interviewees that the goal is to understand, not to criticise. Explaining how notes will be used and confirming that individuals will not be named without consent helps build confidence. Listening carefully to junior staff can be just as valuable as speaking with managers, because those working at the edges often notice problems first.

Group interviews present particular challenges. Escorts sometimes insist that managers be present, which can inhibit candour. Where possible, consultants should seek one-to-one or small-group conversations. If this is not feasible, informal exchanges during a walk-through or break can still provide valuable insights. In group settings, consultants should also watch non-verbal cues such as hesitation, silence, or glances between participants.

Consistency checking is a core discipline. Statements should not be taken at face value but compared across stakeholders. If managers claim daily checks are performed but frontline staff describe otherwise, the discrepancy merits investigation. Differences may reflect constraints, misunderstandings, or cultural factors rather than deliberate misrepresentation.

Cultural dynamics shape how information is shared. In some settings, staff may avoid criticising superiors directly. In others, hierarchy discourages acknowledging procedural gaps. Consultants working internationally must adapt style accordingly: indirect questioning or scenario-based prompts may work better in high-context cultures, while direct enquiry may suit low-context ones. Sensitivity to these nuances helps avoid alienation.

Recording interviews needs careful consideration. While some clients allow it, it often discourages people from speaking openly. GDPR[5] and liability concerns add further risk, as organisations may be held responsible for what a participant says if a recording exists. There are also practical problems: equipment can fail, files can be lost or leaked, and the very presence of a recorder can make staff feel observed rather than respected. For these reasons, recording is generally best avoided. Written notes are the safer and more reliable option, provided they are structured and accurate. They should capture not only what was said but also how it was said, since tone, hesitation, or contradictions can be as revealing as the words themselves. Reviewing notes immediately after the discussion ensures clarity while details are still fresh.

Interviews should not be treated as isolated events but as part of cross-checking. A propped-open door observed onsite may be explained by staff as a habit, a maintenance issue, or a policy gap. Similarly, claims of chronic understaffing should be checked against rosters or incident logs. Insights from people are strongest when validated against other evidence.

Effective interviews transform fieldwork from inspection into investigation. They expose the human dynamics behind technical systems, reveal the gap between policy and practice, and provide early warnings of resistance that may undermine future recommendations. By preparing carefully, questioning with sensitivity, respecting cultural context, and validating findings, consultants can gather insights that no desktop analysis could match. Interviews, when done well, are both an act of respect and one of the consultant's most powerful tools in the field.

Recording and Validating Observations

Observations are only valuable if they are captured accurately and preserved in a way that supports later analysis. Consultants who rely on memory risk distorting details or overlooking nuances. Effective fieldwork therefore requires structured recording methods and disciplined validation to produce evidence that is reliable, defensible, and usable.

The first principle is clarity. Notes should distinguish between what was observed directly and what is interpretation. Writing *"the gate was open at 14:15 with no guard present"* is a factual observation. Writing *"possible lack of supervision"* is interpretation. Both matter, but they should be recorded separately so that analysis remains grounded in evidence rather than assumption.

Structured formats help. Many consultants use observation forms with columns for time, location, detail, and follow-up. Others prefer a two-column notebook: one for facts, one for comments. The format matters less than consistency. Notes taken under pressure are often messy, but a clear structure reduces the chance of losing critical points.

Photographs and sketches add weight to written notes. Where permitted, photographs should be deliberate, annotated with time and place, and linked to specific findings. A single image of a damaged fence can be more compelling than a paragraph of description. Where photography is restricted, quick sketches can capture layouts, routes, or equipment positions that words alone cannot.

The level of detail must be balanced. Over-recording floods the record with noise, while under-recording risks missing key insights. A practical rule is to prioritise observations that relate directly to the scope of work or that contradict stated policy. Consultants should also capture anomalies even if their significance is unclear – small details often connect later into meaningful findings.

Validation is just as important as recording. Observations made in passing can be misleading if treated as stand-alone facts. A door found unsecured once might be a rare lapse or a regular habit. Staff claims should be checked against rosters, logs, or direct observation. Comparing information from different sources, such as interviews, documents, and physical inspection, reduces the risk of basing conclusions on a single weak piece of evidence.

Team validation makes the record stronger. When several consultants attend a visit, they should compare notes before leaving the site. One may have focused on technical systems while another noticed cultural dynamics, and reconciling impressions straight away creates a fuller picture. A personal debrief is recommended for solo consultants: taking time to review shorthand, clarify impressions, and write a brief summary before leaving ensures nothing important is lost.

Sensitive material must also be managed responsibly. Site surveys often expose vulnerabilities that clients would not want widely known. Notes, sketches, and photographs should therefore be treated as confidential, stored securely, and never left unattended. Digital material should be encrypted and devices password protected. Where information may enter legal or regulatory processes, a clear chain of custody helps preserve credibility.

A useful final step is to prioritise findings. Before leaving, consultants should flag high, medium, or low significance against their notes. This does not replace detailed analysis later, but it prevents urgent issues from being buried in detail and guides where to focus deeper investigation. It also helps structure any immediate debrief with the client by highlighting what requires early attention.

Observations are not just technical artefacts but part of a narrative. Each note, sketch, or photograph contributes to a story about how the site operates and where risks lie. Recording and validating observations is therefore not only about accuracy but about creating an evidence base that can withstand scrutiny. Consultants who work systematically, validate carefully, and handle information responsibly ensure that their fieldwork stands up to challenge and builds client trust. Those who do not risk undermining their own credibility – and in consultancy, credibility is the strongest currency.

Practice Guide

Fieldwork is where consultancy moves from planning into real practice. This chapter has addressed its objectives by demonstrating how consultants can prepare effectively for site visits, conduct disciplined surveys, resist stage-management, engage stakeholders constructively, and capture and validate observations with integrity. It has also shown that credibility in consultancy is won or lost not in the office but in the way the consultant listens, observes, and responds in the field.

The pitfalls are easy to fall into yet costly. Consultants who allow escorts to control the itinerary see only a curated version of the site. Those who focus too narrowly on technical systems neglect the cultural dynamics that shape security behaviours. Overconfidence leads to missed details, while poor note-taking or lax handling of sensitive material undermines credibility. Equally damaging is the tendency to rush, ticking boxes without probing deeper, or to accept stage-managed performances as authentic. Each of these traps produces distorted evidence and weakens recommendations.

Good practice requires preparation, structure, and respect. Consultants who research thoroughly before arrival, assemble the right tools, and plan their time demonstrate professionalism from the outset. Once on site, they must balance disciplined observation with flexibility, probing when anomalies appear and listening to those whose daily experiences often reveal more than official narratives. They must separate fact from interpretation in their notes, validate findings through multiple sources, and manage sensitive data responsibly. By doing so, they create an evidence base that withstands scrutiny and builds client confidence.

The broader lesson is that fieldwork is not just about what consultants see, but about how they are seen. Every site visit is both an investigative exercise and a performance of credibility. Clients judge professionalism by how prepared, attentive, and respectful the consultant is. Staff form impressions that shape candour and cooperation. The consultant who combines curiosity with tact, structure with adaptability, and authority with humility produces insights that are both accurate and actionable.

Fieldwork is only the beginning. The observations captured onsite must now be analysed and translated into design, risk assessments, and recommendations that influence decision-making. As the next chapter shows, it is the ability to convert raw evidence into structured analysis that completes the bridge from field practice to professional impact.

Chapter 16 – Analysis and Design

Fieldwork generates the raw material of consultancy – the observations, interviews, and data that reveal how a site truly operates. But information on its own does not create value. Unless it is interpreted, tested, and converted into workable designs, it remains little more than a record of what was seen. At this stage, the consultant's task is to move from evidence to insight and from insight to solutions that can be implemented. Doing so calls for technical skill, a structured approach to analysis, and the creativity to propose measures that are both effective and practical.

Analysis is the discipline of making sense of complexity: identifying patterns, tracing causes to consequences, and testing hypotheses to ensure conclusions are sound. Design is the act of synthesis: turning those conclusions into recommendations that clients can adopt, operate, and sustain. The two are inseparable. Weak analysis leads to poor designs; ambitious designs without evidence cannot withstand scrutiny. Mastering both is what turns consultancy from observation into impact.

By the end of this chapter, you will be able to:

- Organise and interpret raw data from fieldwork in a way that is systematic, structured, and defensible.
- Apply hypothesis-driven methods to link evidence with risk, need, and opportunity.
- Generate multiple design options, evaluating trade-offs and feasibility rather than defaulting to a single solution.
- Translate analytical conclusions into implementable designs that meet technical, cultural, and regulatory requirements.
- Validate proposed solutions through stress-testing, stakeholder engagement, and iterative refinement.
- Avoid common errors such as over-analysis, over-engineering, and failing to align designs with client objectives.

Introduction

Having gathered the raw material of consultancy through fieldwork, the consultant's task now is to turn observation into insight and insight into action. Notes, sketches, interview transcripts, and photographs are valuable only if they are interpreted and translated into solutions that the client can implement. Without this step, consultants risk becoming mere reporters of what they saw rather than interpreters of what it means.

Analysis is more than cataloguing data. It is the process of sense-making. It requires sorting, questioning, and connecting evidence to uncover patterns, causes, and implications. A single propped-open door might seem trivial; linked with accounts of staff shortages and maintenance delays, it reveals systemic weakness. Analysis turns fragments into coherent narratives and explanations.

Design follows from analysis. Clients do not just want to know what is wrong; they want to know how to fix it. Design must therefore be the disciplined conversion of analysis into solutions that are practical, defensible, and aligned with context. A consultant who leaps to design without proper analysis risks prescribing expensive systems that solve the wrong problem, while one who never moves beyond analysis leaves the client with data but no path forward.

The strength of consultancy lies in balancing these two disciplines. Analysis anchors recommendations in evidence; design gives them tangible form. Together, they produce solutions that can be justified technically, implemented operationally, and sustained over time.

This chapter shows how to make that transition. It covers the organisation of raw data, the use of hypothesis-driven analysis to avoid bias, and the development of multiple options rather than a single answer. It then explains how to design for implementation, validate proposals, and stress-test them under realistic scenarios. The goal is to equip consultants with a disciplined process that turns fieldwork into credible, actionable outcomes.

Making Sense of Raw Data

The fieldwork stage leaves the consultant with an abundance of material: hastily scribbled notes, annotated floor plans, transcripts of conversations, sketches, photographs, and impressions captured in the moment. On their own, these fragments have limited value. The task now is to transform them into structured evidence that can underpin sound recommendations. Making sense of raw data is the first and most critical step in that process – and it should be done within a recognised framework. For security consultancy, that framework is typically the Threat, Vulnerability and Risk Assessment (TVRA) model.

The challenge is scale and coherence. Even a modest site visit can generate dozens of pages of notes and hours of interviews. Larger projects involving multiple facilities, stakeholders, and site visits may produce thousands of discrete observations. Without structure, this volume can overwhelm. Consultants who fail to organise their data early risk becoming lost in the detail, unable to see patterns or prioritise meaningfully. The goal is therefore to impose order without losing nuance – to create a system that captures the richness of fieldwork while allowing insight to emerge.

Organising the material is the starting point. This often begins with simple collation: typing up handwritten notes, renaming and filing photographs, and storing sketches in a logical sequence. Digital tools can help, whether basic spreadsheets or more advanced qualitative analysis software. What matters is consistency and traceability. Every observation should be linked to its time, location, and context. Without this discipline, consultants may later struggle to justify how a particular recommendation was derived. A photograph of an open gate, for example, is far more persuasive when it is tied to a timestamp and corroborated by interview notes from the same period.

Once collated, the data must be categorised. Consultants use a variety of frameworks for this, but TVRA provides a particularly valuable lens. In TVRA, observations are not recorded as isolated incidents but mapped onto three key elements: threats, vulnerabilities, and potential impacts. For example, a malfunctioning CCTV camera is not just a technical fault; it is a vulnerability that could be exploited by a specific threat (unauthorised entry, insider theft), leading to defined consequences (asset loss, reputational damage). Categorising findings in this way ensures that analysis remains tied to risk, rather than drifting into an unstructured list of issues.

Coding observations is a further refinement. Coding involves tagging each piece of data with keywords or labels that capture its significance. A single interview statement might be tagged as "staffing shortage", "shift handover", and "training gap", but under TVRA it would also be linked to potential vulnerabilities (weakened monitoring during transitions) and threats (intruders exploiting reduced vigilance). This allows consultants to later sort, filter, and cross-reference data efficiently. Coding also reduces reliance on memory, ensuring that less obvious but important threads can be rediscovered during analysis.

At this stage, consultants must also distinguish between fact, assumption, and narrative – and again, TVRA provides a way to discipline thinking. Facts are what was directly observed or documented: the number of guards on duty, the existence of a broken lock, the wording of a policy. Assumptions are interpretations: the belief that low staffing levels are due to budget cuts, or that the broken lock indicates weak maintenance culture. Narratives are the stories told by stakeholders, which may reflect perceptions, agendas, or biases. All three are valuable, but their role in risk analysis differs. Facts provide evidence of vulnerabilities, assumptions may point to underlying systemic issues, and narratives may reveal perceived threats or cultural drivers that shape behaviour. Keeping them separate avoids blurring subjective accounts with objective findings.

Consultants should also be attentive to anomalies and contradictions. Often, the richest insights come not from what is consistent but from what does not fit. If most staff describe a procedure one way but one person describes it differently, that inconsistency is worth probing. If a site appears compliant with standards but day-to-day behaviour suggests otherwise, the tension must be noted. In TVRA terms, such anomalies often indicate unrecognised vulnerabilities or mismatches between documented controls and operational practice. Treating anomalies as distractions is a common mistake; in reality, they are often the early indicators of deeper risk.

The organisation of raw data is not purely mechanical. It also requires judgement about significance. Not every observation is equally important. A minor procedural lapse in a low-risk area may be less significant than a cultural practice that undermines perimeter security. TVRA supports this prioritisation by linking vulnerabilities to the likelihood and impact of specific threats. This allows consultants to distinguish between cosmetic issues and those with serious implications for resilience. The framework therefore provides both structure and proportionality, ensuring that analysis leads to meaningful priorities rather than a long, undifferentiated list.

Another discipline is ensuring traceability. Every recommendation should be able to be traced back to specific evidence – and through TVRA, also to the specific threat and vulnerability it addresses. This not only strengthens credibility but also protects the consultant if recommendations are challenged. Clients are far more likely to act on advice that is demonstrably linked to observed fact and structured risk analysis. Traceability also ensures accountability within the consulting team. When multiple consultants contribute to fieldwork, traceable evidence prevents disputes about interpretation and reinforces collective ownership of findings.

The process of sense-making is iterative. Rarely does a consultant move from raw data to final conclusions in a straight line. Instead, patterns emerge gradually as data is reviewed, categorised, and re-examined. Initial impressions may change as new connections are made. A practice that seemed benign in isolation may take on new significance when placed alongside related findings. By mapping observations back to threats and vulnerabilities, TVRA helps consultants refine and validate these connections, ensuring that patterns reflect real risk rather than coincidence.

Technology can aid but not replace this process. Qualitative analysis software, digital mapping tools, and risk assessment platforms can all help consultants organise and interrogate their material. Some tools even allow observations to be directly linked to risk registers. But the consultant's judgement remains paramount. Software may identify clusters or trends, but it cannot determine which patterns matter in context. The human task is to weigh evidence, test assumptions, and align findings with both the TVRA framework and the client's objectives.

Making sense of raw data is both a technical and intellectual task. It requires organised collation, clear categorisation, disciplined coding, and a careful distinction between fact, assumption, and narrative. Consultants must notice anomalies, prioritise what matters, and maintain traceability. Applied within the TVRA framework, this process turns scattered observations into a coherent picture of threats, vulnerabilities, and impacts, ensuring that recommendations are not only evidence-based but risk-based, and focused on the issues that matter most.

This stage is not glamorous, and it is often invisible to the client. Yet it is here that consultancy earns its credibility. By bringing order to complexity and tying it to an established risk framework, consultants create the foundation upon which all later recommendations will rest. Without that order, analysis risks becoming superficial, and design risks collapsing under scrutiny. Making sense of raw data is therefore not just a preparatory task; it is the first act of delivering value.

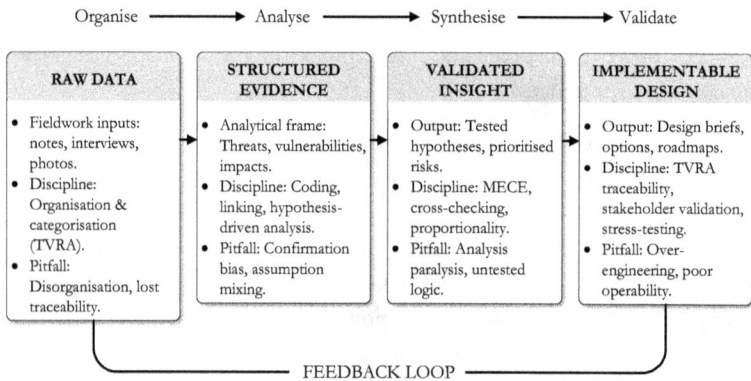

Organise ⟶ Analyse ⟶ Synthesise ⟶ Validate

RAW DATA	STRUCTURED EVIDENCE	VALIDATED INSIGHT	IMPLEMENTABLE DESIGN
• Fieldwork inputs: notes, interviews, photos. • Discipline: Organisation & categorisation (TVRA). • Pitfall: Disorganisation, lost traceability.	• Analytical frame: Threats, vulnerabilities, impacts. • Discipline: Coding, linking, hypothesis-driven analysis. • Pitfall: Confirmation bias, assumption mixing.	• Output: Tested hypotheses, prioritised risks. • Discipline: MECE, cross-checking, proportionality. • Pitfall: Analysis paralysis, untested logic.	• Output: Design briefs, options, roadmaps. • Discipline: TVRA traceability, stakeholder validation, stress-testing. • Pitfall: Over-engineering, poor operability.

FEEDBACK LOOP

Figure 14 Turning evidence into defensible design

Hypothesis-Driven Analysis

Once raw data has been organised and categorised, the consultant must move from description to explanation. This is the essence of analysis: not just listing what was observed but testing why it matters and what risks it implies. A disciplined way to do this is through hypothesis-driven analysis, widely used in professional consulting and especially powerful when anchored in the Threat, Vulnerability and Risk Assessment (TVRA) framework.

A hypothesis is a provisional explanation – a statement linking an observation to a likely cause or consequence. For example, repeated access lapses might lead to the hypothesis: "The site's security vulnerabilities are due to insufficient guard staffing during peak periods, increasing the likelihood of unauthorised entry." The hypothesis connects evidence (staffing levels), vulnerability (weakened access control), and threat (intruder exploitation), and is then tested against rosters, incident logs, and interviews.

Hypothesis-driven analysis prevents being overwhelmed by detail. Fieldwork produces more observations than can be analysed equally, so hypotheses provide a framework for enquiry. Each becomes a question to test: Is this vulnerability significant in the threat environment? Does it create a plausible attack path? What would the impact be? These questions mirror the logic of TVRA and keep analysis structured and relevant to risk.

Hypotheses are best generated from the categories created during data organisation. Grouping findings into themes such as "perimeter integrity", "access control", "control room operations", and "security culture" allows focused framing. Examples include:

- **Perimeter integrity**: "If fence repairs remain delayed, intruders could exploit the gaps to gain access."
- **Access control**: "Shared access cards may allow unauthorised individuals into sensitive zones."
- **Control room operations**: "Operators rely too heavily on alarms; if systems fail, monitoring will collapse."
- **Security culture**: "Staff indifference to tailgating shows weak procedural compliance and underestimation of insider risks."

Testing must draw on multiple sources. A claim such as "contractors share access cards" should be checked against logs, rosters, and interviews. If sources align, credibility grows; if they diverge, the consultant probes further to uncover when and why sharing occurs.

The MECE principle (Mutually Exclusive, Collectively Exhaustive) complements TVRA by ensuring all plausible causes are explored without overlap. For example, weak incident response might stem from (1) policy gaps, (2) training gaps, or (3) technology failures. This prevents focusing too narrowly on a single cause and missing systemic weaknesses.

Guarding against confirmation bias is essential. Assumptions must be tested, not protected. Under-resourcing may look like the cause, but evidence might reveal cultural complacency as the real driver. Hypotheses force these differences into the open and stop recommendations from reflecting the consultant's preferences.

Equally important is avoiding over-analysis leading to delay, producing too many hypotheses and testing them all. TVRA allows prioritisation by risk significance, focusing effort on those with the highest likelihood and impact. Lower priority hypotheses are not ignored, but investigation remains proportionate.

Each validated hypothesis points towards a design response, creating a clear chain from evidence to solution. For example, confirming that shared cards enable uncontrolled access might lead to biometric verification, anti-passback, or tighter contractor management.

Hypotheses also clarify trade-offs. If manual checks during night shifts are identified as a vulnerability, options might include automation, doubling staff, or reconfiguring shifts. Each comes with cost, cultural, and operational implications. This clarity helps clients make decisions that reflect their risk appetite.

Validation should include stress-testing against threat scenarios. TVRA prompts questions such as: What happens if this vulnerability is exploited by an adversary with capability and intent? How severe would the consequence be? This ensures conclusions are proportionate and rooted in real threats, not isolated observations.

Hypothesis-driven analysis serves three purposes: it organises thinking, disciplines testing, and builds a defensible bridge from evidence to design. It is not about proving the consultant "right" but about making conclusions transparent, risk-based, and traceable. Presenting hypotheses and supporting evidence shows clients both the reasoning and the result, strengthening trust and persuasiveness.

Hypothesis-driven analysis is as much a mindset as a method. It demands curiosity, scepticism, and humility. It demands the willingness to revise or discard ideas when evidence requires it. Coupled with TVRA, it transforms analysis from subjective interpretation into a structured, risk-based enquiry that prepares the ground for credible, implementable design.

Developing Options and Alternatives

Analysis is only valuable if it leads to solutions. Yet one of the most common weaknesses in consultancy is the rush to produce a single recommendation too early. Clients are rarely well served by being presented with one "answer," because security challenges are complex, shaped by multiple threats, vulnerabilities, and constraints. The more effective approach is to develop a range of options and alternatives, each grounded in evidence, structured through the Threat, Vulnerability and Risk Assessment (TVRA) framework, and evaluated in terms of feasibility, cost, and long-term impact.

Options represent different pathways for reducing risk. For example, if analysis confirms that access control is undermined by contractors sharing cards, several solutions are possible. The consultant might recommend biometric authentication, issue named photo ID cards with tighter controls, or redesign contractor onboarding and supervision processes. Each addresses the same vulnerability but in different ways, with distinct implications for budget, culture, and user acceptance. By developing and presenting alternatives, the consultant gives the client the ability to weigh trade-offs transparently, rather than being steered towards a single pre-determined answer.

TVRA provides the discipline for framing these options. Each design alternative should map explicitly to the threat it mitigates, the vulnerability it addresses, and the risk reduction it achieves. For example:

- **Threat:** unauthorised access by outsiders.
- **Vulnerability:** uncontrolled use of shared contractor cards.
- **Option A:** introduce fingerprint readers (high cost, strong control).
- **Option B:** issue unique QR-coded temporary passes (medium cost, moderate control).
- **Option C:** restructure supervision and daily pass audits (low cost, cultural emphasis).

When options are presented in this way, the link between design and analysis is clear, and the client can make an informed choice based on appetite for risk and resource constraints.

Creativity in solution design is important, but it must remain anchored in feasibility. Some consultants are tempted to over-engineer solutions, proposing cutting-edge technologies that are impressive on paper but unrealistic in context. Others propose minimal interventions that seem achievable but do not materially reduce risk. Developing alternatives forces a balance between creativity and practicality. It ensures that the consultant explores both innovative and pragmatic responses, but always with reference to the evidence and risk profile established in analysis.

Cost-benefit considerations play a central role. Security measures are rarely implemented without budgetary scrutiny, and clients will expect to see a clear justification for investment. Developing alternatives allows costs and benefits to be compared side by side. A high-cost technical system may deliver strong controls but may not be justifiable if a lower-cost procedural fix achieves similar risk reduction. Conversely, a cheap solution that does little to reduce risk is unlikely to be credible. TVRA supports this assessment by showing how much each option reduces the likelihood of a threat or mitigates its impact.

Another dimension is lifecycle implications. A design that looks attractive in the short term may create long-term burdens in maintenance, staffing, or replacement costs. Consultants should therefore evaluate options not only for their immediate effect, but also for sustainability. For instance, recommending a high-tech biometric system in a location with limited technical support may create more problems than it solves. An alternative option focusing on cultural and procedural reinforcement may prove more durable. Presenting lifecycle considerations alongside upfront cost helps clients make decisions that are resilient rather than short-lived.

Stakeholder perspectives must also be considered. Each option has winners and losers – groups who benefit and groups who may resist. For example, introducing biometric access may improve control but could generate resistance from staff who perceive it as intrusive. A cultural training initiative may be welcomed by management but dismissed by frontline staff as burdensome. By mapping stakeholders against each option, consultants can anticipate resistance and identify strategies to mitigate it. This strengthens the likelihood that the chosen solution will be implemented successfully.

Developing options also allows the consultant to distinguish between incremental improvements and transformative redesigns. Sometimes the most effective path is a modest adjustment that closes specific gaps. Other times, analysis may reveal systemic weaknesses that require a complete redesign of security architecture. By offering both kinds of option, the consultant helps the client understand the spectrum of possible responses, from quick wins to long-term transformations. Clients may choose a phased approach: implementing low-cost procedural fixes immediately while planning for more substantial redesigns over time.

Transparency is critical in this process. Each option should be presented with its assumptions, costs, benefits, and limitations made clear. Consultants should resist the temptation to steer clients towards their preferred solution by overstating advantages or minimising drawbacks. Instead, the role of the consultant is to lay out the evidence, explain the trade-offs, and support the client in making an informed decision. This reinforces trust and ensures that the chosen design reflects the client's context and risk appetite, not just the consultant's preferences.

Options must be framed within the proportionality principle of TVRA. Not every vulnerability warrants a complex or costly intervention. The level of response should match the significance of the risk. For example, if the risk of a vulnerability being exploited is low and its potential impact minor, the most proportionate option may be to accept the risk rather than invest in expensive mitigation. Conversely, where a vulnerability creates high-impact, high-likelihood risks, only robust interventions will be defensible. By grounding design choices in TVRA, the consultant ensures that proportionality remains central and that recommendations can withstand external audit or regulatory scrutiny.

Developing options and alternatives is not about indecision; it is about rigour. It prevents premature closure, balances creativity with feasibility, and ensures that design is explicitly tied to evidence and risk. By presenting multiple, well-structured pathways, consultants empower clients to make choices that reflect their resources, culture, and objectives. This process also builds credibility: the consultant is seen not as prescribing a single solution but as providing a transparent, evidence-based framework for decision-making. In consultancy, that ability to illuminate choices is often as valuable as the recommendations themselves.

Analysis provides the evidence for design; design provides the test of analysis. Credible consultancy depends on connecting both through a transparent, risk-based rationale that can withstand scrutiny.

Designing for Implementation

Developing options and alternatives provides clients with choice, but choice alone is not enough. The consultant's role is to ensure that selected solutions are translated into practical designs that can be implemented, operated, and sustained. A recommendation that looks persuasive in a report but cannot be delivered in reality is of little value. Designing for implementation therefore requires the consultant to balance technical rigour with operational practicality, always within the framework of the Threat, Vulnerability and Risk Assessment (TVRA).

The starting point is to translate analysis into design briefs. Each validated hypothesis and prioritised risk should become the foundation for a clear design requirement. If the analysis shows that perimeter security is undermined by poor lighting, the design brief may specify illumination levels, coverage areas, and integration with CCTV. If insider risks are highlighted, the brief might call for redesigned access rights, monitoring protocols, and cultural reinforcement. This translation ensures that every design element is directly traceable back to observed evidence and the risk logic of TVRA.

Designs must also reflect compliance with standards and regulations. Security is not implemented in a vacuum; it is shaped by international standards such as ISO/IEC 27001:2022[15] and ISO/IEC 22301:2019[12], sector-specific codes, and local regulatory requirements. Consultants must ensure that their designs not only address vulnerabilities but also align with these frameworks. This dual compliance – to both the risk model and the regulatory environment – gives recommendations credibility and defensibility. For example, a design may propose redundant power supplies for a control room not only because analysis revealed a vulnerability to outages but also because ISO/IEC 22301[12] demands continuity of critical functions.

A critical aspect of implementation is operability. Designs must work for the people who use them. Complex systems that require constant attention, specialist expertise, or unrealistic staffing levels often fail once installed. Consultants should therefore consider how recommendations will be operated day-to-day. This means designing processes that are intuitive, training programmes that are achievable, and technologies that can be maintained with available skills. A CCTV system specified with advanced analytics may be technically impressive, but if operators cannot interpret the alerts or if the client lacks the resources to maintain licences and upgrades, it is unlikely to deliver lasting value.

Closely related is maintainability. Security measures degrade over time, whether through equipment failure, procedural erosion, or cultural fatigue. Consultants must anticipate this and design for sustainability. Maintenance schedules, spare-part availability, vendor support, and staff turnover should all be factored into the design. In TVRA terms, a vulnerability mitigated today may re-emerge tomorrow if the solution cannot be maintained. Consultants who design with lifecycle considerations in mind build resilience into their recommendations, rather than offering only short-term fixes.

Another danger is over-engineering solutions. Sometimes this stems from a desire to impress with advanced technologies; at other times, from client pressure to demonstrate the "latest and best." The result is often costly systems that exceed operational needs and create unnecessary burdens. Over-engineering not only wastes resources but can undermine security by overwhelming users. The principle of proportionality, central to TVRA, provides a safeguard: the level of design response must be proportionate to the threat, vulnerability, and risk impact. A high-cost biometric system may be justified for a nuclear facility but excessive for a small logistics hub. Consultants must resist the temptation to design beyond need.

Tools and outputs play an important role in communicating and implementing designs. These may include:

- **Design briefs:** concise statements of requirements linked to TVRA findings.
- **Concept diagrams:** visualisations showing how proposed measures interact within the site.
- **Risk registers:** regularly updated to show how each recommendation mitigates specific vulnerabilities.
- **Implementation roadmaps:** phased plans showing priorities, dependencies, and timelines.

These outputs are not bureaucratic; they are practical aids that ensure clarity and alignment between consultant, client, and contractors.

Stakeholder engagement is critical during design. A technically sound recommendation may fail if it does not account for organisational politics or cultural realities. For example, suggesting armed guards in a context where they are legally prohibited or culturally unacceptable would undermine credibility. Engaging stakeholders during the design stage allows the consultant to test assumptions, refine proposals, and build ownership. A design that reflects stakeholder input is more likely to be accepted, funded, and implemented.

Scenario testing provides another discipline. Consultants should test designs against plausible scenarios to assess robustness. What happens if a power outage coincides with a hostile intrusion? How would the design respond to a mass evacuation? Scenario testing ensures that designs are not only technically compliant but resilient under stress. This reflects the TVRA principle of considering both likelihood and impact: designs must be evaluated against realistic threat scenarios, not just normal operations.

Consultants must recognise that implementation is a process, not a single event. Rarely can all recommendations be delivered at once. Designs should therefore include phased implementation strategies, showing what can be achieved immediately, what requires medium-term investment, and what constitutes long-term transformation. Phasing also allows clients to manage resources and adapt to lessons learned along the way. A roadmap that shows incremental progress towards resilience is often more persuasive than a grand design requiring immediate wholesale change.

Designing for implementation is where consultancy moves from analysis to action. It requires translating evidence into design briefs, aligning with standards, ensuring operability and maintainability, avoiding over-engineering, and presenting solutions in clear, usable formats. It demands sensitivity to culture and politics, rigorous scenario testing, and phased planning. Above all, it requires constant reference back to the TVRA framework, ensuring that every design choice is proportionate, evidence-based, and linked to the client's risk profile. Consultants who design for implementation produce recommendations that not only look credible but also work in practice, building the trust that underpins long-term professional value.

Validation and Stress-Testing

A design that looks persuasive on paper may falter when exposed to real-world constraints. Consultants must therefore validate and stress-test their recommendations before presenting them as credible solutions. Validation ensures that designs are consistent with evidence, objectives, and risk priorities. Stress-testing explores how those designs hold up under pressure, whether from operational challenges, hostile threats, or stakeholder resistance. Together, they provide the final assurance that recommendations are not only theoretically sound but also resilient.

Validation begins with alignment. Every recommendation should be explicitly traceable back to the Threat, Vulnerability and Risk Assessment (TVRA). This means demonstrating which threat is being addressed, which vulnerability is being mitigated, and how the overall level of risk is reduced. For example, if the design proposes biometric access control, validation requires showing that the solution directly addresses the identified vulnerability of shared access cards, that it reduces the likelihood of unauthorised entry, and that this in turn reduces the impact of theft or sabotage. If the alignment cannot be shown, the recommendation might look convincing, but it is not valid.

Validation also requires checking against the original client objectives and scope. Projects often evolve as fieldwork and analysis uncover new issues. Consultants must ensure that final recommendations still meet the agreed objectives. Or, if they extend beyond them, that this is explicitly justified and communicated. Failure to validate against scope risks producing designs that are technically impressive but irrelevant to the client's priorities.

A further step in validation is benchmarking against standards and best practice. Designs should be compared against relevant international frameworks such as ISO 31000:2018[13] (risk management), ISO/IEC 27001:2022[15] (information security), and sector-specific regulations. Benchmarking not only strengthens credibility but also provides defensibility in audits, procurement processes, or regulatory reviews. Where a design exceeds minimum compliance requirements, the consultant should explain the rationale; where it falls short, the justification must be clear and proportionate to the risk context.

Stakeholder validation is equally important. Even technically robust designs may fail if they lack acceptance from those who must implement and operate them. Consultants should therefore test recommendations in stakeholder workshops, tabletop exercises, or pilot programmes. These engagements reveal practical challenges, resource constraints, or cultural barriers that might not have been apparent in analysis. They also build ownership: stakeholders who have helped shape and test a design are more likely to support its implementation.

Stress-testing moves validation a step further by exposing designs to simulated pressure. This can take several forms:

- **Scenario testing:** Consultants model how the design performs under specific threat scenarios, such as insider theft, power outages, or coordinated intrusions. By walking through the sequence of events, they identify whether controls hold, where bottlenecks occur, and whether resilience is maintained.

- **Red teaming and penetration testing:** For critical facilities, independent teams may be tasked with probing weaknesses in the proposed design, either physically or digitally. Their findings provide an external check on assumptions.

- **Operational stress:** Consultants consider how designs perform under everyday strain – during shift changes, peak traffic, or equipment failures. A solution that works only in ideal conditions is not robust.

- **Financial stress:** Cost scenarios are applied to test affordability. What happens if budgets are reduced or if long-term maintenance proves more expensive than forecast? Stress-testing here ensures sustainability.

The consultant's role is not to guarantee perfection because no design can withstand every conceivable stress. However, the consultant can ensure that vulnerabilities have been anticipated, trade-offs understood, and residual risks made explicit. Stress-testing therefore supports transparency as much as resilience.

Validation and stress-testing also provide a safeguard against consultant overreach. It is tempting to present bold designs that look impressive but cannot be delivered. By forcing recommendations through a disciplined process of risk alignment, compliance benchmarking, stakeholder engagement, and scenario testing, consultants ensure that only solutions capable of surviving scrutiny reach the client. This strengthens professional credibility and avoids the reputational damage of failed implementations.

Another benefit is adaptability. Stress-testing often reveals weaknesses, but it also creates opportunities for refinement. A design that struggles under certain scenarios can be adjusted before it is finalised. Phased implementation may be introduced to spread cost and build resilience gradually. Alternative technologies or procedures may be swapped in. The process is iterative, ensuring that the final recommendation is not only strong but also adaptable to the client's context.

Validation and stress-testing remind both consultant and client that security is dynamic. Threats evolve, vulnerabilities shift, and organisations change. A design validated today must still be subject to review tomorrow. Consultants should therefore embed feedback mechanisms – regular audits, incident reviews, or performance dashboards – so that designs remain under continuous scrutiny. This creates a culture of learning and adaptation, rather than treating design as a one-off exercise.

Validation and stress-testing transform design from a theoretical exercise into a credible, resilient set of recommendations. Validation ensures alignment with TVRA, client objectives, and regulatory frameworks. Stress-testing subjects the design to realistic pressures, revealing both strengths and weaknesses. Together, they ensure that recommendations can withstand scrutiny, gain stakeholder acceptance, and deliver real-world value. For the consultant, this stage is the final proof of professionalism: not simply proposing solutions, but ensuring that those solutions are tested, defensible, and ready for implementation.

Practice Guide

Analysis and design are where consultancy shifts from observation to impact. This chapter has fulfilled its learning objectives by showing how consultants can transform raw data into structured evidence, test assumptions through hypothesis-driven methods, generate and evaluate multiple design options, and translate findings into implementable solutions that are validated and proportionate. Together, these disciplines ensure that consultancy is not a matter of opinion but of defensible reasoning that leads to credible outcomes.

The pitfalls at this stage are particularly dangerous. Consultants risk drowning in data without moving to conclusions. Others fall prey to confirmation bias, building recommendations around their assumptions rather than their evidence. Designs can be undermined by over-engineering an elaborate solution that looks impressive but collapses under the weight of complexity, cost, or cultural rejection. Equally risky are designs created in isolation from operators, producing elegant documents that fail in practice. Each of these traps erodes trust and credibility, leaving clients with little more than theory.

Best practice lies in disciplined methods and proportionality. Consultants who use frameworks such as TVRA to structure raw data, hypotheses, and design options create a transparent chain of reasoning from evidence to recommendation. By presenting alternatives, they allow clients to weigh trade-offs explicitly, balancing technical, cultural, and financial considerations. By designing for implementation – operability, maintainability, and sustainability – they ensure that solutions are not only credible on paper but workable in daily operations. Validation and stress-testing strengthen recommendations further, exposing vulnerabilities, testing resilience under pressure, and confirming alignment with both standards and client objectives.

The consultant's role in this stage is to remain rigorous yet pragmatic. Analysis provides credibility, design provides relevance, and validation provides confidence. When combined, these disciplines produce recommendations that clients trust, act upon, and embed into their organisations. The broader lesson is that consultancy must always move beyond observation and reporting. Its value lies in the ability to connect evidence, reasoning, and design into solutions that deliver lasting resilience.

The challenge shifts from producing credible designs to communicating them effectively. Even the strongest recommendations can fail if they are presented poorly. The next chapter addresses this final step: how consultants can write reports that people not only read, but act upon.

Chapter 17 – Writing Reports That People Read

For many clients, the report is the most visible outcome of a consultancy engagement. However rigorous the analysis, if the findings are not presented clearly and persuasively, their value may never be realised. Reports are not neutral records; they are instruments of influence. They shape decisions, justify investments, and guide behaviour. Poorly structured reports risk being ignored, while well-crafted ones give the consultant credibility and ensure recommendations are acted upon.

The craft lies in balancing accuracy with accessibility and tailoring messages for different audiences. Executives need strategic clarity, engineers expect technical depth, and operators require practical guidance. Techniques such as storyboarding, the Pyramid Principle[17], and plain English help consultants turn complex analysis into decisions clients can use.

By the end of this chapter, you will be able to:

- Structure consultancy reports for clarity, persuasiveness, and lasting impact.
- Apply *The Pyramid Principle*[17] to lead with the main point and build supporting logic.
- Tailor communication effectively for different audiences – executives, engineers, and operators.
- Use storyboarding methods to organise and refine reports before drafting.
- Write in a style that is authoritative, accessible, and free from unnecessary jargon.
- Avoid common pitfalls such as data-dumping, over-technical language, and poorly constructed executive summaries.

Introduction

In consultancy, the written report is more than a deliverable – it is the currency by which value is measured. However, many site visits have been conducted, interviews held, or hours of analysis completed, the client ultimately judges the consultant by what is placed on their desk or inbox at the end of the process. Reports become the tangible proof of effort, the visible record of expertise, and the medium through which decisions are shaped.

This is why poor reporting can undermine otherwise excellent consultancy. A report that is dense, unfocused, or filled with jargon leaves clients disengaged. Executives may not read beyond the first page. Engineers may struggle to extract the technical substance buried in text. Operators may never see the practical implications intended for them. In such cases, the consultant's effort fails at the final hurdle: insights are generated but not communicated, recommendations are made but not implemented. Reports that are unreadable or unconvincing are wasted opportunities.

By contrast, a clear, well-structured report can amplify the consultant's influence. Executives pressed for time can grasp the essence in a page, engineers can find the specifications they need, and operators can act on step-by-step guidance. A strong report achieves more than recording facts – it shapes perceptions, clarifies choices, and compels action. In some cases, it may influence policy, determine investment, or alter the course of an organisation's security posture.

Yet clarity and influence do not come by accident. Reports are often written under time pressure, at the end of demanding engagements, when energy is low and deadlines loom. Without discipline, the result is too often a "data dump": a collection of observations and appendices with little structure or prioritisation. Consultants who approach reporting as a mechanical output rather than a persuasive act risk producing documents that tick contractual boxes but fail to deliver real value.

This chapter argues that reports should be seen as acts of design in their own right. Just as a security system must be engineered for use, so too must a report be crafted for readability and influence. Techniques such as *The Pyramid Principle*[17] – beginning with the main message and then supporting it with evidence – give reports logical clarity. Storyboarding ensures that the flow of argument is planned before writing begins. Tailoring content for different audiences ensures that executives, engineers, and operators each find what they need without compromise.

A consultant's credibility is inseparable from their reports. A weak report can damage reputation even if the underlying work was sound. A strong report can elevate a consultant's standing, building trust and opening the door to further engagements. In this sense, reports are more than a conclusion: they are a continuation of the consultant's influence, extending beyond the project into the decisions and behaviours of the client organisation.

This chapter will therefore focus on how to write reports that people actually read – and, more importantly, act upon.

The Purpose of a Consultancy Report

At its core, the consultancy report is a bridge between analysis and decision. It translates weeks or months of work – site surveys, interviews, data analysis, and design – into a document that the client can use to act on. Its purpose is not simply to document what was done, but to make the consultant's findings intelligible, persuasive, and actionable for people who were not present during the work. Reports must therefore be written with clarity of intent: they are not archives of information, but instruments of influence.

The first and most obvious purpose is to enable decision-making. Clients commission consultants to provide clarity where complexity or uncertainty exists. A well-crafted report distils evidence into a set of conclusions and recommendations that guide the client's next steps. This might mean approving a capital investment, adjusting operational procedures, or preparing for regulatory compliance. If the report does not support timely and confident decisions, it has not fulfilled its purpose.

Equally important is the role of the report in building credibility and trust. A report represents the consultant's professionalism in written form. Clear structuring, logical arguments, and plain English communicate competence and reliability. Conversely, a report cluttered with jargon, disorganised sections, or vague recommendations raises doubts about the consultant's thoroughness, even if the underlying work was sound. Clients often share reports with senior stakeholders who may never meet the consultant in person; the report alone shapes their perception of quality.

A third function is to document evidence for accountability. Many consultancy projects involve significant financial or operational consequences. Recommendations may be scrutinised by boards, auditors, regulators, or even legal authorities. The report therefore provides an auditable record, showing not only what the consultant recommends but also how those recommendations were derived. In security consultancy, where risks and costs can be high, the ability to trace each recommendation back to observed evidence and structured analysis is critical.

Finding / Observation	Supporting Evidence Source	Analytical Inference	Design Recommendation	Residual Risk / Audit Note
CCTV coverage in loading bay incomplete.	Site survey photos; camera layout drawing Rev C.	Blind spot between dock doors 3–5 allows unmonitored vehicle movement.	Add additional PTZ camera; re-align fixed camera C3-05.	Medium – residual risk until installation verified.
Access control server shares IT switch with open VLAN.	Network diagram; IT audit log.	Compromised network could allow unauthorised access-log manipulation.	Segregate network via dedicated VLAN and firewall rules.	Low – requires periodic network review.
Visitor processing queue exceeds screening capacity.	Observation × 3 days; access-log time analysis.	Congestion increases tailgating risk at peak hours.	Add second screening lane; schedule staggered arrivals.	Medium – review effectiveness after 1 month.
Security officers bypass dual-auth procedure during shift change.	Interviews; CCTV time stamps.	Cultural drift undermines procedural enforcement.	Retrain and re-brief; introduce biometric check at shift-change.	High – monitor compliance weekly.
Lighting at east perimeter below 10 lux average.	Lux meter survey results.	Poor illumination reduces deterrence and camera visibility.	Replace fittings with 15 lux LED standard; link to motion sensors.	Low – verify after upgrade.
Emergency exits open directly to unsecured parking.	Floor plan; door hardware schedule.	Direct escape route exposes site to reverse entry threat.	Re-route exit path; add one-way hardware and intrusion sensor.	Low – inspect quarterly.

Table 7 Evidence-to-Recommendation Chain

Reports also serve to align multiple stakeholders. Complex projects often involve executives, engineers, operators, regulators, and contractors. Each group has different priorities and levels of technical literacy. A report provides a single reference point that integrates these perspectives and establishes a shared understanding of the issues. For example, executives may focus on strategic risks, engineers on technical compliance, and operators on practical procedures. A well-designed report ensures that all groups are addressed in one coherent narrative, preventing misalignment that could derail implementation.

The consultancy report also functions as a change management tool. Recommendations often require shifts in behaviour, budget allocation, or organisational culture. A persuasive report can make the case for change, highlighting the risks of inaction and the benefits of adopting new measures. Narrative devices such as scenarios ("What happens if this vulnerability is exploited?") or comparative examples ("Similar organisations that acted avoided losses, those that did not suffered consequences") can strengthen the case. The report thus becomes not only a record of analysis but a lever for transformation.

Reports must be written with discipline of purpose. A common pitfall is treating the report as a catch-all repository of information. Clients may receive documents hundreds of pages long, filled with background detail but lacking clear conclusions. Such "data dumps" obscure the main message, overwhelming readers rather than informing them. The purpose of a consultancy report is not to demonstrate how much work was done, but to convey what matters. Appendices can contain supporting evidence, but the main body must remain focused and usable.

The implicit contract between consultant and client is therefore clarity, honesty, and usability. Reports should be written to inform, not to impress. They should highlight limitations as well as strengths, uncertainties as well as conclusions. A consultant who acknowledges gaps in evidence or constraints in recommendations will build more trust than one who masks uncertainty with vague language. The client's confidence comes not from being told what they want to hear, but from knowing that the consultant's advice is grounded, proportionate, and transparent.

It is also important to recognise that reports serve a longer lifespan than the engagement itself. Long after the consultant has departed, the report may continue to shape decisions. New staff may refer to it, auditors may review it, regulators may request it. A report written solely for immediate consumption risks becoming obsolete once personnel change or memory fades. Reports that clearly explain findings, context, and rationale remain useful well beyond their initial presentation.

The purpose of a consultancy report is not simply to record what the consultant discovered, but to ensure that discovery leads to action. It is the document that translates professional expertise into client outcomes. A well-crafted report is therefore both a conclusion and a beginning: the conclusion of analysis, and the beginning of client decisions that create change.

Structuring for Clarity and Influence

No matter how thorough the analysis or valuable the insight, if the argument is buried in a poorly organised document the message will be lost. Structure is the framework that allows information to be absorbed quickly, judged credible, and acted upon. In consultancy, it is not optional; it is the difference between a report that records information and one that shapes decisions.

The foundation of strong structure is the Pyramid Principle[17], developed by Barbara Minto. Its logic is simple but powerful: start with the answer, then show the reasoning. Executives rarely have the patience to sift through background detail in search of conclusions. They want to know immediately what the consultant recommends, before deciding whether to examine the supporting arguments. Reports that delay their message until the end risk being set aside before the most important points are reached.

Applying the Pyramid Principle[17] means distilling the core message into a clear opening statement, followed by arguments grouped beneath it in a logical hierarchy. Evidence, examples, and data sit at the base of the pyramid, supporting the reasoning above. In this way, the same report can meet the needs of multiple audiences: an executive can grasp the headline conclusion within moments, while engineers and operators can read further into the layers of justification and technical depth.

Alongside the Pyramid Principle[17] sits the discipline of MECE structuring – Mutually Exclusive and Collectively Exhaustive. This ensures that findings are grouped into categories that are distinct, with no overlaps, and comprehensive, leaving no gaps. For example, weaknesses in a security programme might be presented under physical infrastructure, electronic systems, and procedural or cultural practices. Each point fits in one place only, and together the categories describe the full picture. Without such discipline, reports often become repetitive, fragmented, or incomplete.

Within this overarching logic, the executive summary is decisive. Many senior readers will never progress beyond this page, yet they will form their impression of the entire engagement from it. The summary is not an abstract or preface but a condensed report in miniature. It must state why the work was undertaken, what was found, what is recommended, and what the consequences are of acting or failing to act. A useful test is simple: if this is the only page the client reads, would they know what to do next? If the answer is no, the summary has failed in its purpose.

The body of the report should then unfold in a logical sequence that balances transparency with impact. A common order is: introduction and purpose, methodology, findings, analysis, recommendations, and next steps. The introduction frames the issue, the methodology establishes credibility, the findings set out the evidence, the analysis interprets it, and the recommendations turn it into actionable guidance. Closing with practical next steps gives momentum to implementation rather than leaving the client with static advice.

Visuals can support structure when chosen carefully. Tables that link each vulnerability to its corresponding recommendation provide immediate traceability, and flow diagrams can clarify sequences of action. Charts and matrices may also help illustrate patterns, but they must be used with care. Heat maps, for example, have the advantage of showing relative priorities at a glance, which is why they are popular with decision-makers. However, they can also be misleading if they oversimplify complex risks or create a false sense of precision. Where they are used, their limitations should be explained and supported by the underlying analysis. The guiding question should always be whether the visual makes the message clearer, not whether the software makes it possible.

Another discipline of structure is separating fact, inference, and recommendation. Many reports blur the distinction. A statement such as "the control room is inadequately staffed" confuses observation with judgement. Clarity comes from stating the fact that "the control room had one operator during peak traffic periods" then drawing the inference, "this level of staffing may be insufficient to manage simultaneous incidents", and finally presenting the recommendation, "increase staffing to at least two operators at peak times." Separating these elements makes reasoning transparent and defensible, enabling clients to see exactly how conclusions were reached.

Different audiences engage with reports in different ways, and structure must anticipate this. Executives skim, managers read to understand the reasoning behind the recommendations, engineers scrutinise technical details, and operators look for practical instructions. A layered design meets these needs by providing an accessible executive summary, a clear main body of findings and analysis, and annexes or appendices containing the technical or operational depth. Each layer stands alone for its audience, but together they form a coherent whole.

Tone is inseparable from structure. Clear organisation is undermined if the writing itself is cluttered or hesitant. Concise sentences, confident but proportionate language, and plain English keep the focus on meaning rather than style. Technical terms should be explained where necessary, ensuring that even a reader unfamiliar with the project can follow the logic, while specialists still find the analysis credible.

Structure is a form of respect for the reader. Clients often juggle competing priorities and limited time. A consultant who leads with the answer, groups arguments coherently, makes evidence accessible, and layers information to suit different audiences shows that respect. The result is a report that does more than inform; it persuades, builds trust, and drives action.

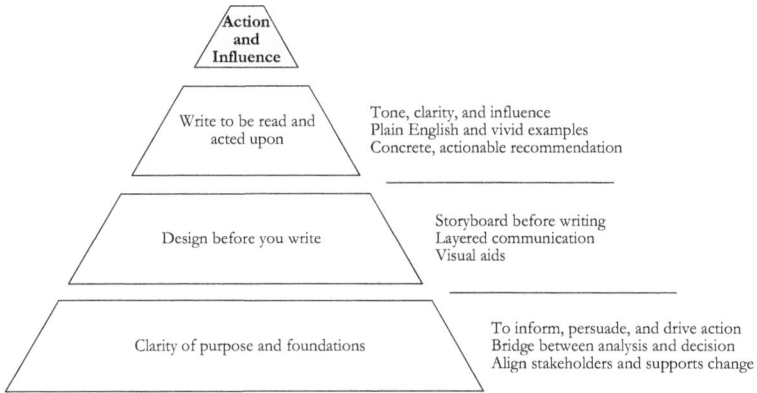

Figure 15 The Architecture of an Effective Consultancy Report

Storyboarding Reports Before Writing

Good reports are rarely created by sitting down at a keyboard and typing from start to finish. They are designed before they are written. Storyboarding is the consultant's equivalent of architectural sketching: a planning tool that lays out the flow of the report, the order of arguments, and the evidence required to support them. It allows consultants to see the shape of the report before committing words to paper, ensuring that the final product is coherent, purposeful, and free of unnecessary detours.

At its core, storyboarding is about treating the report as a narrative. Consultancy reports are not novels, but they do tell a story: the story of the client's challenge, the investigation undertaken, the findings uncovered, and the solutions proposed. If this story is not thought through before writing, the report risks becoming a patchwork of disconnected sections – each technically accurate but lacking in flow. Storyboarding forces the consultant to decide in advance: what is the central message, how will it be delivered, and what sequence of logic will support it?

The process typically begins with identifying the main message. Using the Pyramid Principle[17], this should be articulated as a short, declarative statement: "The organisation's resilience is undermined by weak incident response procedures, and we recommend a phased redesign of training, governance, and monitoring." Once this message is clear, the storyboard can map how supporting points will unfold. Each point becomes a "chapter" or section, with evidence and recommendations linked beneath.

A practical way to build storyboards is through visual mapping. Some consultants use sticky notes on a wall or whiteboard; others use digital tools such as mind-mapping software or slide decks. The method matters less than the principle: each sticky note or box represents a finding, argument, or piece of evidence. By arranging and rearranging them, the consultant can experiment with different flows until a logical and persuasive sequence emerges. For instance, should the report lead with external regulatory drivers, or begin with internal cultural weaknesses? Should recommendations be grouped by threat category, or by organisational function? These decisions are best tested visually before drafting begins.

Storyboarding also serves as a defence against scope creep and redundancy. Reports often expand uncontrollably because some consultants try to include everything they observed. By mapping findings to the storyboard, it becomes clear which points support the central message and which do not. Peripheral details can be relegated to annexes or omitted entirely. Similarly, redundancy is reduced because each point has its place; if a finding does not fit anywhere on the board, it either needs reframing, or it does not belong.

Another strength of storyboarding is its role in team alignment. Large consultancy projects often involve multiple contributors, each responsible for sections of analysis. Without a storyboard, drafts can arrive in different voices, with overlapping content and conflicting emphasis. A shared storyboard acts as a blueprint, ensuring that each contributor knows the intended flow and their place within it. This improves coherence and reduces the editing burden later.

Working alone, storyboarding provides a form of self-discipline. It prevents the common error of starting with background context, wandering through findings, and eventually arriving at conclusions after dozens of pages. Instead, it encourages writing with the destination in mind. The storyboard reminds the consultant: begin with the answer, support with logic, and resist digression.

Storyboarding is also invaluable for time management. Many reports are written under deadline pressure. A storyboard allows the consultant to allocate word counts, visuals, and priorities before writing, ensuring that the executive summary is not an afterthought squeezed in at the end. It also prevents the common trap of spending excessive time drafting detailed background sections while leaving insufficient time for conclusions.

Storyboarding encourages clarity of communication. By designing the narrative visually, consultants see immediately if sections are overloaded or if logic is unbalanced. If one level of the pyramid is disproportionately detailed while another is thin, it signals where more evidence is needed or where unnecessary complexity can be cut. This clarity improves not only the writing but also the subsequent delivery of presentations based on the report.

Storyboarding is not an optional creative flourish; it is a discipline that saves time, enhances coherence, and improves persuasiveness. It ensures that reports tell a clear story, remain focused on the client's needs, and present findings in a logical, compelling sequence. Consultants who adopt storyboarding consistently deliver reports that are not only read but acted upon.

Reporting is the final act of consultancy discipline. Clarity, structure, and proportion turn analysis into influence – ensuring that evidence does not end at understanding but results in action.

Tailoring Reports to Different Audiences

Consultancy reports rarely have a single reader. They move between executives, managers, engineers, operators, regulators, and sometimes external partners. Each group comes with different priorities, levels of technical knowledge, and expectations of detail. The consultant's task is to design one report that can serve all of them without diluting its integrity or overwhelming those who need clarity above all. This requires deliberate tailoring – not by writing multiple reports, but by structuring and layering a single document so each audience can extract what it needs.

For executives, and especially the chief executive suite (C-suite), brevity and strategic focus are paramount. Senior leaders want outcomes, not process. They ask: What are the risks? How serious are they? What options exist? What is recommended? And what are the consequences of action or inaction? Anything that does not address these questions is likely to be ignored. The executive summary therefore becomes the consultant's most valuable tool. It should stand alone, ideally no more than a page, presenting the problem, the evidence, the recommendations, and the implications with absolute clarity.

Often this distillation reduces a technical report of dozens of pages to a handful of points that can be absorbed in a board meeting. These points typically cover the main risks, the priority recommendations, the investment required, the benefits gained, and the risks of inaction. This is not about oversimplifying but about sharpening: providing leaders with the essence so they can make confident decisions under pressure. Consultants who master this skill greatly increase the likelihood that their recommendations will be acted upon.

Engineers require a different emphasis. They will test assumptions, check calculations, and probe feasibility. A report that satisfies executives but fails to provide depth for technical readers risks being dismissed as superficial. Annexes and technical sections should therefore provide schematics, compliance references, risk matrices, and calculations. These details must be available without cluttering the main narrative, allowing the engineer to validate the work while keeping the overall report accessible. Layered structuring serves this purpose: the headline conclusions are visible to executives, but engineers can dive deeper into appendices for the underpinning.

Operators, in turn, need practical guidance they can apply day-to-day. A high-level recommendation such as "enhance incident response protocols" is not enough. It must be translated into steps: who does what, when, and how. Practical checklists, flow diagrams, or one-page job aids are often more useful than long paragraphs of description. Reports that include "operational annexes" are more likely to drive behavioural change at the frontline, where small adjustments can make the greatest difference to resilience.

The challenge is to serve all these audiences within one coherent document. The most effective method is layered communication. This involves structuring the report in tiered levels: an executive summary for decision-makers; a main body with findings, analysis, and recommendations for managers; and annexes or appendices with technical data and operational guidance for engineers and operators. Each layer must stand alone for the reader who uses it most, while remaining part of an integrated whole.

Tailoring also extends to presentation. Reports are often supported by briefings to boards, steering committees, or operational teams. A presentation should not repeat the report but distil it. The consultant must decide: if I had five minutes, what would I want the client to remember? That essence must be captured in a few slides or sentences, supported if needed by appendices or discussion. Decision-makers cannot act on what they cannot grasp.

Different reading behaviours add another dimension. Some readers scan headings, charts, and tables; others read line by line. Reports should therefore be designed to reward both approaches. Informative headings, captions, and summary tables help the scanner; coherent paragraphs and logical argument serve the detailed reader. This dual design prevents frustration when clients struggle to find what matters to them.

Cultural expectations also shape how reports are received. In some environments, brevity and directness are valued; in others, formality and detailed substantiation are expected. Consultants should adapt tone and presentation to the client's organisational culture while still adhering to universal principles of clarity and proportionality.

Tailoring, then, is not about producing different reports for different groups. It is about designing one report that is accessible at multiple levels – from boardroom to control room. This demands discipline in structuring, skill in layering, and care in summarising. Without tailoring, reports risk being too long for executives, too thin for engineers, or too abstract for operators. With it, they become documents that are read widely, trusted deeply, and used to drive change.

Tailoring is an act of empathy. It asks the consultant to step into the shoes of each reader and consider: What does this person need to know? How will they use it? How much time do they have? And what format will make it most useful? When these questions are answered honestly, the report stops being a static record and becomes a dynamic tool – shaping decisions at the top, guiding projects in the middle, and supporting action on the ground.

The Art of Persuasive Writing

Even the best structure cannot compensate for poor writing. A consultancy report must not only be logically sound but also persuasive in tone and style. Persuasion here does not mean manipulation; it means presenting evidence and recommendations in a way that engages the reader, builds trust, and prompts action. The consultant's credibility rests as much on how ideas are expressed as on the strength of the underlying analysis.

Tone and style are the first considerations. Reports should be authoritative but not arrogant, confident but not dogmatic. The language must convey expertise without alienating readers. This balance is achieved by grounding every conclusion in evidence and presenting it plainly. Overly tentative language ("it might be possible that…") erodes confidence. Overly absolute statements ("this will guarantee security") undermine credibility. A persuasive tone sits in the middle: firm, evidence-based, and proportionate.

Plain English is a hallmark of professionalism. Consultants sometimes assume that jargon, acronyms, or dense technical phrasing demonstrate expertise. In reality, they alienate non-specialist readers and slow comprehension. Persuasive writing avoids unnecessary complexity. A phrase such as "egress routes exhibit suboptimal operational functionality" can and should be replaced with "exit routes are difficult to use." Plain English does not mean simplistic; it means clear, precise, and accessible language.

At the same time, persuasive reports use narrative techniques to make risks and recommendations vivid. Humans respond to stories more readily than to abstract data. A consultant might write: "If this vulnerability were exploited during a peak event, evacuation could be delayed, with severe consequences for safety." This scenario-based phrasing helps the client imagine real-world impact, not just theoretical probability. Similarly, referencing comparative cases "a similar organisation that ignored this risk experienced a major outage" can strengthen urgency.

Another persuasive technique is designing for quick reading. Not every reader will study the report line by line. Many will scan headings, charts, or summary tables. Persuasive writing therefore uses signposting to make key points visible. Headings should be meaningful, not generic ("Access

Control Failures" rather than "Findings, Section 2"). Bullet points can be used sparingly to highlight recommendations or summarise risks. Captions on charts and tables should explain the insight, not just the content ("Figure 3: Access logs show 20% of entries lacked proper authentication, indicating systemic control failure"). This design supports readers who skim while still rewarding those who read deeply.

Persuasive writing also depends on proportionate emphasis. Consultants must judge which points deserve prominence and which can be summarised briefly. Reports that give equal weight to minor and major issues dilute their own message. A vulnerability that exposes critical assets should be described in more detail and positioned prominently, while minor compliance gaps can be handled concisely or placed in an appendix. The discipline of emphasis ensures that the client's attention is drawn to what matters most.

Conciseness is another discipline. Reports are often padded with background detail, lengthy methodology, or repeated findings. Persuasive writing trims this excess, focusing on what the client needs to know. Methodology can often be summarised in a paragraph and detailed in an appendix. Background context should be no longer than necessary to frame findings. Redundancy should be ruthlessly edited. Brevity signals respect for the reader's time.

A persuasive report also addresses resistance in advance. Clients may be wary of cost, sceptical of disruption, or reluctant to accept shortcomings. Reports that ignore these objections leave space for them to fester. Reports that acknowledge them build credibility. For example: "While upgrading all perimeter fencing may appear costly, the investment is offset by reduced incident risk and lower insurance premiums." Anticipating resistance and responding directly strengthens the consultant's position and reassures the client that recommendations are realistic.

Persuasion requires clarity of recommendation. Too often, reports end with vague suggestions such as "improve procedures" or "enhance resilience." Persuasive writing makes recommendations concrete, specific, and actionable: "Introduce a quarterly incident drill programme, with scenarios rotated across natural hazard, technical failure, and hostile threat." Clear, practical actions show professionalism and stop the client from dismissing the report as too abstract.

Persuasive writing is not about embellishment but about clarity, confidence, and impact. It avoids jargon, tells compelling stories, makes key points visible, emphasises what matters, respects the reader's time, anticipates objections, and delivers actionable recommendations. Consultants who master this craft produce reports that do more than inform – they influence. They ensure that analysis translates into action, and that the consultant's effort creates lasting change.

Illustrative Example: The Report That Changed Nothing

A major organisation responsible for several high-value facilities experienced a series of minor security incidents. Concerned that these signalled deeper weaknesses, leadership commissioned a consultancy to carry out a comprehensive risk review. The team did exactly that: surveys were conducted, staff were interviewed, and systems were assessed. The analysis was thorough, and the findings were clear. Weaknesses in control room staffing, outdated perimeter technology, and inconsistent incident response were all identified. The recommendations – phased technology upgrades, stronger governance, and renewed staff training – were proportionate and well considered.

The problem was not the work itself but how it was presented. The consultancy delivered a report that exceeded 200 pages, dominated by detailed methodology, raw transcripts, and lengthy technical descriptions. Key findings were scattered through the document and often buried in dense paragraphs. Recommendations were listed at the end in general terms, without sequencing or prioritisation. The executive summary – the page most likely to be read by senior decision-makers – amounted to half a page of bland statements such as "security could be improved in several areas." No urgency was conveyed, no risks were quantified, and no consequences were described.

The reaction was predictable. Executives read only the summary, found little of value, and set the report aside. Managers dipped into the body of the document but could not identify clear priorities. Engineers, frustrated by vague justifications, questioned the robustness of the recommendations. Operators never even saw the report. What could have been a catalyst for improvement became a forgotten file. Within a year, a serious incident occurred – precisely the kind of event the recommendations had sought to prevent.

Four failures stood out. First, the report followed the consultant's workflow rather than the client's decision-making needs, placing methodology before conclusions. Second, it treated all audiences the same, when in reality executives, engineers, and operators required different levels of detail. Third, its tone lacked persuasion: cautious phrases and abstract language failed to make the risks real. The recommendations were presented as an undifferentiated list, leaving managers paralysed by indecision.

The report could have been transformed by applying the very principles outlined in this chapter. Leading with a clear conclusion – that weak incident response and outdated perimeter systems left the organisation exposed – would have captured executive attention. A layered communication approach could have provided a one-page summary for the board, a structured body of analysis for managers, and annexes with technical and operational guidance. Persuasive writing, including scenario-based illustrations of the risks, would have added urgency. Most importantly, prioritisation and phasing would have turned a static list into a roadmap for action.

Good analysis alone does not create value; it must be communicated in a way that informs, persuades, and guides. Without structure, tailoring, persuasion, and prioritisation, even the best work can be ignored. In this case, the consultancy produced a report that documented the risks but failed to influence the client. It became, in effect, the report that changed nothing.

Practice Guide

Reports are the consultant's most visible deliverable, and their impact often extends far beyond the project itself. A report may be reviewed months or even years later, long after the consultant has departed. As a discoverable document, its contents can be evaluated in audits, investigations, or legal proceedings. This scrutiny can work in the consultant's favour if the report is clear, proportionate, and professional, but it can just as easily damage reputation if it is vague, overloaded, or poorly structured.

This chapter has shown how effective reports must be structured for clarity and influence, tailored to executives, engineers, and operators, and written in a persuasive, accessible style. It has demonstrated the value of the Pyramid Principle[17] and MECE logic, the discipline of storyboarding, the layering of communication for different audiences, and the techniques of persuasive writing that make findings not only readable but actionable.

The pitfalls to avoid are well known yet widespread. Reports that become "data dumps" confuse volume with value. Those that follow the consultant's workflow – methodology first, conclusions last – leave clients without a clear path to decision. Jargon alienates readers, weak executive summaries lose critical audiences, and unprioritised recommendations leave managers uncertain where to begin. Each of these missteps undermines influence and wastes the effort of analysis.

Good practice lies in discipline and empathy for the reader. Reports should lead with the answer, structured through the Pyramid Principle[17], supported with MECE logic, and storyboarded before drafting. Layered communication ensures each audience finds what it needs – concise clarity for executives, technical depth for engineers, and practical guidance for operators. Persuasive writing relies on plain English, vivid scenarios, proportionate emphasis, and clear prioritisation, while also anticipating resistance and addressing it directly.

The consultant's credibility is tested in how findings are communicated. Reports that are clear, structured, and persuasive build trust, shape decisions, and drive change. Those that fail in these qualities risk being ignored, however strong the underlying analysis. The lesson is simple but critical: in consultancy, communication is inseparable from value. By mastering the craft of reporting, consultants ensure their work continues to have influence long after the project closes, turning a single engagement into part of a lasting professional legacy.

Reflections – From Process to Impact

Part 3 has shown how consultancy is delivered in practice, moving from the conditions in which projects take place through to the outputs that shape client decisions. If Part 1 established the consultant's mindset, and Part 2 equipped the reader with analytical tools, then Part 3 demonstrated how these attributes come alive in live engagements. Consultancy is not defined by abstract knowledge alone, but by the disciplined application of that knowledge in complex, contested, and time-bound contexts.

The first chapter examined the consultant's place in the project ecosystem. No consultant works in isolation; success depends on navigating a web of clients, contractors, regulators, and integrators. The lesson was not only technical but relational – knowing when to lead, when to advise, and when to step back. Trust, credibility, and political awareness were shown to be as important as technical expertise in sustaining influence across a project's life cycle.

From there, attention shifted to winning the work. Engagements begin with reputation, proposals, and the ability to frame value in ways that clients recognise. Credibility rests on clarity and proportionality: consultants who overpromise or under-price may win contracts but erode trust, while those who scope with discipline and link fees to outcomes build durable relationships.

The discussion then moved from brief to plan. Client briefs are rarely complete or neutral; they carry assumptions and internal tensions. The consultant's role is to interrogate, surface hidden agendas, and convert ambitions into achievable deliverables. This stage highlighted the importance of stakeholder engagement, early planning, and contracting as disciplines that create clarity rather than passively receive it.

Fieldwork brought consultancy into the lived realities of sites and organisations. On-site observation and stakeholder interviews provide the raw material of professional judgement, but only when approached with discipline. The risks of stage-managed visits and superficial surveys were contrasted with the value of structured preparation, careful observation, and sensitive interviewing. Evidence, it was stressed, must capture both systems and culture if credibility is to be sustained.

Analysis and design transformed that evidence into insight and recommendations. Here the emphasis was on structure: using frameworks such as TVRA, applying hypothesis-driven methods to reduce bias, and developing alternatives that allow clients to weigh trade-offs. Analysis without design leaves consultancy academic; design without analysis leaves it fragile. Durable recommendations emerge only when evidence is bridged with feasible, proportionate solutions.

The final chapter focused on reports – the medium through which consultancy endures beyond the engagement. Reports are not neutral archives but instruments of influence. Using principles such as the Pyramid Principle[17] and storyboarding, consultants must structure content clearly, tailor it to different audiences, and write persuasively. The example of *The Report That Changed Nothing* illustrated how poor communication can neutralise otherwise strong analysis, underscoring that credibility is inseparable from the clarity of written outputs.

Taken together, these chapters showed how to position within the project ecosystem, win work through credibility, convert vague briefs into structured plans, gather authentic field evidence, transform it into analysis and design, and communicate findings in reports that compel action. Each stage links to the next: credible proposals shape briefs, clear briefs guide fieldwork, evidence informs analysis, analysis underpins design, and design is only as strong as the report that carries it into decisions.

The pitfalls of process are equally clear: overpromising in bids, accepting briefs at face value, conducting superficial site visits, analysing without designing, or producing reports that are unreadable or unpersuasive. Good practice lies in discipline and empathy – building trust in proposals, interrogating briefs, gathering evidence with rigour, applying structured analysis, and writing reports that are clear, tailored, and persuasive.

The theme of this part is that consultancy is a process of translation: from ambiguity to clarity, from evidence to insight, from insight to influence. Tools and mindsets alone do not create value; value comes from the disciplined process through which they are applied, balancing rigour with empathy, and technical skill with political awareness.

As we move into Part 4, the focus shifts from process to practice at scale. Having explored how individual projects are delivered, the next part considers how consultants sustain performance across portfolios, develop long-term client relationships, and navigate the commercial, ethical, and organisational challenges of building a career. If Part 3 was about process, Part 4 is about practice – the strategies that turn individual engagements into a sustainable professional identity and lasting impact.

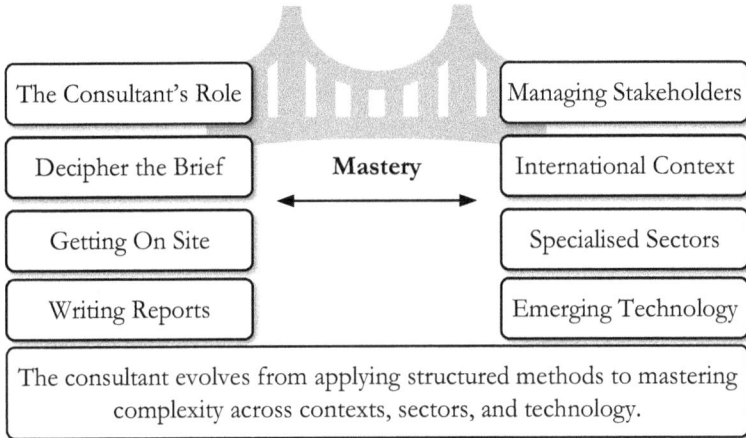

The Consultant's Role		Managing Stakeholders
Decipher the Brief	**Mastery**	International Context
Getting On Site		Specialised Sectors
Writing Reports		Emerging Technology

The consultant evolves from applying structured methods to mastering complexity across contexts, sectors, and technology.

Figure 16 Part 3 Reflections Bridge

Part 4 – Advanced Practice

At higher levels, consultancy faces challenges that are larger, more varied, and less forgiving. Projects become larger, risks more varied, and environments less forgiving. In these contexts, the fundamentals of consultancy – analysis, engagement, design, and communication – still apply, but they must be exercised with greater discipline, judgement, and adaptability. Part 4 explores this advanced practice, where the stakes are higher and the consultant's credibility is tested more severely.

This section traces the situations where consulting practice must stretch beyond the routine. It begins with stakeholder management in environments where agendas compete and integrity is constantly tested. It then considers international and high-risk settings, where cultural awareness and personal resilience matter as much as technical skill. From there, the scope turns to specialised sectors such as critical national infrastructure and data centres, where sector fluency and proportionality become decisive. Emerging technologies and threats, from artificial intelligence to climate pressures, are then examined, showing how foresight and adaptability underpin resilient advice. The section concludes with hybrid and remote consulting, where digital tools extend capacity but never replace the presence and contextual awareness that secures credibility.

Taken together, these chapters show that advanced practice does not replace the fundamentals of consultancy but applies them under greater pressure. Independence, integrity, and proportionality remain the foundation blocks, yet success comes from adapting methods to complex and shifting realities. Advanced practice is less about accumulating knowledge and more about applying sound judgement when certainty is in short supply.

Chapter 18 – Managing Complex Stakeholders

Consultancy outcomes depend not only on analysis and design but on how effectively stakeholders are engaged. Success requires more than technical skill; it rests on trust, impartiality, and the ability to navigate competing agendas. This chapter focuses on the principles and methods consultants need to manage these relationships constructively.

By the end of this chapter, you will be able to:

- Build and maintain trust while managing multiple, often conflicting, stakeholder agendas.
- Recognise common forms of resistance and respond constructively rather than defensively.
- Balance authority, diplomacy, and influence in environments with diverse power dynamics.
- Apply structured methods such as stakeholder mapping, RACI models, and communication plans to organise engagement.
- Sustain professional independence and integrity while navigating political and organisational pressures.
- Avoid common pitfalls, such as over-aligning with one faction or neglecting quiet but influential voices.

Introduction

Every consultancy project is influenced as much by people as by technical detail. However, detailed the analysis or innovative the design, outcomes still depend on whether stakeholders are prepared to listen, support, and act on the consultant's advice. Stakeholders are not something to be dealt with afterwards – they form part of the environment in which consultancy takes place. Success depends as much on navigating this environment as on technical expertise.

Stakeholder complexity arises because every group has its own aims. Clients commission work to achieve organisational goals, but inside the client there may be differences between executives, managers, and operational teams. Contractors often focus on budgets and schedules, regulators on compliance, and operators on day-to-day practicality. In large or politically sensitive projects, external players such as investors, community representatives, or the media may also have a voice. No single perspective is enough on its own, and no agenda is left unchallenged.

This mix creates risks but also opportunities. Poor handling of stakeholders can derail progress with conflicting instructions, hidden vetoes, or quiet resistance can all undermine a project. Well-handled stakeholders, on the other hand, can become allies who promote the consultant's recommendations and clear the way for implementation. Consultants who treat stakeholder management as a core discipline, not a distraction from "real work," are far more likely to make a lasting impact.

At the centre of stakeholder management is trust. Without trust, access is restricted, information is filtered, and recommendations are questioned. With trust, stakeholders share openly, cooperate in testing ideas, and support change even when it is difficult. Trust must be earned through openness, consistency, and responsiveness, and it can be lost quickly if consultants appear biased or dismissive.

Some stakeholders may push back against findings, delay decisions, or agree in meetings while blocking progress outside of them. Consultants should expect resistance, understand the reasons behind it, and respond constructively rather than defensively. Often it signals hidden worries, competing pressures, or organisational weaknesses that must be surfaced and addressed.

Managing stakeholders also demands judgement. Consultants must balance authority with diplomacy, pressing their case strongly enough to be credible but tactfully enough to maintain relationships. They must avoid being pulled too far to one side, keeping their independence while still showing empathy. These are not "soft skills" in the optional sense; they are central consulting skills, every bit as critical as technical analysis or design.

This chapter explores how consultants can work in such environments with integrity and effectiveness. It shows that stakeholder management is not an add-on to consultancy but the context in which all consultancy takes place.

Understanding Stakeholder Complexity

To manage stakeholders effectively, consultants must first understand who they are, what they want, and how they exert influence. Stakeholders are not a homogenous group; they differ in power, interest, expectations, and the degree to which they can shape project outcomes. Recognising this complexity is essential for building realistic strategies for engagement.

Identifying stakeholder groups is the starting point. At a minimum, every consultancy project involves the client organisation, regulators, and operators. In large or politically sensitive projects, additional stakeholders may include investors, auditors, insurers, communities, and even the media. Each group brings a different perspective: clients commission work to achieve organisational objectives, regulators ensure compliance, and operators focus on day-to-day feasibility. External parties such as investors may concentrate on financial performance, while communities focus on environmental or social impacts. The consultant's task is to recognise that these groups coexist and may pull in different directions.

A useful tool here is power/interest mapping. Stakeholders can be plotted on a matrix according to their level of power (ability to influence outcomes) and interest (level of concern with the project). Those with high power and high interest – typically client executives or regulators – must be managed closely. Those with high power but low interest, such as external financiers, must be kept satisfied but not overloaded. Stakeholders with low power but high interest, such as frontline operators, should be kept informed and consulted, as they often have critical practical knowledge. Those with low power and low interest require minimal attention but should not be ignored entirely, as their position can shift over time.

Beyond formal roles, consultants must also watch for hidden stakeholders. These can include informal influencers and people with a quiet power of veto. For example, a project manager may not have formal authority but might control access to key data, meaning their cooperation is essential for progress. A senior figure who rarely attends meetings may still hold veto power if displeased. Cultural dynamics also matter: in some organisations, informal networks and personal relationships shape decisions as much as formal hierarchies. Consultants who fail to identify these hidden stakeholders' risk being blindsided by unexpected opposition.

Complexity also arises from conflicting agendas. Executives may prioritise strategic outcomes, such as reputational assurance or regulatory compliance. Operators may resist changes that add workload or require retraining. Regulators may push for strict adherence to standards, even where flexibility would be more proportionate. None of these positions is inherently wrong; they reflect different perspectives. The consultant's role is to understand and mediate between them, crafting recommendations that balance feasibility with effectiveness.

Stakeholder Group	Typical Motivation / Priority	Engagement Risk	Consultant's Best Approach
Client Executives / Project Sponsors	Strategic success, reputation, compliance assurance.	Over-promising or political pressure may distort risk appetite.	Frame recommendations in business outcomes; use concise summaries.
Contractors / Integrators	Delivery efficiency, profit margin, programme completion.	May resist changes or perceive security as delay or cost.	Use deliverable-friendly language; align with quality and handover benefits.
Regulators / Authorities	Compliance enforcement, public accountability.	Adversarial stance if engaged late or superficially.	Engage early; demonstrate understanding of intent behind standards; align documents.
Architects / Design Teams	Aesthetic integrity, spatial function, client satisfaction.	See security as constraint on creativity.	Collaborate visually; show how measures enhance design intent.
IT / OT Managers	Network performance, uptime, cybersecurity governance.	Conflict over device standards, bandwidth, or control ownership.	Use shared language; highlight mutual benefits.
Operations / FM Teams	Functionality, maintainability, user convenience.	May bypass or disable measures that hinder work.	Involve them early; emphasise usability and lifecycle savings.
Finance / Procurement	Budget control, audit transparency.	Narrow focus on upfront cost; undervaluing risk reduction.	Quantify return on resilience; show cost of incidents avoided.
End Users / Occupants	Comfort, convenience, personal safety.	Non-compliance from perceived over-control.	Communicate purpose clearly; use environmental cues not enforcement.

Table 8 Stakeholder Typology and Typical Engagement Approach

Global projects introduce another layer of complexity: cultural and political variation. In some settings, stakeholders expect direct, assertive communication; in others, deference and consensus-building are essential. In some countries, regulators are powerful and independent; in others, they may be politically constrained. Consultants working internationally must therefore adapt their stakeholder approach to context, avoiding the mistake of assuming that methods effective in one environment will translate seamlessly to another.

A further source of complexity is stakeholder change over time. Projects often last months or years, during which leadership may change, political priorities may shift, or economic conditions may alter. A supportive executive may be replaced by one with different objectives. A regulator may issue new guidance midway through implementation. Communities may become more vocal as projects become more visible. Consultants must recognise that stakeholder management is dynamic: today's allies may be tomorrow's obstacles, and strategies must be flexible enough to adapt.

One practical method for handling this fluidity is the stakeholder register. This living document records key details: who stakeholders are, their role, their power and interest level, their agenda, and the current status of engagement. It also tracks changes over time. By maintaining and updating this register, consultants ensure that complexity is captured, monitored, and managed deliberately rather than reactively.

Complexity is not only about difficulty; it can also be a source of resilience. When stakeholders are diverse, they bring different knowledge and perspectives. Operators may notice vulnerabilities missed by executives. Regulators may highlight risks overlooked by operators. Communities may anticipate social or reputational challenges the project team had not considered. Consultants who engage widely and constructively can harness this diversity to improve the quality of recommendations.

Yet stakeholder diversity also creates the risk of conflicting expectations about the consultant's role. Some stakeholders may see the consultant as a neutral advisor, others as an advocate for their perspective, and still others as a potential obstacle. Misalignment here can create tension. The consultant must therefore define their role clearly and consistently, reinforcing independence and impartiality. Consultants who are perceived as captured by one faction quickly lose credibility with others.

Stakeholder complexity must be understood as part of the political landscape of consultancy. Projects are rarely politically neutral. Decisions about security, investment, or compliance often intersect with organisational politics, resource struggles, or external scrutiny. Consultants who attempt to avoid politics entirely risk naivety; those who engage too directly risk entanglement. The balance is to recognise the political dimension, remain sensitive to it, and maintain professional independence while still engaging with the realities of influence and power.

Stakeholder complexity is multi-dimensional. It arises from the variety of groups involved, the differences in power and interest, the presence of hidden influencers, the conflicts between agendas, the variations in cultural and political context, and the changes that occur over time. Understanding this complexity is the first step towards managing it. Without such understanding, consultants risk wasted effort, missed opportunities, or outright project failure. With it, they can design engagement strategies that build trust, mediate conflicts, and create the conditions for recommendations to be heard and acted upon.

Stakeholder management is a discipline of structure and integrity. Mapping influence, clarifying roles, and sustaining impartiality convert political complexity into professional order.

Building Trust in Diverse Agendas

Consultancy depends on trust more than any tool or method. Without it, access is restricted, information is filtered, and recommendations are questioned or ignored. With it, stakeholders share candid insights, cooperate in testing assumptions, and support changes that may otherwise meet resistance. For consultants managing diverse and often conflicting stakeholder agendas, building and sustaining trust is not optional – it is the central condition of influence.

Trust begins with credibility. Stakeholders judge consultants not only on their technical expertise but also on their reliability, impartiality, and responsiveness. A consultant who provides accurate information consistently, follows through on commitments, and communicates clearly builds a reputation for competence. Conversely, a consultant who misses deadlines, changes their message, or is evasive when questioned quickly loses standing. Credibility is cumulative: it is built through dozens of small interactions, but it can be lost in a single misstep.

A critical part of credibility is transparency. Stakeholders are more likely to trust consultants who explain their methods, clarify their assumptions, and acknowledge limitations. Admitting uncertainty does not diminish authority; it demonstrates honesty. For example, if data is incomplete, the consultant should state this openly and explain how it affects confidence in recommendations. Attempts to overstate certainty may appear persuasive in the moment but often backfire when stakeholders discover gaps or contradictions later. Transparency reassures stakeholders that the consultant's goal is accuracy, not self-promotion.

Trust also depends on independence and impartiality. In environments where agendas conflict, stakeholders watch closely to see whether the consultant is aligned with one faction. If consultants are perceived as advocates for one group, their credibility with others diminishes sharply. Maintaining impartiality does not mean avoiding judgement; it means basing recommendations on evidence and risk logic rather than stakeholder pressure. Consultants must be careful in how they interact, ensuring that access to one group does not appear as bias. Documenting interactions, sharing findings openly, and applying consistent criteria across groups all reinforce impartiality.

Another dimension of trust is responsiveness. Stakeholders want to feel that their concerns are heard and considered. This does not mean agreeing with every viewpoint but acknowledging input and explaining how it was addressed. Even when recommendations cannot accommodate a stakeholder's preference, taking time to explain why builds respect. For example, if operators object to additional procedures, the consultant might explain how risk analysis demonstrates the necessity and explore ways to minimise operational burden. Stakeholders may not like the outcome, but they are more likely to respect it when they feel engaged rather than dismissed.

Building trust also requires sensitivity to stakeholder identity and values. People place greater confidence in consultants who show awareness of their role, pressures, and professional culture. Engineers respond positively to precise technical reasoning; executives appreciate concise strategic framing; operators value practical respect for day-to-day realities. By tailoring communication to reflect these differences, consultants demonstrate empathy and relevance. Ignoring stakeholder identity, by contrast, risks alienation. A consultant who overwhelms executives with technical jargon or patronises operators with generic statements quickly loses credibility.

Trust is reinforced by consistency and confidentiality. Stakeholders notice whether consultants stick to their principles or change under pressure. While analysis may shift as new evidence emerges, core commitments to accuracy, openness, and impartiality must remain constant. At the same time, stakeholders will only share openly if they believe information will be handled responsibly. Consultants must protect sources, record and report ethically, and follow clear protocols on how information is used. Even an unintended breach can cause lasting damage. Together, consistency and confidentiality show reliability, especially in long or politically sensitive projects where trust is repeatedly tested.

Resistance can test trust more than anything else. When stakeholders challenge findings, delay decisions, or quietly block progress, consultants may feel defensive. But resistance is not always rejection; it can be a chance to build trust. If handled well – by surfacing concerns, listening, and reframing issues – resistance can turn into dialogue. Stakeholders who feel their objections are acknowledged are more likely to trust the consultant, even if they do not fully agree.

Trust rests on integrity. Consultants who uphold ethical standards under pressure strengthen credibility; refusing to endorse unsafe options or resisting attempts to downplay risks may cause short-term friction but builds long-term respect. Stakeholders may not always agree with recommendations, yet they value consultants who act with integrity. Building trust therefore requires credibility, openness, impartiality, responsiveness, empathy, consistency, confidentiality, and integrity. Trust is not an abstract idea but the condition that makes stakeholder engagement possible – without it, consultants remain outsiders, and with it, they become trusted advisors whose insights shape decisions and drive change.

Dealing with Resistance Constructively

Where there are stakeholders, there will likely be resistance. Consultants often encounter it in forms both obvious and subtle: challenges to findings, reluctance to share information, delays in decision-making, or passive agreement followed by inaction. Resistance is a natural feature of consulting, not a sign of failure. Indeed, as Peter Block's *Flawless Consulting*[3] emphasises, resistance should be expected, recognised, and engaged with constructively. It signals that the consultant has touched on issues that matter, and that stakeholders are wrestling with change. The question is not whether resistance occurs, but how it is handled.

Recognising resistance is the first step. Some forms are direct: open disagreement, public criticism, or outright refusal. Others are indirect: stakeholders cancelling meetings, providing minimal information, or agreeing in principle while quietly obstructing implementation. Resistance may also take the form of tokenism – offering superficial compliance to satisfy appearances without altering behaviour. Consultants who mistake these signals for apathy or bad faith miss the underlying dynamic: resistance usually reflects deeper concerns about control, risk, or trust.

Block suggests that resistance is often a sign of unspoken fears. Stakeholders may fear loss of status, exposure of weakness, disruption of routines, or accountability for problems. Operators may worry that recommendations will make their jobs harder; managers may fear being blamed for gaps; executives may fear reputational or financial consequences. Resistance is rarely about rejecting the consultant personally; it is about protecting interests or identities in the face of change.

To address resistance constructively, consultants must first surface it openly. Ignoring resistance does not make it disappear; it drives it underground, where it becomes more damaging. The consultant's role is to name what is happening in a respectful, non-confrontational way: "I sense there may be concerns about how this will affect day-to-day operations. Could you share what those are?" By creating space for honest conversation, the consultant legitimises resistance as part of the process.

Listening is critical. Consultants who respond to resistance by pressing harder with evidence or authority often reinforce defensiveness, whereas listening carefully, reflecting concerns, and showing understanding builds respect and uncovers deeper issues. A complaint about cost, for example, may really stem from concerns over resources or political exposure. Once surfaced, concerns can often be reframed as opportunities. Stricter procedures can be presented as investments in staff safety, and new technology as a route to efficiency. Reframing does not dismiss the concern but connects it to outcomes that stakeholders value.

Where resistance reflects genuine limits, negotiation may be required. Operators worried about extra reporting can be supported through phased implementation or automation; contractors concerned about cost may be reassured by prioritising essential measures and deferring others. Negotiation shows flexibility while keeping focus on essentials. Sometimes, shared resistance reveals deeper cultural or organisational issues, such as long-standing neglect of safety, that must be addressed systemically rather than treated as personal reluctance. Recognising these patterns prevents misdiagnosis and enables more constructive solutions.

Not all resistance is negative. Healthy challenge tests assumptions and improves recommendations, while obstruction simply delays progress without adding value. The consultant's task is to distinguish between the two: to encourage challenge that strengthens credibility and quality, but to contain obstruction so it does not paralyse the process.

Illustrative Example: Turning Tailgating into Awareness

A consultant working with a transport operator faced resistance from frontline staff who rejected recommendations for stricter access control. Staff argued that tailgating was a harmless shortcut. Rather than insisting, the consultant asked staff to describe what would happen if an unauthorised person gained access during a high-traffic period. This shifted the conversation from rules to consequences, leading staff to acknowledge risks. By reframing, the consultant turned resistance into engagement and helped staff see the value of the recommendation.

Resistance also tests the consultant's emotional resilience. It can be uncomfortable to face criticism or dismissal, particularly when time is short or stakes are high. Consultants must resist the urge to become defensive or authoritarian. Professionalism requires maintaining composure, focusing on the client's interests, and recognising that resistance is not rejection of the consultant personally. Developing emotional resilience allows consultants to persist in dialogue without losing credibility.

Constructive engagement with resistance can, paradoxically, strengthen trust. Stakeholders who see that their concerns are taken seriously are more likely to support implementation, even if they do not fully agree with every recommendation. Resistance becomes a catalyst for dialogue and adjustment, rather than a barrier. This reinforces the principle that consultancy is not about imposing solutions but about co-creating them with stakeholders.

Consultants must know when resistance requires escalation or withdrawal. Some stakeholders may remain entrenched despite best efforts. In such cases, escalation to higher authority may be necessary, presenting the issue transparently and allowing the client to decide. In extreme cases, where resistance is rooted in unethical pressure or demands for compromised integrity, the consultant may need to withdraw rather than endorse flawed outcomes. Constructive handling of resistance does not mean endless accommodation; it means balancing flexibility with professional boundaries.

Resistance is not an obstacle to be eliminated but a signal to be understood. By recognising its forms, surfacing it openly, listening carefully, reframing constructively, negotiating where possible, and distinguishing between healthy challenge and obstruction, consultants can turn resistance into a productive force. Drawing on *Flawless Consulting*[3], the lesson is clear: resistance is not failure – it is feedback. When handled with empathy, resilience, and integrity, it deepens trust, strengthens recommendations, and increases the likelihood of lasting impact.

Balancing Authority, Diplomacy, and Influence

Consultants rarely hold formal authority within a client organisation. They cannot compel stakeholders to act, enforce compliance, or issue binding instructions. Their effectiveness depends instead on a careful balance of authority, diplomacy, and influence. Authority comes from expertise and contractual mandate, diplomacy from interpersonal skill, and influence from credibility and trust. Mastering this balance is essential for navigating complex stakeholder environments without undermining independence or alienating key groups.

Authority for consultants is both formal and informal. Formal authority is derived from the terms of reference or contractual scope: the client has engaged the consultant to perform specific tasks, evaluate risks, or provide recommendations. This authority legitimises access to sites, data, and personnel. Yet it is limited – consultants cannot usually dictate decisions. Informal authority, by contrast, emerges from the consultant's reputation, demonstrated competence, and ability to add value in conversations. A consultant who explains risks clearly, interprets data convincingly, or frames trade-offs in ways that resonate with executives earns informal authority that extends beyond the contract.

Diplomacy becomes critical when authority alone is insufficient. Stakeholders often have competing priorities, entrenched positions, or sensitivities about scrutiny. Consultants who push too hard risk being excluded; those who hesitate risk being ignored. Diplomacy is the art of pressing the case firmly while maintaining relationships. It involves choosing words carefully, recognising timing, and showing empathy without compromising on substance. For example, rather than bluntly stating, "Your team has failed to comply with procedure," a more diplomatic phrasing might be, "We observed challenges in how procedures are applied consistently. What obstacles might staff be facing?" Diplomacy reframes critique as collaboration, reducing defensiveness while still surfacing issues.

Influence, meanwhile, is the outcome of sustained credibility. It is the ability to shape decisions without direct control. Influence grows when consultants provide insights that stakeholders recognise as valuable, demonstrate impartiality in balancing agendas, and show persistence in following through. Crucially, influence is cumulative: small acts of reliability, clear communication, and thoughtful engagement build a reservoir of trust that can be drawn upon when difficult recommendations must be delivered.

Balancing these elements requires constant judgement. Consider the challenge of managing up, across, and down.

- **Managing up (executives):** Consultants must present clear, concise insights that support decision-making. Authority here is limited; executives decide. Diplomacy is crucial in framing recommendations in terms of strategic impact rather than technical detail. Influence is gained by demonstrating that recommendations support organisational goals.

- **Managing across (contractors and peers):** Consultants often work alongside contractors with overlapping or competing interests. Here authority may be ambiguous. Diplomacy involves building cooperative relationships without becoming aligned with one party. Influence is achieved through fairness and technical clarity, positioning the consultant as an honest broker.

- **Managing down (operators and staff):** Consultants may have more apparent authority as staff are often expected to cooperate with surveys or interviews. Yet true influence depends on respect. Diplomacy requires acknowledging operational realities, listening actively, and avoiding condescension. Recommendations gain traction when operators believe they reflect genuine understanding of their environment.

One of the greatest risks is becoming captured by a single stakeholder group. When consultants appear too close to executives, contractors may distrust their impartiality. When they align with operators, managers may see them as disruptive. When they adopt a regulator's perspective too strongly, clients may perceive them as inspectors rather than advisors. Consultants must therefore maintain balance, demonstrating empathy without alliance, and impartiality without detachment. Independence is the currency of influence; once lost, it is difficult to regain.

Timing also plays a role in balancing authority and diplomacy. Consultants must judge when to press an issue and when to pause. Pushing too early, before stakeholders are ready to hear criticism, can entrench resistance. Waiting too long can allow vulnerabilities to persist or decisions to be taken without input. The art lies in sensing when conditions are right for a message to land – often during moments of heightened awareness after an incident or regulatory review.

Communication style is another lever. Authority can be reinforced through clarity of recommendation: precise, actionable statements that show confidence. Diplomacy shapes how those statements are delivered: firm but respectful, tailored to the audience, and avoiding unnecessary provocation. Influence grows when communication is consistent across audiences, reinforcing trust that the consultant's position is evidence-based rather than politically expedient.

Ethics underpin the balance. Authority should not be abused, diplomacy should not slide into manipulation, and influence should not be used to advance personal agendas. Consultants must constantly ask: is my approach aligned with the client's best interests, defensible if scrutinised, and consistent with professional standards? Influence is sustainable only when grounded in integrity.

Balancing authority, diplomacy, and influence is not about compromise but about proportion. Authority provides legitimacy, diplomacy sustains relationships, and influence secures outcomes. Too much reliance on authority risks alienation; too much diplomacy risks dilution; too much emphasis on influence without evidence risks overreach. The consultant that masters the balance ensures that their voice is heard, their recommendations respected, and their independence preserved – even in the most complex stakeholder environments.

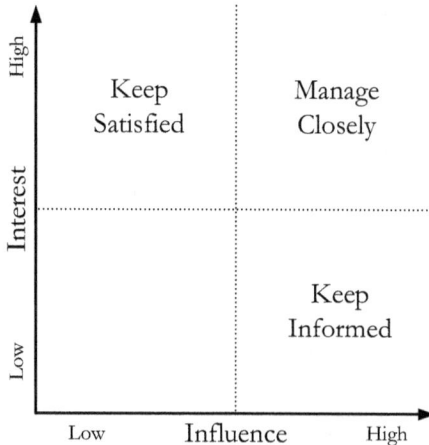

Figure 17 The Stakeholder Power – Interest Map

Tools and Methods for Stakeholder Engagement

Managing stakeholders requires not only interpersonal skill but also structured methods that bring consistency and clarity. Tools help capture complexity, monitor progress, and ensure that no important voice is overlooked. They do not replace judgement or diplomacy, but they give consultants a framework for systematic engagement in environments that might otherwise feel chaotic.

One of the most useful tools is the stakeholder register – a living document that records stakeholders, their role, power and interest, expectations, and status of engagement. It should also note any risks or opportunities and be updated as people, influence, or attitudes shift. Mapping complements the register by showing these relationships visually. Power/interest matrices, for example, allow consultants to focus attention where it matters most and explain engagement strategies to clients transparently.

Role clarity can be reinforced with the RACI model – identifying who is Responsible, Accountable, Consulted, and Informed for each activity. Applied to consultancy, RACI prevents confusion and disputes about ownership. Alongside this, a communication plan ensures that information flows consistently to the right people, in the right way, at the right time. It should also set out how issues will be escalated if stakeholders resist or obstruct, so concerns are surfaced constructively rather than left unresolved.

Workshops and dialogue methods provide space for stakeholders to share perspectives and build consensus. Well-designed sessions, using techniques such as facilitated roundtables or scenario exercises, encourage balanced discussion and help stakeholders take ownership of outcomes. Digital platforms for sharing documents and tracking progress can support this process, especially in global projects, but they must complement rather than replace human engagement.

These tools only add value when they are applied with judgement. Registers must reflect reality, communication plans must adapt to events, and RACI assignments may need review. Consultants should avoid treating tools as ends in themselves; their purpose is to support deliberate, responsive engagement. Documentation also plays a role by creating an audit trail that shows concerns were heard, resistance addressed, and decisions made fairly. These tools are protection for both consultant and client in sensitive environments.

Tools such as registers, maps, RACI models, communication plans, and workshops are not bureaucratic add-ons but essential instruments for managing diverse agendas. Used with integrity and flexibility, they turn stakeholder complexity from a source of risk into a resource for stronger outcomes.

Ethics and Integrity in Stakeholder Management

A consultant's credibility depends as much on integrity as on technical skill. In political environments with competing agendas and hidden pressures, independence must be preserved. Ethics are not an optional extra but the foundation that sustains trust and ensures advice remains defensible.

A frequent challenge is conflicts of interest. Stakeholders may attempt to co-opt the consultant into supporting their preferred position, whether by emphasising certain findings, downplaying others, or tailoring recommendations to align with internal agendas. For example, a project sponsor may ask the consultant to endorse a favoured solution despite evidence that it is unsafe or disproportionate. Yielding to such pressure might satisfy one stakeholder in the short term but will erode trust with others and compromise the consultant's reputation. The ethical stance is to remain impartial: to base recommendations on evidence and structured analysis, not stakeholder preference.

Another ethical challenge arises when consultants face pressure to bias findings for political or reputational reasons. Executives may seek to present risks as under control, contractors may resist exposing compliance gaps, and regulators may prefer to emphasise strengths over weaknesses. Consultants must recognise these pressures and resist them. Transparency is essential: if data is incomplete, assumptions uncertain, or risks higher than some stakeholders wish to acknowledge, these limitations must be stated openly. Diluting or concealing reality not only undermines credibility but exposes the client to greater long-term risk.

Professional integrity also requires managing confidentiality responsibly. Stakeholders may share sensitive information in the expectation it will be handled discreetly. Consultants must protect this trust, ensuring that disclosures are recorded and reported appropriately, without exposing individuals to undue blame. At the same time, consultants must balance confidentiality with the obligation to report material risks. If an operator reveals a dangerous practice, the consultant cannot ethically ignore it. The challenge lies in addressing the issue in a way that corrects the risk while protecting the integrity of the source.

Ethics are tested further when consultants must say "no" to a client's request. This may mean declining to endorse an inadequate solution, refusing to suppress findings, or stepping back from a project that demands compromised standards. These decisions are rarely easy, they may mean loss of income or strained relationships, but they protect professional credibility. In consultancy, reputation is the most valuable currency. Sacrificing it for short-term gain is ultimately self-defeating.

A useful discipline is to ask: *Would I be comfortable defending this recommendation in front of a regulator, auditor, or court of law?* If the answer is no, the consultant must reconsider. This "defensibility test" provides a practical guide for navigating ethical dilemmas when pressures are high.

Consultants must avoid the temptation of false neutrality. While independence is essential, neutrality cannot mean silence in the face of unacceptable risk. Consultants who present all perspectives without judgement abdicate their responsibility to provide clear advice. Integrity requires making reasoned recommendations, supported by evidence, even when they are unwelcome. Stakeholders may disagree, but they are more likely to respect a consultant who takes a principled stance than one who avoids clarity.

Ethics and integrity are not side issues in stakeholder management; they are the basis of professional credibility. Conflicts of interest, pressure to bias findings, confidentiality dilemmas, and demands for neutrality all test the consultant's judgement. By maintaining independence, communicating transparently, and prioritising defensibility, consultants navigate these pressures while protecting both client and professional standing. In complex environments, where agendas conflict and stakes are high, integrity is not only the right choice, it is the consultant's most powerful source of influence.

Practice Guide

Stakeholder management is not an accessory to consultancy – it is its operating environment. This chapter has met its learning objectives by showing how consultants understand complexity, build trust, handle resistance, balance diplomacy with authority, apply structured methods, and sustain integrity. It has demonstrated that technical expertise alone cannot deliver results unless relationships, agendas, and expectations are managed with equal discipline.

The common pitfalls are well known. Consultants often over-align with one faction or the loudest voice, alienating others and eroding impartiality. They may overlook quiet stakeholders – operators, informal influencers, or hidden veto players – whose daily actions determine whether recommendations succeed. Some mistake access for influence, assuming that visibility or attendance equals impact. Others compromise independence by yielding to pressure, softening findings, or avoiding conflict. Each of these behaviours weakens credibility and trust.

Good practice starts with systematic engagement. Consultants should identify and map stakeholders early, assessing their power and interest, then revisit this mapping as projects evolve. Listening is as important as advising – particularly to those with limited authority – because their insights often reveal operational realities. Communication must be clear, consistent, and adapted to each audience, while remaining anchored in evidence to preserve objectivity. Resistance should be viewed as feedback, surfaced and reframed constructively in terms that align with stakeholder values. Above all, integrity is non-negotiable: every recommendation should pass the defensibility test – could I stand by this before a regulator, board, or court?

Mastering stakeholder management moves consultants from the margins of influence to the centre of decision-making. It is within this arena of competing agendas that credibility and independence are most tested. By treating stakeholder engagement as a disciplined professional practice rather than an adjunct skill, consultants convert potential barriers into alliances, sustain authority through trust, and ensure that their advice is not only respected but implemented. This maturity in stakeholder management prepares the foundation for the advanced consultancy practices explored in subsequent chapters.

Chapter 19 – International and High-Risk Environments

Consultancy in international and high-risk environments takes the consultant beyond familiar ground. Such projects are shaped by cultural expectations, political sensitivities, and heightened risks. Working across borders or in unstable regions demands more than expertise – it calls for adaptability, resilience, and the ability to function under uncertainty. Challenges may include navigating unfamiliar legal systems, corruption, weak governance, or operating where security is uncertain. Even in less hostile settings such as remote facilities or fragile infrastructure, added pressures of logistics, health, and safety remain. A cultural misstep can erode credibility, while poor preparation can expose both consultant and client to serious harm.

Success depends on disciplined preparation, situational awareness, and professional integrity. Consultants must recognise that risk cannot be eliminated but must always be managed proportionately. Their responsibility is twofold: to deliver value for the client while safeguarding their own wellbeing and that of those they work alongside.

By the end of this chapter, you will be able to:

- Explain the distinctive demands of international and high-risk consulting environments.

- Distinguish and evaluate the layers of risk at personal, organisational, and operational levels.

- Apply structured preparation through risk assessment, logistical planning, and personal resilience.

- Adapt communication and behaviour to cultural, political, and legal contexts without losing professional integrity.

- Demonstrate effective practice in hostile, hazardous, and unstable environments while maintaining independence.

- Implement measures that protect yourself, clients, and local partners through security, safety, and ethical safeguards.

- Anticipate and avoid common pitfalls, including cultural insensitivity, weak preparation, and underestimation of environmental threats.

Introduction

Most consultancy takes place within environments that, while complex, are relatively stable: boardrooms, regulated industries, predictable political contexts. Yet many projects extend beyond these familiar boundaries. International and high-risk environments present a different order of challenge, where cultural differences, political pressures, and physical hazards combine to test the consultant's adaptability and resilience. Working in such settings is not an occasional exception but increasingly a regular feature of global consultancy.

The globalisation of critical infrastructure, supply chains, and technology means that consultants are often required to operate in regions with unfamiliar legal systems, underdeveloped regulatory frameworks, or heightened physical and political risks. A project to assess a data centre in Western Europe may demand one form of preparation; a similar project in a fragile state, a conflict-adjacent region, or a remote desert facility demands another entirely. The consultant's task is not simply to transfer expertise from one setting to another but to adapt practice to context, recognising that what works in one environment may fail in another.

In hostile environments, consultants may face threats from terrorism, armed conflict, or civil unrest. In hazardous environments, such as offshore platforms, remote mines, or extreme climates, the physical dangers are significant. In politically sensitive contexts, consultants may have to navigate corruption, censorship, or hidden agendas. Even in less extreme cases, such as a remote logistics hub with poor infrastructure, or an international project spanning multiple jurisdictions, the demands on the consultant extend well beyond technical analysis. Logistics, personal safety, cultural awareness, and ethical judgement all become integral to success.

The consequences of underestimating these challenges can be severe. A cultural misstep may erode trust with local stakeholders, undermining months of work. Failure to anticipate logistical risks can delay delivery or compromise safety. Misreading political sensitivities may endanger both consultant and client. The margin for error in such contexts is narrow, and the costs of mistakes are often higher than in stable environments.

Yet international and high-risk contexts also provide opportunities for consultants to demonstrate distinctive value. Clients often lack the internal capacity to operate effectively in these environments. Consultants who can navigate complexity, build cross-cultural trust, and maintain resilience under pressure become indispensable. By demonstrating competence in high-risk settings, consultants enhance not only the project outcome but also their professional reputation.

This chapter therefore addresses the realities of consulting beyond the comfort zone. It explores how international contexts shape stakeholder engagement, how high-risk environments create unique vulnerabilities, and how consultants can prepare, operate, and protect themselves and their clients. It also examines the ethical and professional responsibilities that arise when conditions are difficult, showing that integrity is as critical abroad or in high-risk environments as it is in stable, familiar ones.

The aim is not to create fear but to equip the consultant with frameworks and practices that enable safe, effective, and principled engagement, even in the most challenging environments.

Understanding the International Context

International consultancy demands more than transferring expertise across borders. It requires an appreciation of how cultural norms, legal systems, political dynamics, and local expectations shape the consulting process. The consultant who assumes that methods effective at home will work equally well abroad risks missteps that damage credibility, delay projects, or even create personal danger. Understanding the international context is therefore the first step in operating effectively outside familiar environments.

Cross-cultural communication is a primary challenge. Consultants often work in environments where language, hierarchy, and communication styles differ significantly from their own. What seems like clear, direct language in one culture may be perceived as blunt or disrespectful in another. Silence may signal agreement in some contexts but discomfort or resistance in others. Gestures, body language, and tone can also carry unintended meanings. The risk is not only misunderstanding but also loss of trust if consultants are seen as insensitive. Successful cross-cultural communication requires patience, humility, and active adaptation. It also demands awareness that one's own style is not neutral but culturally shaped.

Cultural approaches to authority and hierarchy can also alter how consultancy is received. In some regions, junior staff may be reluctant to challenge managers openly, meaning that consultants must interpret carefully whether apparent agreement reflects genuine consensus. In other contexts, direct challenge is expected and respected. A consultant who fails to adjust may misread the level of support for recommendations or overlook unspoken resistance. Recognising these dynamics allows consultants to adapt their engagement methods, encouraging honest dialogue without placing undue pressure on stakeholders.

Regulatory environments differ widely between jurisdictions. In highly regulated regions such as the European Union, consultants must account for strict data protection laws, health and safety directives, and industry-specific compliance frameworks. In other parts of the world, regulatory frameworks may be weak, inconsistently enforced, or subject to political influence. This inconsistency creates both challenges and risks. Consultants must be careful not to assume that the absence of regulation equates to freedom; often it implies higher exposure to liability, corruption, or reputational damage. The consultant's role is to understand both the written regulations and how they are applied in practice.

Political sensitivities present another layer of complexity. International projects may touch on issues of national pride, economic strategy, or political legitimacy. A security assessment, for instance, might reveal vulnerabilities that governments or operators prefer to downplay. Consultants must therefore tread carefully, presenting findings in a way that addresses risks without embarrassing stakeholders or appearing politically partial. Neutrality is critical: consultants who are perceived as favouring one political faction risk being excluded or even endangered. Maintaining independence and framing advice in terms of professional standards rather than politics is the safest path.

Working internationally often involves reliance on translators, fixers, and local partners. These intermediaries can bridge cultural and linguistic gaps, provide critical local knowledge, and help navigate bureaucratic processes. Yet they also introduce new dynamics: the consultant must choose them carefully, manage confidentiality, and be alert to possible conflicts of interest. A translator who is aligned with a particular stakeholder may subtly alter meaning, while a local partner may have interests that diverge from the client's. Building trust with local intermediaries while maintaining vigilance is essential.

The physical and logistical context also affects consultancy. In some international environments, consultants may have to operate with unreliable infrastructure, poor connectivity, or limited access to resources. A methodology that relies on constant digital connectivity may fail in remote regions with intermittent power. Consultants must therefore adapt methods to the realities of the environment, ensuring that tools, data collection, and communication strategies are robust under local conditions.

Understanding the international context also requires awareness of social expectations and norms. Issues such as gender roles, religious practices, and community relations can shape how consultants are perceived and whether they are accepted. Ignoring these norms can create barriers. For example, failing to respect prayer times, dietary restrictions, or local dress codes may alienate stakeholders. Demonstrating cultural sensitivity signals respect and increases cooperation, even if consultants remain outsiders.

Importantly, risk perception varies by culture. What one culture sees as a critical vulnerability, another may view as acceptable or unavoidable. For instance, attitudes towards workplace safety or data privacy can differ significantly. Consultants must therefore not only identify risks but also frame them in ways that resonate with local priorities. A report that emphasises reputational consequences may carry more weight in one environment, while another may respond more to cost or regulatory compliance.

The consultant's own identity becomes part of the international context. Nationality, language, and organisational affiliation all influence how stakeholders perceive the consultant. In some regions, foreign consultants are seen as authoritative; in others, they are regarded with suspicion. Awareness of how one is perceived – and adapting accordingly – is part of working internationally. Consultants must leverage the authority their identity affords while mitigating any biases or barriers it creates.

Understanding the international context means recognising that consulting is not simply about transferring expertise across borders. It is about adapting practice to local conditions – cultural, regulatory, political, logistical, and social. Success requires humility, preparation, and sensitivity. Consultants who approach international work with openness and adaptability not only avoid missteps but also build the trust and credibility that make their recommendations effective.

High-Risk Environments Defined

Not all international contexts are equally demanding. Some involve little more than adapting to different business customs, while others expose consultants to significant personal, organisational, or operational risk. High-risk environments are those where hazards – physical, political, or social – elevate the stakes of consultancy beyond the normal. Defining these environments clearly helps consultants prepare, recognise boundaries, and adopt proportionate safeguards.

Hostile environments are those where deliberate threats exist from conflict, terrorism, or organised crime. Consultants working near active conflict zones may face risks from armed groups, checkpoints, or targeted violence. Even in regions without open warfare, terrorism or kidnapping may pose credible dangers. In such settings, security is not a background concern but a primary factor shaping how consultancy is planned and delivered. Movement may require escorts, intelligence briefings, and strict protocols. Hostile environments test not only professional competence but also personal resilience and ethical judgement.

Hazardous environments expose consultants to natural or industrial risks. Extreme climates – deserts with searing heat, polar regions with sub-zero conditions, or tropical zones with high disease prevalence – all impose physical strain and logistical challenges. Remote industrial facilities such as oil rigs, mining sites, or large construction projects add further dangers, from heavy machinery to chemical exposure. Unlike hostile environments, where threats come from people, hazardous environments demand vigilance against natural forces and operational hazards. The risks may be less politically charged, but they can be equally life-threatening if underestimated.

Socially unstable environments present risks that are less visible but no less disruptive. Corruption, weak governance, community hostility, or fragile institutions create conditions where consultants must navigate uncertainty carefully. In such contexts, bribes may be expected, contracts may not be enforceable, and local communities may view projects with suspicion or outright opposition. Consultants may find themselves caught between client expectations and social realities. While the threats may not involve overt violence, the risks to professional integrity, project success, and personal safety are significant.

High-risk environments often combine these categories. A consultant assessing port infrastructure in a fragile state, for example, may face hostile risks from insurgent groups, hazardous risks from under-maintained facilities, and social risks from communities protesting economic inequality. The overlapping nature of these risks makes preparation complex and reinforces the need for systematic analysis.

Identifying the different risk layers is a useful discipline. Consultants should distinguish between:

- **Personal risks:** threats to the individual consultant's health, safety, or wellbeing. These include physical violence, disease, exhaustion, or psychological strain.

- **Organisational risks:** threats to the consulting firm, such as reputational damage, legal liability, or loss of client trust if incidents occur.

- **Operational risks:** threats to project outcomes, including disrupted timelines, incomplete data collection, or compromised recommendations due to constrained access.

Recognising these layers helps consultants frame preparation and mitigation measures. Too often, firms focus narrowly on operational risks – ensuring deliverables are produced – while neglecting personal risks to consultants in the field. A more holistic view ensures that safety, ethics, and professional outcomes are all protected.

It is also important to appreciate that risk is dynamic rather than static. A location considered safe today may become hostile tomorrow due to political events, natural disasters, or sudden social unrest. Similarly, hazardous conditions can escalate unexpectedly – a stable industrial site may experience an accident, or a region considered low risk may face a sudden outbreak of disease. Consultants must therefore treat risk assessment as a continuous process, not a one-time activity.

Consultants must confront the reality that some environments may be beyond acceptable risk. No project is worth severe injury, unlawful detention, or loss of life. Part of professionalism is recognising when risk cannot be mitigated to an acceptable level and advising clients accordingly. Declining assignments, postponing fieldwork, or recommending alternative methods (such as remote assessments) may be difficult conversations, but they are necessary to uphold duty of care.

High-risk environments can be defined as hostile, hazardous, or socially unstable – often in overlapping combinations. They pose risks at personal, organisational, and operational levels, and these risks shift over time. Consultants who understand these categories, and who acknowledge when risk exceeds acceptable limits, are better equipped to prepare for the challenges ahead. Clarity of definition is the first safeguard: it allows consultants to plan proportionately, to protect both themselves and their clients, and to ensure that expertise is not undermined by exposure to unnecessary danger.

Preparation and Risk Assessment

Operating in international and high-risk environments requires preparation of a different order. Consultants cannot rely on improvisation or assume that standard routines will suffice. Risks are magnified, resources are constrained, and mistakes carry heavier consequences. Careful preparation and rigorous risk assessment are therefore essential not only to safeguard the consultant but also to protect the client and ensure that projects can be delivered with credibility.

Threat and vulnerability analysis is the foundation of preparation. Just as consultants apply frameworks such as TVRA to client sites, they must also apply structured analysis to their own deployment. Threats may include armed conflict, terrorism, natural hazards, disease, or political instability. Vulnerabilities may include travel routes, accommodation, or reliance on local partners. By mapping threats against vulnerabilities, consultants can identify where exposure is greatest and what mitigation is required. For example, if the threat is kidnapping and the vulnerability is unprotected movement between airport and site, mitigation might involve secure transport or alternative travel routes.

Medical and logistical preparation is another priority. Consultants should ensure they have appropriate vaccinations, medical supplies, and insurance coverage for emergency treatment. Evacuation insurance, which covers transport to a safe location if serious illness or injury occurs, is particularly important in remote or unstable regions. Logistical preparation extends to travel documentation, reliable communication devices, cash reserves in appropriate currencies, and contingency planning for disrupted supply chains. A consultant stranded without essentials quickly becomes a liability rather than an asset.

Personal resilience, both mental and physical, is also part of preparation. High-risk environments are often physically demanding, with extreme climates, poor infrastructure, or long hours under pressure. Fatigue and stress can erode judgement at the very time when decisions matter most. Consultants must therefore manage their health proactively: adequate rest, nutrition, and exercise before deployment; pacing and stress-management techniques during it. Mental preparation is equally important. Consultants should anticipate culture shock, isolation, or exposure to distressing situations. Developing coping strategies in advance reduces vulnerability in the field.

Duty of care obligations extend beyond the individual consultant to the consulting firm and the client. Firms sending staff into high-risk environments must provide appropriate training, security briefings, and support structures. Clients have responsibilities too, particularly when local arrangements create risks, for example, inadequate transport or insecure accommodation. Consultants should be clear about these obligations in contracts, ensuring that safety is not treated as a personal issue but as a shared responsibility. Clear escalation protocols – who is contacted, in what order, and under what circumstances – should be agreed before deployment.

A critical part of preparation is crisis planning and evacuation protocols. Consultants should plan for scenarios such as sudden civil unrest, natural disaster, medical emergency, or loss of communication. This means knowing in advance:

- Where the nearest safe haven is located.
- How to contact embassies or consular support.
- Which airlines or transport routes remain operational in crisis.
- Who holds decision-making authority for evacuation.

Rehearsing these scenarios may feel excessive, but in high-risk environments it can make the difference between controlled withdrawal and dangerous improvisation.

Information security must also be part of risk assessment. In unstable regions, consultants may face heightened risks of cyber intrusion, surveillance, or data theft. Protecting devices with strong encryption, using secure communication platforms, and maintaining strict data hygiene, such as not leaving devices unattended, limiting sensitive data carried in the field, are essential safeguards. Information leakage can compromise both consultant safety and client confidentiality.

One of the most important disciplines is distinguishing between acceptable, mitigated, and unacceptable risk. Acceptable risk is inherent to consulting in challenging contexts; it cannot be removed entirely. Mitigated risk is reduced to a tolerable level through preparation and controls. Unacceptable risk is that which remains beyond control, where the likelihood or potential impact is disproportionate. Consultants must be honest about these distinctions. Attempting to mask or downplay unacceptable risks places lives and reputations in jeopardy. Professionalism sometimes means advising the client that conditions make the project unworkable.

Preparation also involves stakeholder engagement before deployment. Local partners, fixers, or community representatives can provide critical intelligence about conditions on the ground. Consulting with them in advance allows for more realistic planning. However, reliance on local input must be balanced with independent verification. Stakeholders may understate risks for commercial or political reasons, or exaggerate them to extract concessions. Cross-checking multiple sources ensures accuracy.

In addition to physical and logistical measures, preparation requires ethical clarity. High-risk environments often involve exposure to corruption, coercion, or client pressure to overlook hazards. Consultants should be clear in advance about the professional boundaries they will not cross before departure. Establishing in advance what compromises are unacceptable – whether safety standards, financial practices, or reporting integrity – strengthens resilience when pressures arise in the field.

Lastly, preparation should not end once deployment begins. Risk assessment must be dynamic, updated continuously as conditions evolve. Consultants should adopt a routine of regular check-ins, situational updates, and re-evaluation of assumptions. A context considered safe one week may deteriorate rapidly; conversely, mitigation measures may reduce risk over time. Treating risk assessment as a living process ensures that consultants remain adaptive and alert.

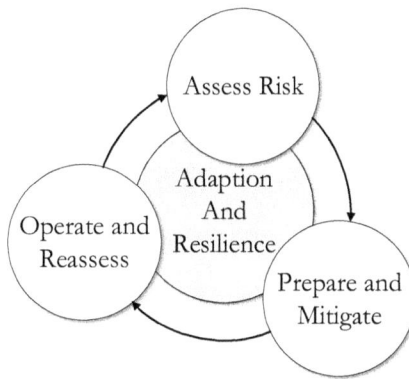

Figure 18 The Operational Resilience Loop

Preparation and risk assessment are not peripheral tasks but a fundamental of international and high-risk consultancy. Threat and vulnerability analysis, medical and logistical readiness, resilience, duty of care, crisis planning, information security, and ethical clarity together provide the foundation for safe and effective practice. Above all, consultants must distinguish between acceptable, mitigated, and unacceptable risks, recognising that professionalism sometimes requires saying no. With careful preparation, consultants can operate confidently even in the most demanding environments, delivering value to clients while safeguarding themselves and those they work with.

Effective practice in international and high-risk environments depends on disciplined preparation and ethical clarity. Adaptability without compromise protects both consultant and client when certainty cannot be guaranteed.

Operating Effectively on the Ground

Preparation provides the foundation for safe consultancy in high-risk environments, but effectiveness is tested once the consultant is in the field. Operating on the ground requires a balance of adaptability, situational awareness, cultural sensitivity, and professional discipline. The environment may be unpredictable, infrastructure unreliable, and stakeholders divided. The consultant's ability to function under such conditions determines whether preparation translates into impact.

Building trust with local stakeholders is often the first challenge. In high-risk contexts, external consultants may be greeted with suspicion. Communities may associate them with foreign influence, regulators may see them as potential critics, and operators may fear that findings will expose weaknesses. Winning trust requires humility, respect for local knowledge, and demonstration of good intent. Small signals such as observing local customs, listening attentively, or acknowledging the expertise of local staff, help reduce barriers. Trust is not given automatically; it is earned through consistent behaviour.

Adapting behaviour to cultural norms is equally important. What is considered professional conduct in one culture may be perceived as arrogance in another. For example, direct criticism may be seen as efficient in some contexts but as disrespectful elsewhere. In hierarchical cultures, bypassing senior figures to speak directly with junior staff may be viewed as undermining authority. The consultant must adapt without compromising principles, tailoring communication style and interaction patterns while remaining anchored in professional standards.

Managing projects with limited infrastructure or unreliable data is a common reality. In remote or fragile environments, access to records may be incomplete, data may be outdated, and systems may be inconsistent. Consultants must therefore cross-reference multiple sources, combining observation, interviews, and available documentation. They must also be realistic in framing findings, acknowledging gaps openly rather than overstating certainty. Operating with imperfect data is challenging, but transparency about limitations maintains credibility.

Navigating corruption and ethical dilemmas is another recurring test. In some high-risk environments, bribes, facilitation payments, or political influence may be commonplace. Consultants may be asked to overlook irregularities or endorse unsafe practices. The temptation is to "go along" for expedience, but doing so undermines independence and can expose the consultant to liability or reputational damage. Ethical clarity, established before deployment, is essential. Where corruption pressures are insurmountable, the consultant may need to withdraw rather than compromise integrity.

Client pressure can add further complexity. Clients may want to downplay risks to secure investment, accelerate timelines, or protect reputations. In high-risk contexts, these pressures may be intensified by political stakes or financial urgency. Consultants must resist being co-opted into biased reporting, even at the risk of friction. Professional responsibility is to provide accurate, evidence-based advice, even when it is unwelcome.

Field decision-making often requires flexibility. Conditions on the ground may shift rapidly due to unrest, weather, or logistical breakdowns. Consultants must decide when to press ahead, when to pause, and when to escalate to clients. This requires situational awareness, reliable communication, and the confidence to adapt plans. Importantly, decisions should be documented, both to create accountability and to support later explanation if outcomes are questioned.

Personal conduct under stress is part of effective operation. High-risk environments often involve long days, uncertainty, and exposure to distressing scenes. Consultants must manage stress without letting frustration show in interactions. Losing composure in front of stakeholders erodes credibility. Simple disciplines such as maintaining rest when possible, avoiding alcohol in unsafe contexts, managing communication with family, all contribute to resilience.

Another essential element is protecting local staff and partners. Consultants often rely on drivers, interpreters, or fixers who may face greater risks than expatriates. Protecting them means ensuring fair treatment, respecting confidentiality, and avoiding placing them in compromising situations. Consultants must recognise that while they may depart at the end of an assignment, local partners remain in the environment and may face repercussions.

Adapting methodology to context is a mark of professionalism. For example, surveys that require large-scale data collection may be impractical in unstable regions; structured interviews or focus groups may provide more reliable input. Likewise, reliance on technology may be unrealistic where power supply is unstable. Consultants must therefore be flexible, adjusting methods while ensuring that recommendations remain evidence based.

Maintaining communication discipline is also crucial. In high-risk contexts, information may be sensitive and surveillance more likely. Consultants must use secure communication channels, limit sensitive data transfer, and remain alert to what is said in public. A careless conversation in a hotel lobby or unsecured message may expose both consultant and client to risk.

Operating effectively requires constant recalibration of risk. Conditions can change quickly: a peaceful environment may deteriorate overnight, or logistical routes may become unsafe. Consultants should maintain a habit of daily reassessment: what has changed, what risks have increased, and what actions are needed to remain safe and effective. This discipline prevents complacency and ensures that consultants remain proactive rather than reactive.

Effectiveness on the ground is defined by adaptability, cultural awareness, ethical clarity, and situational resilience. Building trust, adapting behaviour, managing imperfect data, resisting corruption, handling client pressure, protecting local staff, and recalibrating risk are all part of the consultant's daily practice. High-risk environments amplify challenges, but they also highlight professionalism. Consultants who can operate effectively under such conditions deliver value not only through technical expertise but through their capacity to function credibly and safely in the most demanding contexts.

Protecting Consultants and Clients

In high-risk environments, protecting both consultants and clients is not an optional consideration but a fundamental duty. Projects succeed only if the people delivering and receiving consultancy remain safe, resilient, and able to operate. Security and safety measures therefore form an integral part of professional practice. Protecting consultants and clients requires a layered approach that addresses travel security, cybersecurity, local staff welfare, and the balance between safety and delivery.

Travel security protocols are often the most visible part of protection. Movement in high-risk environments carries significant exposure, whether to targeted attacks, opportunistic crime, or accidents. Consultants should conduct route assessments before every journey, identifying choke points, alternative paths, and safe havens along the way. Secure transport – vetted drivers, well-maintained vehicles, and, where necessary, security escorts – reduces vulnerability. Accommodation should also be chosen with care, favouring reputable providers with robust security measures, controlled access, and reliable emergency procedures. The principle is not to eliminate mobility but to manage it deliberately, ensuring that each movement is justified, planned, and monitored.

Cybersecurity is an equally critical, though less visible, dimension. In hostile or politically sensitive regions, consultants may be targeted for data theft, surveillance, or digital intrusion. Protecting devices with encryption, using secure communication platforms, and employing VPNs are essential safeguards. Consultants should limit the data carried on devices to what is strictly necessary and assume that networks may be compromised. Sensitive conversations should not take place over unsecured channels. For clients, protecting digital assets may mean ensuring that consultancy reports, risk assessments, and system details do not fall into the wrong hands. Cybersecurity is therefore both a personal and organisational obligation.

Safeguarding local staff and partners is often overlooked but is a critical ethical responsibility. Drivers, interpreters, fixers, and contractors may face greater risks than visiting consultants, as they remain embedded in the environment long after the consultancy ends. Consultants should avoid placing local staff in compromising situations, respect confidentiality, and ensure that protective measures extend to them as well. This may include providing appropriate personal protective equipment, offering fair pay that reflects risk exposure, and ensuring they are not asked to perform tasks beyond their capacity or safety. Protecting local staff reinforces trust and demonstrates professionalism to clients and communities alike.

Balancing operational demands with personal safety is a constant tension in high-risk environments. Clients may push for accelerated timelines, additional site visits, or greater access, sometimes underestimating risks. Consultants must be clear that safety takes precedence over speed. Saying no to unnecessary exposure is not unprofessional; it is a mark of competence. At the same time, consultants must show that safety and delivery are not opposing goals but complementary: careful risk management ensures continuity, reduces liability, and sustains project credibility. A consultant injured or incapacitated through preventable risk undermines delivery far more than a cautious adjustment of schedule.

Emergency preparedness underpins protection. Consultants should know evacuation routes, emergency contacts, and contingency plans for medical, political, or environmental crises. Clients should also be briefed on these plans, ensuring alignment in case of disruption. Emergency protocols must be rehearsed, not just documented, so that all parties know how to act when stress and confusion strike. For example, Consultants and clients alike should understand designated assembly points, communication protocols if networks fail, and decision-making authority during a crisis.

Psychological protection is another dimension that is easily neglected. High-risk environments expose consultants and clients to stress, fatigue, and sometimes trauma. Long periods in uncertain or threatening conditions can erode morale and impair judgement. Consultants should monitor their own wellbeing and that of their teams, recognising early signs of burnout or stress. Clients should be encouraged to consider mental resilience measures – from reasonable rest schedules to access to counselling support after exposure to particularly challenging conditions. Protecting psychological health is as important as protecting physical security, since impaired decision-making undermines both safety and effectiveness.

The last point to note is that protection requires shared responsibility. Consultants, firms, and clients each have a role to play. Consultants must follow protocols, exercise vigilance, and maintain discipline. Firms must provide training, insurance, and logistical support. Clients must honour duty of care by facilitating safe movement, providing adequate resources, and respecting security recommendations. Protecting consultants and clients is not the burden of one party but a collective commitment that ensures consultancy can be delivered safely and credibly.

Protecting consultants and clients in high-risk environments involves more than defensive measures. It is about embedding safety and security into the practice of consultancy itself. Travel security, cybersecurity, safeguarding local staff, balancing safety with delivery, and preparing for emergencies all contribute to resilience. When consultants and clients share responsibility for protection, they create the conditions for projects to succeed even in the most demanding contexts. Protection, in this sense, is not a constraint but an enabler: it allows consultancy to deliver value without compromising those who provide or receive it.

Illustrative Examples: Lessons from the Field

Example 1 – Conflict-Adjacent Infrastructure: A consultancy team was engaged to assess the resilience of a critical transport hub located near an active conflict zone. The site itself was not under attack, but sporadic violence in surrounding areas created a volatile environment. Initial plans assumed access would be straightforward; however, checkpoints and curfews severely restricted movement. Local staff were reluctant to speak openly, fearing repercussions if their comments were overheard. The consultants adapted by shortening site visits, using discreet interviews, and combining observations with remote monitoring data. Their recommendations emphasised redundancy in transport routes and contingency planning for sudden closures. The key lesson was that conflict, even when indirect, shapes both the consultant's access and the client's operational assumptions.

Example 2 – Corruption Pressures: A consultant working in a resource-rich but politically fragile state was tasked with auditing site security for a multinational client. During the project, local officials hinted that approval of recommendations would be expedited if "facilitation fees" were provided. At the same time, contractors attempted to steer the consultant towards endorsing cheaper but non-compliant security measures. Yielding to either pressure would have compromised independence and exposed the consultant to liability. The consultant documented all interactions, reported them transparently to the client, and framed recommendations in terms of international standards and duty of care. Though this approach delayed implementation, it preserved credibility. The lesson was that corruption pressures are best managed through transparency, defensibility, and an unwavering commitment to professional standards.

Example 3 – Remote Industrial Facility: A consultancy assignment in a remote mining operation illustrated the risks of hazardous environments. The site was several hours from the nearest town, with poor medical facilities and unreliable communications. During initial visits, consultants discovered that evacuation protocols were theoretical only; the nearest "emergency airstrip" was in disrepair. Data records were incomplete, and many safety practices existed only on paper. The consultants shifted their methodology, relying heavily on direct observation and staff interviews rather than documentation. They also prioritised recommendations around medical readiness, communication resilience, and practical evacuation measures. The lesson was that remoteness magnifies ordinary risks, turning logistical oversights into critical vulnerabilities.

Cross-Cutting Lessons: Though these examples differ in context, they share common themes. Consultants must expect conditions to be more restrictive than anticipated, must resist pressures that compromise independence, and must adapt methodology when infrastructure or data is weak. In each case, effectiveness depended less on technical frameworks alone than on adaptability, ethical clarity, and practical problem solving. These lessons reinforce that high-risk environments are not theoretical constructs but realities where consultants' judgement is tested daily.

Practice Guide

International and high-risk environments demand more than technical expertise; they test preparation, adaptability, and integrity. The key is to approach each assignment with humility, respect for local context, and disciplined risk management.

The most common pitfalls are overconfidence, cultural insensitivity, weak preparation, and ethical compromise. Consultants who assume that practices from stable environments will transfer directly, or who downplay risks to satisfy client pressure, undermine both safety and credibility. These traps are best countered through rigorous preparation, transparent decision-making, and a clear sense of professional boundaries.

Good practice lies in treating preparation as central, not peripheral. Structured risk assessments, realistic logistics planning, and continuous reassessment allow consultants to stay effective even as conditions change. Listening to local voices, adapting methods to context, and protecting the welfare of clients and partners reinforce trust and resilience. Above all, establishing ethical red lines in advance ensures independence under pressure.

Mastering these disciplines enables consultants to turn high-risk assignments from liabilities into opportunities to demonstrate value. The next chapter explores how consultants sustain effectiveness under pressure, ensuring that resilience and credibility extend beyond individual projects to long-term professional practice.

Chapter 20 – Specialised Sectors

While general principles of analysis, design, and reporting apply across many projects, each sector brings distinct demands shaped by risks, regulations, and culture. Critical national infrastructure, nuclear facilities, maritime ports, aviation systems, and data centres are environments where security is paramount, stakes are high, and mistakes can have national or global consequences. Credibility rests not only on transferable skills but also on grasping the nuances of these specialised contexts.

Consultants who rely on a single generic method risk oversimplifying complex environments and losing stakeholder confidence. Those who adapt established frameworks to sector-specific challenges deliver advice that is rigorous and relevant. Sectoral expertise is therefore the basis for trust, influence, and impact. This chapter explores how the consultant's role shifts across specialised domains, examining implications for risk assessment, stakeholder engagement, and design, while showing how international frameworks, cultural dynamics, and proportionality shape effective practice.

By the end of this chapter, you will be able to:

- Recognise the unique consulting demands of critical national infrastructure, nuclear, maritime, aviation, and data centre sectors.
- Understand the regulatory, operational, and cultural nuances that shape each sector.
- Apply consulting frameworks proportionately to specialised environments.
- Anticipate sector-specific threats, vulnerabilities, and stakeholder dynamics.
- Tailor analysis, design, and recommendations to sectoral context without compromising independence or integrity.
- Avoid common pitfalls such as over-generalisation or neglect of regulatory scrutiny.

Introduction

Consultancy is often presented as a set of transferable skills: the ability to analyse problems, engage stakeholders, design solutions, and communicate persuasively. These capabilities are indeed essential. Yet they are not sufficient when working in highly regulated or high-stakes sectors such as nuclear, aviation, or maritime. Each of these environments brings its own language, culture, and expectations. For consultants, recognising and adapting to these differences is what separates generic advice from credible, actionable recommendations.

Specialisation matters because risks are not evenly distributed across sectors. A data breach in a retail business may damage reputation and revenue; a breach in a nuclear facility could create national security consequences. Similarly, delays in implementing recommendations in an office setting may cost money; delays in aviation security could risk lives. Clients in specialised sectors therefore expect consultants to demonstrate not only general consulting competence but also fluency in the specific risks, regulations, and standards that define their industry.

Regulation further intensifies the need for sectoral expertise. Critical national infrastructure operates under detailed frameworks such as the EU's Directive 2022/2557, NCEMA 7000[18] in the UAE, or NERC CIP[21] in North America. Aviation security is shaped by ICAO[10] and IATA standards; maritime operations by the IMO[11] and ISPS Code; nuclear projects by IAEA[9] guidance and national regulators. Consultants who cannot reference or align with these frameworks risk producing outputs that lack legitimacy. Sector-specific regulations are not optional extras; they are the baseline against which consultancy is judged.

Specialisation also affects how stakeholders engage. In nuclear environments, consultants may face highly technical engineers accustomed to zero-tolerance safety cultures. In aviation, they may deal with multiple competing stakeholders – airlines, airports, regulators, and passengers – each with different priorities. In maritime projects, consultants may encounter overlapping jurisdictions and international politics. In data centres, clients may include global hyperscalers, regulators concerned with cyber resilience, and operators balancing cost against uptime. In each case, credibility rests on understanding the nuances of the sector's culture and pressures.

Specialisation also influences the consultant's own positioning. Sectoral expertise builds trust and opens doors to high-level engagements. Consultants recognised for depth in nuclear, aviation, or data centre work are more likely to be invited to projects where stakes are highest. Specialisation is therefore not just about delivering effective projects; it is also about career trajectory and reputation.

This chapter explores how consultancy principles are applied within specialised sectors. It shows that while frameworks such as TVRA remain valuable, they must be adapted to context. Each sector demands its own blend of technical literacy, regulatory awareness, and cultural sensitivity. Understanding these differences enables consultants to move beyond generic advice and deliver solutions that are credible, defensible, and impactful.

Sectoral expertise transforms consultancy from method to mastery. Understanding regulation, culture, and interdependency allows frameworks to be adapted credibly and proportionately across specialised environments.

Critical National Infrastructure (CNI)

Critical National Infrastructure (CNI) refers to those assets, systems, and services that are essential to the functioning of society and the economy. Power generation and distribution, water treatment, transport networks, telecommunications, health systems, and financial services all fall within this category. When CNI is disrupted, the consequences are often severe: widespread public harm, economic losses, and potential threats to national security. For consultants, working within this sector demands a heightened level of awareness, as recommendations influence systems upon which millions of people depend.

Defining CNI is not straightforward, as the designation varies between nations. In the United Kingdom, the National Protective Security Authority (NPSA) provides guidance and definitions, while in the European Union the NIS2[6] Directive and Directive 2022/2557[7] set frameworks for resilience. In the United States, the Cybersecurity and Infrastructure Security Agency (CISA) identifies 16 critical sectors.

Despite these variations, common themes emerge: dependency, resilience, and proportionality. Dependency highlights how modern economies rely on interconnected systems; resilience stresses the need to withstand shocks; proportionality requires that security measures match the scale of risk.

Consulting in the CNI space is shaped by regulation and oversight. Authorities expect consultants to demonstrate fluency in relevant frameworks, such as NCEMA 7000[18] in the UAE, NERC CIP[21] for North American energy systems, or sector-specific safety codes. Recommendations that fail to align with these standards risk dismissal. Consultants must therefore integrate regulatory requirements into every stage of analysis and design, framing advice not only in terms of risk reduction but also compliance. Clients value consultants who can translate dense regulatory language into practical, actionable measures.

Stakeholder complexity in CNI is particularly acute. Projects may involve government ministries, regulatory agencies, private operators, contractors, unions, and local communities. Each stakeholder has legitimate but sometimes conflicting interests. For example, a government regulator may insist on stringent controls to meet national security objectives, while an operator may resist due to cost implications. Local communities may support projects for economic benefits but oppose perceived environmental risks. The consultant must mediate these tensions, ensuring that recommendations are defensible across constituencies. Neutrality and independence are critical; consultants seen as favouring one side risk exclusion or reputational harm.

Risk assessment in CNI goes beyond the boundaries of single sites. Interdependency means that failure in one system can cascade into others. A power outage can disrupt hospitals, transport, and telecommunications. Consultants must therefore adopt a systems view, mapping dependencies and identifying where resilience measures should be prioritised. Scenario-based planning is invaluable: modelling how disruptions ripple through interconnected networks enables proportionate recommendations.

Continuity and resilience are central themes. In CNI, the objective is not only to prevent incidents but to ensure continuity of service during and after disruption. This shifts the consulting focus from pure protection to resilience: redundancy, recovery, and adaptability. For example, in advising a water utility, a consultant might recommend layered perimeter security, but also continuity measures such as backup power supplies, mutual aid agreements with neighbouring utilities, and pre-planned incident response drills. The consultant's credibility rests on recognising that absolute prevention is impossible; resilience ensures society continues to function even when incidents occur.

Public trust adds another layer of complexity. CNI operators are often scrutinised not just by regulators but by the media and the public. A single incident, whether a blackout, data breach, or transport failure, can quickly escalate into a reputational crisis. Consultants must therefore frame recommendations with public trust in mind. This means not only addressing real risks but also demonstrating transparency, proportionality, and fairness. For example, an energy-sector recommendation may need to balance the cost of grid redundancy with the need for resilience, ensuring that critical services remain reliable without imposing unsustainable financial burdens.

Consulting methods must adapt accordingly. Generic risk frameworks provide a starting point, but consultants must tailor them to the sectoral context. For instance:

- In the energy sector, analysis may focus on redundancy in grid systems and protection against insider threats.
- In telecommunications, emphasis may be on cyber-physical resilience and continuity during natural disasters.
- In transport, consultants must integrate security with passenger flow and operational efficiency.
- In healthcare, continuity of life-critical services is paramount, requiring consultants to prioritise resilience over efficiency savings.

Each sub-sector has its own regulatory foundations, technical cultures, and operational realities. Consultants must be conversant with these nuances, ensuring that recommendations are not only technically sound but also sector-appropriate.

Applied Scenario – Energy Sector Resilience: A consultancy team tasked with assessing an electricity grid could find strong perimeter measures but weak contingency for cyber-physical threats. Their recommendations could include not only upgrades to intrusion detection but also investment in redundant control centres and cross-training staff for rapid response. Regulators could support such measures because they align with NERC CIP[21] requirements, while operators could value the emphasis on operational continuity. Credibility would rest on marrying regulatory alignment with practical, resilience-led design.

Applied Scenario – Transport Network Dependency: In a metropolitan rail project, consultants could discover that a single point of failure in the signalling system might disrupt the entire network. Rather than recommending only technical fixes, they could advise a broader resilience strategy: decentralised control nodes, pre-agreed rerouting protocols, and public communication strategies. This approach could deliver not just technical robustness but also continuity of service and protection of public trust.

Balancing regulatory demands, sector-specific risks, and operational realities creates pressures. For consultants working in CNI, these translate into challenges such as:

- Balancing proportionality: avoiding both over-engineering and under-protection.
- Mediating between conflicting stakeholders without losing independence.
- Managing cascading interdependencies across systems.
- Translating complex regulatory frameworks into actionable measures.
- Maintaining credibility under public and political scrutiny.

Consulting in CNI requires more than applying generic frameworks. It demands a systems perspective, regulatory fluency, and sensitivity to stakeholder and public trust dynamics. Consultants must demonstrate that they understand both the technical and societal stakes, delivering recommendations that are defensible, proportionate, and resilient. By doing so, they contribute not only to the success of individual projects but to the stability and security of the societies that depend on them. Importantly, consultants must also recognise that CNI never operates in isolation: transport depends on energy, telecommunications enable healthcare, and data centres underpin finance and government services. A weakness in one sector can quickly cascade into another, making interdependency analysis a critical part of the consultant's role.

Nuclear Sector

Few sectors illustrate the weight of responsibility in consultancy more clearly than nuclear. The nuclear domain is unique in its combination of technical complexity, stringent regulation, and high public sensitivity. A single incident, whether an operational accident or a security breach, can have profound consequences for health, the environment, and public trust. For consultants, operating in the nuclear sector demands not only technical literacy and risk competence but also exceptional integrity and independence.

The uniqueness of nuclear lies in its zero-tolerance culture. Unlike many industries where small failures can be tolerated, nuclear operators adopt a mindset in which every deviation is treated as potentially catastrophic. Consultants must adapt to this culture of precision, where language, assumptions, and recommendations are scrutinised in detail. In nuclear environments, credibility is judged not just by the quality of insights but by their defensibility under the highest levels of scrutiny.

International frameworks and regulation define much of the consultant's context. The International Atomic Energy Agency (IAEA) sets global safety and security standards, while the World Association of Nuclear Operators (WANO) fosters peer review and continuous improvement. National regulators, such as the U.S. Nuclear Regulatory Commission or the UK's Office for Nuclear Regulation, impose rigorous requirements. Consultants must be fluent in these frameworks, aligning recommendations with international standards while respecting national regulations. Unlike other sectors where compliance may be one element among many, in nuclear it is the baseline.

The consultant's role is to bridge technical, organisational, and governance dimensions. For example, a consultancy project might involve reviewing the security of a nuclear facility. Technical aspects could include access controls, surveillance systems, and perimeter resilience. Organisational aspects might address insider threats, culture of safety, and incident drills. Governance dimensions include board oversight, regulatory reporting, and transparency. Consultants must integrate these elements into coherent recommendations that satisfy technical standards, align with regulatory expectations, and are implementable by the operator.

Ethical imperatives are particularly acute in nuclear consultancy. Stakeholders may pressure consultants to downplay vulnerabilities, emphasise compliance over resilience, or endorse cheaper but less robust solutions. Yielding to such pressure compromises both safety and credibility. Integrity requires consultants to present findings transparently, acknowledging uncertainties and limitations. In this sector, defensibility is critical: every recommendation should be something the consultant is prepared to justify under audit, legal review, or public inquiry. Ethical clarity provides not only moral protection but also professional credibility.

Public perception and trust shape the nuclear sector in ways that extend beyond technical considerations. Nuclear projects attract public attention and, often, controversy. Communities may oppose facilities on environmental or political grounds; media coverage amplifies even minor incidents. Consultants must therefore recognise that their reports may be scrutinised not just by clients and regulators but by the public. Recommendations should therefore be communicated with clarity, transparency, and proportionality, avoiding both alarmism and minimisation.

Applied Scenario – Insider Threats in Nuclear Facilities: A consultancy engagement at a nuclear plant could reveal strong perimeter and surveillance measures but insufficient controls against insider threats. Staff access rights might be broad, and monitoring of critical areas could be limited. The consultants could recommend a layered access control system, enhanced background checks, and a culture programme reinforcing insider vigilance. Regulatory inspectors could endorse such an approach, and operators might implement it in phases. Insider risks can determine the true scale of vulnerability; external threats are only part of the picture.

Applied Scenario – Community Engagement: In a project assessing a proposed nuclear waste storage site, consultants could recognise that community opposition might derail implementation. They could advise the client to adopt a transparent communication strategy, including regular town hall meetings, publication of non-technical summaries, and community advisory panels. By addressing public trust alongside technical resilience, the project could gain broader acceptance. Trust must be treated as a design parameter, not a communications afterthought.

Balancing safety culture, regulatory scrutiny, and the unique risks of nuclear environments creates distinct pressures. For consultants, these translate into challenges such as:

- **Complexity of regulation**: multiple, often overlapping international and national standards.
- **Cultural adjustment**: working within a zero-tolerance environment where scrutiny is intense.
- **Balancing independence**: resisting pressures to bias findings.
- **Managing public sensitivity**: recognising that credibility rests as much on perception as on technical accuracy.
- **Integrating multiple dimensions**: operational, technical, organisational, and governance factors must be addressed together.

Consultancy in the nuclear sector demands rigour, independence, and a holistic approach. Consultants must be fluent in international standards, sensitive to public trust, and uncompromising in ethical integrity when commercial or political pressures mount. Recommendations should be framed so they can withstand audit, legal scrutiny, and public inquiry, acknowledging uncertainties without minimising risk. Credibility depends on showing that technical, organisational, and governance measures work together, and that any compromises do not weaken defensibility.

Maritime Sector

The maritime sector is the backbone of global trade, with more than 80 per cent of international goods transported by sea. Ports, shipping lines, and logistics hubs form critical nodes in global supply chains, linking producers and consumers across continents. For consultants, the sector presents both opportunities and challenges. It is global by nature, heavily regulated at the international level, and subject to persistent threats ranging from piracy to smuggling and terrorism. Effective consultancy in this sector requires not only technical and security expertise but also a deep appreciation of the political and economic complexities that surround maritime activity.

The maritime sector faces a wide range of threats. Piracy remains a threat in certain regions, particularly in parts of West Africa and Southeast Asia. Smuggling, including narcotics, arms, and human trafficking, exploits weaknesses in port security and customs processes. Terrorism, while less common, poses catastrophic risks if ports or ships are targeted. Insider threats are also significant: port employees or contractors may be coerced or corrupted into facilitating illicit activities. Consultants must therefore take a layered approach, addressing both external and internal risks.

Regulatory frameworks shape maritime consultancy. The International Maritime Organization (IMO[11]) sets global standards, most notably through the International Ship and Port Facility Security (ISPS) Code, which mandates security assessments and plans for ships and ports. Consultants working in this sector must demonstrate fluency in ISPS requirements and their application, as well as familiarity with national regulations that adapt international standards to local contexts. Beyond security, environmental frameworks such as MARPOL (pollution prevention) also influence consultancy, as reputational risks increasingly include environmental compliance.

Operational challenges are acute because of the sector's scale and complexity. Ports are vast, with thousands of employees, contractors, and daily visitors. Cargo volumes are enormous, and the imperative of efficiency means that delays caused by security measures can face resistance. Consultants must therefore design recommendations that enhance security without impeding trade flows. This balance is particularly delicate: too little security exposes ports to exploitation, while too much can disrupt supply chains and alienate stakeholders.

Stakeholder dynamics in maritime projects are complex and multi-layered. A single port may involve port authorities, private terminal operators, shipping companies, customs agencies, coast guards, and local communities. International shipping lines add further layers of complexity, bringing diverse national regulations and expectations into play. Consultants must act as facilitators, ensuring that stakeholders with differing priorities – trade efficiency, revenue, compliance, or safety – converge around workable solutions.

Applied Scenario – Port Security Audit: A consultancy engagement in a major international port could reveal strong perimeter fencing but inadequate cargo screening. Smuggling networks might exploit this gap, inserting illicit goods into containers. Consultants could recommend a risk-based screening approach, focusing on high-risk cargo categories and origin routes, supported by enhanced staff training. Such recommendations could be adopted if framed not only in security terms but also in relation to reputational protection and regulatory compliance. Focusing checks on high-risk cargo is more effective than applying blanket controls that slow down operations.

Applied Scenario – Piracy Risk in Shipping: A consultancy team advising a shipping line operating in high-risk waters could conduct a review of vessel security protocols. They might find inconsistent application of best practices across crews. Their recommendations could include standardising ship security plans, conduct scenario drills, and adopting non-lethal deterrence measures such as water cannons and acoustic devices. The consultancy could also facilitate workshops to build crew confidence. Procedure and culture need equal weight to hardware.

Consulting in maritime environments can demand sensitivity to international politics. Ports are gateways to national economies and symbols of sovereignty. Security recommendations may therefore be politically sensitive, particularly if they imply vulnerability. Consultants must present findings diplomatically, emphasising resilience and international best practice rather than weakness. Neutral, evidence-based framing helps ensure that advice is received constructively.

Cultural sensitivities, political pressures, and personal safety concerns all shape the consulting environment. For consultants, this creates challenges such as:

- Navigating overlapping jurisdictions between national, regional, and international authorities.
- Balancing security with efficiency in environments where throughput is paramount.
- Addressing insider threats in large, complex workforces.
- Overcoming political sensitivities about vulnerabilities in critical national gateways.
- Integrating environmental, reputational, and security considerations into coherent advice.

The maritime sector highlights the interplay between global regulation, local implementation, and practical realities of scale. Consultants must bring technical expertise, fluency in international standards, and skill in stakeholder management. They must frame security not as an obstacle to trade but as an enabler of safe, efficient, and credible operations. By doing so, they help protect not only individual ports and shipping lines but the global supply chains upon which modern economies depend.

Aviation Sector

Aviation is one of the most visible and heavily scrutinised security domains, combining operational efficiency with stringent protective measures. The history of hijackings, bombings, and the September 11 attacks placed aviation security at the forefront of global consciousness. Airports and airlines are now among the regulated environments in the world, combining operational efficiency with stringent protective measures. For consultants, aviation offers both complexity and visibility: projects are technically demanding, politically sensitive, and often highly public.

The regulatory landscape is extensive and global. The International Civil Aviation Organization (ICAO[10]) sets standards and recommended practices through Annex 17 of the Chicago Convention, covering security measures for international aviation. The International Air Transport Association (IATA) supplements these with operational guidance. National aviation authorities, such as the U.S. Transportation Security Administration (TSA) or the UK Civil Aviation Authority (CAA), impose their own frameworks. Consultants must be fluent in these regulations, as aviation operators are regularly audited, and recommendations must stand up to international scrutiny. Unlike many sectors, aviation is characterised by near-universal regulatory harmonisation, creating high expectations for compliance and professionalism.

Threats to aviation remain diverse and evolving. While hijacking and terrorism remain critical risks, insider threats, cyber vulnerabilities, and disruptive passengers now also feature prominently. Airports are attractive targets because of their symbolic status and the concentration of people. Consultants must assess risks across the entire spectrum, from airside access control to passenger screening, baggage handling, cargo, and cyber-physical systems that underpin flight operations.

Stakeholder complexity is acute. Airports are ecosystems in themselves, hosting airlines, airport authorities, regulators, ground handlers, security companies, law enforcement, concessionaires, and passengers. Each group has different priorities: airlines prioritise on-time performance, regulators focus on compliance, and passengers expect both safety and efficiency. Consultants must mediate these interests, ensuring that recommendations are proportionate and achievable. The political sensitivity of aviation adds another dimension, as failures can quickly escalate into national or even international crises.

Operational challenges stem from the need to balance security with passenger experience. Excessive delays or intrusive screening undermine public trust and the commercial viability of airlines and airports. Consultants must therefore design measures that are both robust and efficient. This often involves introducing risk-based screening approaches, using intelligence to target resources where risk is greatest. Recommendations must integrate seamlessly into passenger flow and operational systems to avoid creating bottlenecks.

Applied Scenario – Passenger Screening Innovation: A consultancy engagement with a major hub airport could reveal long queues at security checkpoints, leading to passenger frustration and reputational harm. The consultants could recommend adopting automated screening lanes and expanding the use of behavioural detection officers. By piloting these measures, the airport could reduce waiting times without compromising security. Efficiency gains and security gains can be achieved together.

Applied Scenario – Cyber-Physical Risks: An assessment of an airline's operational systems could highlight vulnerabilities in flight planning and crew scheduling platforms. Although physical security might be robust, cyber resilience could lag behind. Consultants could recommend integrating cyber threat monitoring into the airline's operational control centre and training staff in incident response. Regulators could welcome such an approach as forward-looking, while the airline might gain reassurance that business continuity was protected. Operations control should treat cyber monitoring data as just as important as other safety information.

The role of emerging technology in aviation consultancy is growing. Biometric identification, AI-based screening, and automated border control are transforming passenger management. Consultants must understand these technologies, evaluate their risks, and advise on proportional adoption. At the same time, they must recognise that technology alone cannot solve every problem; cultural change, training, and process integration remain critical

The combined demands of safety, regulation, and operational complexity in aviation create particular challenges for consultants, including:

- Balancing compliance with efficiency in highly regulated contexts.
- Managing multiple stakeholders with conflicting priorities.
- Addressing insider threats in large, complex workforces.
- Adapting to rapid technological change while ensuring proportionality.
- Recognising aviation's symbolic status, which heightens reputational and political risk.

The aviation sector combines high visibility, global regulation, and operational complexity. Consultants must be fluent in international standards, alert to evolving threats, and skilled at balancing safety with efficiency. Recommendations must protect not only passengers and infrastructure but also the reputations of airlines, airports, and governments. Aviation consultancy is therefore both technically demanding and symbolically significant – a domain where credibility is tested at every stage, and where successful recommendations have global impact.

Data Centres

Data centres have become the critical infrastructure of the digital economy. They underpin financial transactions, government services, healthcare records, and the daily communications of billions of people. Hyperscale facilities support global cloud providers, while colocation centres host the systems of multiple clients, and edge data centres extend digital capacity closer to end-users. For consultants, this sector represents a rapidly expanding field where physical and cyber domains converge, regulatory expectations are evolving, and client trust is paramount.

Threats to data centres arise from both physical and cyber vulnerabilities. Physical risks include unauthorised access, sabotage, insider threats, and reliance on utilities such as power and cooling. Cyber risks range from data breaches to ransomware and state-sponsored attacks. Converged security threats – where physical and digital risks intersect – are increasingly evident across many sectors, from aviation to critical national infrastructure. They are especially pronounced in data centres, where physical intrusion can enable large-scale cyber compromise, and cyber failures can disrupt local power management or fire suppression. Consultants must therefore approach security holistically, bridging both domains.

Regulatory foundations are increasingly important. The European Union's NIS2[6] Directive extends obligations on operators of essential services, including digital infrastructure. ISO/IEC 27001:2022[15] establishes international standards for information security, while local authorities such as Dubai's SIRA[4] or Abu Dhabi's ADMCC[1] impose additional physical security requirements. Clients expect consultants to align recommendations with these frameworks, providing assurance that facilities meet both global and local expectations. In some jurisdictions, compliance is a prerequisite for licensing; in others, it helps protect organisations from legal liability.

Stakeholder complexity varies depending on facility type. In hyperscale data centres, the client may be a global technology provider with high technical expectations and established global standards. In colocation centres, consultants must navigate the needs of multiple tenants, each with different risk appetites, compliance obligations, and contractual arrangements. Edge facilities typically involve local operators working with limited budgets, requiring consultants to balance proportionality with resilience. In all cases, stakeholder trust is critical: clients are entrusting consultants with advice that affects the protection of highly sensitive assets.

Threat, Vulnerability, and Risk Assessment (TVRA) is the foundation of all security consultancy, but in data centres it becomes especially critical. Consultants must evaluate not only physical perimeters and access controls but also operational dependencies such as energy resilience, redundant cooling, and supply chain security. Because data centres consume vast amounts of energy, any disruption to power or cooling can escalate rapidly into outages with global consequences. Recommendations therefore often include investment in redundant systems, integration of renewable energy, and close partnerships with utility providers.

Applied Scenario – Colocation Facility Risk Assessment: A small consultancy team assessing a colocation facility could find that while perimeter controls were robust, separation between tenant areas was weak. This could create the risk that one client's staff might reach another's racks, exposing the facility to malicious action. The consultants could advise redesigning access zoning, strengthen monitoring, and clarify responsibilities within tenant contracts. These measures could ensure that zoning and accountability reduce the likelihood of tenant-on-tenant risk.

Applied Scenario – Power and Cooling Resilience: At a hyperscale facility, consultants could find that while redundancy for power supply was robust, cooling systems were vulnerable to single points of failure. Given the facility's size, even minor cooling disruption could have catastrophic consequences. Recommendations could include diversifying cooling methods, enhance predictive maintenance, and integrate smart monitoring systems. The operator could adopt a phased programme, recognising that resilience is as much about thermal stability as electrical redundancy.

High availability requirements, strict standards, and client pressures in data centre projects create specific challenges for consultants, including:

- Balancing investment with proportionality in a competitive industry where margins matter.
- Integrating physical and cyber perspectives into coherent, actionable recommendations.
- Navigating multiple tenants with diverse risk appetites in colocation environments.
- Ensuring operational resilience against energy and cooling dependencies, which represent systemic vulnerabilities.
- Aligning with fast-evolving regulatory frameworks across multiple jurisdictions.

The role of trust is especially pronounced in data centres. Clients may already be highly sophisticated in cyber domains but rely on consultants to provide independent assurance of integrated resilience. Credibility depends on the consultant's ability to engage confidently with both technical specialists and business executives, translating security recommendations into business continuity outcomes. Reports must therefore communicate not only technical adequacy but also assurance of resilience, compliance, and reputational protection.

Consultancy in data centres sits at the intersection of critical infrastructure, technology, and global commerce. Alongside physical–cyber convergence, emerging pressures – AI-driven automation, energy and cooling constraints amplified by climate risk, and geopolitics affecting hardware supply chains – must be factored into resilience planning. Consultants need the fluency to translate these pressures into proportionate controls, operational continuity measures, and clear accountability between operators and tenants, so that resilience, compliance, and reputation are all protected.

Illustrative Examples: Sectoral Lessons

Taken together, the applied scenarios throughout this chapter show that consultancy in specialised sectors is not about applying generic tools in isolation but about tailoring responses to the distinctive conditions of each environment. In energy and transport, resilience depends on anticipating interdependencies and preventing single points of failure. In nuclear facilities, credibility comes from addressing both technical rigour and societal trust. Maritime engagements reveal the importance of balancing security with operational efficiency, while aviation examples highlight the need to manage risks without undermining passenger confidence or business continuity. Data centre examples highlight the convergence of physical and cyber domains and the critical role of resilience in energy and cooling systems.

The common thread is that consultants succeed when they integrate regulatory compliance with proportionate, practical measures that stakeholders can support. Across all sectors, the lessons emphasise vigilance against insider threats, sensitivity to public perception, the need for operational continuity, and the value of framing recommendations in terms of resilience rather than only protection. Above all, these examples demonstrate that credibility is earned by showing an ability to adapt frameworks, bridge stakeholder interests, and translate complex risks into solutions that are both defensible and trusted.

Practice Guide

Working in specialised sectors demands more than generic consulting tools. Credibility depends on sector fluency, regulatory awareness, and cultural sensitivity, applied in proportionate and defensible ways. The discussion across CNI, nuclear, maritime, aviation, and data centres demonstrated how consultants can recognise sector-specific demands, anticipate risks, and avoid the trap of generic advice.

Consultants can stumble by treating highly regulated or high-stakes environments as though they were interchangeable with corporate projects. Over-generalisation leads to recommendations that lack legitimacy. Neglecting regulatory foundations, whether ICAO[10] in aviation, ISPS in maritime, or IAEA in nuclear, undermines credibility. Overlooking human and cultural factors is another recurring mistake: insider threats in nuclear facilities, workforce dynamics in ports, passenger experience in aviation, and tenant trust in data centres all show that technical measures alone are insufficient. Over-engineering is also a risk, with consultants sometimes proposing costly or disproportionate measures that fail the test of sustainability.

Best practice flows from recognising these pitfalls. Consultants should immerse themselves in sector-specific standards before beginning assignments, demonstrating not only technical competence but fluency in the frameworks that govern the environment. Recommendations should translate dense regulation into clear, proportionate, and defensible measures. Human factors and stakeholder dynamics must be treated as integral to risk management, not secondary considerations. Independence and impartiality remain vital, particularly when mediating between multiple stakeholders with competing priorities. Above all, proportionality should guide practice – ensuring that solutions are effective, feasible, and aligned with sectoral culture.

The consultant who develops genuine sectoral expertise becomes far more than a technical adviser: they become a trusted interpreter between regulation, operational reality, and strategic objectives. Specialisation is therefore both a safeguard against irrelevance and a pathway to influence. In a world where infrastructure, technology, and society are increasingly interdependent, consultants who adapt their craft to the demands of specialised sectors are those whose advice will be sought, trusted, and implemented.

Chapter 21 – Emerging Threats and Technologies

The consulting landscape does not stand still. New threats emerge as technology evolves, geopolitical conditions shift, and environmental pressures intensify. Yesterday's solutions are often inadequate for tomorrow's risks. For consultants, the challenge lies in recognising these developments early, assessing them with rigour, and advising clients with clarity and proportion. Emerging threats and technologies must be understood not as isolated novelties but as forces that reshape the environment in which organisations operate.

Artificial intelligence, drones, climate change, small modular reactors, and the rise of smart cities are only some of the drivers of change. Each offers opportunities for resilience and efficiency, yet each also introduces vulnerabilities, regulatory challenges, and ethical dilemmas. Consultants must guide clients through this shifting terrain, helping them distinguish between hype and substantive risk, between innovation worth embracing and threats that require mitigation.

The consultant's role is not to predict the future with certainty but to help organisations prepare for uncertainty. This involves combining technical awareness with strategic foresight, ensuring that recommendations are not only responsive to current risks but adaptive to those on the horizon. It also requires embedding feedback loops into consulting practice so that risk management evolves in step with emerging conditions.

By the end of this chapter, you will be able to:

- Recognise the range of emerging threats and technologies most relevant to consultancy, including AI, drones, SMRs, smart cities, and climate-related disruption.
- Distinguish between opportunities and risks in adopting new technologies.
- Apply structured consulting approaches to evaluate emerging threats before they become mainstream.
- Anticipate ethical and reputational challenges posed by new technologies.

- Integrate practical resilience and proportionality into recommendations addressing new risks.
- Design feedback loops and adaptive systems, drawing on *High Output Management*, to ensure security measures remain relevant over time.
- Avoid common pitfalls such as chasing hype, underestimating secondary risks, or neglecting ethical considerations.

Introduction

Threats to organisations, infrastructure, and society are not static. They evolve as technology advances, as political and environmental pressures intensify, and as adversaries adapt. For consultants, this presents a constant challenge: frameworks and methods that were sufficient yesterday may be inadequate tomorrow. The role of the consultant is therefore not only to analyse current risks, but also to anticipate emerging ones, helping clients adapt before vulnerabilities become crises.

Emerging threats are characterised by uncertainty. Their probability, scale, and impact are often difficult to quantify, and their pathways of disruption may be indirect. For instance, artificial intelligence can strengthen surveillance and detection capabilities, yet it can also enable disinformation, deepfakes, or automated cyber intrusions. Drones have revolutionised logistics and industrial inspection, but they are equally capable of smuggling contraband, conducting hostile reconnaissance, or disrupting airports. Small Modular Reactors (SMRs) offer the promise of clean, reliable energy for critical infrastructure, but they raise unique questions of security, regulation, and public trust. Consultants must approach these innovations with both openness and scepticism, recognising opportunities while rigorously testing assumptions.

Environmental factors are also emerging as critical drivers of risk. Climate change brings more frequent and severe weather events, from floods to heatwaves, which disrupt infrastructure and supply chains. These physical impacts are often accompanied by social consequences: resource scarcity, population displacement, and unrest. Consultants who fail to account for environmental disruption in their risk assessments risk leaving clients exposed to widespread disruption.

Smart cities, built on interconnected data and automation, illustrate the convergence of opportunity and vulnerability. Integrated transport, energy, and communication systems promise efficiency and sustainability. Yet interconnectivity creates pathways for cascading failure: a single cyber intrusion or infrastructure fault can spread rapidly across systems. Consultants must therefore advise on governance and resilience, ensuring that efficiency gains do not come at the cost of fragility.

The pace of change creates another challenge: distinguishing between hype and reality. Not every emerging technology will transform risk landscapes, and not every predicted threat will materialise. Consultants must filter claims carefully, grounding their advice in evidence and proportionality. Overreaction wastes resources; underreaction leaves clients vulnerable. The skill lies in balancing foresight with restraint, preparing for what is plausible while avoiding distraction from what is not.

The consultant's role is to help organisations navigate uncertainty. This involves not only identifying risks but also designing adaptive systems capable of learning and adjusting. Embedding feedback loops ensures that clients remain resilient in the face of evolving threats. Emerging risks are not problems to be solved once; they are conditions to be managed continually.

This chapter explores some of the most pressing emerging threats and technologies facing consultants today: artificial intelligence, drones, climate-related disruption, small modular reactors, and smart cities. It also examines how feedback systems can be integrated into consulting practice to ensure that security strategies evolve in step with change.

Artificial Intelligence – Opportunity and Misuse

Artificial Intelligence (AI) has emerged as both a transformative enabler and a disruptive threat in the security landscape. For consultants, AI is no longer an abstract research domain; it is a practical force reshaping surveillance, analytics, and risk management. Yet its power cuts both ways. The same tools that enhance resilience can also be misused by adversaries for deception, intrusion, or exploitation. Understanding this duality is essential for consultants seeking to advise clients responsibly.

AI as an opportunity lies primarily in its ability to process vast amounts of data quickly and identify patterns that human analysts might miss. In physical security, AI-driven video analytics can detect anomalies such as unattended baggage, unusual movement patterns, or perimeter breaches in real time. In cyber domains, machine learning models can flag abnormal network activity, detect intrusions, and adapt to evolving attack patterns. Predictive analytics can even help organisations anticipate maintenance failures or forecast likely threat scenarios, enabling proactive responses. For consultants, these capabilities translate into opportunities to recommend smarter, more efficient systems that improve both security outcomes and operational performance.

Another strength of AI is automation. Tasks that were once labour-intensive, such as access verification or log analysis, can now be handled at scale with minimal human intervention. This frees personnel to focus on higher-value decision-making while reducing the risk of human error. For clients with large, complex operations, such as airports, ports, or data centres, automation can significantly improve efficiency. Consultants who can evaluate, design, and recommend AI-based solutions demonstrate not only technical fluency but also awareness of industry trends.

However, AI introduces significant risks and vulnerabilities. One concern is bias in algorithms. AI systems learn from data; if the data is biased, the outcomes will be too. In surveillance, this can manifest as disproportionate false positives for certain demographic groups, creating reputational and ethical issues for clients. Consultants must therefore stress the importance of dataset quality, transparency in algorithm design, and human oversight. Blind adoption of AI without addressing bias risks undermining trust.

Another vulnerability lies in adversarial attacks. AI systems can be manipulated by malicious actors who deliberately feed them misleading data. For instance, subtle changes to images or patterns may cause facial recognition systems to misidentify individuals or mislead autonomous vehicles into unsafe behaviour. These weaknesses are often overlooked by organisations eager to embrace AI. Consultants must be aware of adversarial risks and recommend safeguards such as redundancy, testing under hostile conditions, and layered security controls.

AI can also be misused as a weapon. Adversaries already exploit AI to create deepfakes, which are highly realistic but false images, audio, or video that can be used for disinformation, fraud, or reputational attacks. Automated bots driven by AI can amplify propaganda, manipulate public opinion, or overwhelm systems with false data. Criminal groups are experimenting with AI-driven malware that learns and adapts to defences. Consultants must advise clients that AI is not only a defensive tool but also a threat vector in itself.

The ethical challenges of AI extend beyond bias and misuse. Delegating security decisions to algorithms raises questions of accountability. If an AI system denies access incorrectly, misidentifies a threat, or makes a decision that harms individuals, who is responsible? Clients may be eager to embrace automation but reluctant to confront these questions. Consultants have a role in ensuring that governance structures are in place, with clear accountability and human oversight of AI systems. Transparency and explainability should be guiding principles: if a system cannot explain its decisions, its reliability is limited.

Applied Scenario – Video Analytics in Airports: A consultancy team advising a major airport could consider adopting AI-based video analytics for passenger flow monitoring and anomaly detection. Trials could show improved detection of unattended baggage and reduced queue times. However, the system might also generate disproportionate false positives for certain groups, raising reputational risks. The consultants could recommend retaining AI for operational efficiency but ensuring human review for all security alerts. AI can enhance capability but requires safeguards to ensure fairness and proportionality.

Applied Scenario – Deepfake Fraud: A corporate client could experience an attempted fraud in which criminals use an AI-generated voice to impersonate a senior executive and request a wire transfer. Even if the attempt were thwarted, it could highlight new forms of deception. Consultants could use such an incident to advise on staff awareness training, multi-factor verification for sensitive transactions, and monitoring for emerging fraud techniques. AI misuse requires not only technical countermeasures but also cultural adaptation.

Rapid innovation, regulatory uncertainty, and the risk of over-reliance on vendor claims create distinct challenges for consultants considering AI, such as:

- Evaluating vendor claims in a rapidly evolving market where hype often exceeds reality.

- Balancing efficiency gains with ethical and reputational considerations.
- Integrating AI with legacy systems and human processes.
- Ensuring transparency, accountability, and proportionality in AI adoption.
- Anticipating adversarial use of AI by malicious actors.

The key is to adopt a balanced perspective. AI is neither a universal solution nor an uncontrollable threat; it is a powerful tool whose value depends on design, governance, and context. Recommendations should therefore emphasise proportionate adoption: where AI adds genuine value, clients should embrace it, but with safeguards for bias, accountability, and misuse. Where AI is hyped but not yet reliable, consultants should advise caution.

AI represents both opportunity and misuse. Consultants must recognise the potential of AI to improve detection, prediction, and efficiency, while remaining alert to its vulnerabilities, ethical implications, and potential for adversarial exploitation. By framing AI in terms of both benefits and risks, consultants provide clients with guidance that is realistic, defensible, and resilient in the face of a rapidly changing technological landscape.

Drones and Unmanned Systems

Unmanned aerial vehicles (UAVs), commonly known as drones, along with other unmanned systems such as ground or maritime platforms, have rapidly transitioned from niche technologies to mainstream tools. They are now integral to industries as varied as logistics, agriculture, filmmaking, and infrastructure inspection. At the same time, their misuse presents a growing security challenge. For consultants, drones symbolise the dual nature of emerging technologies: enablers of efficiency and innovation but also vectors for disruption and harm.

Legitimate applications of drones highlight their potential. Organisations use drones for surveying pipelines, inspecting high structures, monitoring agricultural output, and delivering goods. For critical infrastructure operators, drones provide cost-effective and safe ways to monitor perimeters, assess storm damage, or inspect otherwise inaccessible areas. These applications increase efficiency, reduce risk to personnel, and enable real-time monitoring at scale. Consultants should acknowledge these benefits, as clients may be eager to capitalise on them.

Yet drones also present significant security threats. They can be used for hostile reconnaissance, collecting imagery of sensitive sites such as airports, power plants, or government facilities. Criminal groups use drones to smuggle contraband into prisons or across borders. Terrorist organisations have demonstrated the use of weaponised drones, capable of delivering explosives or hazardous substances. Even amateur operators can disrupt critical services, as seen in incidents where drones forced the suspension of flights at major airports. For consultants, these risks must be considered credible, not hypothetical.

Counter-drone technologies are emerging in response. These include radar and acoustic detection, RF jamming, net-firing systems, and directed-energy weapons. However, no single solution is universally effective. Drones are small, agile, and often difficult to detect, especially in urban environments. Legal frameworks also restrict countermeasures: jamming signals or shooting down drones may contravene aviation laws. Consultants must therefore advise clients carefully, balancing technical capability with regulatory and reputational constraints. In many cases, layered measures combining detection, procedural response, and liaison with authorities, provide the most realistic approach.

Regulatory gaps remain a challenge. While agencies such as the International Civil Aviation Organization (ICAO[10]) set broad guidelines, national regulations vary widely. Some jurisdictions impose strict licensing and operational limits, while others lack robust enforcement. Consultants must be fluent in local legal requirements and ensure that recommendations are compliant. Overlooking regulation risks exposing clients to liability even if countermeasures are technically sound.

Applied Scenario – Airport Disruption: A major international airport could experience repeated drone incursions that force flight delays and cancellations. Consultants could advise on a multi-layered strategy: radar and RF-based detection, rapid response protocols for halting runway operations, and coordination with law enforcement for interdiction. Importantly, they could emphasise communication planning to maintain public confidence. Drone threats cannot always be eliminated, but their impact can be mitigated with proportionate planning and coordination.

Applied Scenario – Prison Security: In a consultancy project for a national prison service, drones could be identified as the primary vector for smuggling contraband. Consultants could recommend installing detection systems, enhancing perimeter patrols, and introducing controlled airspace designations in cooperation with civil aviation authorities. They could also advise staff training to respond quickly to drone sightings. Counter-drone measures require both technology and organisational adaptation.

The rapid spread of drone technology, for both legitimate and malicious use, creates challenges for consultants, including:

- Distinguishing between nuisance incidents and credible threats.
- Advising proportionately in an environment of rapidly evolving technology.
- Navigating legal and regulatory constraints on counter-drone actions.
- Balancing investment in countermeasures against the likelihood and impact of incidents.
- Integrating drone risks into broader security frameworks rather than treating them in isolation.

A proportionate realism is required in approaching drone risks. Drones are here to stay, and their use will expand. Clients must be encouraged to adopt the benefits while preparing for misuse. Recommendations should emphasise layered defence: early detection, clear response protocols, and engagement with regulators and law enforcement. Consultants must also guard against hype. While some vendors market counter-drone systems as universal solutions, consultants should help clients evaluate claims critically and adopt solutions that are practical, proportionate, lawful, and scalable.

Drones and unmanned systems are both opportunity and threat. Consultants must help clients embrace their potential for efficiency and safety while addressing their capacity for disruption. The duality of drones exemplifies the broader theme of emerging technologies: they are not inherently good or bad, but their impact depends on how they are used, regulated, and managed. By advising proportionately, consultants can help clients navigate this complexity with credibility and confidence.

Climate Change and Environmental Disruption

Climate change is increasingly recognised not only as an environmental issue but as a fundamental driver of security and continuity risk. Rising global temperatures, extreme weather events, and resource pressures all disrupt infrastructure, supply chains, and social stability. For consultants, the challenge is clear: climate-related risks can no longer be treated as background context – they must be integrated into mainstream consulting practice.

Physical risks are the most visible. Floods, storms, wildfires, and heatwaves now occur with greater frequency and intensity. These events threaten the integrity of infrastructure directly: power grids overloaded by heat stress, transport networks disrupted by flooding, or data centres disrupted when storms cause power loss or cooling failures. Consultants must incorporate these physical hazards into risk assessments, asking not only how systems perform under normal conditions but also how they withstand extreme events. Scenario planning becomes essential: What happens if a hospital loses power for 48 hours? How quickly can a logistics hub recover after a flood?

Secondary risks emerge from the cascading effects of environmental disruption. Resource scarcity, whether of water, energy, or food, can drive conflict and unrest. Migration pressures from climate-affected regions may strain urban infrastructure. Insurance markets may become unsustainable in high-risk zones, leaving clients exposed. Consultants must therefore broaden their perspective, recognising that climate-related risks ripple across sectors, often in unpredictable ways.

Integrating climate resilience into consultancy means expanding traditional frameworks. A Threat, Vulnerability, and Risk Assessment (TVRA) cannot stop at security incidents; it must include environmental stressors. For example, a consultant assessing a data centre should consider not only intrusion risks but also the site's exposure to flooding, temperature extremes, or utility dependency. Recommendations may then include locating facilities outside flood plains, investing in renewable microgrids, or designing redundant cooling systems. This is not an add-on but part of holistic resilience.

Applied Scenario – Flood Risk to Data Centres: A consultancy project assessing a cluster of data centres in Northern Europe could identify that several facilities are located in areas increasingly prone to flooding. Historical data might underestimate risk because climate change could alter rainfall patterns. Consultants could recommend investment in flood barriers, relocation of critical backup systems to higher levels, and partnerships with local authorities for flood response planning. Historical assumptions are insufficient in a changing climate; risk assessments must be forward-looking.

Applied Scenario – Heat Stress on Power Grids: In a project for a Middle Eastern utility, consultants could examine the resilience of the electricity grid under rising temperatures. They might find that heatwaves reduce transformer efficiency and increase demand for cooling. Recommendations could include phased upgrades of equipment to heat-resistant models, diversification into renewable energy, and demand-management programmes. Climate change does not create new vulnerabilities alone; it intensifies existing ones.

Rising environmental pressures, regulatory expectations, and client demands for sustainability create challenges for consultants in climate resilience, including:

- Access to reliable climate data, which may vary in quality across regions.
- Uncertainty in predicting the exact scale or timing of impacts.
- Balancing long-term resilience investments with short-term client priorities.
- Convincing stakeholders who may see climate risk as remote or secondary.

Consultants can add value by framing climate resilience in terms that resonate with client priorities. For executives, this may mean highlighting reputational risks and regulatory expectations. For operators, it may mean showing how resilient systems reduce downtime and protect staff. For investors, it may involve demonstrating that resilient assets retain value longer. By linking climate resilience to tangible outcomes, consultants can shift the conversation from abstract concern to actionable planning.

Climate change and environmental disruption are not optional considerations. They represent systemic risks that affect every sector, from nuclear and aviation to maritime and data centres. Consultants who ignore these factors risk leaving clients dangerously exposed. Those who integrate climate resilience into their analysis and recommendations provide not only technical insight but also strategic foresight. In a world of accelerating environmental change, this foresight is becoming a marker of professional credibility.

Small Modular Reactors (SMRs) and Energy Innovation

Energy resilience is a central concern across all sectors of critical infrastructure. Reliable, low-carbon power is essential not only for environmental goals but for national security and continuity of services. Against this backdrop, Small Modular Reactors (SMRs) are increasingly presented as a potential solution. They promise clean, dependable energy in a compact and scalable form. For consultants, SMRs exemplify both the opportunity and the challenge of emerging technologies: significant potential benefits, but equally significant security, regulatory, and reputational considerations.

SMRs are nuclear fission reactors designed to be smaller and more flexible than traditional large-scale plants. Their modular construction allows components to be manufactured off-site and assembled at location, reducing build time and cost. SMRs typically generate between 50 and 300 megawatts of power, making them well suited for applications such as powering remote communities, industrial facilities, or data centres. For infrastructure operators, SMRs offer the possibility of continuous, carbon-free power independent of fragile national grids.

Opportunities for clients are clear. SMRs provide baseload power without the intermittency challenges of renewables such as solar or wind. They are more scalable and deployable than traditional reactors, enabling phased investment. Their smaller footprint reduces land requirements, and their passive safety features promise enhanced resilience compared to earlier nuclear designs. For data centres, in particular, SMRs could provide long-term stability in an era where energy dependency is a critical vulnerability. Consultants advising in this space must be able to articulate these benefits while also framing them within realistic constraints.

Security challenges are central. While SMRs are designed with advanced safety systems, they remain nuclear facilities. This brings risks of proliferation, sabotage, insider threats, and terrorism. Even a small-scale incident at an SMR could undermine public trust in nuclear energy broadly. Consultants must therefore apply the same zero-tolerance mindset used in conventional nuclear projects: rigorous access control, layered physical protection, insider threat management, and robust emergency preparedness. Recommendations must be defensible under regulatory and public scrutiny.

Regulatory uncertainty is another critical issue. While the International Atomic Energy Agency (IAEA[9]) provides overarching guidance, national regulators are still developing frameworks specific to SMRs. Some countries may adapt existing nuclear regulations, while others may lack sufficient capacity altogether. Consultants must stay abreast of evolving standards, ensuring that recommendations anticipate rather than lag behind regulation. Failure to align with regulatory expectations risks undermining both feasibility and credibility.

Public perception and reputation represent perhaps the greatest hurdle. Nuclear energy remains controversial, with strong opposition in many regions. Even with enhanced safety features, SMRs may be perceived as risky or unwelcome, particularly in densely populated areas. Consultants must therefore recognise that technical feasibility alone is insufficient; projects require community engagement, transparent communication, and proactive trust-building. Consultants who ignore public perception risk advising on technically sound but socially untenable solutions.

Applied Scenario – SMRs for Data Centres: A consultancy project exploring energy options for a proposed hyperscale data centre could assess SMRs alongside renewable microgrids and conventional grid supply. SMRs could offer unmatched energy stability but might raise concerns over licensing, community acceptance, and long development timelines. Consultants could recommend a phased strategy: short-term reliance on renewable integration with grid power, with SMRs considered as part of a long-term roadmap. SMRs may not be immediate solutions, but they should be factored into strategic planning as technologies and regulations mature.

Applied Scenario – Industrial Application in a Remote Region: A mining operation in a geographically isolated region could explore small modular reactors (SMRs) as an alternative to diesel generators. Consultants could highlight the potential benefits of stable, low-carbon power to support continuous extraction and processing, reducing both costs and emissions. At the same time, they could identify significant challenges: the management of spent fuel, the complexity of regulatory approval processes, and the heightened security requirements of operating nuclear technology in a remote location. They could advise early engagement with stakeholders, robust security planning, and collaboration with international regulators to clarify licensing pathways and waste-handling responsibilities. Such a project could show that while SMRs may offer solutions to unique energy challenges, their viability depends on more than technical feasibility. Successful deployment would require alignment across political, regulatory, and community dimensions, together with a defensible approach to long-term waste stewardship.

The unique mix of regulatory scrutiny, public concern, and technical novelty in SMR projects creates challenges for consultants, such as:

- Balancing enthusiasm for innovation with caution about risks.
- Navigating uncertain and evolving regulatory frameworks.
- Anticipating community opposition and reputational consequences.
- Integrating SMRs into wider energy strategies that include renewables and traditional sources.
- Ensuring that recommendations are defensible under scrutiny from regulators, governments, and the public.

Realistic positioning is essential. SMRs are not a stand-alone solution, but they represent an important option in the future energy landscape. Consultants must help clients weigh benefits against risks, recognise uncertainties, and adopt proportionate strategies. This includes advising on transitional energy approaches, embedding resilience through redundancy, and preparing for a future where SMRs may become more widely accepted and regulated.

SMRs illustrate the consultant's broader role in emerging technologies: to separate promise from hype, to frame adoption within security and regulatory contexts, and to ensure that clients act proportionately. Whether powering data centres, industrial sites, or communities, SMRs offer significant potential, but only if deployed with integrity, foresight, and respect for public trust.

Smart Cities and Connected Infrastructure

Smart cities represent the convergence of digital technology, urban development, and critical infrastructure. By integrating sensors, data analytics, and automation into transport, energy, utilities, and governance, smart cities promise greater efficiency, sustainability, and quality of life. For consultants, however, they also present a new frontier of risk. The same interconnection that enables efficiency also creates pathways for cascading failure. Advising clients on smart cities requires balancing innovation with resilience, ensuring that enthusiasm for technology does not overshadow security and continuity.

The promise of smart cities is significant. Integrated transport systems can reduce congestion through adaptive traffic management. Smart grids optimise energy distribution and incorporate renewables more effectively. Intelligent water networks monitor consumption and detect leaks in real time. Public services become more responsive through data-driven governance. For investors, developers, and governments, smart cities embody modernity and competitiveness. Consultants must recognise these drivers of adoption, as they often shape client expectations.

Yet the risks are equally pronounced. The interconnection of systems creates dependencies: if one element fails, others may follow. A cyber intrusion into a smart grid could disrupt hospitals, transport, and communications simultaneously. A fault in data management could compromise both privacy and operational continuity. The proliferation of Internet of Things (IoT) devices multiplies vulnerabilities, as each sensor or node can become a point of entry for attackers. Consultants must therefore adopt a systemic perspective, advising not only on individual technologies but on the resilience of the whole ecosystem.

Governance challenges add another layer. Smart cities blur traditional lines of responsibility. Who is accountable if a citywide sensor network fails: the municipality, the vendor, or the systems integrator? Consultants must help clients clarify governance structures, ensuring that accountability for security and resilience is embedded into contracts, regulations, and organisational design. Without clear governance, smart cities risk becoming unmanageable in crisis.

Applied Scenario – Cascading Failure in Transport Systems: A consultancy review of an integrated transport project could find that adaptive traffic lights, dependent on centralised servers, lack redundancy. A single server outage could cause gridlock across the city within an hour. The consultants could recommend decentralising control, introducing backup systems, and conducting scenario-based drills. Centralisation without redundancy magnifies vulnerability.

Applied Scenario – IoT Device Proliferation: A smart city pilot project could deploy thousands of sensors for environmental monitoring. Consultants could discover that many devices lack adequate encryption and patching protocols, creating potential entry points for attackers. Their recommendations could include vendor standards, regular vulnerability testing, and integration of IoT security into citywide monitoring. Weak endpoints can undermine even sophisticated systems.

Consulting in smart cities demands sensitivity to public trust. Residents expect convenience but also privacy and fairness. Surveillance systems, facial recognition, and predictive policing technologies may enhance efficiency but risk creating perceptions of intrusion or bias. Consultants must therefore address not only technical resilience but also ethical implications, advising clients on proportionality, transparency, and community engagement. Public trust is as critical to sustainability as technological robustness.

International variation complicates matters further. Some governments adopt smart city initiatives as flagship projects, investing heavily in infrastructure but sometimes neglecting resilience. Others prioritise privacy and community acceptance, slowing adoption but strengthening legitimacy. Consultants must adapt advice to local political and cultural contexts, recognising that smart cities are not purely technical projects but political and social ones.

The interconnected technologies, governance demands, and competing stakeholder interests in smart city development create challenges for consultants, including:

- Balancing innovation with resilience in highly interconnected systems.
- Addressing privacy and ethical issues alongside technical risks.
- Navigating unclear governance and accountability frameworks.

- Managing vendor complexity and ensuring security across supply chains.
- Adapting to political, cultural, and regulatory variations across regions.

The key for consultants is integrated perspective. Recommendations must span cyber and physical security, governance, ethics, and resilience. Consultants should advise on layered defence, redundancy in infrastructure, segmentation of networks, and rigorous incident response planning. They must also highlight the importance of continuous monitoring, recognising that threats evolve as technologies proliferate.

Smart cities and connected infrastructure embody both promise and peril. They demonstrate how emerging technologies can enhance efficiency and sustainability but also how interdependence magnifies risk. Consultants who understand these dynamics, and who frame advice in terms of resilience, governance, and trust, provide critical value. Smart cities are not simply about deploying technology; they are about designing systems that remain safe, adaptive, and reliable under pressure.

Consultants add value not by predicting the future but by preparing organisations to adapt. Structured foresight, proportional analysis, and continuous feedback ensure that advice remains relevant as threats and technologies evolve.

Building Feedback Loops into Consulting Practice

Emerging threats and technologies are dynamic by nature. What is novel today quickly becomes routine, and risks that once seemed speculative can evolve into immediate challenges. Static security frameworks, especially those that focus only on meeting prescriptive compliance requirements, struggle to keep pace. For consultants, the challenge is to design systems that are resilient not at a single point in time but across time, adapting to new data, changing threats, and shifting contexts. Feedback loops provide the mechanism for this adaptation. Drawing on the principles of *High Output Management*, they ensure that organisations can monitor performance, detect emerging risks, and adjust accordingly.

Why compliance alone is not enough is a lesson that consultants must often reinforce. Many sectors are governed by detailed regulations and standards, whether ICAO[10] for aviation, ISPS for maritime, or ISO/IEC 27001:2022[15] for information security, which is widely adopted in data centres. Alongside it, sector-specific infrastructure frameworks such as ISO/IEC 22237:2021[16] or TIA-942-B:2017[22] provide benchmarks for data centre facilities and telecommunications resilience. While compliance with these frameworks is essential, it is not the same as security. Regulations and standards are often prescriptive, specifying minimum controls or processes that reflect conditions at the time of drafting. Threats, however, evolve more quickly than regulations. A system that is "compliant" may still be vulnerable to new forms of attack, insider manipulation, or cascading failures. Consultants must therefore encourage clients to go beyond compliance, treating it as a baseline rather than the objective. Feedback loops enable this by continuously testing whether controls remain effective against current threats, not just against written standards.

Designing feedback loops begins with defining meaningful indicators. Consultants must guide clients in selecting metrics that genuinely reflect risk and resilience rather than superficial compliance checks. For example, a tick-box audit confirming that CCTV cameras meet regulatory specifications may not reveal whether they are monitored effectively, integrated with access controls, or maintained for reliability. In contrast, a feedback metric might track average detection time for perimeter breaches, or the frequency of system outages. These indicators demonstrate whether security functions in real life, not just on paper.

Timeliness and responsiveness are equally critical. Prescriptive compliance frameworks often rely on annual or periodic reviews. By the time an audit identifies deficiencies, vulnerabilities may already have been exploited. Feedback loops ensure continuous monitoring, supported by real-time alerts and rapid escalation pathways. For example, a data centre might track in real time the resilience of redundant power supplies, flagging anomalies before they become outages. The principle is that early detection and timely response reduce both risk and cost.

Feedback loops also create opportunities to learn from disruption. Incidents, whether minor anomalies or major crises, generate valuable data. After-action reviews, red teaming exercises, and crisis simulations allow organisations to capture lessons, analyse root causes, and adapt processes. Consultants can help design these frameworks so that they become systematic rather than ad hoc. Without them, organisations risk repeating mistakes or assuming that because a process is compliant, it is also effective.

Applied Scenario – Beyond Audit Compliance at an Airport: A consultancy team could introduce feedback loops into an airport security programme. Regulators might audit the airport annually, with reports consistently confirming compliance with ICAO[10] requirements. Yet performance data could reveal a rising trend in false positives from screening technology, slowing passenger throughput and undermining confidence. Weekly dashboards tracking queue times, detection accuracy, and randomised drills could expose such issues months before regulators identified them. The consultants could recommend recalibrating systems and enhancing staff training. This would show that while compliance signals adequacy, feedback loops signal reality.

The consultant's role could be to embed feedback as part of organisational culture. Leadership would need to see metrics not as instruments of blame but as tools for resilience. Consultants could help frame continuous monitoring as assurance, enabling organisations to remain ahead of threats rather than simply meeting external expectations. This cultural shift is vital: without executive commitment to act on feedback, even the most sophisticated systems could degrade into box-ticking exercises.

Compliance is necessary but insufficient. Prescriptive regulations define minimum standards, but they cannot anticipate every emerging risk. Feedback loops provide the adaptive capacity to test whether controls remain fit for purpose, to detect vulnerabilities early, and to incorporate lessons from disruption. By embedding monitoring, measurement, and review into consulting practice, consultants can ensure that their advice continues to deliver value long after the report is written. In a world where threats evolve faster than standards, feedback loops are not optional, they are the essence of sustainable security.

Illustrative Examples – Lessons from Emerging Threats and Technologies

When addressing emerging risks, consultants encounter recurring themes that cut across sectors and technologies. In one case, the deployment of

AI-driven access control created frustration through false positives, showing how new technologies can erode trust if not applied proportionately. In another, reliance on high-cost counter-drone measures proved inadequate until consultants recommended a layered approach that combined training, regulatory coordination, and selective use of technology. Climate risk assessments revealed vulnerabilities that could disrupt entire supply chains, underlining the importance of integrating environmental resilience into security planning. Work on advanced energy projects showed how community opposition can undermine even the most rigorous technical designs, highlighting the need for transparent communication and stakeholder engagement. Smart city initiatives demonstrated that interoperability and governance are as critical as the technologies themselves when multiple systems and agencies converge.

Taken together, these scenarios demonstrate that the consultant's role is not to promote technology for its own sake but to contextualise it within resilience, proportionality, and trust. The common thread is that emerging threats are rarely solved by a single intervention. Consultants must anticipate convergence, weigh operational and societal impacts, and translate complex risks into advice that is both defensible and credible. The lessons show that effective consultancy in new domains rests as much on governance, communication, and adaptability as it does on technical innovation.

Practice Guide

This chapter has shown how emerging threats and technologies reshape the environment in which consultants operate. Effective consultancy depends on recognising new risks, distinguishing substance from hype, applying structured approaches, and anticipating ethical as well as reputational challenges. The discussion of artificial intelligence, drones, climate change, small modular reactors, and smart cities illustrated how resilience must be integrated and how feedback loops ensure advice remains relevant as conditions evolve.

The key pitfall is treating novelty as certainty. Consultants sometimes chase hype, adopting vendor claims or media narratives without critical examination. Others underestimate secondary risks, focusing on immediate technical impacts while overlooking systemic consequences such as migration pressures from climate change or cascading failures in smart cities. Neglecting ethics is another danger: AI bias, privacy concerns in surveillance, or public trust in SMRs can make technically sound advice socially untenable. Over-reliance on compliance is equally hazardous; relying on prescriptive standards as a proxy for resilience leaves clients vulnerable when threats evolve faster than regulations. Omitting feedback loops results in static systems unable to adapt in dynamic conditions.

Good practice comes from turning these lessons around. Consultants add value by filtering hype with evidence and proportionality, ensuring clients invest in what is real and urgent rather than what is fashionable. They frame compliance as a starting point, embedding continuous monitoring and review to keep security relevant. They anticipate systemic impacts by thinking in terms of interconnected risks rather than isolated events. They address ethics and public trust head-on, ensuring recommendations are defensible not only technically but politically and socially. They embed feedback loops into consulting practice so that resilience is not a one-off deliverable but an adaptive capability.

The consultant who thrives in emerging risk landscapes is not the one who predicts the future most accurately but the one who prepares clients to adapt. By combining technical awareness with foresight, independence with proportionality, and resilience with ethics, consultants become interpreters of uncertainty. This ability to help organisations navigate change credibly and sustainably ensures that their advice remains trusted and their role indispensable as the environment continues to evolve.

Chapter 22 – Hybrid and Remote Consulting

Hybrid and remote delivery have moved from being an occasional workaround to a routine element of consulting practice. Digital platforms, collaborative tools, and virtual methods allow consultants to continue projects across regions, bring dispersed stakeholders together, and maintain momentum when site access is constrained. These capabilities are now embedded in the profession and can add real value when applied with discipline.

At the same time, the limits are clear. Consultancy depends on credibility, and much of that comes from presence: observing conditions directly, engaging with stakeholders face-to-face, and testing assumptions against the reality of the environment. Remote methods cannot replace this, but they can extend and support it. The consultant's task is therefore to master the balance, knowing when digital methods will add efficiency, reach, and resilience, and when physical presence remains essential for trust and accuracy.

By the end of this chapter, you will be able to:

- Recognise when remote or hybrid methods are appropriate, and when on-site presence is essential.
- Apply digital platforms to enhance analysis, design, and reporting without undermining credibility.
- Build and maintain trust with clients and stakeholders in virtual and hybrid contexts.
- Manage the risks of remote delivery, including security, confidentiality, and digital fatigue.
- Adapt traditional consulting frameworks to hybrid environments while maintaining rigour and independence.
- Avoid the pitfall of treating remote engagement as a replacement for fieldwork.

Introduction

Remote consulting is not a new phenomenon, but its prominence has increased dramatically in recent years. The global COVID-19 pandemic forced consultants and clients alike to adapt rapidly to digital platforms, proving that elements of consultancy could be delivered without physical presence. While those conditions were exceptional, they accelerated a trend that has remained. Today, hybrid and remote consulting is not an emergency workaround but an established capability.

It is important to distinguish between what can be done and what should be done. Remote consulting should not be seen as a replacement for on-site practice. At its heart, consultancy depends on presence: walking sites, observing behaviours, sensing dynamics, and engaging with stakeholders face-to-face. These elements build credibility and uncover insights that digital platforms cannot replicate. Remote methods, however sophisticated, cannot fully substitute for the depth of understanding gained in the field.

Where remote consulting adds value is in reach, efficiency, and resilience. It allows consultants to maintain progress when travel is restricted, to engage stakeholders across different regions without excessive cost, and to facilitate collaboration between dispersed teams. It also offers tools for data analysis, visualisation, and reporting that can enhance understanding and communication. Used proportionately, these methods strengthen consultancy.

Remote delivery brings its own risks. Digital interactions can erode trust if clients perceive the consultant as distant or disengaged. Confidential discussions may be compromised if platforms are not secure. Consultants and clients alike are vulnerable to digital fatigue, reducing the quality of interaction. Over-reliance on remote methods risks diluting the consultant's value to little more than a facilitator of online meetings.

The consultant's responsibility is therefore to treat remote consulting as a supplementary capability: one that adds resilience and adaptability but never replaces the core practices of fieldwork and engagement. This chapter explores how to use digital tools effectively, how to build trust at a distance, how to adapt analysis and reporting for virtual delivery, and how to guard against the risks of over-reliance. It reinforces the principle that hybrid methods extend consultancy's reach but must always be integrated with the consultant's physical presence and professional judgement.

The Digital Toolkit – Enhancing, Not Replacing

Hybrid and remote consulting is enabled by a wide range of digital tools. These platforms can extend reach, streamline collaboration, and provide new ways of analysing and presenting information. Yet their value depends on how they are used. Technology alone does not create effective consultancy; it must be integrated thoughtfully into established methods. The consultant's task is to harness the benefits of technology while recognising the limitations.

Collaboration platforms are at the heart of remote delivery. Video conferencing systems such as Zoom, Microsoft Teams, or Webex allow consultants to meet with clients, conduct interviews, and facilitate workshops without being physically present. Shared workspaces like SharePoint, Google Drive, or secure client portals enable document review and version control. These tools provide continuity when site visits are impractical, but they require careful management. Consultants must ensure that access is restricted appropriately, that sensitive material is encrypted, and that client expectations for confidentiality are met.

Project management and workflow tools offer further value. Platforms such as Asana, Trello, or Jira allow distributed teams to coordinate tasks, track progress, and visualise dependencies. Dashboards give clients visibility of progress, reinforcing transparency and accountability. For consultants managing multi-country projects, such tools reduce reliance on lengthy status reports, providing real-time updates instead. The danger is that digital dashboards can create an illusion of control: colourful charts may look impressive but mask underlying complexity. Clients benefit most when these tools are used to support, rather than replace, critical analysis and judgement.

How consultants run virtual sessions is crucial for effective stakeholder engagement. Workshops can be conducted online using interactive whiteboards, polling tools, and breakout rooms. Platforms such as Miro or MURAL allow brainstorming and mapping exercises that mimic the collaborative nature of in-person sessions. Used well, these tools can broaden participation, enabling input from stakeholders who might not attend in person. Yet they also carry risks. Digital fatigue can reduce engagement, while cultural differences in communication may be amplified online. The consultant must adapt facilitation techniques by keeping sessions shorter, clearer, and more focused than their in-person equivalents.

Data analysis and visualisation tools expand the consultant's capacity to process and present information. Software such as Power BI or Tableau enables the creation of interactive dashboards, turning complex datasets into accessible insights. For example, risk assessments can be visualised as heat maps that clients can filter by geography, asset, or threat type. Such tools enhance comprehension and provide clients with ongoing value beyond the report. But they must not be mistaken for analysis itself. Data visualisation is only as strong as the assumptions behind it. Consultants must ensure that datasets are reliable, methodologies sound, and conclusions defensible.

Digital twins and simulation platforms represent another area of growth. These technologies create virtual models of infrastructure, allowing consultants to test scenarios such as equipment failures, environmental stressors, or even certain forms of cyber intrusion, though the results are limited by how complete and realistic the model is. Good quality digital twins can enrich consultancy by providing dynamic insights, especially for data centres, utilities, or transport networks. Yet they also risk detaching analysis from reality if not grounded in site visits and operational knowledge. A model may simulate conditions perfectly in theory while failing to capture the human or organisational factors that shape real outcomes.

Security and confidentiality safeguards must underpin all use of digital tools. Remote platforms are vulnerable to interception, misconfiguration, or misuse. Consultants dealing with sensitive information must adopt secure channels, multi-factor authentication, and data minimisation. They must also be alert to jurisdictional risks: cloud platforms may store data in countries with different legal protections, exposing clients to liabilities. It is not enough to adopt the latest tool; consultants must demonstrate that its use is proportionate, secure, and aligned with client expectations for confidentiality.

The digital toolkit enhances but does not replace consulting practice. Collaboration platforms, project management tools, virtual workshops, dashboards, and digital twins all expand the consultant's capacity to deliver value at a distance. Yet they must be used with discipline: ensuring confidentiality, avoiding over-reliance, and ensuring outputs are validated against real conditions. The consultant's credibility rests not on the sophistication of tools but on the wisdom with which they are applied. Digital platforms should extend the consultant's presence, not substitute for it.

Hybrid and remote methods extend consultancy – they do not redefine it. Presence, observation, and direct engagement remain the foundations of credibility, while digital tools enhance reach, efficiency, and resilience when used with discipline.

Building and Sustaining Trust Remotely

We have established, in earlier chapters, that trust is the cornerstone of consultancy. It allows stakeholders to share candid insights, clients to accept difficult recommendations, and teams to align around a shared course of action. In traditional contexts, trust is built through presence: walking sites, observing behaviours, and engaging stakeholders face-to-face. Remote and hybrid delivery make this process more difficult. Physical cues are weaker, informal conversations are fewer, and digital interactions are vulnerable to distraction or fatigue. Yet remote environments are now a routine part of consultancy, and consultants must therefore learn how to cultivate and sustain trust at a distance.

The challenge of distance is partly perceptual. Clients and stakeholders may perceive remote consultants as less invested or less credible than those who are physically present. A consultant on a screen may be perceived as an outsider, removed from the realities of the environment. This perception is not entirely unfounded: remote work does limit the ability to observe context and to build rapport through informal interactions. The consultant must therefore work harder to demonstrate attentiveness, reliability, and empathy.

Preparation and professionalism become even more important when operating remotely. Meetings that would allow for spontaneity in person require more structure online. Consultants must arrive with clear agendas, concise materials, and tested technology. Technical glitches or poor preparation damage credibility more severely in virtual settings than in person, as stakeholders are quicker to disengage. Conversely, smooth delivery signals competence and respect for participants' time, gradually building trust.

When working through digital platforms, consistency and responsiveness are critical. Stakeholders need to see that the consultant communicates reliably, is punctual, and remains attentive despite the distance. Trust is built through repeated interactions where reliability is demonstrated over time. In online settings this means clear communication across channels, prompt follow-up, and timely responses to questions or concerns. When body language is harder to read, trust can also be reinforced by explicitly acknowledging stakeholder views and showing that every voice is recognised.

Creating presence in virtual meetings requires deliberate effort. In person, presence is conveyed through body language, eye contact, and attentiveness. Online, these cues are diminished. Consultants must therefore adapt by using clear, deliberate speech, maintaining eye contact by looking into the camera, and limiting distractions. The tone of voice becomes a substitute for body language, conveying confidence, respect, or empathy depending on context. Visuals also play a role. Well-designed slides or diagrams can capture attention, but overloading screens with text diminishes engagement.

Cultural barriers can be amplified in remote settings. In some cultures, silence is respectful; in others, it may signal disengagement. Hierarchical dynamics may discourage junior staff from speaking up in virtual calls, even more so than in person. Consultants must remain alert to these nuances, using inclusive facilitation techniques such as structured rounds, polling tools, or breakout sessions to ensure diverse voices are heard. Cultural empathy is vital: shaping communication and facilitation to fit local expectations, while still maintaining professional standards.

Hybrid models often work best. Trust is rarely built entirely through remote means, but once initial rapport is established in person, it can be maintained through digital channels. For example, an initial site visit may allow consultants to build relationships and observe context. Subsequent workshops, interviews, or follow-ups can then be delivered remotely with less risk of disengagement. Consultants should therefore advocate for hybrid approaches wherever possible, balancing efficiency with credibility.

Openly managing confidentiality is another dimension of trust. Stakeholders may hesitate to speak openly if they fear that online platforms are insecure. Consultants must therefore establish and communicate security protocols: using encrypted platforms, clarifying how information will be recorded and stored, and offering anonymity where appropriate. Demonstrating control over confidentiality reassures stakeholders and encourages openness.

Transparency and honesty also strengthen trust at a distance. Consultants should be open about limitations: acknowledging what cannot be assessed remotely, what requires site validation, and where assumptions are made. Pretending that remote engagement is equivalent to in-person assessment risks damaging credibility if clients later discover gaps. Being open and honest shows integrity, and this often matters more to stakeholders than pretending to have all the answers.

Empathy and human connection remain central to effective stakeholder relationships. Remote interactions can feel transactional, reducing opportunities for informal rapport. Consultants must therefore be intentional in demonstrating empathy: allowing time for informal conversation, acknowledging challenges stakeholders face, and showing appreciation for contributions. Simple acts, such as remembering details from previous interactions or tailoring communication to individual concerns, make it clear that the consultant is listening and committed.

Sustaining trust over time requires maintaining momentum. Remote engagements risk losing energy if interactions are sporadic or unfocused. Consultants should design structured communication plans, with regular check-ins, progress updates, and clear next steps. Predictability reinforces reliability. Where momentum dips, consultants must proactively re-engage stakeholders to prevent drift.

Sustaining trust requires discipline, structure, and deliberate effort. Without this, virtual relationships can quickly weaken or lose direction. These realities create specific challenges for consultants, such as:

- Overcoming perceptions of detachment or lack of commitment.
- Maintaining attention and engagement during digital fatigue.
- Managing cultural differences without the richness of in-person cues.

- Ensuring confidentiality across digital platforms.
- Balancing efficiency with the need for rapport and presence.

Building and sustaining trust remotely requires deliberate action. Preparation, consistency, responsiveness, presence, cultural empathy, confidentiality, transparency, and empathy all contribute to credibility at a distance. Hybrid methods offer the strongest balance, combining the depth of in-person engagement with the reach of digital tools. Consultants who treat remote interaction as an extension of, rather than substitute for, traditional engagement can maintain trust even in constrained circumstances. Trust is a major currency of consultancy, and with deliberate practice, it can be earned and sustained, even when physical proximity is not possible.

Analysis and Design in Hybrid Contexts

Analysis and design are central functions of consultancy, providing the foundation for credible recommendations. Traditionally, these stages rely heavily on a site presence: observing environments directly, gathering first-hand data, and engaging stakeholders in person. Hybrid and remote contexts alter this dynamic. Consultants may need to conduct analysis with partial or delayed access, relying more on digital tools, remote data sources, and virtual collaboration. While these methods expand reach and efficiency, they also risk detachment from reality if not anchored in field evidence. The consultant's task is to integrate digital methods with on-site verification, to keep the work accurate and relevant.

Remote data gathering has become more sophisticated. Clients can provide digital documentation, site plans, video feeds, and access to sensors or monitoring systems. Drones can capture imagery of facilities, while IoT devices provide real-time data on operations. Consultants can analyse this material from afar, saving time and reducing travel costs. For example, digital twins of industrial facilities allow consultants to test different design scenarios without setting foot on site. These tools increase efficiency, but they must be complemented with contextual awareness. A camera feed may show infrastructure, but it cannot capture informal practices, staff behaviours, or the cultural dynamics that shape risk

Validating data remotely presents challenges around completeness, accuracy, and independence. Information provided by clients may be incomplete, outdated, or framed to reflect organisational preferences. Without physical presence, consultants risk basing analysis on curated material rather than objective observation. To counter this, consultants should cross-reference multiple data sources, cross-check with stakeholders at different levels, and be transparent about limitations. Where possible, they should request live demonstrations or remote walkthroughs rather than static documentation. For clients to trust the analysis, they need both sound technical detail and evidence that the consultant's findings are unbiased and independent.

Designing solutions remotely also requires adaptation. Collaborative platforms enable design workshops where consultants and clients can co-create solutions in real time. Interactive whiteboards, modelling software, and scenario simulations can replicate many aspects of in-person sessions. These tools often broaden participation, allowing geographically dispersed stakeholders to contribute. However, complex design discussions may suffer in virtual environments, particularly where trust is still developing or sensitive issues are at stake. Consultants should therefore use hybrid models: initial design workshops in person to build alignment and trust, followed by remote sessions to refine details.

The risks of over-reliance on digital analysis must be recognised. Consultants may be tempted to treat remote methods as sufficient, particularly when clients are cost-sensitive or reluctant to support travel. Yet desk-based analysis, however sophisticated, cannot substitute for on-site experience. Observing site culture, inspecting physical conditions, and experiencing the environment directly reveal vulnerabilities that digital tools may obscure. For example, a site plan may indicate clear evacuation routes, but a site visit might reveal that staff routinely block them with equipment. The difference between design intent and actual conditions is only visible on the ground.

Hybrid analysis as best practice balances efficiency with accuracy. Consultants should structure projects to combine remote and on-site phases. Initial desk-based reviews can narrow focus, saving time during site visits. Remote workshops can prepare stakeholders for engagement, ensuring that in-person sessions are efficient and productive. Site visits can then validate assumptions, provide first-hand experience, and build the trust necessary for sensitive findings. Hybrid delivery does not diminish rigour; if well designed, it can enhance it by integrating multiple perspectives and tools.

Getting this balance right is not straightforward. While hybrid delivery can increase efficiency and enrich analysis, it also introduces pressures that must be managed carefully. These pressures create specific challenges for consultants, including:

- Ensuring independence when reliant on client-provided data.
- Managing limitations of digital tools without overstating their value.
- Deciding which phases of analysis require physical presence and which can be remote.
- Convincing clients that some level of on-site validation is essential, even when remote tools appear comprehensive.
- Balancing efficiency gains against the risk of detachment from context.

Hybrid contexts reshape how analysis and design are delivered but do not alter their essence. Consultants must use digital tools to enhance efficiency while insisting on site presence for validation. Remote analysis provides breadth, while in-person engagement provides depth. Together, they ensure recommendations are both evidence-based and contextually grounded. Consultants who master this balance can deliver effectively in hybrid environments, maintaining credibility while adapting to modern constraints.

Reporting and Presenting in Digital Formats

Reports are the consultant's primary deliverable – the tangible evidence of analysis and judgement. In hybrid and remote contexts, the way reports are delivered and received changes significantly. Clients no longer expect to read only printed documents or sit through lengthy in-person presentations. Increasingly, reports must be adapted for digital-first delivery, designed to capture attention quickly and to work effectively in different formats, from slide decks and dashboards to mobile devices and formal documents. Consultants who cannot adjust to this risk seeing their work ignored, regardless of its quality.

Adapting reports for digital delivery requires a shift in mindset. Long written documents still have their place, particularly for regulators, auditors, or technical specialists. But executives and operational managers often engage with reports through digital summaries, interactive dashboards, or short virtual briefings. Consultants must therefore create layered deliverables: comprehensive written reports for depth, supported by concise digital formats for decision-making.

Interactive dashboards have become a popular medium. Tools such as Power BI or Tableau allow clients to explore data dynamically, filtering risks by geography, system, or impact level. Dashboards provide ongoing value, remaining relevant beyond the final report by updating as new data emerges. Yet they are not a substitute for human analysis. Consultants must ensure that dashboards are built on rigorous methods and accompanied by clear interpretation. A colourful chart is useful only if it reflects defensible evidence.

Distilling complexity into clarity is even more important in digital settings. Executives may allocate only five minutes to a briefing. Consultants must therefore be able to compress findings from a 100-page report into five clear points or five compelling slides. This does not mean oversimplifying but structuring information according to priority: leading with the main message (in line with the Pyramid Principle[17]), then providing supporting logic only as required. The discipline of clarity becomes essential when attention spans are limited.

Consultants must adapt the way they manage digital presentations to suit shorter attention spans and the limits of virtual interaction. Online meetings are less forgiving of rambling delivery or poorly structured slides. Consultants should design presentations with brevity, visual clarity, and interactivity in mind. Shorter sessions with clear objectives are more effective than long monologues. Incorporating polls, Q&A, or breakout discussions can sustain engagement. Presentation style matters: confident tone, steady pacing, and visible attentiveness substitute for the body language that may not translate through a screen.

Addressing digital fatigue is another challenge. Clients may already spend much of their day in virtual meetings. Consultants must therefore ensure that their reports and presentations stand out by being concise, relevant, and tailored. Overloading stakeholders with lengthy slide decks or dense documents risks disengagement. Reports should be modular, allowing readers to access detail when needed without overwhelming them.

The risks associated with the over-reliance on digital formats must also be acknowledged. Some consultants fall into the trap of producing increasingly flashy dashboards or animated presentations, mistaking style for substance. Others assume that a digital report can substitute for direct engagement. The most effective reporting combines strong analysis with clear communication, supported by discussion that allows stakeholders to interrogate findings. Consultants must resist the temptation to let technology overshadow content.

The risks of over-reliance make it clear that technology should never overshadow substance. To keep reports effective and credible, consultants must navigate several challenges, such as:

- Balancing depth with brevity for different audiences.
- Ensuring that visual outputs are evidence-based, not cosmetic.
- Managing confidentiality and data security in cloud-delivered reports.
- Avoiding disengagement caused by digital fatigue.
- Maintaining interactivity and presence despite physical distance.

Reporting and presenting in digital formats require discipline, clarity, and adaptability. Consultants must design deliverables that meet the needs of different stakeholders: full reports for specialists, concise summaries for executives, and interactive tools for ongoing use. They must also present findings in ways that sustain engagement in virtual contexts, recognising the limits of attention and the risks of fatigue. Done well, digital reporting does not dilute consultancy but extends its impact. It ensures that recommendations are not only read but acted upon.

Risks, Limits, and Safeguards

Remote and hybrid consulting brings clear benefits, but it also carries risks that can undermine credibility, compromise security, or damage relationships if not managed carefully. Consultants must be alert to these limits, recognising that digital delivery is a complement rather than a substitute for on-site presence. Safeguards are essential to protect both clients and consultants in this environment.

Security and confidentiality are the most obvious concerns. Digital platforms may be vulnerable to interception, misconfiguration, misuse, or accidental disclosure. Sensitive discussions held over video calls, or confidential documents shared through cloud services, can be exposed to unauthorised parties. Consultants must therefore prioritise secure platforms, multi-factor authentication, encryption, and access controls. They must also respect jurisdictional issues: some cloud services store data in countries with weaker protections, creating legal and reputational risks. It is essential to clarify with clients where data will be stored, who will have access, and how it will be protected.

Confusing compliance with security is a common danger. Many organisations assume that using a platform certified to certain standards (such as ISO 27001[15] or SOC 2) guarantees security. In practice, certification indicates a baseline, not a guarantee. Security is situational: a platform may be compliant but still poorly configured or misused. Consultants must emphasise that security requires ongoing vigilance, training, and feedback loops, not just reliance on prescriptive standards.

Digital fatigue is another limit. Remote engagements often involve long hours in front of screens, leading to reduced attention, engagement, and retention. Stakeholders may become passive or disengaged, particularly in lengthy workshops or presentations. For consultants, fatigue can also erode the quality of delivery. Safeguards include structuring shorter, focused sessions, incorporating breaks, and varying the format with interactive tools. Consultants must also remain sensitive to stakeholder capacity, ensuring that engagement remains constructive rather than burdensome.

Erosion of trust and presence is harder to measure but no less important. Consultancy relies on credibility, much of which is built through informal interactions, observation of context, and non-verbal cues. Remote delivery reduces opportunities for this depth of engagement. Over time, relationships risk becoming transactional. Consultants must guard against this by maintaining regular, structured contact, by investing in hybrid methods where possible, and by being transparent about what cannot be observed remotely. Integrity requires acknowledging these limits, not pretending they do not exist.

Over-reliance on digital data can undermine analysis. Digital platforms provide access to dashboards, sensors, and models, but without validation these may present a distorted picture. For example, a digital twin of a facility may simulate systems accurately yet fail to capture human practices or cultural dynamics. Consultants who rely solely on digital data risk missing critical vulnerabilities. Safeguards include cross-referencing multiple data sources, insisting on site visits for validation, and being clear with clients about assumptions and limitations.

Wellbeing and duty of care are often overlooked. Remote working may seem safer than travel to high-risk environments, but it carries its own strains: isolation, long hours, blurred boundaries between work and rest, and the psychological impact of dealing with sensitive material from afar. Consulting firms must recognise that digital delivery does not remove the need for duty of care. Clear schedules, workload management, and access to support are as important in remote contexts as in the field.

Managing risks in remote and hybrid delivery is not just about technical safeguards, it also demands discipline, judgement, and clear communication. These demands create specific challenges for consultants, including:

- Convincing clients of the limits of remote delivery when they perceive it as cheaper or more efficient.
- Ensuring that technical safeguards (encryption, authentication) are matched by human discipline (training, vigilance).
- Balancing efficiency with credibility, ensuring that hybrid methods preserve presence.
- Recognising that resilience requires proportionality: remote methods are valuable, but not universally applicable.

Remote and hybrid consulting introduces risks that cannot be ignored. Security and confidentiality must be actively managed, digital fatigue mitigated, and trust sustained through deliberate effort. Consultants must guard against over-reliance on digital data, clarify that compliance does not equal security, and ensure that wellbeing and duty of care are respected. By acknowledging limits and embedding safeguards, consultants can use remote delivery effectively without compromising the essence of consultancy: credible, independent, and contextually grounded advice.

Illustrative Example: Hybrid Resilience in Practice

A consultancy team was engaged by a multinational client to deliver a risk assessment and stakeholder alignment exercise during a period of restricted travel. Full site access was impractical, so the team adopted a hybrid model. Local associates conducted site surveys, while central consultants facilitated workshops and interviews online. The client also provided access to a digital twin of one critical facility, enabling scenario testing without physical disruption.

This approach demonstrated several clear strengths. Progress was maintained despite restrictions, wider stakeholder groups could participate virtually, and the digital twin provided rapid insights into system resilience. The client valued the efficiency of reduced travel costs and the inclusivity of involving colleagues from multiple regions.

However, the weaknesses became equally clear. Reports from local associates varied in quality, requiring additional verification. The digital twin was technically impressive, but on later site visits, consultants discovered that routine staff practices, such as blocking fire exits or bypassing security protocols, were not reflected in the model. Virtual workshops also proved less effective for resolving sensitive stakeholder conflicts, where cultural dynamics and interpersonal trust would have been better managed face-to-face.

The outcome showed that while hybrid methods offer efficiency and continuity, they also carry risks if not managed with discipline. What went well was the speed, inclusivity, and resilience gained through digital platforms. What did not go well was the lack of depth in cultural and behavioural insights, and the over-reliance on digital models without ground validation. The "why" lies at the heart of consultancy: credibility is built through observation, context, and presence – the things that technology cannot fully replace.

This example highlights the chapter's central lesson. Hybrid consulting should be treated as a powerful supplement, not a substitute. Digital tools extend reach and efficiency, but only when balanced with site visits, direct observation, and trusted human interaction.

Practice Guide

Hybrid and remote delivery have become a normal part of consulting practice, bringing both opportunities and risks. Used well, they can broaden participation, reduce costs, and keep projects moving when circumstances limit travel. Used poorly, they can erode trust, weaken credibility, and leave critical risks unnoticed. The consultant's task is to strike the right balance: applying digital tools to extend capability while ensuring that core value continues to come from presence, observation, and direct engagement.

The pitfalls are clear. Consultants damage their credibility when they oversell digital delivery as equivalent to being on site. They risk losing stakeholder trust if they fail to invest in relationship-building, and they expose clients to vulnerabilities if they treat mainstream platforms as secure without safeguards. Overloading clients with lengthy online briefings or overdesigned dashboards is another recurring trap, as is relying too heavily on digital twins, models, or dashboards without validating findings against actual conditions. Each of these missteps erodes the independence and authority on which consultancy depends.

Good practice flows naturally from these lessons. Consultants should position hybrid delivery as a supplement, never a substitute, emphasising that digital tools extend capacity but do not replicate the depth of engagement achieved in person. They should invest deliberately in building trust at a distance through structure, responsiveness, and empathy, and they should be transparent about the limits of remote methods. Secure platforms, disciplined protocols, and clarity on data storage and confidentiality are essential to reassure clients. Deliverables should be layered: concise, visual summaries for executives supported by full reports for specialists, all adapted to the realities of digital attention spans. Above all, consultants must validate digital findings with on-site presence wherever possible, ensuring that their analysis remains anchored in first-hand evidence.

Consultants who master hybrid methods while maintaining professional integrity will sustain their authority in an environment where digital platforms are inescapable. Hybrid consulting is about proportion. It's about using technology to broaden participation, reduce costs, and maintain resilience, while protecting the credibility that comes only from presence, observation, and direct engagement. By holding these disciplines in balance, consultants ensure that their work remains rigorous, trusted, and effective in a world where physical and digital practice must coexist.

Reflections – Advanced Practice

Part 4 has explored how consultancy evolves in environments defined by complexity, scale, and uncertainty. The core skills of analysis, engagement, design, and communication remain constant, but their application must be adapted where stakes are higher, risks more diverse, and contexts less forgiving.

Chapter 18 examined stakeholder management in complex settings. Influence depends not only on technical knowledge but on balancing authority, diplomacy, and independence amid competing agendas. Trust, resistance, and integrity emerged as the key elements: consultancy succeeds not when all stakeholders agree, but when they respect the consultant's impartiality and defensibility.

Chapter 19 extended the focus to international and high-risk environments, where cultural, political, and personal safety factors amplify responsibility. Preparation, resilience, and ethical clarity were shown to be as vital as technical skill. Professionalism in such contexts means delivering value to clients while safeguarding the wellbeing of consultants, partners, and communities.

In Chapter 20, the lens turned to specialised sectors – critical national infrastructure, nuclear, maritime, aviation, and data centres – each with unique frameworks, cultures, and vulnerabilities. The principle of proportionality ran throughout: credibility depends on adapting frameworks to the sector's specific risks and regulations. Sectoral fluency and practicable recommendations mark the difference between theory and value.

Chapter 21 explored emerging threats and technologies, from artificial intelligence and drones to climate change and smart cities. These demonstrate that consultancy is dynamic – threats evolve, technologies disrupt, and regulation lags. Consultants must develop foresight, balance innovation with caution, and embed feedback loops so that resilience adapts continuously. Compliance is a foundation, not an endpoint; sustainable security relies on anticipation and adaptation.

Chapter 22 addressed hybrid and remote consultancy. Digital tools extend reach and efficiency but cannot replace physical presence. Trust, credibility, and contextual insight still depend on observation in the field. Digital delivery should enhance, not erode, the human foundations of the craft – independence, presence, and professional judgement.

Together, these chapters show that advanced practice does not abandon the fundamentals of consultancy; it extends them. Stakeholder complexity demands diplomacy, global contexts demand resilience, specialised sectors demand fluency, emerging threats demand foresight, and digital transformation demands proportion. Across all, independence and integrity remain the consultant's compass.

Advanced practice therefore means mastering not only methods but judgement – the ability to adapt frameworks to context, resist pressure while remaining constructive, and deliver defensible advice under scrutiny. Part 4 has shown that the consultant's true value is revealed where uncertainty is greatest. Part 5 now turns inward, exploring how consultants sustain professionalism, identity, and endurance across a demanding career.

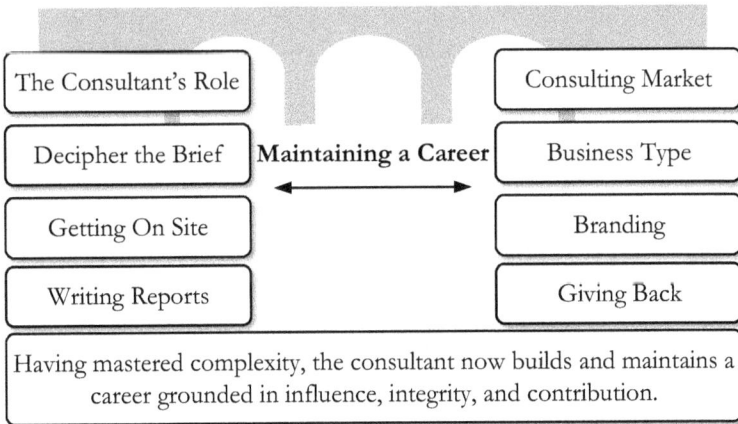

The Consultant's Role		Consulting Market
Decipher the Brief	**Maintaining a Career**	Business Type
Getting On Site		Branding
Writing Reports		Giving Back
Having mastered complexity, the consultant now builds and maintains a career grounded in influence, integrity, and contribution.		

Figure 19 Part 4 Reflections Bridge

Part 5 – The Consultant's Career

Security consultancy is not defined solely by technical knowledge or project execution, but by the ability to sustain a professional life that remains credible, relevant, and that gives back over time. The focus of Part 5 is therefore on the consultant's career itself – how it is built, strengthened, and renewed.

It begins with an examination of how consultants interpret and respond to the markets that shape opportunity. Understanding where demand originates, how it evolves, and what clients truly value forms the foundation of a sustainable career. From there, attention turns to operating models – the professional structures through which consultants work, from independent practice to boutique firms and major consultancies. Each model carries its own balance of autonomy, stability, and reach, and long-term sustainability depends on aligning these with personal values and professional goals. The third chapter addresses professional brand, showing that reputation and visibility are not peripheral concerns but the essence of trust and authority in a competitive field.

The later chapters shift focus from external positioning to personal continuity. They explore the long game of consultancy – maintaining relevance through learning and reinvention, managing energy and resilience, and recognising that longevity depends as much on rhythm and renewal as on ambition. The final chapter broadens the horizon further, reframing consultancy as stewardship. Mentoring, contributing to standards, and sharing knowledge through teaching or publication are presented as hallmarks of professional maturity. Together, these actions ensure that expertise endures beyond individual careers and that the profession itself remains strong, credible, and adaptive.

Chapter 23 – Understanding the Consulting Market

Consultancy thrives when expertise meets real demand. In security, this demand is shaped by external forces such as politics, economics, regulation, and culture. Opportunities vary across regions, sectors, and client types, and entry is often restricted by both formal requirements and informal networks of trust.

This chapter provides tools to navigate that landscape. It examines global and regional markets, highlights valuable niches, reviews revenue models, and considers the barriers that shape participation. It also introduces research methods that help consultants anticipate change and sustain relevance.

By the end of this chapter, you will be able to:

- Analyse global and regional markets for security consultancy, recognising how political, economic, and regulatory forces shape demand.

- Identify the sectors and niches where consultancy services create the greatest value and where growth opportunities are most likely to emerge.

- Understand the commercial models and revenue streams that sustain a consulting practice, and how these vary by client type and region.

- Evaluate barriers to entry, both formal and informal, and develop strategies to overcome them.

- Apply structured research methods, including the considered use of artificial intelligence, to anticipate market shifts and maintain long-term professional relevance.

Introduction

However strong a consultant's technical capabilities may be, they achieve little unless they are applied in a way that matches client demand. Markets decide which services are valued, which models of delivery are viable, and which firms or individuals succeed. For consultants, understanding the consulting market is therefore not an optional extra but a central part of professional competence.

The dynamics of this market are shaped by forces far beyond the control of any one practitioner. Political instability, shifting regulatory frameworks, rapid technological change, and cycles of economic growth or contraction all influence the appetite for consultancy. A surge in regulatory requirements may create sudden demand for compliance audits, while a global recession can just as quickly close off opportunities in sectors such as commercial real estate. Consultants who treat the market as static risk losing relevance; those who monitor and interpret its movements are better placed to anticipate demand and sustain their practice.

Markets are also highly differentiated. A multinational corporate client may expect evidence-based reports that integrate legal defensibility with risk analysis, while a government agency might prioritise compliance with national standards and political accountability. In contrast, high-net-worth individuals may value discretion and personal trust above methodology. Consultants must adapt to these varied contexts, recognising that success in one environment does not guarantee success in another. Understanding where one's skills fit, and how to reposition when conditions change, is part of building a resilient career.

At the same time, the consulting market is not evenly accessible. Barriers to entry exist in the form of certifications, security clearances, and procurement frameworks. Informal barriers such as reputation and insider networks can be just as influential. Navigating these requires a combination of patience, credibility, and strategy. Consultants must learn not only how to deliver technical work but also how to position themselves commercially, build trust, and demonstrate value in ways that clients recognise.

The consulting market is not merely reactive. Consultants who invest in research, who publish insight, and who apply structured methods to track change can influence the shape of demand itself. In this sense, market understanding is not just about survival but about leadership. Those who can interpret trends and frame them for clients often become the trusted advisers who define new areas of practice.

This chapter examines the consulting market in detail. It explores the global and regional landscape, highlights the sectors and niches where opportunities are most promising, and considers the commercial models that sustain practice. It also discusses strategies for market entry, the barriers that restrict participation, and the role of research in anticipating change. With these insights, consultants can align their expertise with real demand and position themselves for long-term relevance.

The Global Market Landscape

The market for security consultancy is broad, diverse, and constantly evolving. It is shaped by external forces that consultants cannot control but must interpret if they are to remain relevant. Political instability, technological change, global supply chain vulnerabilities, and shifts in public trust all influence which services are in demand at any given time. To understand the market, consultants need to look past the technical tasks and recognise the bigger forces that drive clients to ask for advice.

Across the world, demand for security consultancy is concentrated in a few core sectors. Critical national infrastructure is among the most consistent. Energy generation and distribution, water supply, transportation hubs, and telecommunications networks all depend on resilient protective measures. Consultants here are often engaged to conduct threat, vulnerability, and risk assessments, design layered security and advise on regulatory compliance. Engagements can be long-term, as operators prefer continuity and proven expertise, but entry is restricted. Governments and regulators tend to rely on firms with strong track records, clearances, or established reputations.

The corporate sector is broader but more fragmented. Large multinationals typically maintain in-house security teams, yet they often seek external consultants for independent validation, specialist expertise, or during times of organisational change. Mergers, relocations, and market entry into new regions all generate demand for impartial advice. Within this sector, maturity varies widely. Some organisations seek compliance-focused audits, while others expect strategic resilience planning that links security directly to business continuity and reputation. For consultants, adaptability is crucial, as the same client may demand both tactical interventions and longer-term strategic support.

Defence and government projects represent another major market, though with high barriers to participation. Procurement cycles are long, requirements are complex, and work often involves classified information. Consultants are expected to navigate technical specifications, regulatory frameworks, and political sensitivities simultaneously. Success in this environment usually depends on prior defence or government experience, security clearances, or established partnerships with major contractors. While the revenues can be significant, the investment needed to qualify can be prohibitive for smaller firms or individual practitioners.

Alongside these established markets, new growth areas have emerged. Data centres are now among the fastest-growing sectors worldwide, driven by cloud computing, artificial intelligence, and the expansion of digital economies. The security of these facilities is not limited to physical access control and surveillance but extends to integrated cyber-physical resilience. Clients expect consultants to understand both sides of the equation and to advise on governance, compliance, and technical measures. Healthcare is another sector with growing demand, especially after the COVID-19 pandemic exposed vulnerabilities in supply chains, laboratories, and hospital infrastructure. Here, consultants are asked to combine compliance with patient safety and resilience of critical assets.

High-net-worth individuals and family offices represent a smaller but lucrative niche. Services in this segment often include residential security, travel protection, and surveillance countermeasures. Success depends as much on discretion and trust as on technical expertise. Consultants entering this market must demonstrate not only competence but also sensitivity to personal expectations and lifestyle integration.

The drivers of global demand are interconnected. Terrorism and political conflict continue to create requirements for protective design and risk analysis. The expansion of cyber-enabled threats pushes organisations to seek integrated approaches that address both digital and physical vulnerabilities. Regulation – from international directives to local compliance standards – consistently generates opportunities for consultancy. Increasingly, environmental, social, and governance (ESG) frameworks elevate security to board-level concern, linking resilience to reputation and investor confidence. Consultants who can translate technical risk into business terms are especially well positioned, as executives demand clarity on how protective measures safeguard continuity, compliance, and brand value.

The global market is also characterised by cycles. Economic downturns can suppress investment in some areas, such as commercial real estate, but may simultaneously increase demand for resilience, cost optimisation, and efficiency. Crises such as pandemics or natural disasters shift priorities suddenly, eroding some markets while accelerating others. Consultants who monitor these shifts and pivot accordingly demonstrate resilience. For example, during the pandemic, demand for office security consultancy fell sharply, but resilience planning and data centre security grew significantly.

Competition is intense. Large international firms leverage their scale and established reputations, while boutique practices compete by focusing on specialist niches. Differentiation is essential: clients often perceive consultancies as interchangeable, so success depends on articulating a distinct value proposition. Whether through proven expertise, thought leadership, or demonstrable outcomes, consultants must establish why their contribution is unique.

The global consulting market mirrors the uncertainty of the wider world. Risks evolve, regulations tighten, technologies proliferate, and expectations shift. Consultants who treat the market as a living environment are better placed to align their expertise with emerging demand. Technical competence may open the door, but it is market awareness that sustains a career.

Regional Variations

While global forces create broad patterns of demand, regional context determines how consultancy is defined, procured, and valued. A one-size-fits-all approach rarely succeeds. Cultural expectations, regulatory frameworks, and procurement practices vary widely, shaping both opportunities and the skills consultants must bring to the table.

In North America, the consulting market is strongly shaped by compliance and liability. Corporations are motivated by the need to demonstrate due diligence and mitigate legal exposure. Security assessments are often tied to insurance requirements or potential litigation, and consultants are expected to provide detailed documentation, clear audit trails, and evidence that measures meet prescribed standards. Budgets can be substantial, but clients are demanding and expect consultants to integrate seamlessly with legal teams, IT departments, and senior management. Success here depends on structured methodologies, defensible reporting, and the ability to quantify outcomes in terms of reduced liability and improved resilience.

Europe presents a contrasting environment, where regulatory frameworks and cultural attitudes towards privacy dominate. The General Data Protection Regulation (GDPR[5]) and the NIS2[6] Directive are prominent drivers of consultancy work, creating demand for services that combine security, data protection, and compliance. Beyond regulation, organisations are influenced by ethical considerations and reputational pressures. Decision-making is often consensus-driven, requiring consultants to engage with multiple stakeholders and balance technical recommendations with cultural sensitivities. Those who thrive in Europe are not only technically proficient but also skilled facilitators, able to navigate complex governance structures and align diverse interests.

The Middle East is characterised by government-led development and ambitious national strategies. Countries such as the United Arab Emirates and Saudi Arabia invest heavily in critical infrastructure and smart city projects, with security positioned as a central pillar of national planning. Regulatory bodies such as the Security Industry Regulatory Agency (SIRA[4]) in Dubai, Abu Dhabi Monitoring and Control Center (ADMCC[1]), and the federal National Emergency Crisis and Disaster Management Authority (NCEMA[18]) set mandatory standards that consultants must satisfy. Success depends on reputation, trust, and cultural alignment. Relationships often matter more than formal marketing, and consultants must adapt communication styles to hierarchical structures, demonstrating respect for protocol and government priorities. While capital expenditure is high and opportunities are plentiful, credibility is paramount; consultants who fail to adapt to local norms rarely secure repeat work.

The Asia-Pacific region is highly fragmented. At one end are advanced markets such as Japan, Singapore, and Australia, where regulations are mature, client expectations are high, and consultancy is closely aligned with international standards. Consultants here must offer sophisticated, integrated solutions, blending cyber and physical measures with governance frameworks. At the other end, rapidly urbanising countries such as India, Indonesia, and Vietnam present opportunities driven by expansion of infrastructure and urban development. Demand is high, but budgets and regulatory frameworks may be less consistent. Flexibility is critical: consultants must adapt to shifting requirements and be prepared for less predictable client expectations. Cultural context also plays a role. In Japan, decision-making can be consensus-oriented and process-heavy, while in South Asia, agility and responsiveness are often more valued than exhaustive formality.

Africa and Latin America are emerging but increasingly important markets. Political instability, high crime rates, and the desire to attract foreign investment create strong incentives for governments and corporations to demonstrate security and resilience. However, regulatory frameworks may be inconsistent, and enforcement can be uneven. Consultants often find the greatest opportunities in supporting multinational corporations operating in these regions rather than in direct government contracts. Partnerships with local firms can be essential to navigate political and cultural complexities. Corruption, shifting political landscapes, and infrastructure gaps remain challenges, but those who establish credibility and adapt to local realities can carve out important niches.

Cultural expectations shape not just procurement but also definitions of success. In the Gulf, formality, hierarchy, and personal trust dominate; consultants must respect seniority and protocol. In North America, direct communication and assertive positioning are often valued. In Europe, privacy, ethical considerations, and stakeholder consensus carry weight. In Asia, patience and group-oriented decision-making may be decisive, while in parts of Africa or Latin America, building credibility through local networks is essential.

For consultants, the implication is clear: technical expertise travels, but practice must be adapted. A methodology that secures credibility in one region may be ineffective or even counterproductive in another. Success requires both situational awareness and cultural intelligence. The consultant who can flexibly adapt, while maintaining professional standards, will sustain a broader and more resilient practice.

Market awareness is a professional discipline, not a commercial afterthought. Consultants who monitor demand, interpret regulation, and position expertise against real-world priorities sustain relevance when conditions change.

Identifying Sectors and Niches

In a crowded consulting market, few strategies are more important than deciding where to focus. Trying to be all things to all clients rarely works. The breadth of security consultancy means opportunities exist across critical infrastructure, corporate, defence, and government domains, but success often depends on targeting a specific sector or niche where demand is strong and where consultants can demonstrate distinctive expertise.

In recent years, one of the most significant growth niches has been data centres. The rise of cloud computing, artificial intelligence, and digital commerce has created extraordinary demand for resilient facilities. Data centres must integrate physical security with cyber resilience, energy assurance, and regulatory compliance. Consultants are frequently asked to design layered access control, surveillance, and incident response frameworks while ensuring alignment with standards such as ISO/IEC 27001:2022[15]. Clients in this sector tend to be well resourced and acutely aware of reputational risk, making them receptive to high-quality consultancy that can demonstrate measurable value.

Aviation and maritime security remain enduring sources of demand. Airports operate under strict international frameworks, requiring regular assessments, audits, and compliance verification. Airlines also seek advice on resilience, insider threat, and emerging technologies. Maritime ports face threats such as smuggling, terrorism, and organised crime, while piracy remains a major risk to vessels at sea. Together, these create demand for consultants who can blend technical risk analysis with operational insight. Engagements in these sectors often extend beyond compliance into the design of infrastructure and training programmes. Because aviation and maritime are inherently international, consultants with cross-border experience are particularly well positioned.

Healthcare and pharmaceuticals have become increasingly significant. Hospitals, laboratories, and pharmaceutical facilities must protect sensitive data, valuable intellectual property, and critical supplies. Regulation is stringent, and the COVID-19 pandemic highlighted the vulnerability of healthcare supply chains. Consultants are now engaged not only to support compliance but also to build resilience in clinical and research settings. This work often requires balancing accessibility, public perception, and strict protective measures; a challenge that rewards consultants who can integrate human factors with technical controls.

A niche of a very different kind is security for high-net-worth individuals and family offices. Though smaller in scale, this market can be highly lucrative. It requires bespoke solutions – residential protection, travel security, counter-surveillance, and crisis response planning – tailored to personal expectations. Discretion and trust are as critical as technical ability. Consultants who succeed here demonstrate emotional intelligence alongside technical fluency, ensuring that protective measures integrate smoothly with lifestyle.

New specialist niches continue to emerge as risks evolve. The rapid spread of drones has created demand for counter-drone strategies, blending detection, legal compliance, and layered response. Growing concern over insider threats has driven interest in behavioural risk assessments and workforce culture programmes. Consultants who position themselves early in such areas often achieve strong differentiation. Their credibility is reinforced if they combine subject matter expertise with visible thought leadership, such as publishing articles or contributing to professional standards.

The challenge lies in balancing specialisation with adaptability. Over-concentration on a single sector can expose a consultancy to cyclical downturns. At the same time, excessive diversification can dilute credibility. Resilient practices often build around a core niche while retaining the ability to pivot into adjacent markets. A consultant specialising in corporate real estate security, for instance, may adapt to data centres, while one focused on aviation security can extend methods into broader transport resilience. This balance gives consultants depth while reducing the risk of being exposed to sudden market changes.

Structured tools can assist in selecting and evaluating niches. SWOT analysis helps identify strengths and weaknesses relative to emerging opportunities and threats. Porter's Five Forces can illuminate the competitive dynamics of a sector, clarifying whether it is attractive or saturated. Market scanning, using industry reports, regulatory updates, or conference intelligence, ensures consultants remain alert to early signals of change. The value of these tools lies not only in their structure but in how consultants interpret their outcomes considering their own expertise and networks.

Identifying the right sectors and niches is not simply about analysis but about commercial reality. Clients will reward consultants who align services with pressing needs, demonstrate distinctive expertise, and articulate value in terms that resonate with decision-makers. Focus brings clarity, differentiation, and pricing power. Flexibility ensures that expertise can be redeployed when markets shift. Consultants who master both are best placed to sustain relevance and build a practice that is not only profitable but resilient over time.

Market Entry Strategies

For many consultants, the greatest challenge is not delivering value once engaged but securing those initial engagements. Technical capability is necessary but not sufficient; consultancy is purchased as much on perception, reputation, and trust as on competence. Entering the market therefore requires a deliberate strategy, one that blends credibility, visibility, and commercial positioning.

A useful principle comes from Alan Weiss, whose work in professional consulting stresses the importance of focusing on outcomes rather than deliverables. Clients who measure value by the number of pages in a report or the volume of site inspections are often the least profitable and the most demanding. In contrast, clients who value outcomes are willing to pay for expertise because they see a direct return on investment. For consultants, this means framing proposals in the language of business priorities rather than technical activity. Instead of promising "twelve site visits and a detailed report", the message must be that the consultancy will enable continuity of operations, reduce liability, or achieve regulatory certification. Positioning in terms of outcomes elevates the consultant from service provider to strategic adviser.

Establishing authority is another cornerstone of market entry. Generalists tend to be overlooked in competitive environments; those who specialise in particular domains, such as data centre resilience, counter-drone strategies, or insider threat mitigation, are more likely to be recognised. Authority can be built through thought leadership: publishing articles, presenting at industry conferences, contributing to standards bodies, or participating in public consultations. Even small firms or individuals can compete with larger players if they consistently showcase deep expertise in a clearly defined area. This focus creates clarity for clients and reinforces the consultant's ability to command professional fees.

Credibility, however, often rests on prior experience. Those moving into consultancy from corporate or government roles can leverage their history, reframing operational achievements as advisory contributions. A former corporate security manager, for example, can highlight how risk assessments shaped strategic decisions, or how stakeholder engagement supported organisational change. Early projects may require competitive pricing or subcontracting under established firms to gain exposure. Over time, case studies and testimonials become the consultant's strongest currency. Each successful engagement builds a track record that supports the next.

Networking remains critical to early success. Security consultancy is rarely purchased through cold calls or generic advertising. Most engagements are secured through referrals, introductions, or prior familiarity. Professional associations, industry forums, and security conferences provide opportunities for visibility. Digital platforms such as LinkedIn extend this reach, allowing consultants to share insights consistently and to signal expertise in chosen niches. Effective networking is not about collecting contacts indiscriminately but cultivating relationships with decision-makers and influencers who can open doors. In many regions, especially in the Middle East or parts of Asia, personal endorsements carry far more weight than brochures or credentials.

Pricing is another area where consultants often stumble when entering the market. Many assume that lowering fees will attract clients. In reality, under-pricing often signals inexperience and undermines credibility. Clients rarely trust the cheapest option when dealing with sensitive issues of security and resilience. Pricing should therefore be confident and professional, supported by a clear articulation of value. While introductory discounts or packaged services can be useful in establishing initial relationships, they must not lock the consultant into a low-cost position that is difficult to escape. The ability to explain fees in terms of outcomes is central to creating confidence.

Practical entry pathways vary, but common strategies include subcontracting to larger consultancies, collaborating with technology vendors to gain project exposure, or focusing on narrow problem sets where demand is acute. In all cases, consultants must maintain independence in their advice, ensuring that client trust is not compromised by commercial affiliations. Each pathway provides exposure and credibility while allowing new entrants to demonstrate competence. Over time, these experiences can be expanded into fully independent practice. A consultant who begins as a subcontractor on data centre projects, for example, may gradually build enough references to secure direct engagements with operators.

Market entry is about alignment. The consultant must align expertise with demand, pricing with perceived value, and personal credibility with client expectations. It is a cumulative process rather than a sudden breakthrough. Early engagements build a foundation of trust; authority and reputation grow with each visible contribution. Those who succeed are rarely the most technically advanced, but rather those who communicate value effectively, position themselves strategically, and persist in building credibility over time.

Revenue Models in Security Consulting

Every consulting practice depends not only on technical expertise but also on the way its services are priced and delivered. The choice of revenue model influences client expectations, financial stability, and how the consultant is perceived. A poorly chosen model can erode trust or profitability; a well-chosen one signals professionalism and reinforces value.

The most familiar approach is the fixed-fee project. Here the consultant and client agree on a defined scope of work at an agreed price, regardless of the hours required. Clients value the predictability that this offers, particularly in corporate and public-sector contexts where budgets must be allocated in advance. For consultants, fixed fees reward efficiency and experience, since the ability to deliver quickly without compromising quality improves margins. The risk lies in scope creep: clients extending requirements without recognising the additional effort involved. To succeed with fixed fees, consultants must define deliverables precisely and be disciplined in managing expectations.

Another common model is the retainer. Instead of paying for a single project, the client secures ongoing access to the consultant's expertise for a recurring monthly or quarterly fee. Retainers are effective when clients value continuity and immediate advice rather than discrete outputs. A multinational firm entering a high-risk region, for example, might engage a consultant on retainer to provide regular updates, site visits, and on-demand guidance. For the consultant, retainers provide stable income and stronger client relationships. The challenge is to demonstrate continuing value, since clients may otherwise see retainers as open-ended costs. Regular reporting, visible outcomes, and responsiveness are essential to sustain trust.

The time-and-materials model is still widely used, particularly in government and defence sectors. Clients are billed for the hours worked and expenses incurred. This approach offers flexibility, allowing scope to evolve without constant renegotiation, and it protects the consultant against underestimating workload. However, it can create tension, as clients may perceive it as open-ended or inefficient. Maintaining clear communication, accurate records, and disciplined project management is vital to reassure clients that resources are being used effectively.

Less common but increasingly discussed is the performance-based model. Fees are tied to outcomes, such as achieving ISO certification, completing a resilience programme on time and within budget, or demonstrating measurable risk reduction. This model signals strong alignment with client priorities and can build high levels of trust. Yet in security, outcomes are often influenced by factors outside the consultant's control. A fall in incidents may owe as much to external conditions as to improved measures. For this reason, performance-based arrangements work best where outcomes are clearly measurable and attributable, such as compliance with a defined regulatory framework.

Many practices adopt hybrid approaches, blending elements of different models. A fixed fee might apply for an initial risk assessment, followed by a retainer for ongoing advisory work. Implementation phases may be billed on time-and-materials, while milestone achievements trigger performance bonuses. Hybrid models reflect the reality that consultancy is rarely confined to a single type of engagement. They also allow flexibility to meet client expectations while protecting the consultant's financial interests.

The psychology of the client plays a significant role in determining which model works best. Corporate clients generally prefer predictability, favouring fixed fees. Government agencies prioritise accountability and transparency, making time-and-materials contracts more common. Defence contracts often follow rigid procurement frameworks, leaving little room for innovation. High-net-worth individuals may prefer retainers, valuing discretion and immediate access above detailed scoping. Consultants who understand these preferences can align their commercial approach with client expectations, improving the likelihood of securing work.

Benchmarking against other professions also provides perspective. Legal and accountancy firms frequently use time-based billing, which clients have come to expect. Management consultancies, by contrast, often rely on fixed fees or value-based pricing that emphasises outcomes. Security consultancy sits somewhere between the two, sharing the technical precision of engineering services and the strategic positioning of management consulting. Recognising this dual character allows consultants to select models that feel familiar to clients while still signalling expertise and authority.

Revenue models are not static. Early in a career, consultants may accept time-and-materials projects to gain credibility, even if margins are thin. As reputation grows, they can shift towards fixed-fee or retainer arrangements that provide greater control and stability. Over time, mature practices may experiment with outcome-based or hybrid models that signal confidence and align fees directly with client value. What matters is that consultants make conscious choices, positioning themselves deliberately rather than defaulting to whatever clients suggest.

Revenue models are more than financial mechanisms. They shape perception. A consultant who charges by the hour may be seen as a supplier of labour, while one who charges for outcomes is positioned as a strategic partner. Choosing the right model signals to the client how the consultant views their own expertise. Mastery of revenue models is therefore not just about cash flow: it is a core element of professional positioning, shaping both financial sustainability and credibility in the market.

Barriers to Entry

Security consultancy is not an open market where anyone with technical skill can readily establish a presence. Entry is shaped by a mixture of formal and informal barriers that protect standards but also restrict participation. Understanding these barriers is essential for new consultants seeking to establish themselves and for experienced practitioners who must remain aware of the hurdles facing competitors.

Formal barriers are the most visible. Many clients expect consultants to hold recognised certifications such as Certified Protection Professional (CPP), Physical Security Professional (PSP), or Certified Information Systems Security Professional (CISSP). These credentials act as a benchmark of competence and signal commitment to professional standards. In some jurisdictions, local licensing schemes create additional requirements. Dubai's Security Industry Regulatory Agency (SIRA[4]), for example, requires consultants to meet specific criteria before offering services, while in the United States certain contracts require federal clearance or adherence to state-level procurement rules. These requirements raise the cost of entry but also serve to assure clients that only qualified practitioners are operating in sensitive environments.

Equally significant are the informal barriers that revolve around reputation and trust. Security consultancy deals with sensitive information, high-value assets, and vulnerabilities that clients are reluctant to expose to outsiders. As a result, opportunities are often awarded to consultants with proven track records or personal endorsements rather than those responding cold to tenders. Networks of trust therefore become a decisive factor. In some markets, this takes the form of insider communities, such as defence and government projects that require prior service, established clearances, or relationships with major contractors. In corporate sectors, it may be the reputation gained through published work, referrals, or prior collaboration.

Brand recognition functions as another filter. Consultants associated with established firms, or individuals who have published widely in respected forums, enjoy a credibility advantage. Conversely, newcomers may struggle to gain traction even if technically competent. Clients often perceive security consultancy as high-risk, preferring familiar names to unknown entrants. This can create a cycle in which established consultants consolidate their position while new entrants face prolonged struggles to build trust.

Overcoming these barriers requires deliberate strategy. Partnerships and subcontracting provide one route, allowing new consultants to contribute to larger projects while building references. Publishing articles, presenting at conferences, or contributing to professional standards can help build visibility and credibility. Certifications not only meet formal requirements but also signal seriousness and commitment. Patience is essential: consultancy reputations are built incrementally, often through a sequence of smaller engagements that gradually accumulate into recognised authority.

The barriers serve a valuable function. They prevent unqualified practitioners from undermining the credibility of the profession and reassure clients that advice comes from trustworthy sources. For the aspiring consultant, they are not simply obstacles but signals of where investment is required; in certification, in networking, in publishing, and in demonstrating reliability. For established consultants, they are reminders of the privileged position that comes with credibility, and of the responsibility to uphold standards that sustain trust in the profession.

Illustrative Example: Pivoting in a Downturn

Consider a consultancy that built its reputation advising developers and corporate tenants on office security. For many years, the firm prospered by reviewing designs for new towers, planning access control systems, and supporting compliance with building and fire safety codes. Engagements were steady, revenues predictable, and relationships with property owners strong.

This stability unravelled when economic conditions shifted and the demand for office space collapsed. Remote working reduced leasing activity, developers postponed projects, and tenants deferred upgrades. A consultancy that had focused almost exclusively on commercial real estate found its pipeline thinning rapidly. What had seemed like a safe sector proved highly exposed to structural change.

The firm responded by pivoting into adjacent markets where its expertise remained relevant. Data centres provided a logical transition. Like office towers, these facilities required robust access control, layered protective measures, and compliance with regulatory standards. Yet unlike commercial real estate, demand for data centres was accelerating, fuelled by cloud computing and digital transformation. By reframing its capabilities in protective design and compliance, the consultancy began to reposition itself as a partner for digital infrastructure providers. Partnerships with technology vendors and targeted marketing reinforced this shift, allowing the firm to build credibility in its new niche.

At the same time, the consultancy diversified into resilience and continuity planning. While large capital projects were slowing, many corporate clients were willing to invest in strategies to reduce risk and improve efficiency. Fixed-fee packages for continuity planning and crisis response frameworks proved attractive to clients seeking tangible value without long-term commitments. These smaller engagements provided steady revenue and broadened the consultancy's client base.

Thought leadership accelerated the repositioning. By publishing articles on data centre security and hosting webinars on resilience, the consultancy signalled authority in its chosen niches. Even without a long track record in these markets, visible expertise reassured potential clients that the firm was adapting and had relevant insight to offer.

Within two years, the consultancy had stabilised. Data centre projects became a core revenue stream, resilience consulting provided background income, and the firm emerged less vulnerable to downturns in any single sector. The experience illustrated a wider truth: over-reliance on one market is risky, but agility, diversification, and visible expertise can turn disruption into opportunity.

Research Methods and Data Sources

Understanding the consulting market takes more than technical knowledge. Consultants need foresight: the ability to track changes in threats, regulation, and demand, so they can see where opportunities are opening or closing. Without disciplined research, it is easy to misread the market and offer services that no longer match what clients need.

Public sources form the foundation. International bodies such as the UN, INTERPOL, and IMO[11] publish reports on global crime and terrorism, while governments release statistics and regulatory updates. Industry associations add standards and guidance. These sources are accessible but only gain real value when consultants interpret them for specific client contexts. Subscription services offer greater depth. Firms such as Gartner, Frost & Sullivan, and Jane's provide analysis of technologies, geopolitical risks, and sectoral trends. Though costly, they can offer a competitive edge by identifying developments before they reach mainstream debate.

Primary research remains indispensable for understanding demand. Talking directly with clients, attending site visits, or running structured exercises gives consultants first-hand insight into how organisations are thinking and investing. These observations reveal not only operational needs but also the direction of the market.

Informal channels also play a role. Conferences, forums, and networks often surface early signals of regulatory change or emerging risks. Active participation strengthens professional presence while also giving consultants advance notice of shifts in demand.

Artificial intelligence tools can now support this market scanning by summarising reports, scanning news, and detecting trends across large datasets. Used carefully, they help consultants spot patterns that might otherwise be missed. Yet AI is not an authority: outputs must always be validated against original sources, since algorithms can amplify bias or misread nuance.

Research methods are what allow consultants to anticipate market shifts rather than simply respond to them. Those who build structured approaches to gathering, testing, and managing information are better placed to align their services with real demand and sustain relevance in a changing environment.

Practice Guide

The objectives of this chapter were to understand global and regional markets, identify valuable niches, examine revenue models, evaluate barriers to entry, and apply research methods to anticipate change. Each of these has been explored through the lens of how external forces and client expectations shape opportunity.

The main pitfall is to assume that technical skill alone creates demand. Clients buy outcomes, not activity, and they reward consultants who link expertise to pressing business needs. Over-concentration on a single sector is another risk, as markets shift quickly and reliance on one domain can expose consultants to sudden downturns. A further danger lies in undervaluing services: low pricing signals inexperience and erodes trust, while relying on a single source of market intelligence undermines credibility.

Best practice follows from these lessons. Consultants should communicate in the language of outcomes, emphasising continuity, compliance, and resilience rather than deliverables or hours. They should establish authority in chosen niches while remaining flexible enough to pivot into adjacent sectors when demand shifts. Pricing must be confident and transparent, supported by models that balance client expectations with professional sustainability. Market research should be treated as a discipline: combining public, subscription, primary, informal, and AI-enabled sources; cross-checking findings; and managing outputs in ways that feed directly into market positioning.

The consultant who invests in understanding the market is not simply reacting to demand but helping shape it. By aligning expertise with client priorities, demonstrating authority, and maintaining disciplined research, consultants build both immediate opportunities and long-term relevance. This market awareness provides the foundation for the next step in a consultant's career: deciding whether to operate independently, within a boutique practice, or as part of a larger firm.

Chapter 24 – Freelance, Boutique, or Big Firm?

A central decision in a consulting career is which operating model to follow. Freelancers enjoy independence but face volatility. Boutiques combine agility with shared strength but demand management capability. Large firms provide resources and reputation but often limit autonomy. The right choice depends less on an abstract "best" option and more on alignment with personal values, goals, and circumstances.

This chapter explores these models in detail, applying Alan Weiss's principle that solo practices can scale without large teams. It considers the dynamics of boutique practices and the structures of large firms, comparing trade-offs in autonomy, reputation, scalability, and lifestyle.

By the end of this chapter, you will be able to:

- Evaluate the advantages and disadvantages of freelance consulting, boutique practices, and large-firm pathways.
- Assess the trade-offs between independence, support, reputation, and scalability in different career models.
- Apply Alan Weiss's principles on building a solo practice that scales without requiring large teams.
- Understand the financial, operational, and lifestyle considerations associated with each model.

Introduction

Every consultant eventually faces a strategic decision about where and how to practise. Some enter consulting through large firms, drawn by their reputation and stability. Others start as freelancers, valuing independence and direct control over their work. A third path lies in boutique practices, where small teams combine expertise to create a brand that is more than the sum of its parts. Each pathway offers opportunities, but each also requires trade-offs.

This decision is not only professional but personal. It affects how consultants structure their time, manage their energy, and balance their lives. Freelancers often enjoy autonomy but must tolerate uncertainty. Boutique firms require leadership and management skills as well as technical expertise. Large firms provide resources and networks but may constrain individuality. These trade-offs define not only the type of projects undertaken but also the nature of daily work and the rhythm of a career.

The importance of this decision lies in its long-term result. A consultant who builds a strong freelance practice may achieve enviable autonomy but could struggle to take on large-scale projects. One who invests in a boutique practice may create a lasting brand but must also shoulder management responsibilities. A consultant who remains within a large firm may benefit from global opportunities but sacrifice independence. No path is perfect; each is shaped by context, capability, and ambition.

This chapter explores these options systematically. It examines the attractions and risks of freelance practice, the opportunities and challenges of boutique firms, and the structure and trade-offs of large organisations. It then considers financial and lifestyle implications, providing case studies of consultants who have chosen each model. The aim is not to recommend one approach but to provide clarity, enabling readers to align their choices with their goals and to understand the adjustments required over time.

Freelance Practice: Autonomy and Risk

Freelance consulting is often the purest expression of independence in the profession. The freelance consultant operates under their own name, manages their own brand, and accepts complete responsibility for business development, client service, and administration. For some, this independence is the main attraction: the freedom to choose projects, the agility to move quickly, and the satisfaction of working without external constraints. Yet this freedom comes at a price, requiring tolerance of risk, financial uncertainty, and isolation.

The primary advantage of freelance practice is autonomy. Freelancers decide which clients to pursue, how to structure their services, and when and where they work. They are not bound by the methodologies or internal politics of a firm and can adapt approaches to fit client needs directly. This flexibility can be particularly valuable in security consultancy, where projects often demand tailored solutions that do not align neatly with pre-packaged frameworks. Freelancers can respond with speed and creativity, positioning themselves as adaptable partners rather than process-driven suppliers.

Freelancers also retain full ownership of their brand. Every piece of work directly enhances their personal reputation, without dilution by association with a larger firm. For consultants who invest in publishing, speaking, and networking, this creates a clear and recognisable identity. Clients often value this direct association: they know precisely who they are engaging, with no ambiguity about whether junior staff will deliver the work. This directness can strengthen trust and make client relationships more personal and enduring.

Financially, freelance practice has both attractions and risks. With no need to share revenue with partners or firms, freelancers keep what they earn. For those with established reputations and strong networks, this can lead to high margins and rewarding income. However, variability is significant. Freelancers often face feast-or-famine cycles, with periods of intense work followed by quieter months. Building reserves, managing cash flow, and pricing services confidently are essential disciplines. Without them, the freedom of freelancing can quickly turn into anxiety about sustainability.

The lack of scalability is a key limitation. Freelancers can only sell as much work as they can personally deliver. Unlike larger firms, they cannot easily take on multiple projects simultaneously or mobilise teams to cover parallel streams. This limits growth and exposes them to capacity constraints: when demand is high, opportunities may be missed; when demand is low, income falls sharply. Alan Weiss has argued that solo practices can scale without hiring large teams, for example by creating intellectual property, publishing, or designing repeatable products such as toolkits or training modules. Yet this requires deliberate effort to decouple income from direct hours, a transition that many freelancers struggle to achieve.

Operationally, freelancers must wear multiple hats. They are responsible not only for consulting work but also for marketing, administration, invoicing, and compliance. Larger firms provide infrastructure and support; freelancers must build or outsource these functions themselves. While technology and professional service providers make this more manageable, it remains a drain on time and energy. The risk is that consultants spend too much time on administration and too little on value-adding activity.

Isolation is another challenge. Freelancers lack the collaborative environment of a firm where ideas can be tested, knowledge shared, and support provided. This can limit perspective, making it harder to benchmark against peers or to stay updated on emerging practices. Many freelancers counter this by engaging actively in professional associations, building networks of trusted colleagues, or joining informal peer groups. Without such connections, the freelance consultant risks stagnation and reduced credibility.

Lifestyle implications are complex. On the one hand, freelancing provides unparalleled flexibility. Consultants can structure work around personal commitments, avoid unwanted travel, and pursue projects that align with their interests. On the other hand, the uncertainty of income and the pressure of running every aspect of a business can erode quality of life. The boundary between work and personal life is often blurred, with freelancers feeling compelled to remain constantly available. Those who succeed over the long term develop strict boundaries, ensuring that flexibility does not collapse into overwork.

The freelance path is therefore best suited to consultants who value independence, are disciplined in managing risk, and are proactive in building networks. It offers freedom, agility, and direct brand ownership but demands resilience, financial discipline, and tolerance for uncertainty. For some, freelancing is a temporary stage before moving into boutique practices or large firms. For others, it is a lifelong choice that provides fulfilment through autonomy and personal identity. Either way, it represents one of the most distinct models of consulting, combining opportunity with risk in equal measure.

Boutique Consultancy: Building a Firm

Boutique consultancy occupies the space between the independence of freelancing and the scale of large firms. It is typically defined by small teams with a clear focus on niche expertise. Boutiques are agile enough to respond quickly to client needs but structured enough to handle projects beyond the capacity of an individual freelancer. For many consultants, the boutique model represents both an opportunity to expand influence and a way to build something that endures beyond their personal involvement.

The advantages of boutique firms begin with collective capability. A small group of consultants can cover a broader range of skills than any one individual. In security consultancy, for example, a boutique practice might combine expertise in physical security, cyber resilience, and regulatory compliance. This diversity allows the firm to take on complex, multidisciplinary projects that would overwhelm a solo practitioner. Clients often appreciate the ability to access multiple perspectives while still dealing with a lean, responsive organisation rather than a faceless corporation.

Boutiques also allow for a stronger brand presence than freelancing alone. A firm name, however small, signals continuity and stability. Clients gain confidence knowing that delivery does not rely entirely on a single person. At the same time, the boutique brand can be tightly associated with quality, discretion, or innovation, giving it a distinct identity in the marketplace. Many boutiques thrive by carving out strong reputations in narrow niches. For example, advising data centre operators about resilience, or supporting governments with regulatory compliance. Specialisation allows them to differentiate against both freelancers and large firms.

Control of culture is another strength. Unlike large firms, which must accommodate diverse internal priorities, boutiques can shape their values and working practices deliberately. Founders can decide how they wish to engage clients, balance work and life, or invest in professional development. For consultants who value autonomy but also enjoy collaboration, boutique firms provide the best of both worlds: independence from corporate bureaucracy combined with the camaraderie of a small team.

However, boutiques also face distinctive challenges. Building and sustaining a team requires leadership and management skills that many consultants have not developed. Technical expertise may have carried them far as individuals, but running a firm requires attention to finance, human resources, marketing, and administration. Without these capabilities, boutiques risk becoming unstable or overly reliant on founders who struggle to let go of control.

Financial risk is significant. Boutiques carry overheads such as office space, salaries, insurance, that freelancers can often avoid. These costs increase pressure to maintain a steady flow of projects. During downturns, boutiques are vulnerable: they must cover expenses even when revenue dips. Founders often find themselves juggling the dual role of consultant and business owner, balancing delivery with the constant need to secure new work. While success can bring healthy margins, failure to manage overheads can quickly destabilise the business.

Scalability is a recurring dilemma. Growth creates new opportunities but also new pressures. Some boutiques aspire to become mid-sized firms, expanding into multiple regions or service lines. Others prefer to remain small, preserving culture and focus. Alan Weiss argues that consultants should consider scaling their practices without necessarily building large teams, for example by packaging knowledge into training courses, toolkits, or licensing models. This approach allows boutiques to expand impact and revenue without multiplying headcount, reducing risk while retaining independence.

Boutiques must also manage succession carefully. Because their identity is often closely tied to founders, clients may question continuity if key individuals depart. Building second-line leaders, delegating visibility, and sharing responsibility are therefore critical for long-term survival. Without succession planning, boutiques risk collapsing when founders retire or exit.

Lifestyle implications are mixed. Founders of boutiques may initially find themselves working longer hours than freelancers, managing both delivery and operations. Over time, however, successful boutiques can provide stability and continuity, reducing personal dependency on every project. For consultants seeking balance between independence and collaboration, boutiques often offer a satisfying middle path, provided they are managed with discipline.

Boutique consultancy represents an appealing but demanding model. It combines agility with collective strength, specialisation with brand presence, and independence with collaboration. Yet it also requires investment in management, tolerance of overhead risk, and attention to succession. For consultants willing to shoulder these responsibilities, boutiques offer the chance to build practices that reflect personal values, deliver specialised impact, and outlast individual careers.

Large-Firm Pathway: Scale and Structure

Large consulting firms occupy a distinct place in the professional landscape. Their size, resources, and reputation allow them to operate on a scale that freelancers and boutiques rarely achieve. For consultants, joining or remaining within such firms provides stability, access to major clients, and opportunities to work on complex, high-profile projects. Yet these advantages come with trade-offs in autonomy, individuality, and control. Understanding the dynamics of large-firm consulting is essential for those weighing it against freelance or boutique alternatives.

The most obvious advantage is brand recognition. A well-known firm carries credibility that precedes the consultant into the room. Clients often assume that established firms bring quality, rigour, and reliability simply because of their reputation. For junior or mid-career consultants, this brand can open doors that would otherwise remain closed. A government agency or multinational corporation may prefer to hire a globally recognised firm even when individual freelancers or boutiques offer similar expertise. Being part of such an organisation provides access to markets and opportunities that would be difficult to secure independently.

Resources are another benefit. Large firms can draw on extensive internal networks of experts, proprietary methodologies, and research departments. A consultant in a large firm rarely works in isolation; they can access colleagues with deep specialisms across multiple domains. This not only strengthens delivery but also accelerates learning. Exposure to diverse teams and approaches broadens perspective, providing experience that can later be leveraged in independent practice.

Training and development are often more structured in large firms. Many invest heavily in professional development, offering formal programmes, certifications, and international secondments. For consultants early in their careers, this provides a foundation of skills and experience that would be difficult to acquire alone. Even for experienced professionals, the ability to refresh knowledge and stay current with best practice is a significant advantage.

Large firms also offer scale in delivery. They can mobilise teams across regions, handle multi-year programmes, and deliver to clients with global operations. This capacity makes them attractive to clients who require breadth and consistency. For individual consultants, being part of such delivery offers exposure to large-scale projects and the chance to develop experience in managing complex programmes.

However, these strengths come with costs. The most obvious is reduced autonomy. Consultants in large firms must align with established methodologies, reporting structures, and corporate policies. Creativity and agility can be constrained by standardised approaches designed to maintain consistency across teams. For consultants who value independence, this can feel restrictive.

Client relationships are often controlled by the firm rather than the individual. Senior partners may hold primary responsibility, with junior or mid-level consultants playing supporting roles. This means that individual consultants may contribute significantly to delivery but have little visibility or ownership of the client relationship. Building personal brand can be difficult when credit is shared with or attributed to the firm.

Bureaucracy is another challenge. Large firms necessarily operate with layers of management, internal reviews, and compliance processes. While these provide rigour, they can also slow decision-making and reduce flexibility. Consultants accustomed to rapid problem solving may find the environment frustrating. For some, the security and order of a large firm outweighs these drawbacks; for others, bureaucracy is a strong push towards independence.

In financial terms, large firms offer consultants predictable salaries and benefits, but with limited potential for entrepreneurial gains. Consultants typically receive salaries and bonuses rather than direct returns on projects. This reduces personal financial risk but also caps reward. For those seeking profit-linked returns, the large-firm model can feel limiting. For others, the predictability of income and benefits provides a reassuring foundation, particularly when personal commitments require stability.

Lifestyle implications vary. Large firms often demand long hours, extensive travel, and high levels of commitment, particularly in senior roles. While this can be stimulating, it also carries risks of burnout. At the same time, the support structures of large firms can ease the burden in ways that freelancers or boutique founders cannot replicate. The lifestyle trade-off is therefore between intensity and support, prestige and autonomy.

Overall, the large-firm pathway suits consultants who value stability, structured development, and access to scale. It offers prestige, resources, and global opportunities but requires acceptance of bureaucracy, reduced autonomy, and capped entrepreneurial upside. For some, it is a lifelong career home; for others, it is a stage that provides training and credibility before a transition into boutique or freelance practice. Either way, the large-firm model remains a defining option in the consulting landscape, shaping not only careers but also the profession's reputation at large.

Trade-Offs and Decision Points

Choosing between freelance practice, a boutique firm, or a large consultancy is not simply a technical decision about business models. It is a deeply personal choice that reflects values, ambitions, and circumstances. Each pathway offers real opportunities, but each demands trade-offs that must be understood clearly if the consultant is to thrive rather than struggle.

Autonomy is the most immediate trade-off. Freelancers enjoy complete independence: they decide which projects to pursue, which clients to accept, and how to deliver their services. Boutiques offer partial autonomy, with founders shaping culture and approach but also needing to accommodate partners, staff, and shared decision-making. Large firms offer the least autonomy, requiring alignment with corporate policies and established methodologies. Consultants must therefore ask themselves how much independence they truly value, and whether they are prepared to sacrifice some of it in exchange for resources, reputation, or stability.

Reputation is another factor. Freelancers rely entirely on personal brand. Success or failure attaches directly to their name, which can be powerful but fragile. Boutiques develop collective brands, which can provide stability and visibility beyond one individual but also require effort to maintain coherence across the team. Large firms benefit from established reputations that precede individual consultants, opening doors and providing immediate credibility. Yet this comes at the cost of personal recognition, as client trust is often placed in the firm rather than the individual.

Support structures differ significantly across models. Freelancers must build or outsource all administrative, financial, and compliance support. Boutiques carry overheads but can provide internal infrastructure once established, often through shared resources. Large firms provide comprehensive support, but these come with obligations to comply with corporate rules and procedures. Consultants must weigh the value of support against the restrictions it imposes.

Scalability also varies. Freelance practice is limited by personal capacity unless intellectual property is packaged, as Alan Weiss suggests. Boutiques can scale by hiring, diversifying services, or expanding geographically, but growth carries financial and managerial risk. Large firms offer the greatest scale, able to deliver multi-year, multi-country programmes, but individual consultants may find their influence diluted within vast structures. The decision point here is whether a consultant seeks to maximise personal autonomy, build an enduring firm, or operate within a platform that enables global delivery.

Financial considerations provide further contrasts. Freelancers keep what they earn but face volatile income. Boutiques may generate higher total revenue but must cover salaries, office costs, and other overheads, leaving founders exposed to financial risk. Large-firm consultants usually receive stable salaries and bonuses, reducing risk but limiting direct returns on projects. Lifestyle choices intersect with these financial realities. Freelancers may enjoy flexibility but also live with uncertainty. Boutique founders often work the longest hours, balancing delivery with management responsibilities. Large-firm consultants may receive stable income but often face demanding travel schedules, long hours, and corporate expectations.

Career stage influences the choice. Freelancing may suit experienced consultants with strong networks who value independence, but it can be difficult for those without reputation or connections. Boutique practices often emerge mid-career, when consultants have sufficient credibility and networks to attract projects but still have the energy to manage a growing business. Large firms can be ideal early in a career, providing structured training and exposure, or later as a stable platform after years of independent work. Transitions are also common: many consultants move from large firms into boutiques, or from freelancing into boutique partnerships, as priorities shift.

What matters most is alignment between the model and the consultant's own goals, values, and risk tolerance. Consultants must consider their appetite for risk, their tolerance for bureaucracy, their desire for recognition, and their personal circumstances. For some, independence is worth volatility. For others, stability is worth sacrificing autonomy. Still others see the boutique model as the best compromise, providing both independence and collective strength. There is no universally superior model; each has its merits when matched to the right consultant at the right stage of life.

The key is to approach the decision deliberately. Consultants who drift into a model without recognising the trade-offs risk frustration and underperformance. Those who reflect carefully on values, priorities, and long-term goals are more likely to choose models that sustain them, not just professionally but personally. The decision is not final; it can be revisited as careers and circumstances change. Being clear at each stage helps make sure the chosen model supports growth instead of holding the consultant back.

Career models are systems of trade-off. Autonomy, stability, scale, and recognition each carry costs as well as benefits – the consultant's task is to align professional ambition with sustainable practice.

Financial and Lifestyle Considerations

Consultants often frame the choice between freelance practice, boutique firms, and large organisations in professional terms: autonomy, reputation, scalability. Yet the financial and lifestyle consequences are just as significant. How income is earned, how predictable it is, and how it aligns with personal priorities all shape whether a model proves sustainable. Misjudging these factors can lead to stress, burnout, or dissatisfaction, even when professional work is successful.

Freelance practice offers the greatest flexibility in income but also the greatest volatility. Freelancers can set their own fees, retain all earnings, and enjoy high margins when projects flow steadily. For established consultants with strong networks, this can be lucrative. However, income is rarely consistent. Projects may arrive in bursts, leaving lean periods in between. Freelancers must therefore manage cash flow carefully, building reserves to cover expenses during quieter months. The ability to tolerate financial uncertainty often determines whether freelance practice is liberating or anxiety-inducing. Lifestyle considerations mirror this dynamic. Freelancers can choose when and where to work, structuring careers around family or personal commitments, but this flexibility comes at the cost of living with unpredictability.

Boutique firms face a different balance. Revenues may be higher in total, as small teams can deliver larger projects and capture more market share. Yet overheads are significant: salaries, office space, insurance, and compliance costs all eat into margins. Founders often find themselves covering payroll during lean months, carrying stress that freelancers can avoid. Profitability is possible, but only with disciplined financial management and a consistent pipeline. Lifestyle implications are complex. In the early years, founders often work long hours, balancing delivery with management tasks. Over time, successful boutiques may provide greater stability, distributing workload across teams and allowing founders to step back from constant client delivery. The lifestyle appeal is therefore delayed, arriving only once the firm is sufficiently established.

Large-firm consultants typically enjoy the most financial stability. Salaries, bonuses, and benefits provide predictable income, insulating individuals from the risks of fluctuating markets. For many, this stability outweighs the limited upside. The trade-off is that personal earnings are capped compared with the potential of entrepreneurship. Lifestyle implications also vary. Large-firm roles often involve long hours, significant travel, and high expectations of availability. While firms may provide generous benefits, the intensity of workload can erode personal balance. For some consultants, the prestige and global exposure compensate for the demands. For others, the lifestyle proves unsustainable over the long term.

Taxation and legal structures also influence financial outcomes. Freelancers often operate as sole traders or through personal companies, taking responsibility for tax compliance but retaining flexibility in how income is drawn. Boutique firms require more complex structures such as partnerships, limited companies, or even holding entities, each with implications for liability and tax. Large-firm employees avoid these responsibilities but have little control over how income is structured. Understanding these frameworks is essential for aligning financial expectations with chosen pathways.

Lifestyle considerations extend beyond workload. Travel is a normal element in consultancy, but its impact varies. Freelancers can often choose local projects, limiting disruption, though at the cost of reducing scope. Boutique consultants may be more selective once their brand is established but often accept significant travel early to secure growth. Large-firm consultants frequently travel internationally, sometimes with little choice, which can strain personal life. The ability to tolerate or even enjoy travel is often a deciding factor in career model.

Family circumstances also matter. Freelancing provides flexibility to work around family needs but exposes households to income variability. Boutique firms may offer stability once mature but can create intense stress during growth phases. Large firms provide secure income but often demand time and presence that reduce family availability. Each pathway therefore requires honest reflection on personal commitments and tolerance for disruption.

Financial and lifestyle considerations cannot be secondary to professional aspirations. A consultant may choose freelancing for autonomy, a boutique for impact, or a large firm for prestige, but if the model misaligns with financial resilience or personal priorities, the career will eventually strain. The most successful consultants are those who make choices with eyes open, balancing professional ambition with sustainable lifestyles.

Practice Guide

The objectives of this chapter were to show that there is no single "best" model for consulting. Freelance practice, boutique firms, and large organisations each offer distinct advantages and impose particular constraints. The learning objectives – to evaluate different career models, to assess trade-offs in autonomy, support, reputation, and scalability, to apply principles of solo scaling, and to understand financial and lifestyle considerations – have been addressed through the analysis provided.

The pitfalls are common but avoidable. Freelancers may underestimate the volatility of income, confuse autonomy with sustainability, or neglect the discipline of continuous marketing. Boutique founders may overextend, hiring too quickly or failing to build systems that sustain growth, leaving them burdened by overheads. Consultants in large firms may allow their identity to be absorbed into the corporate brand, sacrificing personal visibility and autonomy without a clear plan for progression. In each case, the risk is not in the model itself but in pursuing it without clarity or preparation.

Sustainable approaches address these risks directly. Freelancers succeed when they combine independence with disciplined business habits, building reserves, nurturing networks, and creating intellectual property to reduce reliance on billable hours. Boutique firms thrive when they focus on a clear niche, manage growth carefully, and invest in succession to ensure continuity beyond the founders. Large-firm consultants prosper when they leverage the brand, resources, and training available, while also developing personal credibility that can sustain them if they later transition to independence. Across all models, alignment with personal values, appetite for risk, and stage of life is the foundation of sustainability.

The decision is not permanent. Many consultants move between models as circumstances evolve – gaining training and networks in a large firm, establishing independence as a freelancer, and eventually building a boutique practice. What matters is clarity at each stage: recognising the trade-offs, choosing deliberately, and adapting when priorities shift.

Whichever model is chosen, its success depends on clarity, discipline, and the strength of personal brand, which together sustain credibility and trust over the long term.

Chapter 25 – Your Professional Brand

A consultant's professional brand is one of their most powerful assets. In a field where clients face uncertainty and risk, trust is shaped as much by perception as by technical competence. Reputation, visibility, and credibility combine to create the image of a consultant who can be relied upon, making brand central to long-term success.

This chapter explores how to build and sustain that brand. It looks at identity, visibility, thought leadership, digital presence, networking, authenticity, and ethics. It also considers how brand influences opportunities, pricing, and engagement, and how it evolves over time to help consultants remain relevant throughout their careers.

By the end of this chapter, you will be able to:

- Understand the importance of professional branding in security consultancy and how it shapes credibility, visibility, and client trust.

- Build a distinctive professional identity that differentiates from competitors.

- Leverage digital platforms, publications, and thought leadership to enhance authority.

- Apply strategies for networking, public speaking, and professional associations to strengthen reputation.

- Recognise and avoid common pitfalls in personal branding, ensuring consistency, authenticity, and ethical integrity.

Introduction

Brand is one of the foundations of credibility in consultancy, shaping how clients perceive value before any work begins. While technical knowledge and methodology are vital, they only translate into opportunity when clients believe the consultant can deliver value. In practice, that belief is guided by perception – the professional brand. A consultant with a clear, consistent identity and visible authority is more likely to be trusted, invited to bid, and able to command professional fees. One who lacks visibility or credibility may struggle to secure even modest assignments, regardless of technical skill.

In security consultancy, brand matters more than in most professions because it represents trust. The work involves sensitive information, strict regulations, and the protection of valuable assets. Clients must choose advisers carefully, often with little chance to test their capability beforehand. A consultant who has published widely, spoken at respected conferences, or been recommended by peers provides a clear signal of reliability that reassures decision-makers.

Building a professional brand is therefore essential. It is a deliberate process of defining how one wishes to be perceived, aligning that perception with genuine expertise, and making it visible to the right audiences. It involves more than self-promotion; it requires consistency, authenticity, and a willingness to contribute to the profession. When delivered well, branding strengthens client relationships, supports pricing, and creates opportunities that would otherwise remain inaccessible.

At the same time, branding carries risks if mismanaged. Exaggeration, inconsistency, or chasing visibility without substance can damage credibility quickly. In a profession built on trust, reputation is fragile: it is earned slowly but can be lost in a moment. Consultants must therefore approach branding with care, ensuring that it reflects reality and reinforces rather than undermines credibility.

This chapter examines how security consultants can build and sustain their professional brand. It considers the role of brand in consultancy, the steps required to create a distinctive identity, and the ways in which thought leadership, digital presence, and networking contribute to visibility. It also explores authenticity and ethics, presenting branding not as image management but as the disciplined alignment of perception with practice. It addresses how brand can be maintained over time, adapting as careers progress and markets evolve.

The Role of Brand in Consultancy

Brand is the signal that bridges the gap between technical competence and client trust. Clients rarely purchase services purely based on technical specifications. They are instead influenced by perceptions of reliability, authority, and credibility. A professional brand provides these signals, shaping how consultants are perceived before they even enter a room.

Unlike a product-based industry, consultancy deals in intangible value. The client cannot test the service before buying, nor can they easily measure quality until after delivery. This uncertainty places greater weight on reputation and visibility. A consultant with a recognised name, a history of respected contributions, or a visible presence in the profession carries an assurance that mitigates client risk. In many cases, the consultant's brand is the deciding factor in whether an opportunity is offered at all.

Brand also influences how work is framed. A consultant with a strong brand is more likely to be seen as a trusted adviser than as a commodity supplier. This distinction matters because trusted advisers are invited into conversations earlier, are consulted on strategic issues, and can command higher fees. Commodity suppliers, by contrast, are often engaged only after key decisions have been made, with less scope for influence and lower margins. In this way, brand directly affects both the nature of the work undertaken and the professional status of the consultant.

The effect can be seen in procurement. In competitive tendering, multiple firms may present similar methodologies and comparable technical expertise. Differentiation comes not from process but from perception. Clients ask themselves: who do we trust most? Whose judgement carries authority? Which consultant will carry credibility with stakeholders, regulators, or the board? The brand provides the answer, often tipping the balance between otherwise indistinguishable bids.

This dynamic is not unique to security consultancy but is amplified by the nature of the work. Security decisions frequently carry regulatory, reputational, and even life-safety implications. Clients therefore gravitate to consultants whose brand signals reliability and trustworthiness. For example, a consultant who has published on data centre resilience in recognised journals may be perceived as more credible than a competitor who has not, even if both have similar technical qualifications. In practice, the decision is shaped as much by perceived authority as by formal capability.

Brand also affects pricing. Consultants with strong brands can command professional fees that reflect value rather than cost. Clients expect to pay more for recognised expertise, just as they would for a leading legal or medical specialist. In contrast, consultants without visibility or reputation often find themselves competing on price alone. Over time, this distinction has significant consequences. A consultant with a strong brand can sustain profitability and reinvest in their practice. One without must work harder for lower margins, often becoming trapped in a cycle of low-value engagements.

It is important to note that brand is not constructed overnight. It emerges from consistent behaviour over time: delivering on promises, publishing credible insight, speaking at respected forums, and building a reputation for reliability. Each interaction contributes to the brand, whether through the quality of a report, the professionalism of a presentation, or the discretion shown in handling sensitive information. Consultants who treat every engagement as an opportunity to reinforce their reputation gradually builds a brand that grows in value over time.

The reverse is also true. Missteps can damage a brand quickly. Exaggerated claims, inconsistent delivery, or visible failures erode trust. In a profession built on reputation, recovery from such damage is difficult. Consultants must therefore treat brand as a form of stewardship, recognising that it requires care, consistency, and integrity.

The role of brand extends beyond winning work. It also influences the consultant's ability to shape outcomes. Clients are more likely to accept recommendations when they come from a consultant whose authority they respect. A strong brand therefore not only secures engagements but also enhances the consultant's effectiveness once inside the organisation. In this sense, brand is not just about marketing or procurement; it is integral to the practice of consultancy itself.

Brand is not optional decoration but a fundamental element of consulting practice. It shapes who is trusted, how work is defined, and what fees can be commanded. For security consultants, whose work touches on sensitive, high-value, and high-risk domains, brand carries even greater weight. It is the consultant's signal of reliability in an environment where uncertainty is the norm.

Building a Distinctive Identity

A strong brand begins with clarity about identity. Consultants who cannot articulate what makes them distinctive risk blending into a market where many appear interchangeable. Clients often perceive consultancies as offering similar services, methodologies, and outputs. What differentiates one from another is not only technical depth but the clarity with which they present their identity and the confidence with which they express it.

At its core, identity is about positioning. Consultants must ask: what do I want to be known for? Am I a general adviser across many domains, or a specialist in a critical niche? Do I want to be associated with detailed technical design, or with high-level strategic guidance? Clarity here matters, because clients are more likely to remember and recommend consultants who occupy a clearly defined space. A consultant who is "the go-to adviser for data centre resilience" or "a trusted guide on insider threat management" is easier to recall and recommend than one who is simply "a security consultant."

Distinctive identity also involves aligning brand with values and philosophy. Clients increasingly look for consultants who not only provide technical answers but also embody an approach they can respect. A consultant who emphasises integrity, proportionality, and resilience as core principles communicates more than expertise: they signal the character of the advice they will deliver. This alignment helps build trust, since the consultant's brand becomes an extension of their professional values.

Consistency is central to identity. A consultant who presents themselves one way in a proposal, another way online, and yet another way in conversation risks appearing incoherent. Clients notice these inconsistencies and may interpret them as signs of unreliability. By contrast, consultants who project the same core message across all platforms – proposals, websites, LinkedIn, conference presentations – create an impression of reliability. Consistency does not mean repetition; it means coherence, where all elements of the consultant's brand reinforce the same message.

Practical steps can help. The first is developing a clear positioning statement: a short articulation of what the consultant does, for whom, and to what effect. This is not marketing jargon but a disciplined definition of identity. For example, "I help critical infrastructure operators design and test integrated security strategies that align with national standards and ensure continuity of service." Such statements clarify the consultant's role in the market and give clients a direct understanding of where they add value.

Another step is shaping a professional narrative. This involves telling a coherent story about career trajectory, expertise, and the lessons that inform practice. A consultant who explains that their career began in corporate security management, evolved through data centre projects, and now focuses on resilience planning creates a narrative that is both credible and memorable. Narratives give clients context for expertise, turning technical skills into a story of growth and experience that inspires confidence.

Visual identity can also play a role, particularly for firms. While logos, colours, and design should not dominate professional branding, they contribute to coherence. A consultancy whose website, reports, and presentations all reflect the same visual identity appears more professional and organised than one that uses inconsistent formats. For independent consultants, visual identity may be less elaborate but still benefits from consistency: a standard template for proposals, a professional photograph, and a clear style guide all reinforce reliability.

Authenticity must underpin every element of identity. Attempts to manufacture a persona that does not reflect genuine expertise or character quickly unravel. Clients are adept at recognising exaggeration, and in security consultancy the stakes are too high for them to tolerate misrepresentation. Distinctiveness therefore comes not from inventing an identity but from clarifying and expressing what is already real. Consultants who lean into their genuine strengths create a brand that is both credible and sustainable.

Identity is not static. As consultants progress through their careers, their brand should evolve. Early in a career, distinctiveness may come from technical expertise in a narrow domain. Later, it may shift towards broader strategic insight, thought leadership, or mentoring. What matters is that the consultant remains deliberate about this evolution, updating their positioning, narrative, and messaging so that their identity continues to reflect their role in the market. A failure to evolve risks stagnation, where the consultant's brand lags behind their actual capability.

The ultimate aim of building a distinctive identity is to be memorable. Clients, peers, and stakeholders are more likely to recall and recommend consultants who occupy a clear space in their minds. Identity is the foundation of professional brand, shaping how consultants are perceived, trusted, and engaged. By defining what they stand for, aligning this with values, and expressing it consistently and authentically, consultants move beyond being simply one of many and become recognisable as distinctive, reliable, and relevant.

Visibility through Thought Leadership

Visibility is how a consultant's identity becomes recognised beyond immediate client circles. Among the most effective ways to achieve this is through thought leadership. Unlike conventional marketing, which focuses on promotion, thought leadership builds authority by demonstrating expertise, offering insight, and contributing to the wider profession. It signals that a consultant is not only competent but ahead of the curve, able to interpret emerging issues and frame them in ways that influence clients and peers.

Publishing is one of the most visible routes to thought leadership. Articles in professional journals, white papers on emerging challenges, and contributions to edited volumes all reinforce credibility. These publications serve as evidence of expertise that clients can review independently of any sales process. A consultant who has published on topics such as critical infrastructure protection, crisis response planning, or integrated risk frameworks is immediately positioned as a credible authority. Books amplify this further, both by consolidating knowledge and by demonstrating commitment to advancing the field. While writing requires time and discipline, it creates a durable record that strengthens brand long after publication.

Public speaking provides another powerful channel. Presenting at conferences, industry forums, or academic seminars not only shares expertise but also increases visibility among decision-makers and peers. Speaking roles are often remembered more vividly than written publications, as they provide an opportunity for personality and perspective to come through directly. For consultants, these engagements also create opportunities to engage with potential clients in a setting where authority is established by the platform itself. A keynote address at a professional congress or a panel contribution at a regulatory workshop signals credibility in a way few other activities can.

Participation in professional and standards-setting bodies further reinforces visibility. Consultants who contribute to committees, working groups, or regulatory consultations demonstrate both expertise and commitment to the profession. These contributions often shape policy and practice, meaning the consultant's name becomes associated with the standards clients must follow. This visibility is particularly valuable in security consultancy, where compliance and governance are central. A consultant recognised as having influenced a standard is far more likely to be trusted to help clients meet it.

Digital thought leadership has become increasingly important. Blogs, LinkedIn articles, and short-form commentary can extend reach and maintain presence between major publications or speaking engagements. The key here is quality and consistency. Occasional, thoughtful contributions that interpret new regulations, analyse recent incidents, or provide practical advice are more effective than frequent, superficial posts. Clients and peers quickly distinguish between consultants who share genuine insight and those who chase visibility for its own sake. The former build credibility; the latter risk undermining it.

The benefits of thought leadership extend beyond visibility. It also strengthens pricing power. Clients are less likely to question fees when they can see the consultant as a published author, a recognised speaker, or a contributor to professional standards. Authority built through thought leadership positions the consultant as a scarce resource, reducing price sensitivity. In competitive bidding, it often becomes the differentiator that secures selection even when technical proposals are similar.

There are, however, risks. Overextension is one. Consultants who chase every opportunity to publish or speak risk diluting their credibility if their contributions lack depth or originality. Another is inconsistency: sporadic efforts followed by silence suggest a lack of commitment and reduce impact. Most damaging is self-promotion without substance. Audiences quickly detect when contributions serve primarily to market rather than to inform. Authentic thought leadership requires substance and not just visibility.

Good practice focuses on contribution. Consultants should ask what they can add to the conversation that will genuinely help clients, peers, or the profession. This might mean analysing a new regulation, sharing lessons from a project, or framing emerging risks in ways that aid decision-making. When thought leadership is grounded in contribution rather than promotion, it strengthens brand without undermining credibility.

Visibility is not about being known by everyone but about being recognised by the right people for the right reasons. Thought leadership ensures that when clients look for expertise in a particular domain, the consultant's name comes to mind. It transforms identity into authority, positioning the consultant not just as a participant in the market but as a voice that shapes it.

Digital Presence and Online Platforms

In today's consulting environment, a professional brand is incomplete without a digital presence. Even in security consultancy, where discretion is valued, clients and peers increasingly expect to find consultants represented online. Digital platforms act as both shop window and archive: they allow prospective clients to see who a consultant is, what they have contributed, and how they present themselves professionally. The challenge is to use these platforms strategically, balancing visibility with credibility and confidentiality.

LinkedIn is the most important digital platform for consultants. It functions as a professional directory, publishing platform, and networking tool in one. A well-crafted profile, written in clear language and supported by evidence of experience, provides immediate reassurance of credibility. Thoughtful posts or articles can extend visibility, while active engagement with peers reinforces presence in professional communities. Importantly, LinkedIn is often the first point of reference for potential clients conducting due diligence. A sparse or inconsistent profile can undermine confidence before any direct conversation has taken place.

Beyond LinkedIn, consultants may maintain professional websites. A website offers greater control over narrative and branding, providing space to set out services, credentials, and publications. For boutique firms, it can establish identity distinct from larger competitors, while for individual consultants it provides a platform for case studies and client testimonials. Yet websites must be maintained carefully; outdated content or poor design suggests inattention and risks damaging credibility. As with personal presentation, a website communicates professionalism not through extravagance but through clarity, consistency, and accuracy.

Short-form digital media can complement these core platforms. Blogs, newsletters, or podcasts allow consultants to maintain visibility and share insight between major publications. These formats can be particularly effective for consultants seeking to build authority in a niche, as they allow rapid commentary on emerging developments. However, they must be approached with discipline. Frequent superficial content dilutes credibility, while irregular posting suggests lack of focus. The principle is that every digital contribution should reinforce expertise and reflect the consultant's professional identity.

A growing consideration is online reputation management. Clients, regulators, and peers may search beyond curated platforms, finding references on news sites, industry forums, or social media. Negative coverage, disputes, or unprofessional interactions can damage brand significantly. Consultants should therefore monitor their digital footprint and take care with all online interactions, even those intended to be informal. A single careless comment or poorly judged post can undo years of careful brand-building.

Discretion must remain central in security consultancy. While visibility is important, overexposure risks appearing indiscreet or self-promoting in a field that values confidentiality. Consultants must strike a balance: enough presence to reassure clients of authority, but not so much that they appear careless with sensitive knowledge. For example, case studies published online should be anonymised and sanitised to avoid revealing client vulnerabilities. The consultant's brand should be one of insight and professionalism, never of indiscretion.

Digital platforms also carry cultural nuances. In North America and parts of Europe, open sharing on LinkedIn or X (formerly Twitter) is widely accepted. In the Middle East or Asia, however, visibility may be expected to remain more formal, often limited to professional associations or controlled corporate communications. Consultants operating across regions must adapt their digital strategies to align with cultural expectations, ensuring their presence strengthens rather than undermines credibility.

Used well, digital platforms reinforce brand in three ways. First, they provide accessibility: clients can find and verify a consultant's credentials quickly. Second, they demonstrate activity: regular, thoughtful contributions show engagement with current issues. Third, they create continuity: a visible digital footprint assures clients that the consultant is not only established but actively contributing to the profession. Together, these signals make it easier for clients to trust, engage, and justify selecting a consultant.

The pitfall lies in treating digital presence as an afterthought. A weak or inconsistent online identity can create doubt even where capability is strong. Another risk is over-reliance on digital platforms at the expense of direct relationships, which remain central in consultancy. It is good practice to treat digital presence as a complement to personal reputation: a way of reinforcing authority, broadening reach, and demonstrating consistency across all channels.

The question is no longer whether to have a digital presence but how to manage it. Those who treat platforms as extensions of their brand strengthen credibility. Those who neglect or misuse them risk eroding trust. In a market where first impressions increasingly begin online, digital presence is essential; it is a critical element of professional brand.

Networking and Professional Associations

If brand is the consultant's signal of authority, networking is the channel through which that signal is carried. Security consultancy is rarely purchased cold; most engagements emerge from referrals, introductions, or long-standing professional relationships. Networking is therefore not peripheral but central to building and sustaining a professional brand. It creates the trust, familiarity, and visibility that translate technical capability into opportunity.

Professional associations provide structured platforms for networking. Bodies such as ASIS International, the International Institute of Risk and Safety Management, or regional security councils bring together practitioners, regulators, and clients. Membership alone signals commitment to the profession, but active participation adds greater value. Contributing to committees, presenting at conferences, or writing for association publications not only builds visibility but also demonstrates authority within the profession's own forums. For many clients, a consultant who is visibly active in a respected association appears more credible than one who remains unseen.

Networking at industry conferences and events remains one of the most effective ways to connect with decision-makers. These gatherings allow consultants to demonstrate expertise informally, to listen to client concerns, and to establish relationships that may not lead to immediate contracts but build familiarity over time. The impact is cumulative: repeated encounters at events gradually turn acquaintances into trusted contacts. Consultants who attend without expectation of instant return, focusing instead on listening and contributing, often build stronger networks than those who treat events as transactional.

Local networks are just as important as global ones. In regions such as the Middle East or Asia, personal introductions carry more weight than written credentials. Consultants who invest in relationships with local regulators, contractors, or community leaders often find doors opening that would otherwise remain closed. These relationships must be approached with respect for hierarchy and cultural norms. A consultant who demonstrates cultural sensitivity and honours local protocols reinforces both their brand and their credibility.

Digital networking complements in-person activity. LinkedIn allows consultants to maintain visibility with contacts between events, to share updates that reinforce expertise, and to remain present in professional conversations. Yet digital engagement works best when it supports, rather than replaces, personal interaction. A consultant who relies solely on digital posts risks appearing remote; one who combines online presence with in-person engagement creates a more authentic and durable network.

The quality of networks matters more than their size. A handful of trusted relationships with decision-makers and influencers is often more valuable than hundreds of superficial contacts. Effective networking focuses on building depth: cultivating mutual trust, offering help without immediate expectation of return, and maintaining contact over time. Consultants who consistently add value to their networks, whether by sharing insights, making introductions, or providing informal guidance, are more likely to be remembered when opportunities arise.

There are hazards to avoid. One is treating networking as opportunism, pursuing contacts only when work is needed. This creates the impression of self-interest and quickly erodes trust. Another is overexposure: appearing at every event or relentlessly promoting oneself online can lead to fatigue among peers and diminish credibility. It is good practice to participate selectively, focusing on forums where contributions are most relevant and where the consultant can offer genuine value.

Professional associations also demand balance. Membership of too many organisations spreads effort thin and risks superficial engagement. Greater impact comes from committing to a small number of bodies and contributing meaningfully. Serving on a working group or leading a chapter initiative requires time, but it creates visibility and authority that casual attendance cannot match. Clients and peers alike notice the difference between passive members and active contributors.

Networking, at its best, is not about collecting contacts but about building community. Security consultancy thrives on trust, and trust is built through repeated, reliable interaction. Consultants who invest in relationships, respect cultural norms, and contribute authentically to professional forums find that opportunities flow naturally. Their brand is reinforced not only by what they say about themselves but by what others say on their behalf.

Authenticity and Ethics in Branding

A consultant's brand is only as strong as its credibility. While visibility and positioning create awareness, it is authenticity that sustains trust. In a profession built on confidentiality, discretion, and high-stakes decision-making, clients quickly detect when brand is disconnected from reality. The consultant who overstates capability, adopts an inconsistent persona, or pursues visibility without substance risks undermining years of careful reputation-building.

Authenticity means ensuring that brand reflects actual expertise and practice. Consultants should present themselves in ways that are accurate and consistent with their track record. A professional identity built around a supposed specialism that cannot be demonstrated in real projects soon unravels under scrutiny. By contrast, consultants who align their brand with their genuine strengths build credibility that is both resilient and sustainable.

Consistency is a key test of authenticity. Clients observe consultants across multiple touchpoints: in proposals, online profiles, conference presentations, and informal conversations. If each conveys a different message, confidence is eroded. Inconsistency suggests either uncertainty or deliberate image management, both of which undermine trust. When consultants ensure that their messaging, conduct, and delivery all reinforce the same professional identity, they create the impression of reliability.

Ethics play an equally important role. Security consultancy often involves access to sensitive information and influence over significant investment decisions. Consultants must therefore uphold high standards of honesty and integrity in how they present themselves. This means resisting the temptation to inflate achievements, take credit for the work of others, or imply affiliations that do not exist. Even small lapses can have disproportionate impact, since clients expect consultants to embody the same integrity they demand in protective measures.

The pressure to stand out in a competitive market can tempt consultants towards exaggeration. Claims of "world-leading" expertise, "unparalleled" experience, or "unique" solutions may attract attention but rarely withstand scrutiny. When clients test these claims and find them overstated, credibility is damaged not just for the consultant in question but for the profession more widely. It is better practice to let work speak for itself: case studies, references, and published contributions provide more convincing evidence of capability than inflated claims ever could.

Ethics also extend to how consultants use visibility platforms. Publishing articles or presenting at conferences should be about contributing to the profession, not about self-promotion at any cost. Audiences are quick to distinguish between genuine insight and disguised marketing. The consultant who provides clear, practical guidance builds authority; the one who uses every platform as an advert diminishes both credibility and brand.

Another ethical dimension is discretion. In security consultancy, confidentiality is paramount. Consultants must take care not to share client information without consent, even in anonymised form, if there is any risk of identification. Case studies used in marketing should be sanitised and cleared, ensuring that client vulnerabilities are not exposed. A single breach of confidentiality can destroy trust irreversibly. Ethical branding is therefore not only about honesty in claims but also about restraint in communication.

Cultural sensitivity is part of authenticity as well. A consultant who adapts their brand presentation to align with local expectations demonstrates respect without compromising core values. The risk is to adjust so far that identity becomes inconsistent. It is better to express the same professional integrity in culturally appropriate ways, reinforcing rather than diluting brand.

Authenticity and ethics in branding come down to stewardship. A consultant's reputation is an asset built slowly, interaction by interaction, but it can be lost quickly through carelessness or exaggeration. Authenticity ensures that brand rests on solid ground; ethics ensure it can withstand scrutiny. Together they create a brand that not only attracts clients but sustains their trust through the delivery of credible, reliable, and responsible advice.

> *Professional brand is the external expression of internal discipline. Consistency, authenticity, and contribution – not visibility alone – determine whether reputation becomes a durable form of trust.*

Illustrative Example: The Consultant as Author and Speaker

A mid-career consultant specialising in critical infrastructure found themselves competing against larger firms with more established reputations. Despite technical expertise, opportunities were limited because potential clients were unfamiliar with their name. To address this, the consultant began contributing articles to professional journals and association newsletters, focusing on practical issues such as integrating physical and cyber risk assessments and aligning protective design with regulatory frameworks. These early publications provided credibility beyond immediate projects, offering evidence of expertise that was visible to a wider audience.

Encouraged by positive feedback, the consultant developed a series of white papers on resilience in data centres. These papers were distributed through industry forums and shared on professional networks, gradually establishing the consultant as a voice on this subject. Visibility increased further when invitations followed to speak at regional conferences. Presentations on regulatory compliance, crisis management, and operational resilience gave the consultant direct access to decision-makers and peers, reinforcing authority in settings where procurement choices were often influenced.

The combination of writing and speaking began to reshape the consultant's brand. Instead of being perceived simply as one of many technical advisers, they became recognised as an authority on resilience in digital infrastructure. Clients who had read their articles or heard them speak approached them directly for advice, reducing reliance on competitive bidding. Within a few years, the consultant was invited to contribute to a national working group on standards for critical infrastructure, further embedding their credibility.

The outcomes were significant. The consultant's practice grew steadily, with engagements extending beyond initial regions into international markets. Fees increased as clients associated their brand with authoritative expertise rather than commodity services. Importantly, the consultant's visibility created opportunities to influence policy and industry direction, roles that had previously seemed out of reach.

Publishing and speaking create visibility that compounds over time. Each article, paper, or presentation reinforces authority and extends reach, often in ways that cannot be predicted at the outset. Consistency and substance are essential: superficial contributions or over-promotion quickly undermine credibility. But when executed with discipline, thought leadership transforms brand, shifting consultants from participants in the market to recognised voices who shape its direction.

Sustaining the Brand Over Time

Building a professional brand is only the beginning. The greater challenge lies in sustaining that brand over time, ensuring it continues to reflect both capability and relevance as careers progress and markets evolve. A brand that is not maintained risks becoming outdated, misaligned, or forgotten. Sustaining brand is therefore an ongoing discipline.

Brands evolve as consultants move through different stages of their career. Early in practice, distinctiveness may come from technical expertise in a narrow domain: the consultant known for detailed knowledge of access control or regulatory compliance. As experience grows, identity may shift towards broader roles: strategic adviser, thought leader, or mentor. Consultants who do not update their brand to reflect these transitions risk being perceived as specialists in areas they have outgrown, or worse, as outdated in fast-moving fields. Periodic reflection on how one wishes to be perceived is essential to keeping brand aligned with current reality.

Relevance is another critical factor. Markets change, and with them the expectations of clients. A consultant who built their brand around office real estate security, for example, may find that demand has shifted towards critical infrastructure or integrated cyber-physical resilience. Without adaptation, the brand risks placing the consultant in a declining niche. Sustaining visibility requires monitoring market signals, identifying emerging areas of demand, and aligning brand with them before they become mainstream. This does not mean abandoning existing expertise but reframing it in ways that connect with new priorities.

Consistency remains vital, but it must be balanced with renewal. Clients value reliability and expect consultants to maintain continuity of values and messaging. At the same time, they expect to see evidence of growth and adaptation. The consultant who publishes new insights, contributes to evolving debates, or updates their narrative to reflect recent experience demonstrates vitality. One who repeats the same message without development risks appearing stagnant. Sustained brand strength comes from showing both stability and progress.

Networks also play a role in sustaining brand. Relationships built over years reinforce reputation, but they must be maintained through regular contact and contribution. Consultants who remain visible in professional forums, contribute to associations, and mentor emerging practitioners ensure that their brand remains present in the community. Networks naturally evolve, and consultants who refresh their connections, expanding into new sectors or regions, sustain their brand by ensuring it is recognised in the places where future opportunities will arise.

Reputation management is equally important. A single misstep can damage years of careful brand-building. Consultants must continue to uphold ethical standards, maintain discretion, and deliver consistently. The higher the brand climbs, the greater the expectations attached to it. High-profile consultants are scrutinised more closely, and lapses are more visible. Sustaining brand therefore requires vigilance, recognising that reputation is not only an asset but also a responsibility.

Sustained brand supports legacy. For many consultants, later stages of a career involve transitioning into roles as mentors, teachers, or authors. A strong, well-maintained brand makes this possible, providing authority that extends beyond immediate consulting assignments. By continuing to contribute, whether through thought leadership, mentoring, or participation in professional standards, consultants ensure their brand remains influential even as their direct project work reduces.

A common mistake is complacency: assuming that once built, brand will endure without attention. In reality, brand decays if not actively maintained. Treat branding as a continuous process: reassessing positioning, aligning with emerging demand, refreshing contributions, and reinforcing networks. This approach ensures that brand not only endures but strengthens over time, reflecting both the consultant's growth and the evolving needs of the profession.

Practice Guide

Professional brand is central to credibility and trust. Consultants build a distinctive identity by positioning themselves deliberately, maintaining visibility through contribution, and ensuring authenticity and ethics in every interaction.

The greatest danger is to treat brand as surface image rather than substance. Exaggeration, chasing visibility without contribution, or failing to maintain consistency all weaken credibility. Complacency is another trap: a brand does not sustain itself. Markets evolve, careers progress, and expectations change; without adaptation, a consultant's brand soon falls out of step with reality. Neglecting digital presence brings further risk, as today a weak or inconsistent online identity can damage reputation before a conversation even begins.

The most effective approach is to treat brand as stewardship. Consultants should define a clear and distinctive identity and express it consistently across proposals, presentations, and digital platforms. Visibility is best built through contribution such as publishing, speaking, and active participation in professional forums, ensuring that thought leadership is genuine rather than promotional. Networks should be developed patiently and with integrity, focusing on trusted relationships rather than superficial contacts. Above all, authenticity must run through every interaction: credibility comes from aligning brand with real expertise and delivering consistently on promises.

Brand is not fixed but dynamic. Consultants who adapt to new contexts and changing expectations build resilience and authority over time. A strong, authentic brand offers both immediate visibility and long-term sustainability throughout the varied demands of a consulting career.

Chapter 26 – The Long Game

A consulting career is measured in decades, not months or years. What separates those who build enduring practices from those whose influence quickly fades is the ability to sustain relevance, energy, and credibility over time. Security consultancy makes this especially demanding because regulations change rapidly, technology disrupts established approaches, and client expectations evolve constantly. Knowledge has a short shelf life, and consultants must adapt continually if they are to remain trusted.

The long game is not about working endlessly or chasing every opportunity. It is about pacing a career deliberately, focusing on outcomes rather than activity, and investing in renewal and reinvention. This chapter examines how consultants can build careers that endure: avoiding short-termism, measuring results instead of motion, protecting against burnout, and embracing lifelong learning. It also considers resilience, succession planning, and legacy – the practices that allow consultants to remain relevant, respected, and influential across decades.

By the end of this chapter, you will be able to:

- Recognise the risks of burnout and develop strategies for long-term sustainability in consultancy.
- Apply principles of focus, measurement, and discipline to maintain relevance over decades.
- Distinguish between activity and outcomes, using frameworks from *High Output Management* to evaluate effectiveness.
- Build resilience through balance, renewal, and lifelong learning.
- Plan for succession, reinvention, and exit strategies that preserve professional legacy.

Introduction

Consultancy rewards those who can endure. Many practitioners enter the field with energy and enthusiasm, eager to build a reputation and secure early projects. Yet many find that their initial momentum is difficult to sustain, struggling to maintain energy or adapt to shifting markets after the first few years of practice. The demands of irregular hours, constant travel, and high-pressure assignments can lead to burnout if not managed carefully. At the same time, the consulting market evolves quickly, and those who do not continually refresh their knowledge risk becoming outdated.

The challenge is therefore twofold: sustaining energy while also sustaining relevance. The consultant who masters both builds a career that is not only financially viable but professionally fulfilling. This requires deliberate attention to how time, energy, and reputation are managed. It means distinguishing between activity and progress, recognising when reinvention is necessary, and embedding resilience into both personal practice and business structures.

Short-termism is the most common mistake. Consultants who focus only on the next contract or the immediate deliverable may succeed temporarily but risk undermining long-term credibility. Clients quickly detect when advice is transactional rather than strategic. A career built on activity without outcomes soon stalls, leaving the consultant working harder for diminishing returns. In contrast, those who play the long game invest in reputation, networks, and knowledge that compound over time, making each year of practice more valuable than the last.

This chapter examines the principles and practices that enable consultants to thrive across decades. It highlights the importance of measuring outcomes rather than activity, of protecting energy to avoid burnout, and of embracing lifelong learning and reinvention. It also considers how resilience, succession planning, and legacy form part of the long game. The consultant who thinks beyond the next project, and who approaches their career with discipline and foresight, is the one who will remain relevant, respected, and in demand.

Beyond Short-Term Wins

One of the most common traps in consultancy is the pursuit of short-term success at the expense of long-term positioning. Early victories can be seductive: a well-received report, a high-profile assignment, or a prestigious client contract. These moments bring satisfaction and credibility, but when treated as ends in themselves they create a cycle of short-termism that undermines sustained progress. The long game requires a different perspective, one that views each engagement not only as an opportunity but as a contribution to cumulative reputation and authority.

Short-term wins are necessary, particularly in the early stages of a career when credibility must be established and financial pressures are real. A consultant must demonstrate competence and deliver value quickly if they are to gain repeat work and referrals. The danger arises when the pursuit of immediate engagements becomes the default approach. Consultants who focus exclusively on winning the next project often neglect the slower, less visible work of building thought leadership, cultivating networks, and investing in professional development. Without these longer-term investments, their brand remains shallow and vulnerable to shifts in demand.

The market rewards those who are remembered, not just those who deliver. A consultant who provides an excellent service but leaves no lasting impression beyond the project report risks being forgotten once the engagement ends. In contrast, a consultant who positions each assignment within a broader narrative ensures that the impact extends beyond the immediate client. Over time, this creates compounding visibility: each project not only delivers value but also reinforces professional identity.

There is also a financial dimension. Consultants who chase short-term wins often compete on price, undercutting fees to secure contracts in crowded markets. This approach may provide revenue in the moment, but it erodes pricing power and makes it difficult to escape the perception of being a commodity. Clients accustomed to low-cost engagements rarely accept later arguments for premium fees. In contrast, consultants who prioritise long-term brand invest in positioning themselves as authorities whose value is judged by outcomes, not hours. This authority supports sustainable pricing, ensuring that fees rise with reputation rather than stagnating.

Short-termism can also distort professional judgement. Consultants under pressure to secure the next project may be tempted to overstate capabilities, promise unrealistic outcomes, or align too closely with client preferences to secure approval. While these tactics may deliver immediate contracts, they undermine credibility when expectations are not met. The long game demands proportionality and integrity: consultants must be willing to say no to work that falls outside their expertise or compromises their standards. In the moment, this can feel like a lost opportunity; in the long run, it strengthens reputation as a trusted adviser.

Another risk of short-term focus is professional stagnation. Consultants who spend all their time chasing and delivering immediate projects have little opportunity for renewal. They neglect time for study, reflection, or participation in professional forums. The consequence is that their expertise becomes dated, their insights predictable, and their contribution less compelling. Sustaining a career depends on deliberate allocation of time to development. Reading, training, writing, and engaging with peers may not bring immediate revenue, but they build the depth of expertise that sustains relevance.

The analogy of compound interest is useful. Just as small, consistent investments grow significantly over time, so too do consistent professional contributions. Publishing a single article may have limited effect; publishing regularly over a decade builds authority. Speaking once at a local conference may pass unnoticed; contributing consistently to regional or international forums creates recognition that endures. Short-term wins provide immediate gratification, but long-term positioning creates compounding returns that far outweigh the initial effort.

The discipline of looking beyond immediate projects is what differentiates enduring consultants from transient practitioners. Short-term wins are important milestones, but they should be treated as building blocks in a larger career narrative, not as the destination. Consultants who think strategically about how each engagement contributes to reputation, who invest consistently in visibility and learning, and who protect their integrity even under pressure, create brands that endure. Playing the long game means resisting the lure of short-term gratification in favour of cumulative reputation, authority, and trust.

Outcomes over Activity

Busy consultants are not always effective consultants. A calendar filled with client meetings, site visits, and draft reports may create the impression of progress, but without clear outcomes this activity risks becoming little more than effort without progress. The distinction between activity and results is central to the long game. Those who measure their value by how busy they appear burn energy without necessarily building credibility, authority, or long-term positioning. Those who focus on outcomes accumulate trust, reputation, and sustained relevance.

Andy Grove, in *High Output Management*, emphasised that output is the measure of managerial effectiveness, not the number of hours worked, or the number of tasks completed. The same principle applies in consultancy. Clients do not purchase effort; they purchase results. They want reduced risk, regulatory compliance, resilient systems, or strategic clarity. A report is valuable only insofar as it helps them achieve those outcomes. Consultants who understand this align their practice around measurable impact, ensuring that every engagement produces results that matter to the client and reinforce the consultant's brand.

The activity trap is a common pitfall. Consultants under pressure to demonstrate progress often produce excessive documentation, schedule unnecessary meetings, or pursue tasks that satisfy visible effort rather than substantive value. Clients may initially appreciate the activity, but over time they judge consultants by outcomes. A risk assessment that fills hundreds of pages but fails to identify actionable priorities will be forgotten; a concise, targeted analysis that helps the client achieve compliance or mitigate a major vulnerability will be remembered. The long game depends on building a reputation for outcomes, not for volume.

Focusing on outcomes requires clarity at the outset of engagements. Consultants must ensure that both they and the client understand what success looks like. This may involve defining specific deliverables, such as certification under a particular standard, or broader goals, such as improved organisational resilience. By framing assignments around agreed outcomes, consultants avoid drift and maintain focus. They also signal professionalism, reassuring clients that effort will be directed where it adds value.

Measuring outcomes is not always straightforward in security consultancy, where the value of prevention can be difficult to quantify. A successful outcome is often the absence of an incident, which may be invisible to decision-makers. To address this, consultants must develop proxy measures that demonstrate impact: reduced response times, improved detection rates, successful compliance audits, or enhanced staff confidence in procedures. These indicators provide tangible evidence that consulting interventions deliver results, even when major incidents are not the measure.

Outcome orientation also influences pricing and positioning. Consultants who sell activity such as hours worked or reports produced, are treated as suppliers. Their value is capped by the cost of labour and often subject to downward pressure. Consultants who sell outcomes like compliance achieved, risk reduced, or resilience enhanced, are treated as advisers. Their value is judged by the importance of the result, not the time it took to achieve. This distinction directly affects fees, authority, and client relationships. Playing the long game requires moving steadily towards outcome-based positioning, even if early engagements still involve activity-based billing.

Practical tools can reinforce outcome orientation. Consultants can establish key performance indicators (KPIs) for their own practice: the proportion of engagements leading to repeat work, the number of clients achieving compliance or certification, the measurable improvements in client resilience. They can also use outcome-based narratives when communicating with clients. Instead of reporting how many meetings were held or how many pages were written, they can highlight the progress towards the agreed goal. This reinforces the perception that the consultant delivers impact rather than effort.

The psychological shift is equally important. Many consultants derive satisfaction from being busy, equating a packed schedule with professional success. Yet over time, this creates exhaustion without necessarily building reputation. By contrast, consultants who focus on outcomes reserve their energy for high-value contributions, creating more space for reflection, learning, and renewal. They achieve more by doing less but ensuring that what they do is consequential. This discipline is what allows them to sustain careers over decades.

The key to maintaining success is recognising a simple principle: clients remember outcomes, not effort. They rarely recall how many hours a consultant worked, but they remember whether compliance was achieved, whether risks were mitigated, and whether resilience was improved. Consultants who focus on outcomes become trusted advisers; those who confuse activity with progress remain suppliers. By framing their practice around measurable impact, consultants not only enhance client value but also build the credibility and reputation that sustain a career over the long term.

Managing Energy and Avoiding Burnout

A consulting career places unique demands on energy. Long hours, constant travel, shifting time zones, and the pressure of advising clients on high-stakes issues can gradually deplete both physical and mental reserves. While enthusiasm can carry a consultant through the early years, without deliberate attention to sustainability the cumulative effect is exhaustion. Burnout is not only damaging to health; it erodes professional credibility. A consultant who arrives fatigued, distracted, or disengaged is unlikely to inspire confidence. Maintaining resilience requires managing energy as carefully as knowledge or reputation.

Burnout often arises not from a single crisis but from relentless pressure without renewal. The consultant who accepts every assignment, travels continuously, or works late into the night to meet unrealistic deadlines may sustain this for a period, but eventually performance deteriorates. Quality slips, errors increase, and the enthusiasm that once defined the consultant's brand is replaced by irritability or detachment. Clients may not recognise burnout by name, but they notice when a consultant's presence feels diminished. In a profession that depends on credibility, the cost is severe.

Managing energy begins with boundaries. Consultants must recognise that saying yes to every request is unsustainable. Selectivity is not a sign of weakness but of professionalism: it ensures that engagements undertaken receive the attention they deserve. Boundaries also extend to time. Scheduling recovery periods between major projects, limiting back-to-back travel, and protecting space for family or personal commitments allow consultants to sustain energy over decades rather than months.

Physical health is a foundation. Regular exercise, balanced nutrition, and adequate rest are not luxuries but necessities for long-term consulting careers. Travel can disrupt routines, but consultants who prioritise even modest practices like a short run, a disciplined approach to meals, or consistent sleep habits, build resilience. Neglecting health in pursuit of short-term productivity is self-defeating; the resulting fatigue diminishes both the quality of advice and the consultant's ability to engage effectively with clients.

Mental resilience is equally important. Consultancy exposes practitioners to complex risks, client anxieties, and sometimes adversarial environments. Without strategies for recovery, the mental load becomes overwhelming. Activities such as mindfulness, reflection, or simply maintaining hobbies outside work provide balance. Regular debriefs with trusted peers also help, allowing consultants to process experiences and gain perspective. Professional supervision or coaching can provide additional support, reinforcing resilience in the face of sustained pressure.

Managing energy also involves pacing work across the career. Early intensity is common, but consultants must learn to adjust rhythm over time. What is sustainable at 30 may not be sustainable at 50. Experienced consultants often shift from heavy operational involvement towards more strategic roles, using accumulated expertise to add value without the same physical demands. This transition is part of the long game, ensuring that careers adapt to changing personal capacities.

Technology can support energy management. Virtual meetings, collaboration platforms, and digital tools reduce the need for constant travel, preserving energy while maintaining client contact. While face-to-face engagement remains important, the pandemic demonstrated that remote consulting can be credible when used proportionately. Consultants who adopt blended models of delivery can extend their careers by reducing unnecessary strain.

There are dangers to avoid. One is equating busyness with success, wearing exhaustion as a badge of honour. Another is assuming that energy will recover naturally without deliberate effort. A further risk is ignoring early signs of burnout, such as declining enthusiasm, reduced concentration, or irritability. By the time these symptoms are obvious to clients, damage has already occurred. It is good practice is to treat energy as an asset to be managed: monitoring capacity, pacing commitments, and investing deliberately in renewal.

Sustaining a career depends on recognising that consulting is not only intellectual but also physical and emotional work. Sustaining performance depends on managing energy with the same discipline applied to projects or finances. By establishing boundaries, protecting health, building resilience, and pacing careers deliberately, consultants avoid burnout and preserve the presence, clarity, and credibility that define trusted advisers.

Lifelong Learning and Reinvention

Consultancy is a profession defined by change. New technologies, emerging threats, evolving regulations, and shifting client expectations mean that knowledge has a limited shelf life. What was authoritative advice a decade ago may today be obsolete or even misleading. Consultants who fail to update their expertise risk irrelevance, while those who commit to continuous learning remain valuable across decades. Lifelong learning is not an optional enhancement to consulting practice; it is the foundation of long-term relevance.

Learning begins with awareness. Consultants must remain alert to developments in their sectors, monitoring regulatory changes, technological trends, and shifts in geopolitical or environmental conditions. This requires deliberate investment of time. Reading professional journals, attending conferences, and engaging in continuous professional development programmes ensure that knowledge remains current. Many consultants neglect this in favour of billable work, but over the long game it is precisely this commitment to learning that differentiates those who endure from those who fade.

Formal learning has an important role. Certifications, postgraduate study, or executive education provide structured frameworks that deepen expertise. Security consultancy has a range of recognised credentials – CPP, PSP, CISSP, ISO lead auditor qualifications – each of which signals competence and provides access to networks of peers. Completing such programmes also demonstrates commitment to professional standards, reinforcing brand. Yet formal learning alone is insufficient. The pace of change means consultants must also cultivate informal learning habits: staying curious, questioning assumptions, and seeking lessons in every assignment.

Reinvention is the natural partner of lifelong learning. Consultants cannot simply accumulate knowledge; they must adapt their practice in response to what they learn. Reinvention may involve shifting focus from one sector to another, from technical design to strategic advisory, or from regional practice to international engagement. It may also involve adopting new methodologies or integrating adjacent disciplines, such as incorporating cyber resilience into physical security consultancy. Consultants who resist reinvention risk being trapped in niches that decline, while those who embrace it remain relevant in new markets.

Reinvention does not mean discarding past expertise. Rather, it involves reframing it for new contexts. A consultant who built their career in corporate real estate security may pivot towards data centres, highlighting transferable skills in access control, compliance, and continuity planning. Another who specialised in aviation may broaden into wider transport resilience, leveraging regulatory knowledge in a new domain. The long game is sustained not by abandoning what has been learned but by applying it creatively to emerging challenges.

There are practical strategies to support reinvention. Publishing is one. Consultants who write about new developments demonstrate adaptability and signal to the market that they are evolving. Strategic partnerships are another, allowing consultants to expand into adjacent fields by collaborating with specialists in complementary areas. Training and mentoring also support reinvention, as teaching others forces consultants to clarify and refresh their own knowledge. Each of these activities creates opportunities to reposition brand and extend relevance.

There are, however, traps. Some consultants chase every new trend, abandoning established expertise in pursuit of novelty. This dilutes credibility and creates the impression of opportunism. Others resist change altogether, clinging to familiar niches until demand evaporates. The best practice lies between building on established authority while adapting to new realities. Reinvention should be deliberate, informed by market analysis and aligned with core strengths, rather than reactive or indiscriminate.

Lifelong learning and reinvention also contribute to personal fulfilment. Consultancy can become repetitive if practitioners do not seek new challenges. Learning stimulates curiosity, while reinvention provides renewed purpose. Consultants who embrace both often sustain enthusiasm for longer, avoiding the fatigue that comes from delivering the same advice year after year. For many, this vitality becomes a brand in itself: clients recognise not only expertise but freshness of perspective, reinforcing the perception of a consultant who remains engaged and relevant.

The long game depends on the willingness to evolve. Consultants who commit to continuous learning and deliberate reinvention ensure that their expertise remains valued as contexts change. They avoid stagnation, adapt to new opportunities, and extend their influence beyond immediate niches. In a profession where yesterday's solutions are rarely sufficient for tomorrow's risks, learning and reinvention are essential; they are the essence of sustained relevance.

Building Resilience into Practice

Resilience is often discussed as a quality that organisations need to withstand disruption, but it is equally critical for individual consultants and their practices. A consulting career that lasts decades cannot rely solely on energy and expertise; it must be underpinned by structures and habits that allow the consultant to absorb shocks, adapt to change, and continue delivering value under pressure. Building resilience into practice ensures that careers are not derailed by downturns, personal challenges, or market shifts.

Resilience begins with diversification. Consultants who rely on a single client, sector, or service line expose themselves to unnecessary risk. A change in leadership, a downturn in a sector, or the emergence of new regulations can remove entire revenue streams overnight. By maintaining a mix of clients and a balance of project types, consultants create a buffer that allows them to weather fluctuations. Diversification does not mean dilution; it means ensuring that practice is broad enough to sustain income when conditions change, while still maintaining a clear identity.

Another dimension is financial resilience. Consultancy income is often irregular, with periods of intense activity followed by quieter intervals. Consultants who treat revenue as constant may find themselves unprepared for lean months. Establishing financial reserves, managing expenses conservatively, and building recurring income streams such as retainers or advisory roles all strengthen the ability to sustain practice through uncertainty. Financial resilience provides the stability needed to make long-term decisions rather than chasing short-term contracts out of necessity.

Resilience also requires the ability to share load. Consultants who insist on handling every task themselves limit capacity and increase vulnerability to burnout. Forming alliances with trusted peers, subcontractors, or boutique firms allows consultants to extend capability, scale to larger assignments, and maintain service even when personal capacity is stretched. These networks not only reduce personal strain but also reinforce credibility, demonstrating to clients that the consultant is connected, collaborative, and capable of mobilising expertise beyond their own.

Reputation resilience is another pillar. Consultants inevitably face challenges: projects that do not go as planned, disputes with clients, or shifting expectations. A strong reputation built on consistent delivery and integrity provides resilience in such moments. Clients are more likely to forgive occasional setbacks when they trust the consultant's overall credibility. Protecting reputation requires proactive communication, transparency when difficulties arise, and a consistent commitment to ethical standards. Integrity acts as a form of insurance, ensuring that a consultant's brand remains intact even when specific engagements are challenging.

Adaptability is central to resilience. Markets evolve, technologies change, and regulatory frameworks tighten. Consultants who view their methods as fixed become unable to adapt; those who continually refine approaches remain relevant. Embedding adaptability into practice means maintaining curiosity, testing new tools, and being open to feedback. It also means being willing to step back from outdated methods, even if they were once successful. Resilience is not about resisting change but absorbing it in ways that strengthen practice.

Personal resilience must not be overlooked. As explored earlier, energy management is fundamental to sustaining careers. Consultants who neglect health, relationships, or balance eventually find professional resilience undermined by personal fragility. Building resilience into practice therefore requires aligning work habits with personal well-being: protecting time for recovery, maintaining supportive networks outside work, and ensuring that consulting remains fulfilling rather than all-consuming. Clients are quick to detect fatigue or disengagement, and a consultant who projects balance and composure inspires more confidence than one who appears overstretched.

The lesson here is that resilience is not accidental; it must be designed into practice. Diversification, financial planning, collaborative networks, strong reputation, adaptability, and personal well-being are all elements that reinforce long-term stability. The consultant who builds these habits early creates a practice that can withstand disruption, sustain credibility, and continue delivering value even under pressure. Resilience is not only a client deliverable; it is the basis of a career that endures.

Sustained credibility depends on deliberate renewal. Consultants who measure outcomes instead of activity, manage energy as carefully as knowledge, and plan succession with foresight build careers that endure.

Succession and Exit Strategies

Every consulting career has a horizon. For some, this comes in the form of retirement; for others, it means transitioning into advisory, teaching, or non-executive roles. Yet many consultants approach this stage reactively, leaving succession and exit plans vague until circumstances force decisions. A long-term career strategy must address not only how to sustain practice but also how to hand it on, wind it down, or transform it into a new phase of contribution.

Succession is particularly important for boutique practices. Where capability is concentrated in one or two senior consultants, the departure of a founder can jeopardise the entire business. Clients may perceive the firm as inseparable from the individual, making continuity difficult. Effective succession planning requires deliberate steps to transfer authority, cultivate new leaders, and ensure that client relationships extend beyond one person. This may involve mentoring junior consultants, sharing visibility, and gradually shifting responsibility so that trust is built in the next generation.

For solo practitioners, succession may mean a different approach. Some choose to fold practices gracefully, closing projects and completing commitments before stepping away. Others transition into partnerships or mergers, bringing their expertise into a larger firm that can continue serving clients. Even independent consultants can think in terms of legacy: writing, teaching, or contributing to professional bodies ensures that their knowledge endures even if the practice itself does not.

Exit strategies must balance financial, professional, and personal considerations. Consultants who have built sustainable businesses may be able to sell their firms, monetising reputation, client base, and intellectual property. Others may design gradual step-down approaches, reducing hours while maintaining select clients. A common path is to transition towards roles that demand less operational energy but leverage accumulated expertise: advisory boards, non-executive directorships, academic appointments, or part-time mentoring. Each represents a way of preserving influence while adjusting workload.

Planning for exit also means protecting reputation at the final stage of a career. Clients remember the way consultants finish as much as how they begin. Exiting abruptly, leaving projects unfinished, or withdrawing without communication risks damaging years of credibility. It is better to manage transitions carefully: informing clients early, ensuring handovers are complete, and framing departure as part of a deliberate and thoughtful career progression.

Succession and exit planning also connect to personal fulfilment. Many consultants fear that leaving practice means loss of identity, as careers have often defined them for decades. Yet viewing succession and exit as a continuation, a transition into new forms of contribution, helps reframe the process positively. Teaching, mentoring, publishing, or advising allows consultants to remain engaged, ensuring that accumulated experience benefits the profession and society.

The long game requires seeing succession and exit not as endings but as stages of the same career. By planning deliberately, consultants ensure continuity for clients, opportunity for successors, and dignity for themselves. Legacy is not left to chance; it is the product of foresight, integrity, and contribution. Consultants who approach succession and exit strategically reinforce the credibility of their brand, extend their influence, and demonstrate that the values of resilience and foresight apply as much to their own careers as to the clients they advise.

Illustrative Example: The Consultant Who Lasted

A consultant who began their career in the late 1980s offers a clear illustration of what it means to play the long game. Initially trained in perimeter security, their early projects focused on transport hubs and ports. At the time, governments and private operators were investing heavily in new infrastructure, and opportunities were plentiful. Many of their peers thrived in the same space, but few remained active decades later. This consultant endured, not because of luck, but because of deliberate choices that emphasised sustainability, adaptability, and integrity.

From the outset, they treated each engagement not as an isolated project but as part of a career narrative. Reports were designed not only to meet contractual obligations but to give clients tools they could continue using after the consultant had moved on. This focus on outcomes rather than activity built trust and led to repeat work. Instead of chasing every opportunity, they cultivated a reputation for proportionality and practical solutions, reinforcing credibility with each assignment.

By the early 2000s, shifts in global trade and heightened security concerns changed the priorities of operators. Many consultants who specialised narrowly in perimeter defence or access control saw their practices stagnate. This consultant recognised the change early and repositioned. Drawing on transferable expertise in resilience and regulatory compliance, they moved into advising on aviation and cross-border security, areas that were rapidly gaining strategic importance. To support this reinvention, they invested in new learning, participated in international working groups, and published articles on aligning operational security with emerging global standards. The result was a brand refreshed to meet evolving demand.

They also managed their energy carefully. Instead of accepting every assignment, they limited extended deployments and kept international travel within sustainable cycles, ensuring space for recovery and family life. Over time, they shifted from heavy operational involvement to more strategic advisory roles, mentoring junior consultants to handle detailed fieldwork. This not only preserved their own sustainability but created a succession pathway, ensuring continuity for clients.

By the 2010s, they had become recognised as a thought leader in transport and border resilience, contributing to standards committees and serving on international advisory panels. Clients sought them not just for audits but for strategic guidance and credibility with regulators. Their career demonstrated the compounding effect of long-term thinking: each reinvention built on past expertise, each outcome-focused engagement strengthened reputation, and each ethical decision reinforced trust.

Today, they are semi-retired, focusing on mentoring and teaching. Their legacy is not only a body of work but also a reputation for adaptability and integrity. The example in this story shows that by focusing on outcomes, managing energy, embracing lifelong learning, and planning succession deliberately, consultants can sustain relevance and influence across decades.

Practice Guide

Consultancy is a long game, measured not by the volume of projects but by the ability to sustain relevance, energy, and credibility across decades. Success depends less on short bursts of activity and more on building a career that can adapt, endure, and continue to command trust.

The risks are well known but easy to overlook. Some consultants chase immediate wins, prioritising revenue over reputation. Others confuse effort with progress, filling calendars and producing excessive documentation that adds little long-term value. Burnout is a constant danger, particularly when boundaries and health are neglected. Complacency can be just as damaging, with consultants assuming that past expertise will always remain current. A further risk lies in neglecting succession or exit planning, leaving both reputation and client continuity exposed.

Good practice turns these risks into strengths. Playing the long game means focusing on outcomes that deliver measurable value, managing energy with discipline, and maintaining balance across a career. It requires continuous learning and timely reinvention to stay relevant, coupled with adaptability to respond to shifting markets. Resilience must be built into practice through diversification, financial stability, and strong professional networks. Succession planning and carefully managed exits, approached with foresight and integrity, allow consultants to step back on their own terms while leaving behind continuity and legacy.

The long game is ultimately about stewardship. Consultants who view their career as a cumulative narrative, rather than a collection of isolated projects, create reputations that compound over time. Every outcome delivered, every ethical decision made, and every reinvention embraced strengthens a professional identity that endures. Playing the long game is less about extending years of work than about sustaining trust, influence, and relevance.

Chapter 27 – Mentoring and Giving Back

Consultancy is not only about personal success but about sustaining the field for those who follow. Every consultant benefits from the knowledge, standards, and networks created by others, and each experienced practitioner has the opportunity, and responsibility, to contribute in return. Mentoring, coaching, and sponsorship offer direct ways to guide the next generation, while contributions to associations, standards bodies, and academia help ensure that insight is shared and accessible beyond individual careers.

Giving back also renews the consultant. It brings fresh perspective through contact with emerging practitioners, reinforces credibility by demonstrating authority, and offers satisfaction through service to something larger than individual achievement. Legacy is measured not in completed projects but in influence shared and knowledge passed on. This chapter explores how mentoring, knowledge transfer, and contribution to professional communities strengthen both individual careers and the wider consulting discipline.

By the end of this chapter, you will be able to:

- Recognise the role of mentoring in sustaining the profession and supporting future consultants.
- Differentiate between mentoring, coaching, and sponsorship, and apply each appropriately.
- Develop effective strategies for knowledge transfer and capacity building.
- Understand the value of contributing to professional associations, standards bodies, and academia.
- Frame legacy not only as personal reputation but as lasting impact on the consulting community and clients.

Introduction

Every consultant builds on the work of others. The standards followed, the methods applied, and the professional bodies that set expectations are the product of contributions made by earlier generations. To practise consultancy without acknowledging this heritage risks treating the occupation as a transaction rather than a vocation. A sustainable consulting career therefore requires not only personal development but also a commitment to giving back to individuals, organisations, and to the sector as a whole.

Mentoring plays a central role. It is one of the most direct ways experienced consultants can support those entering the field. By sharing lessons learned, offering guidance on challenges, and providing perspective on career decisions, mentors accelerate the development of new practitioners. The benefits, however, are not one-sided. Mentors themselves gain renewed perspective, sharpen their own understanding, and reinforce their professional identity by articulating the principles that guide their work.

Contribution extends beyond mentoring individuals. Consultants can support the industry through participation in associations, contributions to standards bodies, and engagement with academia. These activities help capture best practice, preserve knowledge, and raise the overall credibility of the field. Consultants who contribute in this way extend their influence beyond client projects, shaping the environment in which future work will take place.

Legacy is the connecting theme. Consultants who think only of their own careers may achieve personal success but leave little behind when they retire. Those who mentor, publish, teach, or support professional organisations ensure that their expertise endures. In doing so, they reinforce the credibility of the profession itself and demonstrate that consultancy is not just a career but a community.

This chapter explores the many ways consultants can give back, from one-to-one mentoring to shaping global standards. It shows that contribution is not an afterthought but a defining element of the long game, ensuring that expertise is passed on, the profession is strengthened, and legacy is secured.

The Role of Mentoring in Consultancy

Mentoring is often described as a gift of time and experience, and in consultancy it plays a particularly significant role. Unlike corporate careers with formal hierarchies and structured progression, consultancy is often fluid, independent, and entrepreneurial. New entrants may have strong technical expertise but little understanding of how to navigate client relationships, manage projects, or sustain a career over decades. Mentoring provides the bridge between technical skill and professional practice, ensuring that knowledge is transferred, mistakes are avoided, and the profession remains strong.

For the person being mentored, the benefits are obvious. Having access to an experienced consultant offers guidance on both technical and professional challenges. A mentor can help interpret regulatory requirements, advise on client dynamics, or provide perspective on ethical dilemmas. This accelerates learning by turning another's experience into practical insight, reducing the trial-and-error that can otherwise slow progress. Perhaps more importantly, mentoring provides encouragement. Consulting can be isolating, particularly for those working independently or in small firms. Knowing that someone experienced has faced similar challenges and found solutions helps build confidence and resilience.

For the mentor, the benefits are equally significant. Teaching forces clarity. By explaining processes, decision frameworks, or lessons learned, mentors refine their own thinking and reinforce the principles that guide their practice. Engagement with those being mentored also provides fresh perspective, exposing mentors to new ideas, emerging technologies, and different ways of seeing challenges. Many senior consultants report that mentoring reinvigorates their careers, giving renewed purpose and reminding them of the enthusiasm they had when starting out. The act of giving back also strengthens a consultant's professional identity, demonstrating not only expertise but commitment to the profession.

Mentoring also supports continuity in client service. Senior consultants nearing the later stages of their careers can ensure that knowledge, methods, and relationships are passed on to younger practitioners. This benefits clients, who gain assurance that expertise will not disappear when an individual retires. It also strengthens consultancy firms, providing a pathway for succession and stability. Without mentoring, knowledge risks being lost, and firms may struggle to maintain standards once key individuals depart.

The role of mentoring is not limited to one-to-one relationships. Group mentoring, peer circles, and structured programmes all offer ways to scale its impact. Professional associations often provide platforms where experienced practitioners can mentor those entering the profession, ensuring that guidance extends beyond personal networks. For smaller firms, internal mentoring systems can create continuity and reduce reliance on external recruitment to maintain capability.

The nature of consultancy also means that mentoring must address more than technical competence. It must include guidance on business development, networking, personal resilience, and ethical decision-making. People often seek advice not only on how to deliver projects but also on how to manage energy, position their brand, and balance professional and personal life. In this sense, mentoring supports the holistic development of consultants, preparing them not only to complete assignments but to build sustainable careers.

There are risks. Mentoring that becomes overly directive risks disempowering the person being mentored, turning guidance into control. The purpose of mentoring is to support growth, not to create dependence. Another risk is neglect: agreeing to mentor but failing to provide time or attention. This undermines trust and may damage the recipient's confidence further. Good practice requires mentors to be deliberate, committing time, listening actively, and focusing on the person's goals rather than projecting their own ambitions.

The wider impact of mentoring is cultural. Professions that foster mentoring cultivate shared identity, collaboration, and high standards. In consultancy, where competition can be intense, mentoring reminds practitioners that the profession as a whole benefits when knowledge is shared. Experienced consultants who mentor reinforce the credibility of the field, ensuring that clients encounter practitioners who are better prepared and more resilient. This strengthens not only individual careers but the collective standing of consultancy as a discipline.

Mentoring in consultancy is both a professional responsibility and a personal opportunity. It benefits recipients by accelerating growth, mentors by reinforcing purpose, and clients by ensuring continuity. It sustains the profession by preserving knowledge and raising standards. Mentoring sits at the heart of consultancy, ensuring that expertise and influence continue through those who follow.

Mentoring, Coaching, and Sponsorship

Mentoring is often spoken of as if it were a single practice, but in reality, it overlaps with two other distinct roles: coaching and sponsorship. Each has a place in consultancy, and understanding the differences is essential for both mentors and mentees. Confusing these roles can create unrealistic expectations or lead to relationships that fail to deliver value. Clear distinctions ensure that consultants provide the right kind of support at the right stage of a career.

- Mentoring is the broadest and most developmental of the three. It focuses on long-term growth, career guidance, and the transfer of experience. A mentor provides perspective, helps the person being mentored avoid common pitfalls, and offers encouragement during difficult moments. The emphasis is not on solving immediate problems but on shaping the recipient's approach to the profession. A mentoring conversation may cover how to balance client demands with personal well-being, how to think strategically about positioning in the market, or how to sustain integrity in the face of commercial pressure. The relationship is often informal and evolves over time, based on trust and mutual respect.

- Coaching is narrower and more task-focused. A coach helps the individual improve performance in specific areas: delivering better presentations, writing more effective reports, or managing client meetings with confidence. Coaching tends to be shorter in duration, structured around goals, and evaluated by measurable improvements. For consultants, coaching can be invaluable at key transition points, such as moving from technical specialist to project leader, or from back-office analysis to client-facing roles. While mentors guide overall career development, coaches address particular skills or behaviours. Both are important, but they serve different purposes.

- Sponsorship is different again. A sponsor is not primarily a teacher or adviser but an advocate. Sponsors use their own influence and networks to create opportunities for those they support. In consultancy, this might mean recommending a younger colleague for a project, introducing them to clients, or nominating them for professional recognition. Sponsorship is often less visible than mentoring or coaching, but its impact can be profound. Where mentoring and coaching focus on building capability, sponsorship focuses on opening doors.

Understanding these distinctions helps avoid confusion. Someone seeking guidance but expecting a sponsor to provide detailed skill development may be disappointed, while a consultant offering mentoring when advocacy is what's needed may miss the chance to make a real difference. Ethical clarity also matters. Sponsors should base their support on proven ability, not personal loyalty, and mentors and coaches must avoid overstepping, giving guidance that builds independence rather than dependence.

The three roles are not mutually exclusive. A senior consultant may begin as a mentor, offering broad advice, then act as a coach on specific challenges, and then sponsor the recipient by recommending them for opportunities. The progression often reflects the growth of trust and the development of competence. Early in a relationship, a person may need reassurance and perspective. Later, as capability grows, they may benefit more from targeted skill development. When ready to take on greater responsibility, they benefit most from active advocacy.

For mentors, recognising when to switch roles is part of the responsibility. A good mentor does not attempt to be all things at once but identifies whether the moment calls for encouragement, instruction, or advocacy. For recipients, clarity about what they need is equally important. Asking for sponsorship when one requires coaching may strain a relationship; asking for coaching when what is really needed is mentoring may lead to disappointment.

There are risks. Sponsorship without merit can create perceptions of favouritism, damaging credibility for both sponsor and protégé. Coaching delivered without sensitivity can become directive, undermining confidence rather than building it. Mentoring without boundaries can slip into over-involvement, blurring professional lines. Good practice requires clarity, honesty, and proportionality. Each role must be exercised with awareness of its limits and with respect for the independence of the recipient.

In consultancy, where careers are often less structured than in corporate environments, these roles are especially important. Mentoring provides guidance in navigating ambiguity, coaching strengthens the skills needed to perform effectively, and sponsorship ensures that capable individuals gain access to opportunities they might otherwise miss. Together they form a continuum of support that sustains the profession, ensuring that talent is not wasted and that experience is passed on.

The consultant who engages deliberately in all three roles contributes more than immediate advice: they shape the future of the profession. By mentoring, they preserve knowledge; by coaching, they sharpen performance; and by sponsoring, they ensure that opportunities flow to those ready to step forward. Each role matters, and when exercised with integrity, they together represent one of the most enduring legacies a consultant can leave.

Knowledge Transfer and Capacity Building

Knowledge is the foundation of consultancy, but much of it is unspoken – built up through experience, shaped by practice, and often held in people's minds rather than written down in formal systems. Without deliberate effort, this knowledge risks being lost when consultants move on, retire, or shift focus. For a profession that depends on expertise, the transfer of knowledge and the building of capacity are essential not only for client value but also for the sustainability of consultancy itself.

Knowledge transfer begins at the level of individual projects. Consultants often deliver their final reports that summarise findings and recommendations, but unless the client organisation internalises the reasoning behind those conclusions, the knowledge remains external and perishable. More effective practice involves embedding lessons through workshops, debriefs, and joint analysis sessions. By involving client teams in the reasoning process, consultants ensure that knowledge is retained, not just results. This strengthens client capacity and reduces dependency, reinforcing the consultant's reputation as a trusted adviser rather than a vendor of documents.

Within consultancy firms, capacity building is equally important. Experienced consultants carry insights into how to manage client relationships, deliver under pressure, and interpret complex regulations. Unless these lessons are recorded, they disappear when individuals leave. Firms that build structured processes for knowledge capture through project debriefs, lessons-learned exercises, and knowledge repositories, create institutional memory. Such systems allow newer consultants to learn from past work, accelerate their development, and avoid repeating mistakes. Over time, this collective knowledge becomes a differentiator, demonstrating to clients that the firm offers not just individuals but an accumulated base of expertise.

Unspoken knowledge requires more than documents to transfer. Apprenticeship-style learning, where less experienced consultants shadow senior colleagues, remains one of the most effective methods. Observing how a senior consultant manages a tense client meeting, responds to unforeseen challenges, or frames recommendations provides lessons that no manual can convey. Structured mentoring and pairing systems embed this approach into practice, ensuring that capacity grows systematically rather than informally.

For independent consultants, knowledge transfer can still be deliberate. Publishing articles, contributing to professional standards, or presenting at conferences allows experience to be captured and shared beyond immediate projects. Even where no firm exists to inherit knowledge, the wider profession benefits, and the consultant's legacy is strengthened. Contributing to the development of best practice not only helps others but also enhances visibility and authority, creating reciprocal benefits.

Capacity building also extends to clients. Effective consultants recognise that their role is not only to solve problems but to strengthen the client's ability to solve them in future. This may involve training programmes, tabletop exercises, or the creation of internal guidelines tailored to the client's context. Such contributions elevate the consultant from problem solver to enabler, building trust and increasing the likelihood of long-term relationships. Clients value consultants who leave them more capable, not more dependent.

Technology provides new tools for knowledge transfer. Collaboration platforms, digital knowledge bases, and online training modules allow consultants to share insights more systematically and at greater scale. Artificial intelligence can help organise large volumes of project data into accessible formats. Yet technology is only as effective as the culture that surrounds it. Consultants must encourage habits of recording, sharing, and updating information, ensuring that digital tools support human practices rather than replace them.

However, there are drawbacks. One is the reluctance to share knowledge out of fear that it reduces personal value. In reality, consultants who hoard expertise often limit their influence, as their insights remain invisible beyond immediate projects. Another risk is shallow knowledge transfer, where a project ends with a simple checklist exercise that does little to help lessons stick. True capacity building requires engagement, explanation, and adaptation to the recipient's needs. It also requires humility, recognising that knowledge is most valuable when it empowers others rather than when it remains closely held.

Knowledge transfer and capacity building are acts of responsibility. They ensure that expertise outlives the individuals who hold it, strengthen clients to face future challenges, and elevate the standing of the profession as a whole. Consultants who commit to these practices demonstrate that they see consultancy not as a transaction but as a contribution to resilience, both within client organisations and across the wider field. For those playing the long game, such contributions are among the most enduring legacies.

Professional maturity is measured by contribution. Mentoring, knowledge transfer, and participation in standards turn experience into shared capability – strengthening both individual legacy and the profession itself.

Contributing to the Profession

Security consultancy operates within a profession shaped by shared standards, ethical frameworks, and collective reputation. The credibility of each consultant rises or falls with the reputation of the profession as a whole. For this reason, contributing to the wider field is more than an act of generosity; it helps strengthen the environment in which everyone works. By engaging with associations, standards bodies, and wider professional debates, consultants not only give back but also build authority and ensure that their influence extends beyond individual assignments.

Professional associations provide the most visible platform for contribution. Organisations such as ASIS International and the United Kingdom's Security Institute offer opportunities to shape practice, engage with peers, and raise standards. Membership alone signals commitment, but active involvement creates lasting impact. Serving on committees, writing for association journals, or presenting at conferences demonstrates authority and positions consultants as recognised voices in the field. Over time, these contributions enhance visibility, generate networks, and reinforce brand.

Standards-setting bodies and regulatory consultations represent another avenue for contribution. Security is a field shaped by extensive regulation, from physical protection standards to governance frameworks like data protection, cyber security, and resilience legislation. Consultants who participate in shaping these standards ensure that practical experience informs policy. Their insights help align requirements with real-world conditions, making compliance more meaningful and effective. Involvement at this level also places consultants in positions of influence, ensuring that their names are associated with the frameworks clients must follow. This not only strengthens credibility but demonstrates a willingness to contribute to the public good.

Publishing is a further form of professional contribution. Articles in peer-reviewed journals, thought pieces in industry magazines, and chapters in edited volumes all extend a consultant's influence beyond their immediate clients. These publications collate knowledge, disseminate best practice, and ensure that lessons are shared widely rather than remaining confined to individual projects. Publishing also creates a record of expertise that endures beyond individual careers, reinforcing legacy. For the consultant, writing brings clarity to their thinking, while it adds to the collective pool of knowledge for the wider field.

Participation in conferences and forums complements publishing. Speaking at events provides an opportunity to share insights directly, engage in debate, and connect with practitioners across regions and sectors. Unlike promotional marketing, these contributions are evaluated by substance: audiences quickly recognise whether presentations offer genuine learning or thinly veiled advertising. Consultants who consistently provide thoughtful, practical, and relevant contributions are remembered, respected, and often sought out for collaboration.

Contributing to the profession also involves mentoring at scale. While one-to-one mentoring supports individual careers, involvement in structured programmes run by associations allows consultants to guide cohorts of emerging professionals. Such programmes extend the reach of mentoring and signal commitment to the future of the profession. For consultants later in their careers, participation in these schemes ensures that accumulated experience is passed on, not lost.

The benefits of contributing extend in multiple directions. Consultants gain visibility and authority, clients benefit from more robust standards and better-prepared practitioners, and the profession as a whole gains credibility. Contributions also reinforce ethical standing. By serving the profession rather than only personal interest, consultants demonstrate integrity and responsibility, qualities that clients value in high-stakes engagements.

There are, however, further pitfalls to avoid. Contribution must be substantive. Consultants who join associations but contribute little, or who publish self-promotional pieces lacking depth, undermine their own credibility. Another risk is overcommitment: agreeing to multiple committees or publications without the time to engage fully. This spreads effort thin, dilutes impact, and risks disappointing peers. Good practice requires selectivity by focusing on forums where expertise is most relevant and where contributions can be sustained with quality.

Contributing to the profession is a form of stewardship. It ensures that consultancy remains credible, that standards evolve in line with practice, and that knowledge is shared for the benefit of all. Consultants who engage in this way extend their influence beyond individual projects, shaping the profession itself. For those committed to the profession, such contributions represent one of the clearest ways to give back by strengthening not only their own reputation but the collective credibility on which every consultant depends.

Academia and Teaching

Teaching has always been one of the most enduring ways for consultants to give back. Universities, professional schools, and executive education programmes increasingly draw on practitioners to bring real-world insight into the classroom. Contributing to academia is not just about personal reputation; it is about capturing and sharing knowledge, shaping the development of future practitioners, and bridging the gap between theory and practice.

Academia benefits from the involvement of consultants because it grounds abstract frameworks in real-life experience. Students studying risk management, security policy, or organisational resilience often learn from textbooks and case studies, but hearing directly from practitioners adds depth and relevance. A consultant can illustrate how regulatory frameworks are applied in practice, how board-level decisions are influenced by security considerations, or how theoretical models of resilience are adapted to the realities of critical infrastructure. Such contributions demystify the consulting profession and inspire students to see the field as both rigorous and impactful.

Teaching provides renewal. Preparing to lecture or supervise students forces reflection and clarity. Explaining methods and reasoning to learners compels consultants to articulate ideas that may have become instinctive in practice. In this way, teaching sharpens professional thinking while ensuring that expertise does not remain tacit. Engagement with students also exposes consultants to fresh perspectives and emerging concerns, keeping them attuned to how new generations interpret risk, technology, and professional responsibility.

Executive education and professional development programmes offer additional opportunities. Many universities run short courses for mid-career professionals, and industry bodies develop certification programmes that depend on experienced consultants as instructors. In these contexts, consultants are not only teaching theory but also equipping peers and clients with the skills to improve performance. This has a multiplier effect: by teaching others, consultants extend their influence beyond individual projects, shaping how entire organisations approach security and resilience.

Academic publishing complements teaching. Contributing to peer-reviewed journals or co-authoring with academic colleagues ensures that consultancy experience is recorded in rigorous, accessible formats. This process can be demanding, as it requires adapting practical insights into scholarly language and evidence-based argument. Yet the reward is significant: published research endures as part of the academic record, reinforcing the legitimacy of consultancy as a field of study as well as practice. Consultants who engage with this process enhance both their own credibility and the academic standing of the profession.

There are challenges. Academia values rigour, evidence, and theoretical grounding, while consultancy often prioritises speed, pragmatism, and client-specific outcomes. Consultants must balance these expectations, ensuring that their contributions are both credible and relevant. Time is another constraint. Teaching and publishing require preparation and discipline, which can be difficult to balance alongside client commitments. Consultants who contribute meaningfully to academia do so by treating it not as an occasional activity but as an integral part of their professional identity.

Cultural sensitivity is also important. In some regions, academic institutions expect formal qualifications and structured research output before practitioners are accepted as instructors. Consultants must respect these traditions while demonstrating the value of practical insight. Good practice involves collaboration: working with academics to co-design courses, combining scholarly frameworks with real-world examples. This partnership approach enriches both sides, ensuring that students receive education that is rigorous and relevant.

The involvement of consultants in academia helps close the gap between theory and practice. It ensures that students are exposed not only to abstract models but also to the practical realities of delivering advice under pressure, managing client relationships, and sustaining careers. For individual consultants, teaching provides legacy: a way of embedding experience into the education of others and reinforcing the credibility of consultancy as a discipline.

Academia and teaching represent one of the most powerful ways to give back. They allow consultants to influence future generations, capture lessons learned, and sustain the relevance of the field. While demanding, the rewards extend beyond personal satisfaction. They strengthen the bridge between practice and theory, ensuring that security consultancy evolves not only as a career but as a field of knowledge.

Legacy and Long-Term Contribution

Every consulting career eventually reaches a stage where questions of legacy become unavoidable. Legacy is not about self-promotion or nostalgia; it is about what endures when the consultant has stepped away from day-to-day practice. For some, legacy is found in the people they have mentored, for others in the standards they helped shape or the methods they developed. However it is defined, legacy is an essential part of the consultant's career, ensuring that years of experience contribute to the profession long after individual projects have been completed.

Legacy can take many forms. At its most immediate, it lies in the influence consultants have on individuals. A person mentored who builds a successful career guided by early encouragement represents a living continuation of that consultant's impact. In this way, legacy is multiplied: each new practitioner carries forward not only their own experience but also the lessons inherited from those who supported them.

At a broader level, legacy is created through contribution to institutions. Consultants who participate in professional associations, standards bodies, or regulatory consultations embed their influence in the structures that guide the profession. A clause in a standard, a methodology adopted by an association, or a framework taught in training courses can trace its roots back to the contributions of experienced practitioners. These legacies are often invisible in day-to-day practice but continue to shape behaviour and expectations across time.

Publishing also creates enduring legacy. Books, articles, and white papers record insights in ways that survive beyond careers. A consultant who writes with clarity and authority not only strengthens their own brand but also leaves behind a body of knowledge that others can use. For younger consultants, these works become valuable resources; for the wider field, they form a growing collection that captures and preserves experience. Writing is demanding, but its permanence ensures that contributions are not lost.

Legacy is also about the way consultants are remembered by clients. A practice built on integrity, proportionality, and reliability leaves reputational capital that endures. Clients may forget the details of specific projects, but they remember the consultant who brought clarity in moments of uncertainty, who upheld standards under pressure, or who helped them achieve resilience when it mattered most. This reputational legacy enhances not only the consultant's name but also the credibility of the profession.

There are traps to avoid. Chasing legacy for personal glory weakens credibility and can overshadow genuine achievements. Consultants who prioritise recognition over substance often leave little of lasting value. Others neglect legacy entirely, focusing solely on immediate engagements. Without deliberate effort, knowledge and insight disappear when individuals retire, weakening the profession as a whole. The best practice is to view legacy as service: not as a monument to the self but as a contribution to the community.

Legacy in consultancy is the culmination of a career lived with foresight, integrity, and contribution. It reflects the principle that the profession is larger than any one individual and that experience is most valuable when shared. Consultants who think consciously about legacy throughout their careers by mentoring, collating knowledge, contributing to institutions, and practising with integrity ensure that their influence endures. In doing so, they demonstrate that consultancy is not just a career of individual achievements but a vocation with lasting impact on people, organisations, and society.

Illustrative Example: Passing the Torch

A senior consultant nearing the end of a long career in critical infrastructure security recognised that his greatest contribution would not be the projects completed under his leadership but the people he had helped to develop. Having begun in government service before moving into consultancy, he had accumulated decades of experience, from designing protective measures for power stations to advising on national resilience frameworks. As retirement approached, he deliberately shifted focus from project delivery to mentoring and professional contribution.

Within his firm, he began pairing junior consultants with senior staff on every assignment. Rather than reserving client presentations for himself, he encouraged emerging practitioners to take the lead, guiding them beforehand and debriefing afterwards. This approach slowed immediate delivery but accelerated development, ensuring that younger consultants gained confidence in front of clients. Over time, several of these younger consultants became recognised project leads in their own right, creating continuity for the firm and reassurance for clients.

Outside the firm, he committed significant time to professional associations. He chaired a standards committee within a regional body, contributing to the drafting of new guidelines on resilience for utilities. His experience brought credibility, while his collaborative approach ensured that younger members of the committee felt valued and able to contribute. These guidelines later became reference points across the industry, embedding his influence in a framework that would endure long after his retirement.

He also devoted energy to publishing. Having written sparingly during the busiest years of his career, he spent his later years collecting lessons learned in articles and teaching materials. These writings provided clarity on practical methods for integrating physical and cyber security, drawn directly from decades of consulting. By publishing them, he ensured that future practitioners had access to insights that might otherwise have been lost.

When he eventually stepped back, the transition was smooth. Clients were already familiar with his successors, the profession had benefited from his contributions to standards, and the wider community had access to his published work. His legacy was not centred on his name but on the continuity he had enabled.

This example shows that by deliberately mentoring successors, engaging in professional associations, and sharing knowledge systematically, consultants can pass the torch effectively. Such choices ensure that their influence extends beyond individual projects and careers, strengthening both their organisations and the profession.

Practice Guide

Consultancy is not only about personal success but about stewardship: the responsibility to pass on knowledge, strengthen others, and leave the field in better shape than before. Contribution takes many forms, from mentoring and coaching to teaching and participation in standards and associations. Each reinforces the idea that a lasting career is measured not just by personal achievement but by influence shared with others.

The risks are well known but easy to overlook. Some turn mentoring into control, directing rather than guiding, or fail to follow through on commitments once made. Others blur roles, offering advice when advocacy is needed or seeking visibility rather than meaningful contribution. Knowledge transfer can become a formality, reduced to paperwork that does little to help learning take place. At a wider level, giving back can drift into self-promotion, where personal brand overtakes genuine service. Legacy pursued for recognition rather than impact risks weakening the credibility it aims to secure.

Best practice rests on authenticity and purpose. Mentoring should encourage independence, helping others develop confidence and judgement. Coaching sharpens specific skills, while responsible sponsorship opens doors for those ready to advance. Knowledge sharing must be structured and practical, embedding lessons within client teams and consulting firms alike. Contribution to associations, standards, and academia ensures that insight influences the wider field, while teaching renews understanding and passes on experience in lasting form. Legacy grows not from self-promotion but from strengthening people, methods, and standards that endure.

The long game of consultancy is only complete when expertise extends beyond the individual. Those who mentor, publish, teach, and contribute build continuity and resilience, ensuring that knowledge outlives careers. Legacy in this sense is not an afterthought but the natural result of a life's work carried out with integrity, foresight, and generosity.

With this, Part 5 draws to a close. The chapters together have shown how to build, sustain, and pass on a consulting career from understanding markets to developing brand, from playing the long game to guiding others. They complete the arc of the consultant's journey, reinforcing the idea that expertise achieves its greatest value when it endures beyond the person who holds it.

Reflections – The Consultant's Career

Part 5 has explored the consultant's career as a continuum rather than a series of assignments. It has addressed the inward-facing dimension of consultancy: the endurance, identity, and integrity that allow a professional to practise credibly and sustainably over time. Whereas earlier parts of this book examined skills, tools, and delivery in the field, this final part has focused on the consultant themselves: how they build, protect, and renew the capacity to serve others with clarity and purpose across a lifetime of practice.

Chapter 23 established that no career exists in isolation from its market. It explored how consultants position themselves amid global forces, regional variations, and shifting sectors. The lesson was that technical expertise alone is insufficient: to remain relevant, consultants must understand where demand arises, how it changes, and how their services create value within those dynamics. Awareness of market cycles, niches, and barriers to entry is not commercial trivia but professional survival.

Chapter 24 examined the structural choices that define a consultant's professional life: freelance, boutique, or large-firm practice. Each model offers opportunity and risk. Independence brings freedom but volatility; boutiques provide focus and collective strength but demand leadership; large firms offer reach and stability but constrain autonomy. The central message was that sustainability depends on alignment: choosing the environment that matches one's values, appetite for risk, and stage of life, and revisiting that alignment as circumstances evolve.

Chapter 25 turned to professional brand – the outward signal of credibility and trust. It showed that brand is not image but substance made visible. Identity, thought leadership, and ethical consistency combine to create authority that endures beyond single projects. Visibility without authenticity corrodes credibility; integrity expressed consistently builds it. A strong brand multiplies impact, allowing consultants to influence clients, shape markets, and lead debates rather than merely join them.

Chapter 26 extended the perspective across decades. The long game of consultancy demands energy management, continuous learning, and the capacity to reinvent. Consultants who confuse activity with progress or chase short-term wins at the expense of credibility erode their own foundations. Those who pace their careers, measure outcomes, and invest in renewal sustain both relevance and health. The chapter's central argument that endurance is a discipline tied back to the foundations of resilience and foresight first introduced in Part 1.

Chapter 27 reframed consultancy as stewardship. Mentoring, teaching, contributing to standards, and supporting professional communities are not optional gestures but the means by which the field itself survives. Knowledge has little value if it ends with the consultant who holds it. Legacy is therefore not about recognition but continuity: passing on expertise, strengthening others, and leaving the profession more credible than it was found.

Taken together, these chapters show that sustaining a consulting career requires balance across five dimensions: market awareness, structural alignment, visible integrity, managed endurance, and shared legacy. Each reinforces the others. Market insight provides direction; the right operating model provides stability; brand provides recognition; resilience provides longevity; and contribution provides meaning. To neglect any one of these is to weaken the whole.

This final part also provides a vantage point from which to view the entire book. Part 1 defined the consultant's identity and ethics; Part 2 equipped them with analytical tools; Part 3 demonstrated how those tools are applied in live engagements; Part 4 extended practice to complex, high-stakes, and emerging contexts; and Part 5 has completed the arc by showing how to sustain the person behind the practice. Together, these parts trace the evolution of the consultant from novice to expert, from technician to adviser, from individual practitioner to steward of a profession.

The closing reflection is simple but fundamental: consultancy is not a role, a project, or a brand – it is a discipline of thought and conduct sustained over time. Its success depends on clarity of purpose, ethical independence, proportionality of response, and the humility to keep learning. The true measure of a consultant is not the number of projects delivered but the integrity with which they are delivered, and the influence that endures once they are done.

This book therefore ends where consultancy truly begins: with the individual consultant, equipped not just with methods and models but with identity, resilience, and purpose. When these are sustained, the profession itself is sustained, and the value it creates continues long after the report is written and the engagement has ended.

Reflections from Practice

Looking back across the years, I realise this book isn't just a manual, it's a map of where I've been. Every principle, model, and mindset described here comes from projects that tested them, clients who challenged them, and teams that refined them. In that sense, this is less a book about security than it is a reflection of a career spent trying to make complex things work in the real world.

When I first set up CHQ with my business partners, I wanted it to be more than another consultancy. The goal was to build a niche company – small enough to stay agile, selective enough to work on projects that mattered, and independent enough to speak honestly. Later, with 323 Ltd., I took that same spirit into freelance form: a single practitioner's pursuit of mastery. Each step reaffirmed something I had suspected from the start – that genuine expertise comes not from scale, but from clarity of purpose.

Over time, I've noticed an interesting pattern. Clients often pay for advice, but don't always take it. Early in my career, I used to find that frustrating. Now, I see it differently. Consulting is about influence, not control. The role of the consultant is to illuminate the path, not to force the journey. Still, I've learned the importance of documenting that advice carefully – because when something later goes wrong on site, those records are not just evidence of diligence; they're proof of integrity.

The mindset I described in Chapter 2 – about curiosity, accountability, and professional humility – has guided me through every challenge. It's what turns a good consultant into a trusted one. It's also what drives my desire to give back. After decades of working with exceptional people in demanding environments, it felt right to consolidate what I've learned and make it available to others. This book is part of that process; it is my way of passing on lessons that were once passed to me.

Not every lesson is glamorous. Some are found in the fine print – like the time we specified a global event notification system for a major institution. It was technically brilliant, operationally elegant... and financially unsustainable. The ongoing licensing costs turned out to be astronomical, and when renewal time came, the system was quietly dropped. It was a reminder that affordability isn't just about initial procurement. It's about understanding the true cost of ownership –

maintenance, licensing, staffing, and everything in between. The price of technology is often not in what it does, but in what it continues to demand.

So, if there is one guiding message behind this book, it's this: Security consulting is about connection. Between ideas and action, between technology and people, between purpose and proof. My hope is that this work helps others see those connections more clearly, and that it inspires a few to approach this field not as a checklist, but as a craft.

To everyone who has shared a challenge, a question, or a late-night design call along the way – thank you. You're all part of this map.

— *Martin J. Grigg*

Intentionally blank

Addendum: The Grigg Evolved Equilibrium Resilience Model (GEERM)

GEERM

GRIGG EVOLVED EQUILIBRIUM
RESILIENCE MODEL

Note on Validation and Review

The Grigg Evolved Equilibrium Resilience Model (GEERM) represents an original framework developed through applied consulting and research practice. While the model and its underlying paper have not yet undergone formal peer review, they are being prepared for academic and professional validation through pilot applications and collaborative studies. Readers are therefore encouraged to view the model as a developing contribution to the evolving field of integrated resilience measurement.

The discussion that follows introduces the model as it currently stands – a working framework designed to translate complex security interactions into measurable resilience.

Security has evolved beyond the management of barriers, firewalls, and procedures. In a converged world, resilience is achieved through the coherence of entire systems – the ability of physical, cyber, procedural, and human elements to function as one adaptive whole. The Grigg Evolved Equilibrium Resilience Model (GEERM) has been developed to measure that coherence and to express resilience as something observable, comparable, and improvable over time.

At its core, GEERM represents security as a living ecosystem – a network of interacting forces rather than a stack of discrete defences. It visualises how physical measures, digital safeguards, operational procedures, and human behaviours reinforce one another within a dynamic governance boundary. This interaction produces what the model terms *integration as a multiplier*: the condition in which the combined effect of connected systems exceeds the sum of their individual parts.

The model can be applied to any system or combination of systems – from a single facility to a national network – and with equal relevance to procedures, organisational units, or inter-agency relationships. Its structure is scalable and sector-neutral, suitable for environments as diverse as data centres, border facilities, and corporate enterprises.

Unlike traditional frameworks that offer static snapshots, GEERM introduces a temporal dimension. It recognises that both risk and governance evolve continuously, and that true resilience depends on an organisation's capacity to learn, adapt, and realign faster than its surroundings change. This transforms maturity assessment from a point-in-time audit into a living indicator of resilience trajectory.

The white paper that accompanies the model details it's quantitative scoring system, through which the four domains – Physical, Cyber, Procedural, and People – are assessed across defined maturity dimensions. The results expose strengths, asymmetries, and interdependencies, showing how systems behave as a connected field rather than as isolated controls.

The value of scoring resilience lies not in numbers or measurement for their own sake, but in the clarity, they bring – revealing how resilience performs within the system. It converts professional intuition into measurable insight, giving consultants and executives a shared language for performance, investment, and improvement. Over time, successive assessments show how governance responds to pressure, how culture reinforces systems, and how integration multiplies protection.

GEERM is a framework, not a standard. It complements ISO/IEC 27001, ISO 31000, NCEMA 7000, and NIST CSF, serving as the connective layer between them. Ultimately, GEERM bridges the gap between compliance and capability. It enables resilience to be seen not as a checklist, but as a dynamic equilibrium between risk and governance, structure and culture, prevention and recovery – a living system that can be measured, communicated, and continually improved.

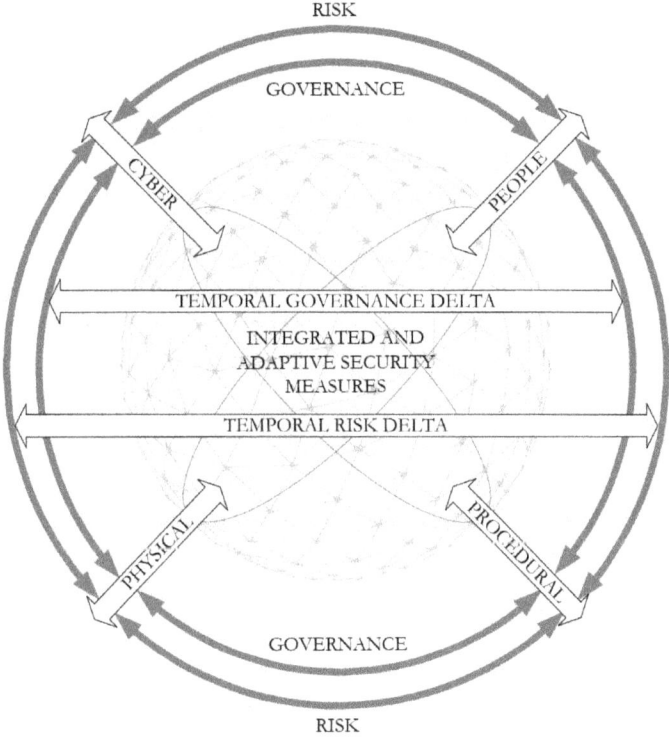

Figure 20 The Grigg Evolved Equilibrium Resilience Model

The GEERM System Dynamics Explained

The diagram visualises the Grigg Evolved Equilibrium Resilience Model (GEERM) as a dynamic ecosystem of interacting forces. It represents how resilience emerges not from isolated controls but from the balance, feedback, and adaptation between internal capability and external pressure.

491

The Outer Fields: Risk and Governance:

At the perimeter of the model, Risk and Governance form two opposing yet interdependent boundary conditions.

- **Risk** acts as an external, omnidirectional pressure – the collective force of threats, uncertainty, and environmental change pressing inward on the system. It represents the evolving field of hazard, intent, and opportunity that continuously challenges stability.
- **Governance**, by contrast, operates as an adaptive feedback boundary. It interprets this pressure and projects stabilising energy back into the system through policy, oversight, and decision-making. Governance does not shield the system rigidly; it flexes and reforms in response to what it learns.

These boundaries are in constant tension. When risk intensifies, the field contracts inward, compressing the four internal dimensions and exposing weaknesses. When governance adapts effectively, the boundary expands, restoring equilibrium and reasserting control. Over time, both fields oscillate – expanding and contracting in response to change – symbolising the temporal cycle of pressure and adaptation that defines resilience.

The Four Axes: Physical, Cyber, Procedural, and People:

Intersecting the model are the four primary axes of security, each depicted as a bi-directional vector.

- The inward direction represents the convergence of defence – controls, processes, and behaviours focusing energy toward the protected core.
- The outward direction projects assurance and influence – the diffusion of security culture, deterrence, and standards into the surrounding environment.

These double-ended arrows express the dual nature of mature security systems: they are both defensive and generative. Protection and influence coexist in balance; inward strength must be matched by outward coherence. None of the axes dominates; all are equal contributors to resilience.

The Core Sphere: Integration and Adaptation:

At the centre lies the sphere of Integrated and Adaptive Security Measures – a visualisation of the organisation's living, adaptive, network of controls, processes, and people. The fine mesh signifies interconnectivity: each node represents a control, and each connecting line a relationship or dependency. The network is dynamic, capable of shifting and rebalancing as conditions change. It is this interconnected adaptability that distinguishes a resilient system from a merely compliant one.

In systems terms, the core behaves as a *multi-vector field*: energy and assurance flow continuously across the network, and resilience emerges from the quality of those interactions. When one area weakens, others compensate; when feedback loops strengthen, the whole system learns.

The Temporal Vectors: Time and Change:

Running horizontally through the model are two key variables – the Temporal Governance Delta (ΔG) and the Temporal Risk Delta (ΔR).

- ΔR tracks how external risk pressure changes over time – whether exposure is rising or falling.
- ΔG measures how governance capability evolves in response – whether oversight is static, reactive, or adaptive.

The space between these two vectors represents the system's current equilibrium. When governance adapts faster than risk escalates ($\Delta G > \Delta R$), resilience strengthens. When risk rises faster than governance can respond ($\Delta R > \Delta G$), vulnerability increases. Tracking these deltas provides a temporal understanding of maturity – not just how resilient the system is, but how it is trending.

The System in Motion:

The model as a whole depicts security as a living, adaptive system.

- Risk and governance create the conditions of pressure and correction.
- The four axes channel energy inward and outward, maintaining equilibrium.
- The core network translates these forces into learning and adaptation.

- The temporal deltas introduce the dimension of time, revealing whether the system is evolving or degrading.

Together, these components express the principle that resilience is dynamic. It flexes, learns, and rebalances under stress, constantly reshaping itself in response to the forces of governance and risk. The Grigg Model therefore moves beyond static assurance: it allows consultants and organisations to see how protection behaves as a living system – converged, temporal, and measurable. It further shows that resilience must be governed, not merely designed: sustained through informed decision-making, continuous measurement, and the disciplined translation of insight into action. By making these dynamics visible, the model transforms resilience from an abstract aspiration into an observable process of governance in motion.

Interpretation:

Viewed holistically, the diagram illustrates that an organisation's resilience depends not on the volume of controls deployed, but on the quality of their interaction and the responsiveness of governance feedback under changing risk. It highlights that in a modern, converged environment, resilience is not a fixed state but a sustained behaviour – one continually shaped by the dialogue between risk and governance, and by the adaptive coherence of the system itself. The aim of the model is to *evolve equilibrium* towards a state of balanced security, where each domain operates in proportion to the others, and the system remains stable yet responsive under pressure.

Glossary of Terms

Term	Definition
Access Control	Processes and systems that govern who can enter areas or use resources
ACFE	Association of Certified Fraud Examiners
ACS	Access control system
ACSC	Australian Cyber Security Centre
ADMCC	Abu Dhabi Monitoring and Control Centre
AI	Artificial Intelligence
Anti-passback	Prevents re-entry without valid credential presentation exit to stop credential sharing
APA	American Psychological Association
ASIS	ASIS International - American Society for Industrial Security - (global security association)
ASTM	American Society for Testing and Materials
BMS	Building Management Systems
BS	British Standard
BSI	British Standards Institution
Business Continuity	Capability to continue operations at acceptable levels during disruption
CAA	Civil Aviation Authority (UK)
CCDCOE	NATO Cooperative Cyber Defence Centre of Excellence
CCTV	Closed-circuit television (video surveillance)
CERT	Computer Emergency Response Team (India)
CIP	Critical Infrastructure Protection (Standards)
CIPD	Chartered Institute of Personnel and Development (UK)
CIPS	Chartered Institute of Procurement & Supply
CISA	Cybersecurity and Infrastructure Security Agency
CISSP	Certified Information Systems Security Professional
CNI	Critical National Infrastructure
CPNI	Centre for the Protection of National Infrastructure
CPP	Certified Protection Professional
CPTED	Crime Prevention Through Environmental Design
Critical National Infrastructure	Assets and systems essential to the functioning and security of a nation
DHS	Department of Homeland Security
EN	European Norm

Term	Definition
ENISA	European Union Agency for Cybersecurity
ESG	Environmental, Social, and Governance
EU	European Union
FEMA	Federal Emergency Management Agency (US)
FERC	Federal Energy Regulatory Commission
FISMA	Federal Information Security Modernization Act (United States)
Five Whys	Root-cause technique of asking 'why?' five times to uncover underlying causes
GDPR	General Data Protection Regulation
HBR	Harvard Business Review
HR	Human Resources
HVAC	Heating, Ventilation, and Air Conditioning
HVM	Hostile Vehicle Mitigation
IAEA	International Atomic Energy Agency
IAPSC	the International Association of Professional Security Consultants
IATA	International Air Transport Association
ICAO	International Civil Aviation Organization
ICS	Industrial Control Systems
IDS	Intrusion detection system
IEC	International Electrotechnical Commission
IEEE	Institute of Electrical and Electronics Engineers
IMO	International Maritime Organization
Insider Threat	Risk posed by trusted individuals who may intentionally or accidentally cause harm
INTERPOL	International Criminal Police Organization
IP	Internet Protocol
ISACA	Information Systems Audit and Control Association
ISO	International Organization for Standardization
ISO/IEC	International Organization for Standardization/International Electrotechnical Commission
ISPS	International Ship and Port Facility Security
IT	Information Technology
ITT	Invitation to Tender
MARPOL	International Convention for the Prevention of Pollution from Ships (Marine Pollution) – the acronym comes from MARine POLlution.
MECE	Mutually exclusive, collectively exhaustive – a way to structure issues without overlap or gaps
NATO	North Atlantic Treaty Organization

Term	Definition
NCEMA	National Emergency Crisis and Disaster Management Authority (UAE)
NERC	North American Electric Reliability Corporation
NIS2	EU Directive on measures for a high level of cybersecurity across the Union (second version)
NISC	Japan National Center of Incident Readiness and Strategy for Cybersecurity
NIST	National Institute of Standards and Technology
NPSA	National Protective Security Authority (UK)
OSAC	Overseas Security Advisory Council
OT	Operational Technology
PCI	Professional Certified Investigator (ASIS International certification)
Perimeter Detection	Measures that detect intrusion attempts at site boundaries
PESTLE	Political, Economic, Social, Technological, Legal and Environmental analysis
PMBOK	Project Management Body of Knowledge
PMI	Project Management Institute
PMI/PRINCE2	Project Management Institute/PRINCE2 Certification
POPIA	Protection of Personal Information Act
PPE	Personal Protective Equipment
PSP	Physical Security Professional
PSR	Protective Security Requirements (New Zealand)
Pyramid Principle	Top–down communication method: start with the answer, then group supporting arguments
RACI	Responsible, Accountable, Consulted, Informed
Red Teaming	Adopting an adversary's perspective to test assumptions and expose vulnerabilities
RFP	Request for Proposal
RIBA	Royal Institute of British Architects
Risk Assessment	Systematic process to identify, analyse, and evaluate risk
Risk Register	Structured log of identified risks, owners, and treatments
Root Cause Analysis	Method to identify the fundamental reason a problem occurs
RPAS	Remotely Piloted Aircraft Systems
SCADA	Supervisory Control and Data Acquisition
SIA	Security Industry Authority
SIRA	Security Industry Regulatory Agency
SMR	Small Modular Reactor

Term	Definition
SOC 2	System and Organization Controls 2.
Socratic questioning	Structured probing questions used to challenge assumptions and reasoning
SP	Special Publication (NIST)
SWOT	Strengths, Weaknesses, Opportunities, and Threats analysis
Tabletop Exercises	Facilitated walk-throughs of scenarios to test plans, roles, and decision-making
Tailgating	Unauthorised entry by following an authorised person through an access point
TIA	Telecommunications Industry Association
TSA	Transportation Security Administration
TVRA	Threat, Vulnerability and Risk Assessment
UAE	United Arab Emirates
UK	United Kingdom
UN	United Nations
UNDSS	United Nations Department of Safety and Security
UNODC	United Nations Office on Drugs and Crime
US	United States
VMS	Video management system
WANO	World Association of Nuclear Operators
WEF	World Economic Forum
WHO	World Health Organization

References

1. Abu Dhabi Monitoring and Control Centre (ADMCC). Physical Security Standards for Critical Infrastructure. Abu Dhabi: Government of Abu Dhabi, 2023.
2. ASIS International. ASIS Code of Ethics. Alexandria, VA: ASIS International, 2022.
3. Block, P. Flawless Consulting: A Guide to Getting Your Expertise Used. 3rd ed. San Francisco, CA: Jossey-Bass, 2011.
4. Dubai Security Industry Regulatory Agency (SIRA). Security Systems Regulations. Dubai: Government of Dubai, 2023.
5. European Parliament and Council. Regulation (EU) 2016/679 (General Data Protection Regulation – GDPR). Official Journal of the European Union, 2016.
6. European Union. Directive (EU) 2022/2555 on measures for a high common level of cybersecurity across the Union (NIS2 Directive). Official Journal of the European Union, 2022.
7. European Union. Directive (EU) 2022/2557 on the Resilience of Critical Entities. Official Journal of the European Union, 2022.
8. Government of India. Computer Emergency Response Team – India (CERT-In) Guidelines. Ministry of Electronics and Information Technology. New Delhi: Government of India, 2022.
9. International Atomic Energy Agency (IAEA). IAEA Safety Standards and Nuclear Security Series. Vienna: IAEA, 2022.
10. International Civil Aviation Organization (ICAO). Annex 17 to the Convention on International Civil Aviation: Security – Safeguarding International Civil Aviation against Acts of Unlawful Interference. Montreal: ICAO, 2017.
11. International Maritime Organization (IMO). Maritime Security and the ISPS Code. London: IMO, 2021.
12. International Organization for Standardization (ISO). ISO 22301: Business Continuity Management Systems. Geneva: ISO, 2019.
13. International Organization for Standardization (ISO). ISO 31000: Risk Management – Guidelines. Geneva: ISO, 2018.
14. International Organization for Standardization (ISO). *ISO 21500:2021 – Project, Programme and Portfolio Management – Context and Concepts.* Geneva: ISO, 2021.
15. International Organization for Standardization (ISO). ISO/IEC 27001:2022 – Information Security Management Systems. Geneva: ISO, 2022.

16. International Organization for Standardization (ISO)/International Electrotechnical Commission (IEC). ISO/IEC 22237:2021 – Information technology – Data centre facilities and infrastructures. Geneva: ISO/IEC, 2021.
17. Minto, B. The Pyramid Principle: Logic in Writing and Thinking. London: FT Prentice Hall, 2010.
18. National Emergency Crisis and Disaster Management Authority (NCEMA). NCEMA 7000: Business Continuity Management Standard. Abu Dhabi: NCEMA, 2017.
19. National Institute of Standards and Technology (NIST). Cybersecurity Framework. Gaithersburg, MD: NIST, 2024.
20. New Zealand Government. Protective Security Requirements (PSR). Wellington: Department of the Prime Minister and Cabinet, 2022.
21. North American Electric Reliability Corporation (NERC). Critical Infrastructure Protection (CIP) Standards. Atlanta, GA: NERC, 2021.
22. TIA. TIA-942-B: 2017 – Telecommunications Infrastructure Standard for Data Centres. Telecommunications Industry Association, 2017.
23. Weiss, A. Million Dollar Consulting: The Professional's Guide to Growing a Practice. 5th ed. New York: McGraw-Hill, 2016.

Bibliography

A

- Association of Certified Fraud Examiners (ACFE). Occupational Fraud: Report to the Nations 2022. Austin, TX: ACFE, 2022.
- Australian Cyber Security Centre (ACSC). Cybersecurity Guidance and Frameworks. Canberra: Australian Government, 2023.
- Allen, T.D., and Eby, L.T. (eds.). The Blackwell Handbook of Mentoring: A Multiple Perspectives Approach. Oxford: Blackwell Publishing, 2007.
- Alley, M. The Craft of Scientific Presentations: Critical Steps to Succeed and Critical Errors to Avoid. 2nd ed. New York: Springer, 2013.
- American Psychological Association (APA). Stress in America 2022: A National Mental Health Crisis. Washington, DC: APA, 2022.
- American Society for Industrial Security (ASIS International). Board Certification Handbook: CPP, PSP, PCI. Alexandria, VA: ASIS International, 2023.
- Argyris, C. "Double Loop Learning in Organizations." Harvard Business Review, September 1977.
- Argyris, C., and Schön, D.A. Organizational Learning II: Theory, Method, and Practice. Reading, MA: Addison-Wesley, 1996.
- Aroles, J., Mitev, N., and Vaujany, F.X. "Mapping themes in the study of new work practices." New Technology, Work and Employment, 34(3), 285–299, 2019.
- ASIS International. Organisational Resilience: Security Convergence Guidelines. Alexandria, VA: ASIS International, 2017.
- ASIS International. Facilities Physical Security Measures Guideline. Alexandria, VA: ASIS International, 2019.
- ASIS International. General Security Risk Assessment Guideline. Alexandria, VA: ASIS International, 2019.
- ASTM International. Standard Test Method for Vehicle Crash Testing of Perimeter Barriers (ASTM F2656/F2656M-15). West Conshohocken, PA: ASTM International, 2017.
- Australian Government. Security of Critical Infrastructure Act 2018 (as amended 2021). Canberra: Government of Australia.

B

- Bazerman, M.H., and Moore, D.A. Judgment in Managerial Decision Making. 8th ed. Hoboken, NJ: Wiley, 2012.
- Bennis, W., and Thomas, R.J. Leading for a Lifetime: How Defining Moments Shape Leaders of Today and Tomorrow. Boston, MA: Harvard Business School Press, 2007.
- Bostrom, N., and Yudkowsky, E. "The Ethics of Artificial Intelligence." In K. Frankish & W.M. Ramsey (eds.), The Cambridge Handbook of Artificial Intelligence. Cambridge: Cambridge University Press, 2014, pp. 316–334.
- Boyatzis, R.E., and McKee, A. Resonant Leadership: Renewing Yourself and Connecting with Others Through Mindfulness, Hope, and Compassion. Boston, MA: Harvard Business School Press, 2005.
- Brundage, M., et al. The Malicious Use of Artificial Intelligence: Forecasting, Prevention, and Mitigation. Oxford: Future of Humanity Institute, University of Oxford, 2018.
- British Standards Institution (BSI). BS EN 50132-7:2012 CCTV Surveillance Systems for Use in Security Applications – Application Guidelines. London: BSI, 2012.
- Brown, B. Dare to Lead: Brave Work. Tough Conversations. Whole Hearts. New York: Random House, 2018.
- Brown, T. Change by Design: How Design Thinking Creates New Alternatives for Business and Society. New York: Harper Business, 2009.
- Bryson, J.M. Strategic Planning for Public and Nonprofit Organizations: A Guide to Strengthening and Sustaining Organizational Achievement. 5th ed. Hoboken, NJ: Wiley, 2018.

C

- Campbell, D.J., and O'Hare, D. Crisis Management in International Settings: Navigating Political and Security Risks. London: Routledge, 2021.
- Carroll, A.B., and Brown, J.A. Corporate Responsibility: The American Experience. Cambridge: Cambridge University Press, 2018.
- Centre for the Protection of National Infrastructure (CPNI). Protective Security: Physical Security Guidance. London: UK Government, 2020.

- Chartered Institute of Procurement & Supply (CIPS). Tendering Guide: Best Practice for Tendering and Procurement. Stamford, UK: CIPS, 2020.
- Christensen, C.M., and Raynor, M.E. The Innovator's Solution: Creating and Sustaining Successful Growth. Boston, MA: Harvard Business Review Press, 2013.
- Cialdini, R. Influence: The Psychology of Persuasion. Revised ed. New York: Harper Business, 2021.
- Clarke, R. "The Internet of Things and Security Governance." Journal of Computer Information Systems, 59(1), 81–91, 2019.
- Clutterbuck, D. Everyone Needs a Mentor: Fostering Talent at Work. 5th ed. London: CIPD, 2014.
- Clutterbuck, D., Megginson, D., and Garvey, B. Coaching and Mentoring: Theory and Practice. 3rd ed. London: Sage Publications, 2016.
- Connell, J., and Rugman, A.M. Safety and Security Management Practices in Challenging and Hostile Environments. Basingstoke: Palgrave Macmillan, 2014.
- Covey, S.R. The 7 Habits of Highly Effective People. 30th Anniversary ed. New York: Simon & Schuster, 2020.

D

- De Geus, A. The Living Company: Growth, Learning, and Longevity in Business. Boston, MA: Harvard Business Review Press, 2002.
- DeLong, T.J., and Vijayaraghavan, V. "Let's Hear It for the B Players." Harvard Business Review, 81(6), 96–102, 2003.
- Deloitte. 2022 Global Corporate Real Estate Survey. London: Deloitte Insights, 2022.
- Drucker, P.F. Innovation and Entrepreneurship: Practice and Principles. London: Routledge, 2015 (original 1985).
- Drucker, P.F. Managing Oneself. Boston, MA: Harvard Business Review Press, 2008.
- Duarte, D.L., and Snyder, N.T. Mastering Virtual Teams: Strategies, Tools, and Techniques That Succeed. 3rd ed. San Francisco, CA: Jossey-Bass, 2011.
- Duarte, N. Resonate: Present Visual Stories that Transform Audiences. Hoboken, NJ: Wiley, 2010.

E

- Eden, C., and Ackermann, F. Making Strategy: The Journey of Strategic Management. London: SAGE Publications, 2013.
- Endsley, M.R. "From Here to Autonomy: Lessons Learned from Human–Automation Research." Human Factors, 59(1), 5–27, 2017.
- European Union Agency for Cybersecurity (ENISA). Threat Landscape Report 2018. Athens: ENISA, 2019.
- European Union Agency for Cybersecurity (ENISA). Cybersecurity for Smart Cities – An Architecture Model for Public Transport. Athens: ENISA, 2021.
- Eraut, M. "Non-formal Learning and Tacit Knowledge in Professional Work." British Journal of Educational Psychology, 70(1), 113–136, 2000.

F

- Federal Energy Regulatory Commission (FERC). Critical Infrastructure Protection Standards (CIP). Washington, DC: FERC.
- Fennelly, L.J., and Perry, M. The Handbook for Facility Security: Protecting High-Risk Facilities. Boca Raton, FL: CRC Press, 2018.
- Finn, R.L., and Wright, D. "Unmanned Aircraft Systems: Surveillance, Ethics and Privacy in Civil Applications." Computer Law & Security Review, 28(2), 184–194, 2012.
- Fisher, R., Ury, W., and Patton, B. Getting to Yes: Negotiating Agreement Without Giving In. 3rd ed. London: Penguin, 2011.
- Flick, U. An Introduction to Qualitative Research. 6th ed. Thousand Oaks, CA: SAGE Publications, 2018.
- Fonner, K.L., and Roloff, M.E. "Why teleworkers are more satisfied with their jobs than office-based workers: When less contact is beneficial." Journal of Applied Communication Research, 38(4), 336–361, 2010.
- Freeman, R.E., Harrison, J.S., Wicks, A.C., Parmar, B.L., and De Colle, S. Stakeholder Theory: The State of the Art. Cambridge: Cambridge University Press, 2010.
- Friedman, A.L., and Miles, S. Stakeholders: Theory and Practice. Oxford: Oxford University Press, 2006.
- Frost & Sullivan. Global Security Services Market Outlook, 2022–2027. San Antonio, TX: Frost & Sullivan Research, 2022.

G

- Gallo, C. Talk Like TED: The 9 Public-Speaking Secrets of the World's Top Minds. New York: St. Martin's Press, 2014.
- Gartner. Market Guide for Security Risk Assessment Services. Stamford, CT: Gartner Research, 2023.
- Garvey, B., Stokes, P., and Megginson, D. Coaching and Mentoring: Theory and Practice. 2nd ed. London: Sage Publications, 2009.
- Gibbs, J.L., Sivunen, A., and Boyraz, M. "Investigating the impacts of team type and design on virtual team processes." Human Resource Management Review, 27(4), 590–603, 2017.
- Gill, M. The Handbook of Security. 3rd ed. London: Palgrave Macmillan, 2021.
- Gillham, B. Research Interviewing: The Range of Techniques. Maidenhead: Open University Press, 2005.
- Goffee, R., and Jones, G. Why Should Anyone Be Led by You? Boston, MA: Harvard Business Review Press, 2006.
- Grove, A. High Output Management. New York: Vintage, 2015.

H

- Haidt, J. The Righteous Mind: Why Good People are Divided by Politics and Religion. London: Vintage, 2012.
- Hammond, J.S., Keeney, R.L., and Raiffa, H. Smart Choices: A Practical Guide to Making Better Decisions. New York: Currency, 2015.
- Harris, M. Artificial Intelligence and the Security Sector: Opportunities and Challenges. London: Routledge, 2022.
- Harvard Business Review. The Succession Planning Handbook for the Modern Leader. Boston, MA: Harvard Business Review Press, 2021.
- Harvard Business Review. HBR Guide to Building Your Business Case. Boston, MA: Harvard Business Review Press, 2015.
- Heath, C., and Heath, D. Made to Stick: Why Some Ideas Survive and Others Die. New York: Random House, 2007.
- Hofstede, G. Culture's Consequences: Comparing Values, Behaviors, Institutions and Organizations Across Nations. 2nd ed. Thousand Oaks, CA: Sage Publications, 2001.
- Hofstede, G., Hofstede, G.J., and Minkov, M. Cultures and Organizations: Software of the Mind. 3rd ed. New York: McGraw-Hill, 2010.
- Hollnagel, E., Woods, D.D., and Leveson, N. (eds.). Resilience Engineering: Concepts and Precepts. Aldershot: Ashgate, 2006.

- Horton, J.L. The Art of Public Speaking *for Professionals*. New York: Harper Business, 2011.

I

- International Air Transport Association (IATA). Security and Facilitation Standards and Guidance. Montreal: IATA, 2023.
- International Atomic Energy Agency (IAEA). Advances in Small Modular Reactor Technology Developments. Vienna: IAEA, 2022.
- International Civil Aviation Organization (ICAO). Manual on Remotely Piloted Aircraft Systems (RPAS). Montreal: ICAO, 2022.
- International Electrotechnical Commission (IEC). IEC 62443 (series): Industrial communication networks – IT security for networks and systems. Geneva: IEC, various parts, latest editions.
- International Organization for Standardization (ISO). ISO 9001: Quality Management Systems. Geneva: ISO, 2015.
- International Organization for Standardization (ISO). ISO 22316: Organizational Resilience – Principles and Attributes. Geneva: ISO, 2017.
- International Organization for Standardization (ISO). ISO 31010:2018 – Risk Management – Risk Assessment Techniques. Geneva: ISO, 2018.
- International Organization for Standardization (ISO). *ISO 10667:2011 – Assessment Service Delivery: Procedures and Methods*. Geneva: ISO, 2011.
- International Organization for Standardization (ISO). *ISO 30401:2018 – Knowledge Management Systems: Requirements*. Geneva: ISO, 2018.
- International SOS. Risk Outlook 2022: The Top Five Predictions for Organisations. London: International SOS Foundation, 2022.
- INTERPOL. Global Crime Trend Report 2022. Lyon: INTERPOL, 2022.
- ISACA. "Overcoming a False Sense of Security." ISACA Journal, Vol. 1, 2021.

J

- Janes Defence. Janes Security and Risk Assessment Reports. Coulsdon: Janes Group, 2023.

- Japan National Center of Incident Readiness and Strategy for Cybersecurity (NISC). Cybersecurity Strategy. Tokyo: NISC, 2021.

K

- Kahneman, D. Thinking, Fast and Slow. London: Penguin Books, 2011.
- Kaplan, R.S., and Norton, D.P. The Balanced Scorecard: Translating Strategy into Action. Boston, MA: Harvard Business Review Press, 1996.
- Karmel, A. "Compliance and security are two sides of the same coin." Security Magazine, 2023.
- Kegan, R., and Lahey, L.L. Immunity to Change: How to Overcome It and Unlock the Potential in Yourself and Your Organization. Boston, MA: Harvard Business Review Press, 2009.
- Kelley, T., and Littman, J. The Art of Innovation: Lessons in Creativity from IDEO. London: Profile Books, 2001.
- Kepner, C.H., and Tregoe, B.B. The New Rational Manager: An Updated Edition for a New World. Princeton, NJ: Princeton Research Press, 2013.
- Kets de Vries, M.F.R. The Hedgehog Effect: The Secrets of Building High Performance Teams. San Francisco, CA: Jossey-Bass, 2011.
- Kets de Vries, M.F.R. The Leadership Mystique: Leading Behavior in the Human Enterprise. 2nd ed. Harlow: Pearson Education, 2006.
- Khalid, N., and Gardner, B. Port Security Management. London: Routledge, 2021.
- Kitchin, R. "The Ethics of Smart Cities and Urban Data." Philosophical Transactions of the Royal Society A, 374(2083), 20160115, 2016.
- Kolb, D.A. Experiential Learning: Experience as the Source of Learning and Development. 2nd ed. Upper Saddle River, NJ: Pearson Education, 2015.
- Kotler, P., and Keller, K.L. Marketing Management. 15th ed. Harlow: Pearson Education, 2016.
- Krueger, R.A., and Casey, M.A. Focus Groups: A Practical Guide for Applied Research. 5th ed. Thousand Oaks, CA: Sage Publications, 2015.
- Krotz, J.L. The Consultant's Quick Start Guide: An Action Plan for Your First Year in Business. Hoboken, NJ: Wiley, 2012.

L

- Lave, J., and Wenger, E. Situated Learning: Legitimate Peripheral Participation. Cambridge: Cambridge University Press, 1991.
- Lencioni, P. The Five Dysfunctions of a Team: A Leadership Fable. San Francisco, CA: Jossey-Bass, 2002.
- Leonardi, P.M., and Neeley, T. "What managers need to know about social tools: Avoiding adoption failures in the workplace." Business Horizons, 60(5), 635–643, 2017.
- Levinson, H. Executive. Cambridge, MA: Harvard University Press, 1981.
- LinkedIn Corporation. LinkedIn Talent Solutions: Global Recruiting Trends Report 2022. Sunnyvale, CA: LinkedIn, 2022.

M

- Maister, D.H. Managing the Professional Service Firm. New York: Free Press, 1993.
- Marotta, A., and Madnick, S. "Convergence and Divergence of Regulatory Compliance." Issues in Information Systems, 22(1), 10–50, 2021.
- McKinsey & Company. How to Write Proposals That Win Business. McKinsey Insights, 2023.
- McKinsey & Company. Resilience in the Age of Uncertainty: A Guide for Companies. New York: McKinsey Global Institute, 2020.
- Mitchell, R.K., Agle, B.R., and Wood, D.J. "Toward a theory of stakeholder identification and salience: Defining the principle of who and what really counts." Academy of Management Review, 22(4), 853–886, 1997.
- Montoya, P., and Vandehey, T. The Brand Called You: Make Your Business Stand Out in a Crowded Marketplace. New York: McGraw-Hill, 2009.

N

- National Institute of Standards and Technology (NIST). Special Publication 800-53: Security and Privacy Controls for Federal Information Systems and Organizations. Gaithersburg, MD: NIST, 2020.

- National Institute of Standards and Technology (NIST). Guide for Conducting Risk Assessments (SP 800-30 Rev.1). Gaithersburg, MD: U.S. Department of Commerce, 2012.
- National Institute of Standards and Technology (NIST). Guide to Industrial Control Systems (ICS) Security (SP 800-82 Rev.2). Gaithersburg, MD: U.S. Department of Commerce, 2015.
- NATO Cooperative Cyber Defence Centre of Excellence (CCDCOE). Cyber-Physical Security of Critical Infrastructure. Tallinn: NATO CCDCOE, 2021.
- Neeley, T. Remote Work Revolution: Succeeding from Anywhere. New York: Harper Business, 2021.
- Nonaka, I., and Takeuchi, H. The Knowledge-Creating Company: How Japanese Companies Create the Dynamics of Innovation. New York: Oxford University Press, 1995.

O

- O'Hern, J., and Noonan, C. Global Aviation Security: Policy, Regulation and Risk. London: Routledge, 2019.
- Olson, J.S., and Olson, G.M. Working Together Apart: Collaboration Over the Internet. Synthesis Lectures on Human-Centred Informatics. San Rafael, CA: Morgan & Claypool, 2017.

P

- Parasuraman, R., and Wickens, C.D. "Humans: Still Vital After All These Years of Automation." Human Factors, 50(3), 511–520, 2008.
- Parasuraman, R., Sheridan, T.B., and Wickens, C.D. "A Model for Types and Levels of Human Interaction with Automation." IEEE Transactions on Systems, Man, and Cybernetics – Part A: Systems and Humans, 30(3), 286–297, 2000.
- Patton, M.Q. Qualitative Research & Evaluation Methods: Integrating Theory and Practice. 4th ed. Thousand Oaks, CA: SAGE Publications, 2014.
- Polanyi, M. The Tacit Dimension. Chicago: University of Chicago Press, 1966.
- Project Management Institute (PMI). A Guide to the Project Management Body of Knowledge (PMBOK® Guide). 6th ed. Newtown Square, PA: Project Management Institute, 2017.
- PwC. Global Data Centre Market Outlook: Building Resilience for the Digital Age. London: PwC Research, 2021.

R

- Raghuram, S., Hill, N.S., Gibbs, J.L., and Maruping, L.M. "Virtual work: Bridging research clusters." Academy of Management Annals, 13(1), 308–341, 2019.
- Ragins, B.R., and Kram, K.E. (eds.). The Handbook of Mentoring at Work: Theory, Research, and Practice. Thousand Oaks, CA: SAGE Publications, 2007.
- Rasiel, E. The McKinsey Way. New York: McGraw-Hill, 1999.
- Reason, J. Human Error. Cambridge: Cambridge University Press, 1990.
- Red Team Journal. Red Teaming Handbook: A Guide to Critical Thinking in Complex Environments. Red Team Journal Press, 2020.
- Redmond, A.D., and Mahoney, P.F. Risks and Challenges in Medical Response to Conflict and Disasters. Cham: Springer, 2018.

S

- Schein, E.H. Career Dynamics: Matching Individual and Organizational Needs. Reading, MA: Addison-Wesley, 1978.
- Schein, E.H. Organizational Culture and Leadership. 4th ed. San Francisco, CA: Jossey-Bass, 2010.
- Scharre, P. Army of None: Autonomous Weapons and the Future of War. New York: W. W. Norton & Company, 2018.
- Schon, D.A. The Reflective Practitioner: How Professionals Think in Action. New York: Basic Books, 1983.
- Security Industry Authority (SIA). Standards of Professional Conduct. London: SIA, 2019.
- Seidman, I. Interviewing as Qualitative Research: A Guide for Researchers in Education and the Social Sciences. 5th ed. New York: Teachers College Press, 2019.
- Senge, P.M. The Fifth Discipline: The Art and Practice of the Learning Organization. Revised ed. New York: Doubleday, 2006.
- Smith, R.G. Cybercrime and Digital Forensics: An Introduction. London: Routledge, 2018.
- Sovacool, B.K., Gilbert, A., and Nugent, D. "An international comparative assessment of construction cost overruns for electricity infrastructure." Energy Research & Social Science, 3, 152–160, 2014.

- South African Government. Protection of Personal Information Act (POPIA) 2013. Pretoria: Government of South Africa.
- Spradley, J.P. Participant Observation. Long Grove, IL: Waveland Press, 2016.
- Stanton, N.A., Salmon, P.M., Rafferty, L., Walker, G.H., Baber, C., and Jenkins, D.P. Human Factors Methods: A Practical Guide for Engineering and Design. 2nd ed. Boca Raton, FL: CRC Press, 2017.
- Susskind, L., and Cruikshank, J. Breaking Robert's Rules: The New Way to Run Your Meeting, Build Consensus, and Get Results. Oxford: Oxford University Press, 2006.
- Susskind, R., and Susskind, D. The Future of the Professions: How Technology Will Transform the *Work of Human Experts*. Oxford: Oxford University Press, 2015.

T

- Thomas, D.C., and Peterson, M.F. Cross-Cultural Management: Essential Concepts. 4th ed. Thousand Oaks, CA: SAGE Publications, 2017.
- Townsend, A.M. Smart Cities: Big Data, Civic Hackers, and the Quest for a New Utopia. New York: W. W. Norton & Company, 2013.
- Transparency International. Corruption Perceptions Index 2020. Berlin: Transparency International, 2020.
- Treviño, L.K., and Nelson, K.A. Managing Business Ethics: Straight Talk About How to Do It Right. 8th ed. Hoboken, NJ: Wiley, 2021.

U

- United Nations Department of Safety and Security (UNDSS). Security Risk Management Manual. New York: United Nations, 2019.
- United Nations Office on Drugs and Crime (UNODC). Global Study on Homicide 2023. Vienna: UNODC, 2023.
- United States Congress. Federal Information Security Modernization Act (FISMA) 2014. Washington, DC: United States Government, 2014.
- United States Department of State. High-Risk Area Security Guidelines. Washington, DC: Overseas Security Advisory Council (OSAC), 2021.

- U.S. Department of Homeland Security (DHS). Cybersecurity and Infrastructure Security Agency (CISA) Guidelines. Washington, DC: U.S. DHS, 2023.

V

(no entries beginning with V in current list)

W

- Waizenegger, L., McKenna, B., Cai, W., and Bendz, T. "An affordance perspective of team collaboration and enforced working from home during COVID-19." European Journal of Information Systems, 29(4), 429–442, 2020.
- Weick, K.E., and Sutcliffe, K.M. Managing the Unexpected: Sustained Performance in a Complex World. 3rd ed. Hoboken, NJ: Wiley, 2015.
- Wenger, E., McDermott, R., and Snyder, W.M. Cultivating Communities of Practice: A Guide to Managing Knowledge. Boston, MA: Harvard Business School Press, 2002.
- Williams, J.M., and Bizup, J. Style: Lessons in Clarity and Grace. 12th ed. New York: Pearson, 2016.
- World Association of Nuclear Operators (WANO). Performance Objectives & Criteria. London: WANO, 2019.
- World Economic Forum (WEF). Global Risks Report 2023. Geneva: WEF, 2023.
- World Health Organization (WHO). Burn-out an "Occupational Phenomenon": International Classification of Diseases. Geneva: WHO, 2019.

Y

- Yin, R.K. Case Study Research and Applications: Design and Methods. 6th ed. Thousand Oaks, CA: SAGE Publications, 2017.

Z

- Zinsser, W. On Writing Well: The Classic Guide to Writing Nonfiction. 30th Anniversary ed. New York: Harper Perennial, 2006.

About The Author

Martin J. Grigg is an international security consultant and subject-matter expert with more than three decades of experience protecting critical assets and environments across the United Kingdom, the Middle East, and beyond.

Beginning his career in military-grade electronics, Martin evolved into one of the foremost practitioners of integrated physical and electronic security, combining deep technical understanding with strategic foresight. His portfolio spans civil nuclear facilities, custodial environments, defence installations, data centres, and national infrastructure – including projects for government agencies, regulators, and major commercial developers in both the UK and the UAE.

As a founder of CHQ, a UK-based niche consultancy, and later 323 Ltd., Martin built independent practices recognised for their work in high-security and critical infrastructure environments. Each was founded on a single principle: that small, expert teams deliver the greatest value – agile enough to innovate, and close enough to understand the client's real-world challenges, while maintaining the independence required to give clear, unbiased advice.

A published technical author, Martin wrote *Integrated Electronic Security: A Layered Approach* – a reference text listed on the University of Central Lancashire's master's programme in Nuclear Security and Safeguards and reviewed by ASIS International and *Professional Security Magazine*. He has also contributed a chapter to the *Oxford Handbook of Nuclear Security* and numerous professional journals on topics including convergence, resilience, and the evolution of data-driven protection.

Throughout his career, Martin has advocated a mindset-based approach to consultancy: that true value lies not only in the advice given but in the discipline of documenting it. As he often notes, clients may not always follow a consultant's recommendations, but clear records ensure accountability, integrity, and learning when projects face real-world tests.

His work also emphasises the full lifecycle of protection: from conceptual planning to operation, maintenance, and renewal. He has seen how systems that appear affordable at procurement can impose unsustainable costs later. These experiences have shaped his conviction that resilience must include not only strength and adaptability, but sustainability.

Now based in Abu Dhabi, Martin continues to advise on critical national infrastructure, smart cities, and converged risk-resilience systems, developing models that link governance, culture, and technology into unified frameworks of assurance. His latest work – the Grigg Evolved Equilibrium Resilience Model (GEERM) – extends this philosophy, offering consultants a method to visualise and measure security maturity across physical, digital, procedural, and human domains.

More than a career, Martin sees his practice as a craft – the disciplined pursuit of protection through understanding, connection, and clarity. This book captures that pursuit: the synthesis of decades spent turning complexity into confidence and helping organisations protect what matters most.